Forensic Psychology

An Inside Perspective on Criminal Thinking and Behavior

Kenneth B. Cairns

Waynesburg University

Sage

FOR INFORMATION:

2455 Teller Road
Thousand Oaks, California 91320
E-mail: order@sagepub.com

1 Oliver's Yard
55 City Road
London, EC1Y 1SP
United Kingdom

Unit No. 323-333, Third Floor, F-Block
International Trade Tower
Nehru Place, New Delhi – 110 019
India

18 Cross Street #10-10/11/12
China Square Central
Singapore 048423

Copyright © 2024 by Sage.

All rights reserved. Except as permitted by U.S. copyright law, no part of this work may be reproduced or distributed in any form or by any means, or stored in a database or retrieval system, without permission in writing from the publisher.

All third-party trademarks referenced or depicted herein are included solely for the purpose of illustration and are the property of their respective owners. Reference to these trademarks in no way indicates any relationship with, or endorsement by, the trademark owner.

Printed in the United States of America

Library of Congress Control Number: 2023028806

ISBN: 978-1-0718-3781-8

This book is printed on acid-free paper.

Acquisitions Editor: Zachary Valladon

Content Development Editor: Cassie Carey

Production Editor: Vijayakumar

Copy Editor: Erin Livingston

Typesetter: TNQ Technologies

Indexer: TNQ Technologies

Cover Designer: Gail Buschman

Marketing Manager: Victoria Velasquez

23 24 25 26 27 10 9 8 7 6 5 4 3 2 1

Forensic Psychology

Sara Miller McCune founded Sage Publishing in 1965 to support the dissemination of usable knowledge and educate a global community. Sage publishes more than 1000 journals and over 600 new books each year, spanning a wide range of subject areas. Our growing selection of library products includes archives, data, case studies and video. Sage remains majority owned by our founder and after her lifetime will become owned by a charitable trust that secures the company's continued independence.

Los Angeles | London | New Delhi | Singapore | Washington DC | Melbourne

BRIEF CONTENTS

DETAILED CONTENTS

PREFACE

This textbook represents an innovative approach to the topic of forensic psychology. As instructors of topics related to forensics and psychology, we face a number of challenges when it comes to selecting a textbook. First, there is the likelihood that many of our students register for a forensic psychology course after binge-watching the numerous television programs and movies that portray this topic, albeit very often in an inaccurate manner. Thus, the beliefs of such students about this topic are distorted at best or completely inaccurate at worst. Secondly, although some instructors are quite comfortable teaching psychology, they may be unfamiliar with the terminology and procedures of the forensic/legal world. Others, of course, have a solid foundation in law and criminal behavior but feel less confident in their understanding of psychology. It is vitally important to find a textbook that helps instructors from "each side of the fence" to be confident in understanding and teaching those aspects of this topic that they may be less familiar with. A third challenge involves the importance of making certain that in the teaching of psychology and law, of criminal justice professionals and offenders, that we do not lose sight of another group that is of (at least) equal importance in the field of forensic psychology: those who have been victimized by offenders or by the criminal justice system itself.

The first challenge faced by instructors of forensic psychology is related to the fact that the students who take our courses often have skewed or even wildly inaccurate beliefs about that field. Many students register for forensic psychology classes after years of watching *CSI, Criminal Minds, Silence of the Lambs*, or any of a host of other programs that purportedly portray the day-to-day happenings in the life of a forensic psychologist. As instructors, we know that although dramatic portrayals of an FBI (Federal Bureau of Investigation) profiler tracking down serial killers are captivating, they are chock-full of inaccuracies and do no justice to the breadth and depth of research and knowledge in the field. This textbook aims to capture student interest by beginning each chapter with a true story from the author's experience working in the Pennsylvania prison system; the theme of that story is then woven into the fabric of the chapter. While maintaining students' attention, the importance of forensic psychologists' use of empirical research, evidence-based practices, and legal precedents in the criminal justice system are emphasized. A primary goal of the present textbook is to utilize real-life examples from the field of forensic psychology to maintain student interest while dispelling media-inspired myths about the topic, replacing those misconceptions with evidence-based principles.

The second challenge that we face as instructors is that many of us who are familiar with the field of forensics perhaps feel less confident in teaching about psychology, while those who are well-versed in psychology feel equally unsure in regard to teaching forensic topics. Existing texts often present the topic of forensic psychology from two different perspectives, with some chapters written by an expert in the law, focusing on courtroom professionals, procedures, and case law but neglecting the role of human thought and emotion in forensic matters. Other chapters in such textbooks are written by an expert in psychology and delve into research concerning human cognition and emotions but may neglect the manner in which this information applies to the field of criminal justice and the law. In such texts, it appears that it is hoped that these two perspectives will somehow meet in the middle and yield a coherent review of the field of forensic psychology. The present textbook, authored by a psychologist with more than 20 years of experience working day-to-day in maximum-security state prisons, endeavors to integrate forensics and psychology, giving students a single coherent viewpoint of the manner in which these two seemingly different fields interact. Along with real-life scenarios from the author's experience, the present textbook incorporates legal case and research citations in every chapter, along with lists of key terms and a glossary to make the textbook more accessible and relevant to both instructors and students.

The third challenge addressed by the present text—that movies, television, and even some research studies and other texts focus intently on the role of criminal justice professionals and the offenders while ignoring the plight of the victim—is addressed in every chapter. Rather than relegating the impact of being victimized to a sidebar or a single chapter, the text infuses the plight of victims into every chapter, focusing on the victim in a wide variety of contexts. Each chapter contains a section titled "Through the Eyes of the Victim": a more intimate portrayal of the physical, emotional, and behavioral impact of crime on innocent parties. These sections serve to remind readers of the lived experience of victims and the importance of forensic psychologists and others in maintaining and providing assistance to those who are suffering through no fault of their own.

INTENDED COURSES AND READERS

Given the current popularity of studies in forensic psychology, this text was designed to appeal to and to be appropriate for a wide variety of undergraduate students. As such, it was designed to be appropriate for students with some education in psychology but whose background in law, criminology, and forensics is still limited. It was also written to be accessible to students on the other side of the coin, that is, those who may be studying prelaw or have some familiarity with criminal justice but whose foundation in psychology is more basic. Lastly, many of the students who register for our courses do so simply because they are fascinated by the forensic psychology–related television shows and movies named earlier in this preface but have no intention of a career in any such field. Therefore, the textbook is also designed for students who are taking the course as a general education elective and are simply interested in the topic to round out their education in another field and to complete their degree requirements.

Because the present textbook is designed to appeal to and be appropriate for such a wide variety of students, it contains a list of key terms at the end of every chapter and a glossary of those terms to help familiarize students with what may be new concepts for them. References, citations, and case law references are also contained at the end of the text for those who wish to delve deeper into particular cases or topics.

ORGANIZATION AND FEATURES

This textbook is comprised of eleven chapters. Each chapter is an independent unit, so instructors can deliver those chapters in any order they wish without disrupting the learning process. Chapter 1 introduces the topic of forensic psychology and provides a broad foundation for the rest of the book with definitions of essential terminology and concepts that will be found throughout the remainder of the book. In Chapter 2, students will be introduced to the role that forensic psychologists play in regard to police, corrections officers, and other first responders, including preemployment screenings, fitness for duty evaluations, and crisis intervention. Chapter 3 focuses on the psychology of investigations and discusses the detection of deception and the importance of being able to distinguish between "normal" and "abnormal" behavior. Juvenile criminal behavior is addressed in Chapter 4, with an emphasis on the manner in which hormonal changes and brain development (or lack thereof) play a role in juvenile impulsive and aggressive behavior. In Chapter 5, the text focuses on the role of both nature and nurture in the development of violent behavior as well as the impact of violence on those who have been victimized. Sexual assault is addressed in Chapter 6, as is the tendency of others to unfairly blame the victims of such assault and the rationale for blaming the victim. Actuarial assessment of sex offenders is also discussed in Chapter 6. Chapter 7 focuses on cases of extreme violence and presents examples of mass murder, spree killing, and serial homicides along with the personality disorders often associated with such offenders. In Chapter 8, the text turns to the topic of behavioral analysis and seeks to dismiss many of the myths associated with criminal profiling while discussing both the methodologies and the shortcomings of such analysis. Chapter 9 introduces students to the terminology and procedures of the court system and provides a foundation for Chapter 10, which delves deeper into the specific role of forensic psychologists in assisting with determinations of competence to stand trial, pleas of not guilty by reason of insanity, and the treatment and disposition of those with mental illness. Lastly, Chapter 11 discusses the manner in which deinstitutionalization of psychiatric hospitals has led to an influx of those with mental illnesses into the correctional system and the manner in which such individuals are treated by that same system.

DIVERSITY, EQUITY, AND INCLUSION

This book was written with an understanding of the tremendous importance of embracing, supporting, and including individuals from a wide variety of backgrounds and belief systems. As with the emphasis on the experience of victims, which is infused throughout the book rather than being relegated to a single chapter or text box, the importance of acceptance and being an ally to underrepresented populations is vitally important. To that end, gendered pronouns are seldom used in this text, except where their use is required because the pronouns refer to a specific individual who uses those pronouns.

It is hoped that exposing students to the concepts of diversity, equity, and inclusion in this textbook will broaden their understanding of the importance of being accepting and supportive of those whose backgrounds and beliefs are different than their own. After all, a key concept in forensic psychology and criminal justice is that "justice is blind" and that everyone involved in the process should be treated in a humane, fair, and impartial manner regardless of gender, sexual orientation, race, ethnic background, or any of a tremendous variety of other individual factors. It is hoped that exposure to such concepts will broaden their perspective not only in the forensic psychology classroom but in their personal lives, professional lives, and beyond.

CHAPTER HIGHLIGHTS AND DETAILS

Chapter 1. An Introduction to the World of Forensic Psychology

- Define the practice of forensic psychology and distinguish it from other fields of psychology and forensics.

- Explain the development of forensic psychology from early cases to the present day.

- Compare and contrast the educational requirements of the master's degree and doctoral degrees as they apply to forensic practitioners.

- Recognize the importance of following ethical guidelines as a psychologist and some of the unique challenges of doing so that are specific to the field of forensic psychology.

- List and describe the various career paths open to those with degrees in forensic psychology.

Chapter 2. First Responder Psychology

- Define *first responders* and examine the stressors that may be associated with such occupations.

- Delineate different types of stress and the impact that stress may have on an individual's body, mood, and behavior.

- Examine the manner in which the Minnesota Multiphasic Personality Inventory-3 (MMPI-3) is utilized to assist in making hiring decisions for first responders and others.

- Explain the importance of diversity, equity, and inclusion in the first responder workplace and in terms of working with members of the public.

Chapter 3. Psychology of Investigations

- Compare and contrast interview and interrogation techniques.

- List and explain the Reid interrogation technique.

- Distinguish between voluntary, compliant, and persuaded false confessions as a result of interrogation.

- Explain the manner in which the polygraph is used to detect physiological changes and review the literature concerning the accuracy of this device in detecting deception.

- Recognize the potential inaccuracies of eyewitness reports.

- Explore definitions and research related to "normal" and "abnormal" human behavior.

Chapter 4. The Juvenile Justice Process

- List and describe the steps involved in the juvenile justice process.

- Describe the role and function of juvenile detention centers and the potential benefits and risks of placing juveniles in such a setting.

- Compare and contrast static and dynamic risk and protective factors for juveniles.

- Summarize social learning theory and the impact of the social environment on juvenile behavior.

- Identify treatment approaches that have been attempted and the relative merits and drawbacks of such approaches.

Chapter 5. Aggression and Violent Behavior

- Define key terms associated with aggression and violence in modern society.

- Explain the phrase "correlation does not imply causation" and the application of this concept to the science of forensic psychology.

- Identify the hormones and brain structures involved in human aggression and violence.

- Summarize of the role of alcohol and other drugs on violent and aggressive behavior.

- Explain the concept of personality disorders and those disorders most often associated with aggressive and violent behavior.

- Define intimate partner violence (IPV) and discuss the risk factors associated with such violence.

Chapter 6. Sexual Assault, Rape, and Child Molestation

- Define sexual assault and rape and discuss the frequency of such offenses and the reasons that such offenses often go unreported by victims.

- Define paraphilias and paraphilic disorders and analyze the difference between the two.

- Review the procedures for psychological assessment of sex offenders and the treatment modalities available for such offenders.

- Explain Megan's Law and the Adam Walsh Act and debate the effectiveness of such measures in reducing the incidence of sex offenses.

- Delineate symptoms of post-traumatic stress disorder and discuss the manner in which victims of sex offenses may experience this disorder.

Chapter 7. Extreme Violence: Mass Murder, Spree Killing, and Serial Killing

- Provide definitions and case examples of mass murder, spree killing, and serial killing.

- Identify commonalities between mass murderers and spree killers.

- Differentiate serial killers in motive and methodology from mass murderers and spree killers.

- Compare and contrast the concepts of antisocial personality disorder and psychopathy.

- Discuss the manner in which modus operandi, ritualistic behavior, and signature may be useful in the behavioral analysis of an offender.

Chapter 8. Behavioral Analysis

- Explain the manner in which early unsolved cases led to use of the scientific method as part of an attempt to apprehend offenders.

- Debunk myths surrounding behavioral analysis and discuss the manner in which television and other forms of media have misled the public about the criminal profiling process.

- Examine the tenets of criminal profiling.

- Describe and compare different methods of criminal profiling.

- Describe the purpose and process of victim–offender mediation.

Chapter 9. Forensic Psychology and the Courtroom

- Provide basic definitions of courtroom participants and the duties and responsibilities of each.

- Discuss basic courtroom procedures and practices, including jury selection.

- Describe the federal and state court systems and the responsibilities of each of these systems.

- Explain civil court and criminal courts as well as the similarities and differences between these two courts.

- Identify and explain the role of the forensic psychologist in courtroom procedures.

Chapter 10. Psychology and the Law

- Identify the impact of deinstitutionalizing psychiatric facilities on the prison system.

- Describe the role, functioning, and purpose of mental health courts, veteran's courts, and other specialized courts.

- Explain the conditions under which a forensic psychologist has a duty to warn others of a potentially dangerous client.

- Define competence to stand trial, the rationale for such assessments, and the manner in which such an assessment may be conducted.

- Define and describe the not guilty by reason of insanity defense and compare that defense to a plea of guilty but mentally ill.

Chapter 11. The Correctional System

- Discuss the relative merits and drawbacks of punishment and rehabilitation in attempting to change maladaptive/illegal behavior.

- Explain the role of intermediate sanctions, including fines, community service, and probation, in making the punishment fit the crime.

- Compare the rates and cost of incarceration in the United States as opposed to other countries.

- Define evidence-based corrections and discuss the importance of using empirical evidence to select programs designed to reduce recidivism.

- Identify the unique challenges of incarcerating those with addictions, mental health challenges, and other special needs.

LEARNING OBJECTIVES

Each chapter begins with a number of learning objectives to assist both instructors and students in being aware of the key concepts that will be presented within that chapter. The learning objectives are framed as verifiable actions that students should be able to demonstrate after reading the material contained in the chapter.

CHAPTER SUMMARIES

Every chapter ends with a concise summary reviewing the learning objectives and reiterating the essential information from that chapter to help reinforce students' understanding and retention of that material.

EXERCISES AND DISCUSSION QUESTIONS

At the end of each chapter is a section of exercises and discussion questions. These questions go beyond the material presented in the chapter by asking the students to consider their personal opinions about a dilemma related to that topic. This is intended to help students consider both sides of an issue in an unbiased manner and invite them to reach their own informed decision. For example, in Chapter 4, students are asked to consider whether suspending students from school for inappropriate behavior actually serves to discourage that behavior or whether the suspended student might see this as a vacation from school and therefore suspension might serve to reward rather than discourage their maladaptive behavior. It is hoped that such dilemmas will serve to foster healthy debate among students while strengthening their critical thinking skills.

DIGITAL RESOURCES

This text includes an array of instructor teaching materials designed to save you time and to help you keep students engaged. To learn more, visit sagepub.com or contact your SAGE representative at sagepub.com/findmyrep.

AN INTRODUCTION TO THE WORLD OF FORENSIC PSYCHOLOGY

LEARNING OBJECTIVES

1. Define the practice of forensic psychology and distinguish it from other fields of psychology and other fields of forensics.

2. Describe the development of forensic psychology from first early cases to the present day.

3. Compare and contrast the educational requirements of the master's degree and doctoral degrees as they apply to forensic practitioners.

4. Recognize the importance of following ethical guidelines as a psychologist and some of the unique challenges of doing so that are specific to the field of forensic psychology.

5. List and describe the various career paths open to those with degrees in forensic psychology.

Many children grow up dreaming of being a firefighter or maybe an astronaut or a singer or a doctor or an actor. Not me. From as early as I can remember, I wanted to be a psychologist. I was fascinated with the workings of the human mind. I managed to find a course or two on the topic in high school and then majored in psychology in college. I did well enough in college to be accepted to a combined master's/PhD program, and I spent the next five years after college grinding away with tests, writing papers, practicums (more papers), and an internship (and even more writing!). Finally, at age 27, having completed all my studies, I entered the workforce as a psychologist. Just a few years after doing so, I was faced with a sad realization. I wasn't happy with the work I was doing. The clients were fine, nice people. It just wasn't what I had pictured or hoped for. To be honest, I was less than thrilled with the idea of continuing to do what I was doing for the next 25 years.

I had always had an interest in criminal behavior, so on a whim, I called the State Correctional Institution at Pittsburgh. After learning that they did indeed employ psychologists and talking to the person in charge of the psychology department, I was invited to visit the prison for a few days to see exactly what it was that psychologists did in that setting. The prison was a grim and foreboding castle-like penitentiary, very much like what you may have seen in Shawshank Redemption *or other prison movies. My guide walked me across the main yard, which also seemed to be straight out of a movie, with several hundred muscular, angry-looking men lifting weights and playing basketball. I asked my guide what kind of offenders were incarcerated in this prison. In a matter-of-fact tone he said, "Oh we got 'em all. Murderers, rapists, and child molesters. Death row. Hell, we got one guy who they say is a cannibal. But I bet you don't want to meet him!"*

But indeed, I did want to meet him. As strange as it may sound, I knew that I had found my calling. For those who want to study the depths of the human mind, what could be more fascinating than to talk to those who have committed the most extreme acts? What compelled these people to do the things they did? What were they thinking and feeling when they committed these acts? And had their thoughts, emotions, and behaviors changed since then? How? And why? So I asked my guide to take me to the man who was reportedly a cannibal, and I did talk to him. And thus began the next stage of my career: as a psychologist in a maximum-security prison.

INTRODUCTION

In 1888, the people of London England were scared—and with good reason. Women were being murdered, and the murders were especially gruesome. The victims were found with their throats slashed and with some of their internal organs removed. At least five women were killed in such a manner, and perhaps more by the same individual. Naturally, people wondered, who was doing this? What kind of person would do such a thing? And why? Speculation ran wild, with one popular theory being that the murderer was a doctor and their medical training was allowing them to cleanly remove the internal organs, though this still did not answer the questions of who was doing so or why they were doing it. Although the term *forensic psychology* did not exist at that time, the case of Jack the Ripper stirred the imagination. This may have been the beginning of the notion that by analyzing the crime, we could learn something about the criminal—a precursor, perhaps, to the ideas of modern forensic psychology.

The crimes of Jack the Ripper, whose true identity is still unknown, frightened the people of London and likely led many to wonder what kind of person would commit such atrocities.

David Levenson / Alamy Stock Photo

For some time now, there has been tremendous interest in movies and television shows about forensics. On TV, millions watch shows such as *CSI, Law and Order: Special Victims Unit, Dexter,* and *Forensic Files.* In the movie theater, people happily munch their popcorn while watching *Silence of the Lambs, Seven, Psycho, No Country for Old Men,* or any of a slew of similar movies. It is vitally important to keep in mind that as fascinating and exciting as these shows are, they are not necessarily accurate representations of forensic psychology or any other aspect of forensic investigation. Many such programs make it seem as though forensic psychology is at least partly supernatural, as if the psychologist has some mysterious ability or magical intuition that leads them to be able to identify the perpetrator. While years of experience may lend some insight, there is not a shred of evidence to suggest that forensic psychologists have any supernatural ability. Forensic science must be based on just that: empiricism and research. Just as we know that superheroes flying through the sky make for great movies but have no basis in reality, it is important for us to keep in mind that media portrayals of forensic psychology may be equally exciting but is no more realistic than the ability to fly like a superhero.

Definitions and the Importance of Keeping an Open Mind

The term **forensics** generally refers to scientific tests or techniques that are used to detect crimes or to solve those crimes. **Forensic evidence** has been obtained by scientific methods and is used to help solve crimes. Forensic evidence may include (but is not limited to) fingerprints, DNA, ballistics, blood spatter patterns, tire tracks, computer data, photos or video, or many other sources of evidence. In the instance of, say, the robbery of a grocery store, the forensic evidence gathered might include images of the offender on the store's security camera, fingerprints, eyewitness reports of the appearance of the offender, and video of the offender's car arriving at or leaving the scene as captured on security cameras in the parking lot. All these pieces of evidence can be collected and analyzed by various forensic experts as part of an effort to apprehend the criminal.

During his career in the department of corrections, the author of the present textbook was taking a break from a meeting with departments lawyers. One lawyer commented that the main thing that lawyers and psychologists have in common is that they begin answering any question with the phrase, "Really, it depends . . ." That truly struck a chord. Upon learning that someone is a forensic psychologist, members of the public frequently announce that they are big fans of television programs and movies about the topic and then launch into a series of questions along the lines of "I've just never understood why someone would kill another person. Why do they do it?" The answer to such a question invariably starts with "Really, it depends . . ." and that is indeed the case.

Such behavior depends whether the (now deceased) individual committed a home invasion in the middle of the night, in which case, the reason for killing them might very well have been self-defense. It depends on whether an ex-lover killed the new lover in a fit of rage, in which case, the reason for the killing might have been jealousy. It depends on whether the offender believed that the victim was the devil and was infiltrating their soul in order to take over the earth, in which case, the reason for the killing may have been a severe mental illness— or a thousand other explanations. It is vitally important for the budding forensic psychologist to remember that the answer to such questions is rarely a simple one, and even when an answer appears to be simple, a competent forensic psychologist will keep an open mind and consider that things may not be as simple as they at first appear to be. As we shall see in this chapter, and in subsequent ones, it is not uncommon for the answer to our questions to begin with "It depends."

THE VARIETY OF FORENSIC PROFESSIONALS

Whether we are aware of it or not, a great deal of what we do and when we do it is stored on our cell phones, computers, and other devices and is subject to forensic analysis. A **forensic digital analyst**, for example, would retrieve and collect evidence related to crimes and cybercrimes. This might involve retrieving hidden or supposedly deleted search history from the accused individuals' computer or phone. In many cases, even the cars we drive integrate our daily technology and collect considerable data about our location, driving speed, where stops were made, and, in some cases, even whether or not our hands were on the wheel. All of this information may be collected and analyzed by a digital analyst in order to aid in solving a crime. A forensic digital analyst might determine the location of a person's cell phone at a given time by identifying the last cell phone tower the phone received a signal or ping from. A forensic digital analyst might also serve as an expert witness when testifying about cybercrime or cyber security.

When we watch the local weather report, we are more likely to be thinking about whether or not we need to have an umbrella with us today than we are thinking about solving a crime. However, a **forensic meteorologist** may use their expertise in the science of weather to reconstruct weather data for a particular place and time and use this in civil or criminal proceedings. For example, a forensic meteorologist might study precipitation patterns, temperature, and other data to reconstruct whether or not weather may have played a role in the fact that a plane crashed during landing. In a criminal case, such an expert might reconstruct the weather data in the area of the crime in order to determine whether or not it is possible that no footprints were left outside the crime scene due to the weather at that time and since then.

If at first glance we don't associate weather with forensics, then it seems likely that we might not initially associate entomology (the study of insects) with forensics. However, **forensic entomologists** can and do provide valuable insight into helping solve crimes. For example, such a professional can use their expertise about insect development and populations to assist in determining how long a body has been exposed and decaying and whether or not that body has been moved or its position changed.

Nursing as we know it is a profession that involves providing care to the sick and injured. Forensic nursing involves nurses who are trained to provide such care to those who have been victims of violence. For example, forensic nurses provide care to those who have been sexually or physically assaulted; such care often involves assisting in the collection of evidence (such as DNA) that will be used in the investigation of such offenses. Forensic nurses may also be used as expert witnesses in some cases.

Definition of Psychologist and Forensic Psychologist

Psychologists, as the name implies, are experts in the field of psychology. In broad terms, they attempt to understand and explain the manner in which people think, the emotions they experience, and the manner in which they behave. In terms of day-to-day activities, depending on their area of specialization, a psychologist may be involved in conducting research, performing evaluations, report writing, or counseling or crisis intervention, among a wide variety of other tasks. The term *psychologist* may only be used by those with a doctoral degree (either a PhD or PsyD or, in a few states, a master's degree) and who have passed the psychological licensing exam in their state. Other clinicians may refer to themselves as counselors or therapists or a variety of other titles, but it would be inaccurate for them to refer to themselves as psychologists.

According to the **American Psychological Association (APA)**, **forensic psychology** involves the application of clinical knowledge and research to the judicial and legal systems (Ward, 2013). More narrowly, a forensic psychologist engages in many of the same activities outlined above for any psychologist but performs these duties in a forensic or legal setting. Forensic psychology, then, might be thought of as the application of psychological practices and principles to those people who work in or come into contact with the legal/criminal justice system. In this text, the terms *forensic psychologist, forensic practitioner*, and *forensic clinician* will be used interchangeably, but it should be noted that these titles are not necessarily identical.

Dr. Martin Reiser was hired by the Los Angeles Police Department in 1968 and may have been the first psychologist to work full-time in a police department, thus opening the door to the notion of forensic psychology. He evaluated officers, helped them learn to cope with stress, and discussed issues related to suicide prevention of those officers. Dr. Reiser was known to keep a bulletproof vest in his car and to assist with hostage negotiations procedures (Chawkins, 2015).

In 2001, the APA first officially recognized forensic psychology as a legitimate subspecialty within the field of psychology. This meant that forensic psychology had generated enough research, data, and literature that it could be distinguished from other areas in the field of psychology (Packer & Borum, 2003). APA now has its own division: Division 41, the American Psychology-Law Society. There are now numerous journals and scholarly articles related to forensic psychology and related topics.

By 2012, there were more than 40 colleges and universities offering degrees in forensic psychology (Burl et al., 2012). However, it should be noted that one does not necessarily have to attend a specialized program in forensic psychology to eventually work in this field. The present author obtained a PhD in 1992, when there were few (if any) programs specializing in forensic psychology. Continuing education, conferences, independent study, and practical experience can (and indeed, should) always be obtained even after the completion of one's master's or doctoral degree. Continuing education is an important and required step to maintaining licensure and competency to practice, and there is no substitute for practical experience in helping one to prepare for a career in forensic psychology.

Educational Requirements

The road to becoming a psychologist is a long one. At a very minimum, a master's degree is required, and this typically takes at least two years after achieving a bachelor's degree. A specialized forensic degree is not necessarily required but the practitioner must make certain they have the necessary training and education to adequately perform the duties they are entrusted with. Indeed, such education, supervision, and training are required by both the APA ethical guidelines and specialty guidelines pertaining to competence; clinicians must only practice in areas in which they are adequately trained.

Students aspiring to a career in forensic psychology often ask if they should obtain a master's degree or a doctoral degree; "Which one is better?" As noted above, a truthful answer to this question might begin with the phrase "Really, it depends . . ." because of a number of factors. Such a decision may depend on one's college grades; master's degree programs are less stringent in terms of who they admit, though good grades and scores on admission tests such as the graduate record exam are still advisable. A master's degree generally requires two years of full-time study after receiving a bachelor's degree and should involve some clinical experiences, practicums, and/or internships as well. It will certainly allow for entry-level jobs and clinical work with some clients. At times, depending on licensure and training, supervision by a doctoral-level clinician may be required. In some programs, people with a master's degree are permitted to teach undergraduate courses. However, some jobs may be limited or not permitted to those without a doctoral-level degree.

A doctoral degree can certainly pave the way for some opportunities that would not be available with a master's degree. As we will discuss, doctoral degrees include the PhD (doctor of philosophy), the PsyD (doctor of psychology), and in some cases, the EdD (doctor of education). The PhD tends to be more research-oriented than the PsyD and can take 3–5 years after the master's degree; the PsyD, which is more clinically oriented than the PhD, may take 2–4 years after the master's degree, including an internship. Doctoral-level training, then, requires a substantially longer commitment of time (and likely money as well!) from the potential student. Such degrees allow employment in a wide variety of areas, from psychological testing to research to graduate teaching to supervising other clinicians to private practice and even expert witnessing.

To the uninitiated, forensic psychiatry may sound much the same as forensic psychology, but these are two separate vocations entirely. Psychiatrists are medical doctors (MDs) rather than PhDs or PsyDs. As such, psychiatrists have attended medical school rather than graduate school and therefore have the ability to prescribe medications and to provide expert testimony on issues related to psychotropic and other medications.

CAREERS IN FORENSIC PSYCHOLOGY

It is not uncommon for those in the field of psychology to change jobs or direction on occasion. The present author, as noted at the beginning of this introduction, did not begin his career determined to be a psychologist in the state prison system; in fact, it was the furthest thing from his mind! Psychology, and specifically forensic psychology, has a much wider scope of practice than one might originally think. Many students interested in forensic psychology have the same goal in mind—to be a criminal profiler in the Federal Bureau of Investigation's (FBI's) Behavioral Assessment Unit. Although that is certainly an admirable goal, it is important to keep in mind that they may go on to participate in a wide variety of other fascinating and rewarding career opportunities available to forensic practitioners.

A question frequently asked by those considering a career in forensic psychology is "What exactly is it that a forensic psychologist does?" Once again, the answer to that question may begin with "Really, it depends . . ." In many cases, it depends on exactly what setting the clinician is working in, and there are a wide variety of such settings.

In a courtroom setting, forensic psychologists may offer expert testimony or may work with a lawyer to help select a jury or prepare a witness to give testimony. Forensic psychologists may be tasked with assessing a defendant and providing a report to the court as to that defendant's competency to stand trial and to assist in their own defense. In still other cases, such a psychologist might be asked to render an expert opinion about any mental health issues the defendant may (or may not) have or may testify in regard to a plea that the defendant is **not guilty by reason of insanity (NGRI)**.

In a law enforcement setting, forensic psychologists may work with police agencies to conduct assessments of officer candidates or officers whose fitness for duty is in question. In this same setting, some practitioners will provide evaluation and assistance to officers who have been involved in critical incidents, such as shootings or suicides. Some forensic psychologists may be involved in educating officers in verbal de-escalation or may provide support to hostage negotiations or other specialized response teams. Still other forensic psychologists might provide education and emotional support to officers or others who have been victims of violent offenses.

Some forensic practitioners, including the present author, are employed in a correctional setting such as a jail or prison. In this type of environment, a psychologist would conduct assessments of incoming inmates, provide consultation to administration of the institution, deliver crisis intervention services, and provide individual and group mental health services to incarcerated individuals with a wide variety of mental health challenges.

In addition to the above career paths, some forensic psychologists choose to work with offenders or accused individuals who have been placed in inpatient psychiatric facilities. Such clinicians may conduct testing, evaluations, provide individual or group counseling, or focus on restoring competency so that the accused may be tried in a court of law.

Some forensic psychologists may choose to work with those who have been victimized as part of an ongoing effort to help those individuals recover from the emotional trauma that they suffered as a result of that victimization. Still others may choose to teach at the college or university level; for those interested in becoming a forensic practitioner, the possibilities are wide and varied.

In discussing forensic psychology careers, it would be remiss not to mention the fact that such careers can be challenging for the clinician. As portrayed in books, movies, and television, a career in forensic psychology appears to be very exciting. Indeed, that may often be the case. However, what is rarely (if ever) portrayed in the media is the fact that such excitement can come at a high price. Testifying in court, counseling those who have been victimized, conducting crisis interventions, and the other responsibilities noted above can take a significant emotional toll on the provider of those services. It is important for the forensic clinician to recognize signs of stress not only in those around them but also in themselves and to have adaptive methods of coping with and alleviating such stresses. Only when the forensic psychologist is taking care of themselves can they adequately do the same for others.

Ethics

Ethics may be thought of as those moral principles that guide one's behavior or the manner in which one conducts oneself and treats others. We would perhaps say that a person who is considerate, compassionate, and fair toward others and who refrains from lying, cheating, or stealing is acting in an ethical manner. On the other hand, we would likely say that a person who is deceitful and cruel and only concerned with their own welfare while disregarding the law and the welfare of others is acting unethically.

The code of ethics for psychologists has been established by the APA. Among other ethical principles, this code holds that psychologists should protect their clients from harm, keep their interactions with clients confidential (with a few exceptions that will be discussed later in this text), and only conduct evaluations, counseling, and other services in cases in which they are trained and fully competent to do so. It is vitally important that psychologists diligently follow these and the remainder of the ethical guidelines established by the APA, as even a single failure to do so can bring harm to their client and can also harm the reputation of mental health clinicians in general. Forensic psychology, as a unique and challenging subspecialty of psychology, does have specialty guidelines for forensic psychology that were adopted by the APA Counsel of Representatives in 2011. These guidelines reinforce the importance of diligence, integrity, and competence among other aspirational guidelines and goals.

Adherence to such guidelines during forensic practice is every bit as important as it is in any other field of psychology, but arguably, it can be more challenging in the stressful and difficult field of forensic psychology. For example, during his career in corrections, the author of the present textbook was the subject of death threats on occasions too numerous to count and was physically assaulted on several occasions during that career. In such cases, the clinician may have no choice but to continue to work with those who have threatened or assaulted them. In such cases, it is imperative that the clinician is able to continue to treat that client in a compassionate and professional manner and provide them with the same quality of services that any client is entitled to, regardless of what may have transpired previously.

In maintaining an ethical practice, it is vitally important for the forensic psychologist to make their client aware of the fact that different guidelines apply in that setting than would apply in a private practice clinical setting. For example, in the latter setting, it is understood that the person coming to the psychologist for evaluation and treatment is the client, that their conversations will be confidential (with a few exceptions, as already noted), and the psychologist might in one way or another be an advocate for that client. In a forensic setting, however, it is important to make clear to the individual that it is the court, parole board, or other agency that is the client and that information discussed during the evaluation or session was requested by that agency and will be disclosed to them. In the forensic setting, it is not to be assumed that the psychologist is necessarily an advocate for the individual but may be a neutral party in that regard, whose job is simply to provide an accurate and unbiased report to the court about the accused's competency, appropriateness for parole, or other relevant issue. In regard to ethical practice, all such matters must be made quite clear to the individual in question.

THROUGH THE EYES OF THE VICTIMS

Many forensic psychology textbooks have a chapter devoted to those who have been victimized in some manner. In this book, we do not have a single chapter devoted to victims. Instead, you will find that most chapters have a section called "Through the Victim's Eyes." The trauma and challenges that victims undergo deserve more than a passing reference or a single chapter. Such experiences are incredibly difficult, complex, and multifaceted and it only does them justice to infuse them throughout the text. The author worked in corrections for 20 years; after talking to both victims and offenders and now teaching classes in victimology, he shares that this is only the beginning of being able to understand the courageous journey of those attempting to heal and grow after having been victimized.

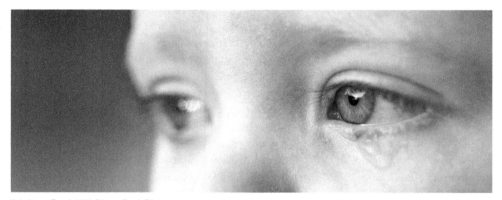

Volodymyr Tverdokhlib/Alamy Stock Photo

First Responder Psychology—Chapter 2

The number of books, movies, and television shows that portray police, firefighters, FBI agents, combat veterans, and other **first responders** (those trained to respond immediately to emergency events) is too numerous to count. Typically, these jobs are portrayed as exciting and glamorous—the FBI agent breaking down a door to rescue a kidnapped child from the arms of a serial killer, a police officer tackling the kidnapper before they can push their victim off the edge of a building, or a firefighter rescuing a child from a burning building. While making for an exciting program, such portrayals do little justice to the reality of being a first responder. In the media, first responders are often portrayed as heroes who respond to crisis situations, resolve those situations, and then bask in the adulation of the crowd around them, without any portrayal of the challenges and stresses of such an occupation. In a movie, we may see the "good cop" shoot a number of "bad-guy criminals" in what appears to be a justifiable situation. The officer then walks away, receiving pats on the back for doing such a great job and appearing unconcerned with the consequences of their actions. In reality, the career of a first responder can be tremendously difficult; the taking of a human life, even when required in self-defense, is likely to have a tremendous impact on the shooter; of course, the impact of that event on the family of the person who was shot will also be incredibly traumatic. First responder careers can take a tremendous physical and emotional toll on first responders and on their families, as we will see in Chapter 2.

As it pertains to first responders, forensic psychologists may assist with interviews and evaluations of those who are applying for such positions. Such evaluations may include psychological testing to help determine whether a particular individual is likely to be well-suited for a first responder occupation. The forensic practitioner may also assess individuals who are already working as first responders in making certain that they are still mentally and emotionally fit to continue to perform such difficult and often hazardous duties. Such practitioners may provide clinical intervention in the case of first responders who are identified as struggling with mental health concerns and/or who have been involved in a critical incident, such as a shooting or other event that is beyond the realm of normal human experience.

In some settings, forensic psychologists provide organizational or operational support to police and other organizations, such as assisting with hostage negotiations or attempting to intervene and verbally de-escalate individuals who are potentially suicidal. They may also provide consultation to supervisory personnel related to issues such as diversity, equity, and inclusion as well as programs and interventions that may assist first responders in reducing and managing stress. Consultation related to reducing alcohol/substance abuse and preventing suicide may be of special importance; as will be discussed in Chapter 2, drug and alcohol abuse, divorce rates, and suicide rates are unfortunately all too common among those who work as first responders.

It is important to know that it is not only uninvolved, innocent third parties who can be victimized. The first responders themselves can be victims as a result of carrying out their job responsibilities. For example, it is not uncommon for police officers to be threatened or assaulted during the course of their duties. This makes them both a first responder *and* a victim. The same is true for a paramedic who is assaulted by the very patient they are trying to care for or a corrections officer who has bodily fluids thrown on them. As one corrections officer told the author of the present textbook, "In this job, it's not a question of will you be assaulted. It's a question of when, and how bad is it gonna be?" We would be remiss not to discuss the role of first responders as victims.

Psychology of Investigations—Chapter 3

It is important for the forensic practitioner to be able to distinguish between so-called normal and abnormal human behavior. On the surface, this may seem easy. We may consider it to be normal to consume meat, to tip the server at a restaurant, to drink alcohol, or any of an almost infinite number of other behaviors. However, such assumptions about what is normal are typically based on our own experience, and it is important for us to understand and accept that such practices are not necessarily the norm for every person or every culture in every time frame.

We might consider it to be normal and even commonplace to assist a person who is injured or in distress. We might also believe it to be normal for a person to refuse to follow the order of an authority figure if that authority was ordering them to cause someone else significant pain. However, as we will see in Chapter 3, an individual stopping to help someone in distress or a person refusing the order of an authority figure to inflict pain on someone are not as commonplace as we might think and, in some cases, may actually represent the exception to the rule. Our perceptions about normal behavior may not always be as accurate as we would like to believe.

In Chapter 3, we will also look at our ability to detect deception in others. We may assume (and that is something a good forensic psychologist should not do!) that we can tell if a person is lying to us. After all, we may reason, such a person will be nervous about the lies they are telling, and that anxiety should manifest itself in some observable way. Surely we will be able to tell from their sweating, their lack of eye contact, and their nervous tics that they are lying . . . won't we? We will examine this assumption and evidence about the accuracy of the polygraph or "lie detector" and its role in conducting investigations.

Eyewitness testimony often plays an important role in findings of guilt. But as we shall see, our memories are quite fallible and may be easily influenced by even a single word in the manner in which a question is phrased. We will also look at what is referred to as the *own race bias* and the difficulty and inaccuracy that people experience in identifying those who are of different ethnic or racial backgrounds than their own.

The Juvenile Justice Process—Chapter 4

Those who work in the mental health fields often debate whether behavior is a product of nature or nurture. That is, does a person (or animal, for that matter) engage in a particular behavior because the genetics, biology, or chemistry of their body lead them to do so (the "nature" point of view)? Or do they engage in that behavior because at some point during their development, they learned to do so (the "nurture" point of view)? We may express the belief that babies cry because over the centuries, those babies that cried were more likely to be fed than those who did not cry, so now their genetics is such that they are programmed to cry. On the other hand, it could be argued that babies quickly learn that crying will be rewarded with a meal of warm milk, thus making them more likely to cry in the future. While it is not certain that this debate will ever be settled once and for all, it is the case that forensic practitioners examine and debate similar nature versus nurture issues when examining the development of juvenile criminal behavior, as we will examine in Chapter 4.

By definition, **juveniles** (usually thought of as those under 18 years of age) are still developing physically, mentally, and emotionally, and therefore represent an especially vulnerable population. Parental behavior such as drug use, drug use while pregnant, and physical, sexual, and emotional abuse or neglect are only a few of the many factors that play a critical role in a child's development. Most people agree that young people represent an incredibly valuable and delicate resource, and forensic practitioners can and often do have a vital role in the decisions that are made in the legal system about how to best manage the young people who come into contact with that system.

Especially with children and juveniles, it is vitally important for the forensic practitioner to help guide court decisions related to rehabilitation versus punishment in changing juvenile criminal behavior. Although some may think on the surface that placement in a juvenile detention center will "scare the kid straight," this should not at all be taken for granted. As we will see in Chapter 4, such placement may very well have the opposite effect. Juvenile detention centers can be violent places with rampant criminal activity and gang membership. It is entirely possible that instead of mending their ways, a young person will instead become more violent in order to adapt and survive in a hostile environment. Clearly, this is the opposite of what anyone would want to happen and only increases the chances of that young person re-offending. Instead, targeted programs of rehabilitation, including drug and alcohol treatment, education, mentoring, and a stable living environment, may help to both save taxpayer money and reduce the chances of that young person growing up to commit further offenses.

If and when a juvenile is placed in a detention center, the forensic psychologist may be involved in evaluating incoming youth to determine what mental health services (if any) they might need during their stay and in delivering mental health services in that setting. Such youth have often been physically, sexually, or emotionally abused or have been neglected, and the practitioner may be charged with providing treatment to them in such cases.

Aggression and Violent Behavior—Chapter 5

In Chapter 5, we will also learn that correlation does not imply causation. That is, simply because two factors are related does not necessarily mean that one of those factors caused the other. For example, perhaps there is a case in which a school shooter played violent video games and listened to violent music lyrics before committing the shooting. It would be easy (but incorrect!) to jump to the conclusion that the video games and music caused that person to commit the shooting. An astute forensic practitioner realizes the importance of reaching conclusions based on all the evidence and research that is available to them, not merely based on opinions, coincidences, or assumptions.

As mentioned above, the debate about nature versus nurture and their relative influence on human behavior is ongoing in the field of psychology. Forensic psychology is certainly no exception to this rule, especially when it comes to an examination of aggression and violent behavior. Indeed, forensic psychologists have an important role in understanding the conditions under which people engage in violent behavior, and we may find that in some cases, both nature and nurture play a role in aggression and violence. In Chapter 5, we will begin to look at and differentiate between different types of aggressive and violent behavior, and we will discuss the manner in which human biology, brain development, hormonal factors, the use of alcohol and other drugs, and other factors can play a role in influencing such behavior.

As we will also see, research as far back as the early 1960s suggested that when children observed an adult behaving in an aggressive manner, the children tended to imitate that behavior, becoming more aggressive themselves (Bandura et al., 1961). We will also look at violence between intimate partners and within families—what that is and how that can impact not only the direct victim but the indirect victims (such as children) and the intergenerational transmission of violence.

Forensic and other psychologists may work with victims of violent behavior. Being victimized by violence directly or indirectly (such as witnessing a violent act toward others) can have profound and lasting physical, emotional, and psychological impacts on the victim and can lead them to develop mental illnesses, impair their functioning, and destroy relationships. In this chapter, we will learn about the signs and symptoms of **post-traumatic stress disorder (PTSD)**.

Sexual Assault, Rape, and Child Molestation—Chapter 6

In Chapter 6, we will examine the difficult topics of sexual assault, rape, and child molestation. We will examine the differences between date rape, acquaintance rape, stranger rape, and statutory sexual assault. We will also discuss the cognitive, emotional, and behavioral impact on those who have been so victimized, including (but not limited to) mental health concerns such as PTSD.

In many courtroom dramas (and, at times, in actual courtrooms), we will see a defense attorney imply that the victim is at least partly to blame for the fact that they were assaulted. Perhaps the defense attorney questions the victim as to how much they had to drink, what they were wearing, why they were out so late, or other questions that suggest that the victim's own actions contributed to the fact that they were assaulted. We will also discuss the psychological research on why we are so often willing and even eager to blame the victim for the awful thing that was done to them when instead it is the offender who is truly the blameworthy one.

In some settings, a forensic psychologist may conduct a psychological evaluation of an accused sex offender so that they can make a recommendation to the court as to whether the accused, if convicted, should be considered a sexually violent predator (SVP). If such a determination is made, the SVP will be subjected to more frequent and more lengthy sex offender registration requirements. In correctional settings, psychologists also perform sex offender assessments and provide sex offender treatment to those who are convicted of and incarcerated for such offenses. With sex offenders, some members of the public may believe that society should simply lock them up and throw away the key. However, it is important to realize that many such offenders will eventually be released back into the community. When that day comes, does the public want them to be released no better than when they were originally incarcerated, or would the community prefer these offenders to have had some treatment in order to decrease their risk of re-offending?

Forensic and other psychologists will often interact with, assess, and treat those who have been victims of sexual assault. It should be noted that this can be challenging and emotionally difficult work first and foremost for the victim but also to a lesser degree for the therapist. Hearing someone graphically describe the manner in which they were sexually assaulted can be heartrending indeed. In this chapter, we will spend some time discussing the role of working with those who have been so victimized and the courageous battle such individuals fight in regaining their lives and functioning.

Extreme Violence: Mass Murder, Spree Killing, and Serial Killing—Chapter 7

In Chapter 7, we will take a look at extreme violent behavior. So many of the media portrayals that we have already discussed involve depictions and descriptions of incredibly violent offenders. In such depictions, we may see the young FBI agent interviewing the famous serial killer, the police on the scene of a school shooting, or the bomb squad attempting to defuse the explosive before it can erupt in the crowded stadium. Such portrayals are exciting but often have little or no basis in reality.

In the media, we often see or hear the words **mass murderer** or **spree killer** or **serial killer** used interchangeably, but in fact, such terms describe different offenses and offenders. In Chapter 7, we will define each of these terms and learn that mass murderers and spree killers share a number of similarities, but serial killers may be distinctly different than the former two groups. There will also be a discussion of some of the infamous offenders in these categories.

Chapter 7 will also discuss what makes the individuals who commit such offenses so different from most other people. You may be able to imagine yourself reacting with violence if a family member was being threatened or had been assaulted. However, in all likelihood, it would be impossible for you to fathom engaging in multiple acts of violence against people that you barely knew, who had done nothing to you or your family. In Chapter 7, we will discuss the signs and symptoms of what is referred to as **antisocial personality disorder**, which simply means that an individual feels little (or in some cases, absolutely no) remorse for their actions, even when those actions are extremely harmful to others.

Behavioral Analysis—Chapter 8

Movies such as *Silence of the Lambs* and television shows such as *Mindhunter* purport to show us the early days of the FBI's Behavioral Sciences Unit (which have now evolved into the Behavioral

Assessment Units). The Behavioral Sciences Unit (BSU) was originally formed in the early 1970s by Patrick Mullany and Howard Teten and consisted of a handful of agents. Later, John Douglas and Robert Ressler joined the group and the BSU began to collect data on sexual and violent crimes, establishing a database of such offenses and offenders. In the late 1970s and early 1980s, these agents and others began to provide consultation and training to other law enforcement agencies regarding serial sexual and violent offenders. Some of the books that came from this, including Resslers's *Whoever Fights Monsters* and Douglas's *Mindhunter* (among many others) fueled the public's imagination and desire to learn more about the dark side of the human mind.

In this chapter, we will take a deeper dive into the beginnings of criminal profiling and behavioral analysis. We will discuss the notion that the crime tells us about the criminal and the belief of some forensic psychologists that behavior reflects personality. For that reason, some forensic practitioners believe that by studying a crime scene and the behavior of the offender, they will be able to reach some conclusions about the personality of the offender and perhaps the future behavior of that offender. Different methodologies of behavioral analysis will be explained, and we will examine the debate about whether such techniques are empirically grounded and reliable.

We will also discuss the portrayal of forensic psychologists and profilers in the media and the idea that such portrayals are not necessarily (or at all likely) to be accurate. The notion that forensic psychologists have some supernatural or psychic ability, as we will see, is a complete fabrication. Indeed, such profiling has been wildly inaccurate at times, as we will see in the case of the Beltway Snipers; in such cases, such notions can do more harm than good. We will also discuss the fact that despite media portrayals of criminal profiling as commonly accepted and unfailingly accurate, only 10% of forensic psychologists surveyed stated that they had ever engaged in any type of criminal profiling, and only 17% expressed the belief that such profiling was based on scientifically reliable techniques (Torres et al., 2006).

Turning to the victim, we will discuss **victim–offender mediation**, in which the victim of an offense requests to talk with their offender. In such cases, it is hoped that the victim, in cooperation with a state agency specializing in this type of remediation, will be able to obtain some emotional closure and healing by talking to their offender. In some cases, such interactions can also help the offender to understand the impact of their offense on that person and the community.

Forensic Psychology and the Courtroom—Chapter 9

In Chapter 9, we will discuss the legal system and the role of forensic psychologists in that system. The legal system is a world unto itself, and to those unfamiliar with the structure of the court system, terminology, procedures, and professionals in the courtroom, it can be an intimidating and complex world indeed. In this chapter, we discuss federal and state court systems and the difference between criminal and civil matters. We will also discuss the roles of those professionals in the courtroom, referred to as the **courtroom work group**.

The role of the forensic practitioner related to court can be quite varied. Some practitioners might assist a lawyer in picking a jury that they believe will be favorable to their client. Others might help to prepare a witness for the rigors of the witness stand and cross-examination. Some may be used as expert witnesses on topics related to mental health issues or the potential consequences of suffering from abuse or other trauma.

We will also examine what psychologists can teach us about the reliability of memory, the influence of leading questions, and how changing a single word in the way a question is asked can have a significant impact on the answer provided by a witness.

As we will see in this chapter, defendants are to be afforded a jury of their peers. However, there can be debate about exactly what comprises *peers*. With some frequency, defendants who are part of a racial or ethnic minority may find themselves being judged by a jury that is comprised of few (or zero) members who are racially or ethnically diverse. Such diversity, equity, and inclusion in the jury pool is vitally important in helping the jury to understand and appreciate the life experiences of minority group members and to reduce (or ideally, eliminate) any bias or prejudice (Joshi & Kline, 2015).

Psychology and the Law—Chapter 10

Having gained a foundation in the workings of the legal and court system in Chapter 9, in Chapter 10, we take a deeper dive into the intersection of psychology and the legal system and will discuss the complexities (of which there are many!) when these two systems interact. As we shall see, psychology and the law have been intertwined since at least 1843, when Daniel M'Naughten was put on trial for shooting a man he believed to be the prime minister of the United Kingdom. At trial, it was obvious to all parties involved that M'Naughten was very seriously mentally ill. The defense, in cooperation with the prosecution and the judge, found the defendant to be not guilty by reason of insanity (NGRI); he was then committed to a psychiatric institute rather than being incarcerated. We will discuss how this plea is now used in different-

Some forensic psychologists will work and testify in a courtroom setting similar to this one.

keeton12/iStock Photo

ent states, alternatives to this plea, and why it is so controversial. We will also compare and contrast the cases of Jeffrey Dahmer and Andrea Yates as they apply to the NGRI plea.

Forensic practitioners can become involved in the legal process early on, conducting evaluations of the accused's competence to stand trial. As we will see, it is a relatively common practice as legal proceedings begin to make certain that the accused has the mental capacity to understand what they are accused of and the courtroom process itself and that they are able to assist their lawyer in their own defense. The assessment of competence (and attempts to restore the accused to competence when necessary) are vitally important in making sure that the due process rights of the accused are not violated.

In Chapter 10, we will discuss the impact of **deinstitutionalization**, the release of thousands of people from psychiatric institutions into the community, and we will see that this release was followed by a subsequent influx of individuals with mental illness into the criminal justice system and eventually into jails and prisons (Earley, 2007). It is not difficult to imagine that the stark and hostile environment of jail or prison would be counterproductive to the mental health of almost anyone and could certainly exacerbate the severity of mental illness for those who are already suffering from such a disorder. Thus, mental health practitioners have become a vital part of the correctional system, which was ill prepared to assess, treat, and care for those with mental illnesses. As we will see, an increasing number of counties today are implementing various types of specialized courts to divert those with mental illness, drug addictions, and other issues from incarceration into a program of monitored treatment when possible.

Psychologists hold the issue of confidentiality to be of paramount importance. After all, their clients may reveal and discuss deeply personal and difficult issues based on the notion that those discussions will remain confidential. However, especially in forensic settings, there may be exceptions to the boundaries of confidentiality, which the psychologist should make the client aware of in advance. As we shall see, if a client discloses that they are going to harm or kill themselves or have plans to harm or kill a specific other individual, it is important (and required) that the psychologist disclose this information and take steps to inform and protect the individual(s) who have been threatened.

The Correctional System—Chapter 11

In the United States (U. S.), citizens hold their freedom to be of the highest possible importance. With some exceptions, we are allowed to say what we want and go where we want with limited concerns in regard to having those freedoms taken away from us, unless we commit a criminal offense of some type. As we will see, even if a person has a serious mental illness, if they are not committing an offense and pose no identifiable risk of harm to themselves or others, we cannot deprive them of their basic rights and freedoms. In Chapter 11, we will also discuss the process of *involuntary civil commitment*—that is, placing a person in a psychiatric unit or institution against their will—and the manner in which we attempt to balance that individual's due process rights with the safety of those in the community.

Chapter 11 will also focus on the role of psychology for those in the jail and prison system. As we will see, the U. S. has the highest incarceration rate of any nation on the planet, according to the World Prison Brief, a database kept by the Institute for Crime & Justice Policy Research at Birkbeck at the University of London. Some might argue that this is because Americans are tough on crime and will not tolerate criminal offenses while some other countries let people get away with a lot more. On the other hand, it could be that the U. S. is incarcerating people at great expense and, at times, without good reason. A great many of those who are incarcerated in the U. S. are in jail or prison for nonviolent offenses. As we will see, in such cases, taxpaying citizens are often paying more money to incarcerate offenders than they would be paying to send someone to college! We must ask ourselves whether we believe that we need to spend thousands (and thousands!) of dollars per year to incarcerate someone who committed a nonviolent retail theft of items with practically no value.

It is also worth noting that incarceration in the U. S. demonstrates evidence of great racial disparity, with Black Americans being incarcerated at nearly five times the rate of white Americans, and Latinx persons being incarcerated at 1.3 times the rate of non-Latinx white Americans (Nellis, 2021). It goes without saying that such disparity can have devastating, long-lasting consequences, including (but not limited to) children growing up without the emotional or financial support of one (or in some cases, both) parents. The Sentencing Project also found that in 12 states in the U. S., more than half those incarcerated are Black.

Psychologists in the jail and prison setting perform evaluations of incoming inmates to determine their need for mental health treatment or placement in a specialized unit to meet a particular need. Forensic practitioners may also conduct crisis intervention, psychological evaluations on those being considered for release, and routine screening and treatment. In my own experience, when being interviewed by a student who was preparing a paper on the topic of forensic psychology, I was invariably asked "What is an average day like here?" I could honestly answer "That's my favorite part of this job: No two days are the same—ever. Maybe not every day is easy, but it is never boring!"

In this chapter, we will discuss **evidence-based corrections**; that is, what steps can the correctional system take to try to ensure that those who are released will not commit further offenses? Some might say that if the prison environment is truly punishing, it will discourage offenders from committing offenses in the future because they will not want to return. However, others might argue that a punishment-focused environment will only make inmates more angry and violent and perhaps more likely to re-offend after release than they would have been. We will examine the evidence as to whether the correctional system should involve punishment versus rehabilitation.

CONCLUSION

For many years, when a brutal or unusual crime has been committed, people have wondered what kind of person would do such a thing. What could they have been thinking or feeling when they did so? This curiosity about bizarre and violent behavior is natural and perhaps has planted the seed that gradually evolved into the field of forensic psychology. As with the discipline of psychology, and with the subdiscipline of forensic psychology, research and clinical work eventually blossomed into its own discipline, complete with educational requirements, guidelines for practices, and its own set of ethical guidelines for this complex and challenging field. Pioneers such as Dr. Reiser with the Los Angeles Police Department, and the founders of the FBI's BSU opened our eyes to the importance of psychologists working in concert with the legal system to help make decisions that impacted those who practice in these fields and those who come into contact with the forensic system.

At present, we are inundated with books, movies, and television shows purporting to show us forensic psychologists tracking down serial killers and other dramatic storylines. It is important for the student interested in becoming a forensic practitioner to be able to separate facts from the fiction of such dramatic portrayals. Portrayals of criminal profilers as having some magical insight or intuition are erroneous; the field of forensic psychology must depend on research and experience, not nonexistent magic.

As we have seen (and will see in greater depth in the body of this text), forensic psychology offers many opportunities for those who have interests in both psychology and the law. Working with police and other first responders, assisting the courts, counseling victims, and providing assessment and treatment to those who are currently incarcerated are only a few of the opportunities that are available to those who are interested. While the field has grown greatly since its inception, for those who enter this field, there is still a great deal to learn and to discover.

Exercises and Discussion Questions

1. Compare and contrast the profession of forensic psychology to other forensic sciences, including forensic digital analyst, forensic nurse, and forensic entomologist.

2. Describe the differences between a master's degree education in psychology and a doctoral-level education in psychology.

3. Describe several of the ethical challenges that may be faced by a forensic practitioner during the course of their duties.

4. List and describe some of the careers in forensic psychology.

KEY TERMS

American Psychological Association (APA)

Antisocial personality disorder

Courtroom work group

Deinstitutionalization

Ethics

Evidence-based corrections

First responders

Forensic digital analyst

Forensic entomologists

Forensic evidence

Forensic meteorologist

Forensic psychology

Forensics

Juveniles

Mass murderer

Not guilty by reason of insanity (NGRI)

Post-traumatic stress disorder (PTSD)

Serial killer

Spree killer

Victim–offender mediation

2 FIRST RESPONDER PSYCHOLOGY

LEARNING OBJECTIVES

1. Define *first responders* and list the stressors that are often associated with such an occupation.

2. List and explain the different types of stress and the impact that stress may have on an individual's body, mood, and behavior.

3. List and explain the symptoms of post-traumatic stress disorder and some of the therapies utilized to attempt to treat this disorder.

4. Examine the manner in which the Minnesota Multiphasic Personality Inventory-3 (MMPI-3) is utilized to assist in making hiring decisions for first responders and others.

5. Explain the importance of diversity, equity, and inclusion in the first responder workplace and in terms of working with members of the public.

The corrections officer sitting across the prison lunch table looked up at me. We'd been talking about yesterday's pro football outcomes when he suddenly said, "We are the thin gray line between good and evil. We are supposed to be the strong ones. The sheepdogs protecting the flock from the wolves. Nothing is supposed to bother us. But people don't know, they don't see what we see every day. What we do. I saw things in Afghanistan . . . you wouldn't understand unless you were there. And now as a corrections officer . . . you see the evil of society. I won't sit in a restaurant unless I can have my back against the wall someplace where I can see the door. I drink myself to sleep more nights than I care to admit. I'm irritable all the time. I have no patience with my kids. The slightest little thing sets me off. I don't trust people anymore. It changes you. It changes you forever. My wife says I'm not the same. And she's absolutely right."

INTRODUCTION AND DEFINITIONS

As defined in Homeland Security Presidential Directive HSPD-8 (Office of the Press Secretary, 2003), the term *first responders* includes federal, state, and local governmental and nongovernmental emergency, fire, law enforcement, and public safety dispatchers; emergency medical services providers (including hospital personnel); and related personnel, agencies, and authorities. First responders may also include public health and skilled support personnel (for example, heavy equipment operators) who provide immediate support services during disaster response and recovery procedures. First responders may be professionals or volunteers and are typically thought of as the first personnel to arrive on the scene of an emergency, whether that emergency be a natural disaster (for example, a hurricane), a man-made incident (a terrorist act), or an accident (a motor vehicle collision). First responder duties in the early stages of a crisis event may include the protection and preservation of lives, property, and evidence related to that incident.

The number of movies, television shows, podcasts, and similar stories portraying and centered on first responders are too numerous to count. We are bombarded by stories of soldiers at war, hectic emergency rooms, and numerous reality shows about police, prison, and paramedics. Such portrayals glamorize the lives and job responsibilities of first responders. But of course, such portrayals in the media are intended and designed to attract viewers and advertisers and do *not* necessarily provide an accurate portrayal of such jobs. In reality, first responder jobs are far less glamorous than the media would have us believe. Police don't spend all day on SWAT teams kicking down doors and arresting drug dealers; many hours are spent completing paperwork. Prison psychologists don't spend all day talking to serial killers but instead are sometimes worried an inmate is preparing to spit on them.

When we think of first responders, we may think that police are the only first responders who are involved in forensics. That would be a mistake. Firefighters and emergency medical services (EMS) personnel may be called on to testify in court either as witnesses or, in some cases, as expert witnesses. A doctor or nurse on their way to work might be the first one to provide care in the case of an individual who has been assaulted and may also appear in court as an expert witness. Military service people may be subjected to training, combat, and other situations where people's lives are at stake. Corrections officers are challenged on a routine basis with preventing suicide attempts, breaking up fights, and rendering first aid to staff members or inmates who are having a medical emergency. It would be a mistake to believe that police are the only first responders who are impacted by the stressful nature of their jobs and the only ones who may be involved in the justice system. It is also important to keep in mind that some first responders are or have been first responders in more than one field. That is, many law enforcement officers served in the military prior to a career in law enforcement. Some paramedics may also serve as firefighters in their communities, and many first responders in other fields are also required to be trained as emergency medical technicians (EMTs). Those who feel the call to serve in one capacity often feel the call to do so in another capacity as well.

It is important to be inclusive of all these and other professions that serve as first responders. Forensic psychologists will very often come in contact with a wide variety of first responders, whether counseling them in a private practice setting, testifying with them in court, or meeting with them in the course of their professional duties, so it is important for students of forensic psychology to realize that many of the challenges and stressors that apply to police apply to other first responders as well. Furthermore, as is the case with any profession, there are first responders on both sides of the legal fence. That is, there are members of the above professions who are accused or convicted of crimes themselves, so the more familiar a forensic psychologist can be with the culture, responsibilities, and challenges faced by first responders, the better.

First responder duties include unique responsibilities and stressors. By definition, many of the duties of first responders involve emergency situations in which time is in short supply; inadequate performance can have catastrophic results. A police officer is first on the scene of a child who is choking on a piece of hot dog and cannot breathe. The officer has very limited time to act, is perhaps under the scrutiny of a number of bystanders, and, based on what the officer does (or doesn't do), that child may live or die. It is difficult to imagine a more stressful situation. Adding to that stress is the grim reality that even if that officer does exactly what they are supposed to do, it is possible that it will not be sufficient and the child will die in the officer's arms, despite their very best efforts. The stressful and demanding nature of such an occupation cannot be overstated.

Given the above descriptions, it is easy to wonder why anyone would want to be a first responder. It wouldn't appear to be the salary; Military-Ranks.Org shows us that an E-1 Private in the United States Marine Corps makes less than $40,000 per year. Police officers, according to DePietro (2020) in *Forbes*, make an average of $67,600 (only about $15,000 more than the average wage in the United States) for putting their lives on the line every day. EMS workers such as paramedics had an average of less than $39,000 per year in 2019, according to the U.S. Bureau of Labor Statistics (2019a, 2019b) and that same agency reported that the average salary of corrections officers was barely $50,000 per year. Thus, while first responder occupations may pay the bills, it seems highly unlikely that one goes into such a field with the idea of becoming wealthy.

It also wouldn't appear to be the glamour of the job that attracts people to first responder occupations. Such careers may involve becoming involved in physical altercations, witnessing the aftermath of a gruesome motor vehicle accident, or exposure to toxic fumes, chemicals, or even bodily fluids. Such possibilities are less than enticing. We can likely rule out public adulation as a factor, as police, veterans, and other first responders may have as many people who view them as the bad guy as view them as heroes. So why would people willingly seek out an occupation that can and does involve risking one's life for little money and no fame?

When we ask a police officer, prison guard, firefighter, or other first responder why they do what they do, the answers tend to include "I want to help my community," "I've always wanted to help people," "It's just the right thing to do," and "It's kind of a tradition in my family; everyone is a cop/paramedic/Marine/etc." Some say that they want to serve their country or that they want to be able to say "I've saved someone's life" or that they want to make a real difference in the world.

It is important to understand that first responders are often perceived as the strong, silent type of individual, and the public expects them to appear calm and in control of their emotions at all times. As a result, many first responders feel the need to project calmness when that is not what they are feeling; furthermore, they may deny to others (and even to themselves!) that they are bothered by a traumatic incident. They may believe that those who are not first responders couldn't possibly understand the challenges of their job, so they choose not to speak of them to friends, family members, or mental health professionals.

In a general sense, we are aware of the fact that first responders' jobs are inherently dangerous, and the data consistently supports this notion. In 2020, the number of police officers shot in the line of duty hit a record high (George, 2020). Firefighters were found to have sustained 58,250 total injuries in the line of duty in 2019 (Campbell, 2019). Corrections officers fared no better, with one of the highest rates of nonfatal injuries of any profession: 544 such injuries per 10,000 staff members (Konda et al., 2013). We will see later in this chapter that as dangerous as their job duties may be, when it comes to lethality, first responders are actually in greater danger from themselves than they are from others.

In September of 2018, Dallas Police Officer Amber Guyger had just finished her shift when she walked into the apartment of 26-year-old Botham Jean and shot and killed him as he sat on the couch eating a bowl of ice cream. She later testified that she had mistakenly entered his apartment and, thinking that he was an intruder in *her* apartment, had opened fire in what she believed to be self-defense. The jury found her guilty of homicide and sentenced her to ten years in prison. A year and a half later, in March of 2020, police officers made a forcible entry into the apartment of Breonna Taylor as part of an investigation into alleged drug dealing by her boyfriend, Kenneth Walker, who was staying with her. Walker later stated that he believed the police were intruders and fired a warning shot. The police responded by firing 32 rounds, six of which hit and killed Taylor, who was never accused of any wrongdoing; a grand jury did not indict any of the officers for homicide. Just two months later, in May of 2020, Minneapolis police were called to the scene of a convenience store, where George Floyd, a 46-year-old Black man, had allegedly attempted to pay using a counterfeit bill. After some discussion, police cuffed Floyd with his hands behind his back and then placed him face down in the street. Officer Derek Chauvin was observed placing his knee on the back of Floyd's neck for 8 minutes and 46 seconds. A review of Chauvin's record would reveal that he was awarded the Medal of Valor in 2006 but also that there were 18 official complaints against him (Barrett et al., 2020). A jury found Chauvin guilty of homicide, and as a result, he was sentenced to 22 ½ years of incarceration. The cases of Botham Jean, Breonna Taylor, George Floyd, and others led to worldwide protests and accusations of racism, bias, and police brutality. Naturally, these cases also raised the issue of screening of police recruits, training of police, and periodic evaluation of whether or not they are fit to perform their duties in a safe, appropriate, and unbiased manner.

PREEMPLOYMENT SCREENING

The importance of hiring the appropriate personnel to be first responders cannot be overstated. After all, police, firefighters, corrections officers, nurses, and other first responders are responsible for the lives of others, and the decisions they make and the actions they take can literally mean the difference between life and death. But how exactly does the hiring process work? How is it decided who might perform well in such an occupation and who might be unsuitable?

Some researchers have recommended preparedness and assessing the suitability of new staff for the first responder role before they begin work, in order to ensure that their personality and mental health status are such that they can handle the stress of work as a first responder (Brooks et al., 2016). These same researchers have also emphasized the importance of being prepared for the potential psychological impact of the job as well as the importance of providing workers with mental health trainings and briefings.

Given the importance of selecting the appropriate people for employment as first responders, it is perhaps not surprising that some states have established detailed protocols for doing so. The California POST (Peace Officer Standards and Training) commission is one agency dedicated to exactly this mission. The California POST has established a set of minimum standards that must be met in order for an applicant to be hired as a California peace officer. Those standards include (but are not limited to) age, educational level, and the ability to pass a medical exam demonstrating that they are free from any physical condition that would adversely impact their ability to perform their job duties. A bank of oral interview questions is used to assess the candidate's experience, problem-solving ability, communications skills, and other factors.

Additionally, the California POST requires that all applicants have a psychological or psychiatric exam by a qualified practitioner and that exam demonstrates that the applicant is free of any mental health or emotional condition (including bias or prejudice against others) that would impair their ability to complete their job duties. The POST requires that at least two written personality tests are given as part of this exam.

The Minnesota Multiphasic Personality Inventory (MMPI)

The Minnesota Multiphasic Personality Inventory (MMPI) was originally developed by Stark Hathaway and J.C. McKinley in 1943 as a means of assessing personality and psychopathology. Since that time, the MMPI and its subsequent versions (the MMPI-2 in 1989, followed by the

MMPI-2-RF and now the MMPI-3) have become what is quite probably the most frequently used means of assessing personality and mental health issues in the world. The items, scales, scoring, and norms have undergone changes in the eighty years since it was first published, but the goal of the test—to provide information about the personality and potential mental health concerns of the individual to whom it is being administered—remains the same. The number of studies conducted in regard to the validity, reliability, and other aspects of the various versions of the MMPI would be difficult to count; it is safe to say that it represents one of the most studied psychological tests ever developed.

The most recent version, the MMPI-3 (Ben-Porath & Tellegen, 2020) is available in both English and Spanish versions and takes 25–35 minutes to complete when administered on a computer. The MMPI-3 is a self-report measure in which respondents answer True or False to 335 statements about themselves. For example, one statement might be "No one understands me," and another might be "At times, I feel like smashing things" or "Other people have expressed concern about my drinking habits." For each of these items, the respondent would simply respond with True or False.

The MMPI-3 is comprised of 52 scales, providing a wide variety of information about the candidate. Interpretation of these scales and the overall MMPI-3 profile should only be performed by someone who is specifically trained and qualified to do so and usually begins with an examination of the validity scales. The MMPI-3 validity scales provide information concerning the test-taking approach of the individual who completed that measure. For example, these scales would allow the examiner to determine if the candidate was responding to items in a random fashion rather than being thoughtful about each item. Did the candidate appear to be defensive, denying even the most minor faults? Did they appear to blatantly distort the existence of any mental health symptoms, either reporting many fewer or many more symptoms than most people do?

If and when the interpreter of the test, having examined the validity scales, decides that the candidate has approached the test in a thoughtful and accurate manner, they may then turn to interpretation of the clinical scales, which provide data about (but not limited to) substance abuse, aggressiveness, stress, antisocial behavior, anxiety, depression, and many other factors. It is important to note that the MMPI-3 (or any measure, for that matter) should not be used as the sole means of determining whether someone is a suitable candidate for a public safety/first responder position. In addition to any formal psychological testing, a thorough background and records check and personal interview(s) should be performed.

It is also important for the examiner to meet with the examinee to discuss any items that have been endorsed in an unusual manner to make certain that the candidate fully understood that item. For example, the present author on many occasions interviewed candidates who marked True to an item similar to "I hear and see things that others do not hear and see." A True response to such an item might well suggest that the candidate is experiencing a psychotic episode or schizophrenia and is suffering from auditory and/or visual hallucinations. However, in this author's experience, when interviewing the candidates who responded True to this item, they typically said, "Yeah, when I served in Afghanistan, I was in combat; I saw and heard things that most people never experience." Such an explanation demonstrates that the candidate merely interpreted the item differently than it was intended and that there is no psychotic process at work that might contraindicate employment as a public servant.

The MMPI-3 also features public safety candidate interpretive reports. These include the Police Candidate Interpretive Report (PCIR), the Correctional Candidate Interpretive Report (CCIR), and the Firefighter Candidate Interpretive Report (FCIR). These reports allow the examiner to compare a candidate's MMPI-3 profile to those of candidates for a similar position. For example, the PCIR was developed from the profiles of more than 3,900 police candidates and meets the requirement that tests that may be used to disqualify a job candidate do so on the basis that such disqualification is based on evidence that the candidate's ability to perform the essential functions of that job will be limited by the identified impairment (Corey & Ben-Porath, 2020).

TYPES OF STRESS

Stress is typically thought of as mental, physical, or emotional strain that may be triggered by a wide variety of life circumstances. When our senses tell us that we are in danger, our eyes and ears send signals to the amygdala, an almond-shaped group of cells deep within each hemisphere of the brain that is involved in processing emotions. From there, the amygdala relays signals to the hypothalamus, often considered to be the command center of the brain. The hypothalamus in turn activates the sympathetic nervous system, preparing us for fight or flight. The adrenal glands then secrete large amounts of epinephrine (also called *adrenaline*) as part of the stress response. Epinephrine helps to prepare the brain and body to respond to the crisis by increasing the heart rate, blood pressure, respiration, and oxygenation to the brain and significantly energizing the body (Harvard Medical School, 2020).

First responders often find themselves in situations that are dangerous not only to others but also to themselves, and they must sometimes attempt to balance their job duties with maintaining their own safety. A police officer might be dispatched to a bridge as part of an attempt to prevent an individual from jumping to their death. It might occur to the officer to use force to pull the person to safety, but this impulse, as heroic as it may be, must be balanced against the possibility that the individual may struggle and in the course of that struggle, both may fall to their deaths. Decisions such as this must be made quickly and under a great deal of pressure and, in some cases, may be subject to public scrutiny, criticism, and Monday-morning quarterbacking: "If they had just done such-and-such, so-and-so would still be alive today." Furthermore, the reality is that a failure to act or incorrect actions can easily lead one to be the defendant in a civil suit or, worse yet, prosecuted for a criminal offense.

Stress may be experienced physically, emotionally, mentally, and/or behaviorally. Stress can and does vary greatly in terms of frequency, intensity, and duration. Although stress is most often thought to be associated with adverse events such as the illness of a loved one or an important deadline at work, it is also important to know that positive events can and do elicit stress as well. Such stress is called *eustress*. For example, getting married, having a baby, and receiving a big promotion at work are all events that have strong positive associations. However, that does not mean that they are stress-free; far from it! The miracle of being a parent to a newborn baby is nevertheless accompanied by the stress of sleepless nights, increased financial strain, and the knowledge that as parents, we are entirely responsible for the care of another person, which may all weigh more heavily upon our emotions than we expect. Unlike stress, eustress may take us by surprise; we expect being fired to be stressful, but we may well be surprised by the eustress associated with a promotion or with the birth of a child.

Short-Term Stress

Stress may be short-term (acute) in nature or may be long-term (chronic). In either event, the intensity of the stress may vary. For example, **short-term stress** of low intensity might be the stress you feel when you are not sure whether or not you are going to make it to class on time. That stress will be resolved fairly quickly (you will either make it to class on time or you won't) and is likely to me minor in nature, as the consequence of being late to class is likely to be nothing more than a dirty look from your professor. Being late to an important job interview would also be a short-term stress for the same reason but would likely be of much greater intensity, as the consequences of being late could be much greater than a dirty look.

Long-Term Stress

Like short-term stress, **long-term stress** may be of lesser or greater intensity. Being diagnosed with a chronic disease may well trigger long-term stress, as one must continue to deal with the physical and emotional challenges of that disease. If the disease is less serious and fairly well-controlled, perhaps that chronic stress is of relatively low intensity. However, if it is quite serious, the patient (and their family) may suffer intense distress over a lengthy period of time. Chronic stress of any intensity bears the additional burden of what may be referred to as *cumulative toxicity*; that is, the unrelenting nature of that stress inherent in a disease or a job can gradually erode one's ability to cope, just as ocean waves will eventually erode the largest rock into sand.

Few indeed are the types of employment that involve little or no stress. Whether one is working in a factory, in the home, as an accountant, as a manual laborer, or as the CEO of a global corporation, employment is likely to be stressful in one way or another. Whether we are attempting to meet a deadline, produce a certain number of widgets per hour, or make important decisions, nearly every form of employment must be thought to involve at least some stress.

First responder jobs, by definition, can involve tremendous amounts of stress and can take a significant emotional toll on those who are so employed. These jobs may involve threats of harm or actual violence toward oneself or one's coworkers. Injuries may occur, and line-of-duty deaths—while uncommon—are a grim reality of such occupations. The emotional strain of never knowing when the fire bell may ring, when a trauma case will come into the emergency room, or when an offender may try to assault a police or corrections officer is bound to take an emotional toll on the first responder at some point during their career.

Personal Stress

Personal stresses, such as finances, relationships, school, household responsibilities, legal concerns, medical issues, and many other issues can lead us to feel sad, anxious, or uncomfortable. Those working as first responders experience personal stressors in the same manner others do. Just as any other member of the public can become seriously ill, have a loved one pass away, be overwhelmed by bills, or go through a difficult divorce, so too can those who work as first responders. However, in addition to the stresses of daily life, first responders may also face further stressors during the course of their job duties that most people never contemplate, much less experience.

It is a running joke among corrections officers and likely among police as well: "You walk into a crowded restaurant. How do you tell the corrections officer?" Answer: "They are the one sitting in the corner, with their back to the wall, in a place where they can see who's coming in and out the main door." Constant vigilance of one's surroundings and potential threats is a survival skill for corrections officers and other first responders. When they leave the work environment, it is often difficult or impossible for those in such occupations to let their guard down; even in public settings that most people would consider to be safe, first responders find themselves looking to see where the entrances and exits are and observing others for any potential signs of danger. They feel the need to be on guard at all times and in all places, without ever feeling that they can truly relax. Thus, occupational stressors can and do bleed over into areas of the first responder's personal life.

Occupational Stress

Occupational stress is the stress that is associated with one's job duties. For first responders, these stresses may be more varied and intense than they are in many other occupations. First responders are by definition subjected to experiencing traumatic events on a regular basis. No one ever

calls the police because they are getting along wonderfully with their spouse. No one goes to the emergency room to report that they feel great. Firefighters don't get asked to rush into a building that isn't on fire. Such individuals are only called into service when there is an emergency occurring, quite possibly an emergency in which someone's life is in peril or in which the first responder could be putting themselves in considerable danger by attempting to intervene. Such stresses are not common in other occupations. Some of these first responders have the additional emotional burden of knowing that there are people in the world who intend to do them harm. Law enforcement officers and corrections personnel live with the fact that there are people in the world who want to and intend to harm or kill them. This is a daily burden most people cannot comprehend.

The work of police officers, firefighters, and other first responders can be extremely stressful; they may be faced with life-or-death decisions far more often than most other professions.

avstraliavasin/iStockPhoto

Organizational Stress

In addition to the occupational stresses related directly to the performance of their job duties, first responders may also experience significant **organizational stressors**; that is, the stress associated with the organizational demands of their profession rather than with their actual job duties. Organizational stressors might include (but are not limited to) working many hours (including different shifts), disrupting the normal sleep/wake cycle, and policies and procedures that are perceived as counterproductive to the mission. Budgetary constraints, a lack of training or equipment, a perceived lack of support from those higher up in the organization, a tarnished public perception of the profession, and an abundance of paperwork are all common sources of organizational stress.

The impact of stress on one's physical, mental, and emotional well-being should not be underestimated. Stress has been associated with headaches, digestive problems, increased risk of heart attack, high blood pressure, and increased risk of Type II diabetes (Pietrangelo, 2020). Other common effects include difficulty falling asleep or staying asleep, a change in eating habits (and associated weight gain or loss), social isolation, withdrawal, and abuse of alcohol or other drugs, to name a few.

MENTAL HEALTH ISSUES

Depression

When we hear the word *depression*, we often equate it with being sad or bummed out. In fact, according to the **Diagnostic and Statistical Manual of Mental Disorders** (DSM, 5th edition; American Psychiatric Association, 2013), **major depressive disorder (MDD)** involves much more than minor or brief episodes of sadness. MDD is generally thought to involve feelings of sadness or hopelessness for much of the day, every day, for at least a two-week-long period and includes decreased interest in many activities, a significant change in sleep and/or appetite, difficulty thinking, and fatigue, among other factors. In some cases, the individual with MDD has thoughts of death, wishes to die, or experiences suicidal ideation. By definition, these factors must represent a change from the person's previous level of functioning and must impair their ability to function in their daily lives. According to the DSM-5, the overall 12-month prevalence of MDD in the United States is approximately 7%, with women showing 1.5 to 3 times the rate for males, beginning in early adolescence (American Psychiatric Association, 2013).

Depression is commonly reported in firefighters, and studies have found various rates and levels of severity of this disorder in these first responders. One study found that volunteer firefighters reported markedly elevated levels of depression as compared to career firefighters (with an odds ratio for volunteer firefighters of 16.85 and for career firefighters of 13.06; Stanley et al., 2016). The researchers observed that greater structural barriers to mental health care (such as cost and availability of resources) may explain the increased levels of depression observed among volunteer firefighters. That is, volunteer firefighters likely do not have as much access to mental health services as career firefighters do. Additionally, competing demands for volunteer firefighters (such as having to have a separate job) create stress vulnerabilities that contribute to the development or exacerbation of mental health issues. Organizational factors (such as more systematic and stringent recruitment and screening within career departments as opposed to volunteer departments) may contribute to the difference in the levels of behavioral health issues (Stanley et al., 2017). In another study, 22.2% of female career firefighters were at risk of depression, while 38.5% of female volunteer firefighters were at risk of depression (Haddock et al., 2017). According to Jahnke et al. (2012), this could be attributed to social pressures associated with working in a profession that tends to be male dominated. Additionally, although female firefighters reported similar job stressors to male firefighters, they also reported experiencing significantly more occupational discrimination than their male peers.

Military veterans also appear to experience depression at higher rates than those who did not serve in the military. Kerr (2018) found that approximately 14% of those who had served in the military acknowledged feelings of depression and speculated that the actual number could be higher, as some might be experiencing such emotions but are unwilling to report it.

Police officers have also been shown to experience higher rates of depression than those in many other occupations. In a study of 1,400 police officers in three urban areas of Texas, Bishop et al. (2018) found higher than average rates of depression and burnout among officers.

Furthermore, this study suggested that organizational stressors contribute greatly to feelings of anger, depression, and burnout among those officers.

Substance Use Disorders

Substance abuse (including, but not limited to alcohol abuse) is generally referred to as a **substance use disorder (SUD)** in the DSM-5. SUDs are characterized by using larger amounts of the substance than originally intended, unsuccessful attempts to reduce or stop using the substance, craving the substance, and continued use despite physical dangers or impairment in social or occupational functioning. Also noted is a tolerance for that substance (a need for an increased amount of that substance to produce intoxication) and/or withdrawal symptoms such as tremors, irritability, insomnia, and anxiety if the individual ceases use or is unable to obtain that substance.

Stanley et al. (2017) found that career firefighters reported higher levels of problematic alcohol use and **post-traumatic stress disorder (PTSD)** as compared to volunteer firefighters, while the volunteers reported higher levels of depression and suicide attempts and ideation. Recent (past month) heavy or binge alcohol drinking was reported in approximately 50% of male firefighters and driving while intoxicated was reported in 9% of male firefighters (Haddock et al., 2017). Female firefighters account for 5.1% of the total number of firefighters (Jahnke et al., 2012), and in a study evaluating the health of this population, more than 88% of career female firefighters had consumed alcohol in the past month. In another study of female firefighters, more than 60% drank more than the 2015–2020 Dietary Guidelines for Americans recommended; binge drinking was reported in slightly more than 39% in this population (as compared to 12%–15% of the females in the general population) and more than 4.3% admitted driving while intoxicated (Haddock et al., 2017).

A study of medical doctors undergoing monitoring and treatment for SUDs found that physicians were five times as likely as nonmedical personnel to abuse prescription drugs (Merlo et al., 2013). Doctors, of course, have more ready access to prescription medications, and in the Merlo study, doctors stated that they used and became addicted to these substances to relieve physical pain, to mask emotional or psychiatric distress, and as part of an attempt to manage daily stress. They also admitted using such substances for recreational purposes and to avoid any withdrawal symptoms.

When it comes to first responders and substance abuse, police do not appear to be an exception to the rule. A 1988 study by Kraska and Kapeller suggested that one in four police officers had a drug/alcohol issue, with between 20%–30% of them being diagnosable with a SUD as opposed to less than 10% of people in the general population. Most of the officers in this study found to have a SUD had between four and nine years of experience at that job.

Suicide

Suicide occurs when a person intentionally and voluntarily acts in such a manner as to end their own life. Overall, the rate of completed suicides (that is, suicides in which the individual does terminate their own life, as opposed to a *suicide attempt*, in which that individual survives), according to the American Foundation for Suicide Prevention (AFSP), is 13.4 per 100,000 residents in the United States. It should be noted that there is considerable variability in these numbers, with men completing suicide three and a half times more often than women do, and with older white men making up nearly 70% of all completed suicides (AFSP, 2017).

Police and corrections officers daily run the risk of being assaulted or even killed by offenders. Although firefighters, nurses, and EMS professionals may not face such threats as often, assaults on these first responders can and do occur from time to time. Sadly, statistically, the greatest risk to the lives of many first responders is not from others but from themselves; suicide is a tragic and often unspoken-of epidemic among first responders. Davis (2019) noted that the number of police officers dying by suicide was greater than the number of those who died in line-of-duty deaths, with 228 deaths by suicide that year and 132 line-of-duty deaths. Unfortunately, this has been the trend for some time, with 140 law enforcement officer (LEO) suicides in 2017 and 129 line-of-duty deaths that same year (Heyman et al., 2018). Additionally, about half of the LEOs reported personally knowing one or more law enforcement officers who changed after experiencing a traumatic event and about half reported knowing an officer in their agency or another agency who had committed suicide (Fleischmann et al., 2016)

EMS providers were found to be *ten times* as likely as the national average to experience thoughts of suicide and/or suicide attempts (Barber et al., 2015), and Conts (2018) noted that more than one in 20 EMT deaths are the result of suicide. Stanley et al. (2016) found that individuals who had both EMS and firefighting duties showed six times as many suicide attempts as those who had firefighting duties only, suggesting that the stresses of these jobs may be cumulative.

Firefighters are not immune to the trend seen with other first responders. Hayes (2018) found that in 2017, 103 firefighters died by suicide as compared to 93 line-of-duty deaths. Military veterans diagnosed with PTSD are twice as likely to die from suicide and accidental injury as people in the general population (Forehand et al., 2019).

In 2009, the New Jersey Police Suicide Task Force (Governor's Task For on Police Suicide, 2009) found that the suicide rate for men in the general population aged 25–64 was about 14 per 100,000. For police officers, it was slightly higher at approximately 15 per 100,000. For corrections officers, however, the suicide rate was a staggering 34.8 per 100,000—more than double the rate of police officers. "Based on analysis of death certificate data from 21 states that provided information on the occupation of the deceased, it was determined that Corrections Officers' risk of suicide was *39% higher than that of the rest of all other professions combined*" (emphasis added; Denhoff & Spinaris, 2013, p. 8).

The job duties and responsibilities of first responders can take a heavy emotional toll on those professionals.
PA Images/Alamy Stock Photo

There are several factors that may be relevant to the high rates of suicide among first responders. As we have already discussed, levels of stress and emotional difficulties can be high in these occupations. Given the strong, silent culture of first responders, in which many still consider it to be a sign of weakness to discuss their emotions or to admit any emotions at all, many may not seek help by speaking to a professional counselor. Instead, the culturally acceptable outlet for such stress may be alcohol consumption or include the excessive use of medications and/or illegal drugs. Furthermore, by the nature of their profession, police and corrections officers own firearms, as may many other first responders. Thus, in first responders, we have people who are operating under a great deal of personal and professional stress, who may be worsening that stress by their attempts to self-medicate with alcohol or other drugs and who have ready access to firearms; it may only take one brief lapse in judgment or one moment of emotional overload for them to make the irreversible decision to end their own lives.

As if the above statistics are not sad and startling enough already, it should be kept in mind that such numbers are likely to *under*represent the actual numbers of suicides completed by these professionals. That is, equivocal deaths (deaths in which there is no clear precipitating factor) may be classified as accidental in the absence of any clear evidence of suicide. A car running into a bridge abutment resulting in the death of the driver might well be ruled accidental in the absence of any evidence to the contrary. However, it is possible that such an act could have been a suicide. Thus, as shocking as the aforementioned suicide statistics are, the sad reality is that they may represent an underestimate of the actual frequency of suicide in these professions.

Post-Traumatic Stress Disorder (PTSD)

The DSM-5 notes that PTSD may occur in response to an individual being exposed to an event in which someone was seriously injured, killed, or in danger of being subject to violence. That individual may have experienced or viewed such an event as it occurred or such an event may have happened to a loved one of theirs. It is important to note that an individual can experience such a traumatic incident and *not* develop PTSD. The DSM-5 identifies a 12-month prevalence rate of 3.5% for PTSD, and Harvard Medical School (2017) suggests that the lifetime prevalence of PTSD in the general population is 6.8%. Thus, we should not equate experiencing trauma with the automatic development of PTSD. In fact, these studies suggest the opposite: While people may be emotionally upset about a trauma that they have experienced, the vast majority do *not* go on to develop PTSD.

PTSD may be diagnosed when an individual has experienced a trauma and then demonstrates many of the following symptoms: recurrent, distressing memories and/or dreams of the traumatic event; flashbacks in which the individual feels as if they were experiencing the traumatic event all over again; or significant reactions to cues that remind the individual of the traumatic event. For example, as we will talk about more in Chapter 6, some victims of sexual assault may experience extreme emotions or panic if, in the course of their daily life, they happen to smell the same cologne that their offender was wearing when they were assaulted. Some individuals with PTSD will experience significant changes in thinking or mood, especially in a negative or unpleasant direction. Irritability, impulsivity, and an exaggerated startle response are all common signs of PTSD. Individuals with PTSD may attempt to avoid any people, places, or objects that remind them of the traumatic incident; the survivor of a serious traffic accident may go out of their way to avoid the intersection where it occurred, even if that means driving a considerable extra distance to do so.

The DSM-5 suggests that the projected lifetime risk of PTSD by age 75 is 8.7%, but also specifically notes that "rates of PTSD are higher among veterans and others whose vocation increases the risk of traumatic exposure (*e.g., police, firefighters, emergency medical personnel*)" (emphasis added; American Psychiatric Association, 2013, p. 276). Spitzer (2020) noted, "All literature points to the same conclusions. The data suggests that first responders are at increased risk of PTSD."

One of the core risk factors for first responders is the frenetic and unpredictable pace of their work. One moment they may be drinking coffee and discussing the weather, and the next they may be responding to a life-or-death situation. First responders are on the front lines, facing highly stressful and risky calls. This tempo can lead to difficulty in adapting to and integrating work experiences. For instance, according to one study, 69% of EMS professionals have never had enough time to recover between traumatic events (Bentley et al., 2013). Quite simply, there are times when first responders have little or no time to process one trauma before they are called to the scene of another such event. As a result, depression, stress, post-traumatic stress symptoms, suicidal ideation, and a host of other functional and relational conditions have been reported. Stress symptoms and post-traumatic stress symptoms in EMS personnel have been reported in a number of studies. For instance, in a study in Germany, stress was reported in 5.9% of certified EMS professionals, with mild stress being the most common type (3.1%; Bentley et al., 2013).

Police officers are at increased risk of negative mental health consequences due to the dangerous nature of their jobs as well as the greater likelihood that they will experience critical incidents, environmental hazards, and traumatic events (Heavey et al., 2015). In this same study, about three-fourths of the surveyed officers reported having experienced a traumatic event but less than half of them had told their agency about it. In a study following Hurricane Katrina, PTSD was reported in between 7% and 19% of a sample of police officers (McCanlies et al., 2014). After the World Trade Center attack, PTSD was reported in 11% of police responders, and PTSD was noted to be more prevalent among those with fewer social supports. In another study, the prevalence of probable PTSD in police officers following the 9/11 attack was 12.9% (Bowler et al., 2016).

Such statistics are not unique to the United States. In South Korea, 41% of police were noted to be at high risk of PTSD (Lee et al., 2016). One in five Australian police officers were noted to be at risk of PTSD (Skeffington, 2016). Additionally, eight Canadian provinces now have presumptive laws covering PTSD. Such laws mean that Canadian firefighters may be compensated for lost wages and treatment of PTSD that occurs secondary to job-related trauma. The fact that the laws are *presumptive* means that the burden of proof shifts to the employer to prove that the PTSD is not related to trauma that occurred on the job (International Association of Firefighters, 2019).

Critical Incident Stress Debriefing (CISD)

In the early 1980s and for quite a few years thereafter, **critical incident stress debriefing** (CISD; Mitchell & Everly, 1996) was perhaps the most popular intervention intended to decrease the risk of developing PTSD after experiencing a traumatic event. In CISD, first responders who have experienced the same traumatic incident are required to gather in a confidential setting. The facilitators (some of whom are mental health professionals and some of whom are trained peers to the affected group) guide group members through a seven-phase debriefing process involving introduction, fact phase, thought phase, reaction phase, symptom phase, teaching phase, and reentry. Group members are guided through recalling and discussing their role in the incident, their thoughts about the event, and their emotional and physical reactions to what occurred. Then the facilitators provide instruction in coping skills to the group members. Although this technique continues to be utilized in some settings, it does have its detractors. Van Emmerick et al. (2002) suggested that CISD has never conclusively been demonstrated to reduce the probability of an individual developing PTSD. Another study found no relationship between debriefing and decreased incidence of PTSD (Harris et al., 1998). Indeed, as noted earlier, statistics suggest that most people who experience a traumatic event do not go on to develop PTSD, so a debriefing process may not be necessary and could actually pathologize the experience of having done so. The National Institute of Mental Health (2022) no longer recommends CISD as an early intervention technique. The World Health Organization (2003) noted possible negative effects of this technique. Thus, use of this technique is likely to be less popular at present than it once was.

Psychological First Aid (PFA)

Psychological first aid (PFA; Everly, 2018) involves the provision of emotional support after an individual has experienced a traumatic event. Everly compared PFA to a "psychological bandage" provided to those who have experienced a traumatic incident. PFA seeks to stabilize and prevent distress from worsening, to decrease symptoms of active distress, and to provide assistance with accessing ongoing support services for those who might benefit from them. Unlike CISD, where those who have responded to a traumatic incident are required to attend the session, PFA sessions are not required for individuals. Training in PFA is important but it does not have to be administered by a licensed mental health clinician. During the COVID-19 pandemic of 2020 and 2021, the American Red Cross developed and delivered online PFA sessions for those impacted by that disease.

Fitness for Duty Evaluations (FFDE)

Hiring those who appear to be reasonably well-suited for a career as a first responder is only a first step. Once hired, given the numerous personal and professional stresses that such occupations entail, it is important to ensure that these individuals continue to conduct themselves in a safe and professional manner. When one has the authority to handcuff and detain or even use deadly force against a member of the public, we want to be confident that they will not abuse this authority. At times, we may see signs that a first responder is not functioning as well on the job as they once did. A firefighter might come to work smelling of alcohol. A police officer may be observed to punch their locker repeatedly. A correctional employee's hygiene may have deteriorated to a noticeable degree. All these and other signs may raise concerns about that employees' ability to perform their job duties. When these or other issues potentially impact an employees' ability to perform their job, a **fitness for duty evaluation** (FFDE) is indicated. Unlike preemployment screening, FFDE are not utilized with every employee and are only utilized when there appears to be some issue that potentially impacts that employees' ability to perform their job functions.

For law enforcement officers, FFDE guidelines have been established by the International Association of Chiefs of Police (2009). These guidelines suggest that such evaluations be in-depth, including a thorough review of the employee's physical and mental health history, psychological testing, a face-to-face interview, and consultation and referrals when indicated. Also, it is important to keep in mind that such evaluations, as the name implies, must be focused on that officer's ability to perform their job in a safe and effective manner. Thus, if it is determined that the officer is depressed because of an ongoing divorce but that depression cannot be shown to impact their job performance, they cannot be disciplined or sanctioned for this in any manner and should be cleared to resume full job duties (though it might be suggested to them that they voluntarily seek some type of support or mental health treatment).

In other cases, it may be determined that the employee can resume their job duties as long as they follow certain guidelines (sometimes referred to as a *condition of continued employment*) or that they are temporarily unfit to perform their duties until they have undergone some type of treatment or intervention. In some cases, it may be found that the employee is so debilitated that they are unable to perform their job functions and they may be asked to take a different assignment, retire, or be fired. In such cases, it is not unusual for the employee to obtain legal counsel to represent them and argue the case on their behalf.

THE IMPORTANCE OF DIVERSITY, EQUITY, AND INCLUSION

When I met Corrections Officer Vasquez (not his real name), I was not convinced that he was going to be an effective corrections officer. Spanish was Vasquez's first language; English was his second language, and he spoke it with a very strong accent. At times, I had trouble understanding him. It concerned me that if I could not understand him, then many of our inmates would not be able to do so either. However, he had passed all the required exams and had been hired and was working as a corrections officer without any reported difficulties. One day, I got a call to report immediately to the restricted housing unit (RHU), as there was an inmate who was cutting himself with a razor blade. He needed to go to the medical department to be treated but was in his cell, refusing to allow himself to be handcuffed in order to be transported there. Thus, my job was to attempt to talk him into allowing himself to be handcuffed so that we could transport him. If I could not convince him, then we would have a cell extraction team remove him by force, cuff him, and take him for medical care. Cell extraction is a dangerous business at best. The inmate could use the razor blade to attack staff or could accidentally be injured during the process, and staff could be injured as well. It was important that I convince the inmate to allow himself to be handcuffed so that a use of force could be avoided.

When I arrived in the RHU, they told me the name of the inmate and the number of his cell. I was immediately skeptical of my ability to negotiate with this inmate, as I knew from past experience that he spoke little English and I spoke even less Spanish. Determined to give it my best shot, I walked into the housing unit toward his cell. As I approached the cell, I saw that Officer Vasquez was already there, talking to the inmate. Normally, under such circumstances, I inform the officer that I am there, and they leave and allow me to conduct the negotiation. However, this case was different. As I approached the cell, I saw that Vasquez and the inmate were talking quite comfortably, Spanish being the native language of both men. Furthermore, I saw that Vasquez's body posture was relaxed and that the two men were making good eye contact. Most importantly, I saw that although the inmate appeared to have the razor blade still in his hand, he was clearly interested in talking to Officer Vasquez and was no longer in the act of harming himself.

Rather than approach further, I decided to wait and watch. Although I had no idea what they were saying, it was clear to me that their interaction was comfortable and productive. A few minutes later, the inmate put the razor blade down, Vasquez opened the trap door to the cell, the inmate extended his hands through it and allowed himself to be cuffed without further incident. Vasquez and I escorted him down to the medical department, where he received the treatment that he needed.

This moment was an eye-opening one for me. Officer Vasquez, whom I had wrongly thought might struggle in his duties as a corrections officer, taught me the importance of embracing diversity. His challenges speaking English were not *a liability after all; his ability to speak Spanish was a clear asset and served to completely negate what would otherwise have been a very dangerous situation. Especially as first responders, it is incumbent upon us to realize the importance of embracing diversity, equity, and inclusion in order to have the best possible team.*

Diversity, equity, and inclusion are all vitally important when considering first responders. Diversity includes (but is not limited to) race, age, color, educational background, religion, gender, gender identification, sexual orientation, mental and physical abilities, and learning styles. Equity refers to the fair treatment of all, with access and opportunities for all while recognizing and attempting to eliminate any barriers that may prevent the full participation of some groups. Equity includes acknowledging that some groups are historically underserved and underrepresented and that fairness may be needed in order to make sure there are truly equal opportunities for everyone. Inclusion refers to making an actual and genuine effort to bring traditionally excluded individuals into the activities and decision-making processes in a way that provides equal power, resources, and opportunities. The importance of diversity, equity, and inclusion in the ranks of first responders and the respect of these principles in regard to how first responders treat others cannot be overstated.

THROUGH THE EYES OF THE VICTIM: FIRST RESPONDERS AS VICTIMS

Victimology refers to the study of the physical, emotional, and cognitive changes that people may undergo if they have been a victim of a natural disaster, accident, or criminal event. Many students interested in forensics hope to have a career in bringing offenders to justice in one manner or another but may be less interested in the impact on the victims of those offenses. To many, victim impact may seem like the work of social worker, psychologist, or other mental health clinician. However, it is important that anyone planning a career in forensics realize that as a first responder, or nearly anyone involved in the forensic or court system, there is a great likelihood that at some point during their career, *they* will be the victim of some type of trauma or stress. Forensic practitioners can be assaulted, exposed to hazardous substances, threatened, hurt on the job, or even lose their lives in the line of duty. Unfortunately, the probabilities of being victimized in some manner during the course of a 25-year career in such a field would appear to be high.

Resilience

The Oxford dictionary defines *resilience* as "the capacity to recover quickly from difficulties." From a psychological standpoint, we may think of resilience as the ability to face adversity and to rebound from it as strong as (or, in some cases, perhaps even stronger) than one was prior to that challenge. One of the first studies of resilience was conducted by Dr. Emmy Werner in 1971, and she has authored a number of follow-up studies since that time (see Werner, 1992). Originally, she studied children who grew up in extremely challenging circumstances in low-income homes with a parent (or sometimes both parents) who were mentally ill and/or substance abusers. Werner found that approximately two-thirds of these children grew up to demonstrate problematic behaviors of their own, such as substance abuse and chronic unemployment. Interestingly, though, she found that one-third of children raised in these extremely difficult circumstances did not appear to demonstrate significant negative consequences as a result. This was the beginning of many future studies on resilience as the ability to survive or even thrive despite (or perhaps even because of) adversity.

Resilience, however, is not some type of magic emotional armor that makes one impervious to adversity. Instead, it refers to the thought processes and behaviors one may utilize to protect oneself from the negative effects of stress and to promote or enhance personal growth (Robertson et al., 2015). The manner in which a person thinks and acts can allow them to adapt to adversity by changing course, healing, and (hopefully) continuing to have a happy and productive life.

The American Psychological Association (APA) suggests that there are steps that first responders and others can take in order to build their resilience (2022). For example, the APA suggests that people form social bonds and connections with others and that they engage in positive communication and problem solving with those others. Also suggested is the ability to accept change and to reframe change as self-discovery. For example, a person might be able to reframe the loss of a loved one as, "I learned to always hug my friends and family and to tell them that I love them because a day may come when I'm not able to do that anymore." The APA goes on to suggest that resilience is built when we are able to resist maladaptive impulses and to engage in realistic problem solving in regard to our challenges. Avoiding potentially harmful behaviors such as alcohol and nicotine is recommended. Taking care of one's physical health through diet, exercise, and sleep is likely to benefit resilience, as is caring for one's mental health by engaging in a program of mindfulness through prayer, meditation, or relaxation techniques. Just as being physically healthy might help one to resist a medical illness, physical and emotional well-being may help one to be resilient toward trauma and stresses.

Hope for the Weary

Anderson (2020) found that only 56% of first responders said they could manage stress all or most of the time. That suggests that the remaining 44% feel they are not in good control of their stress much of the time. This same study also suggested that the manner in which first responders manage their stress does make a difference: Those who stated that they exercised to manage stress were three times as likely to say that they were able to manage stress well, and those who felt they have a high level of support from their coworkers were six times as likely to report that they were able to manage their stress well. However, those who said they used alcohol to manage their stress were 60% less likely to report having a low stress level. In short, exercise and peer support seem quite helpful, whereas consumption of alcohol appears to make stress worse rather than better. The remaining suggestions in the Anderson study were very much in line with the recommendations of the Centers for Disease Control and Prevention (CDC).

Fortunately, there are things that first responders can do to reduce and better manage the stress of their occupations. According to the CDC, first responders should use a buddy system in which they have peers that they can depend on and talk to. It is also suggested that to the extent possible, first responders don't work an excessive number of hours, hopefully never longer than 12 hours at a time. It is important for first responders to have friends, family, or professional counselors or chaplains that they can talk to about their experiences. Learning and use of muscle relaxation, deep breathing, or meditation techniques can also be helpful, as can limiting or avoiding the use of caffeine, nicotine, and alcohol. Self-care is important, meaning that such individuals should make an effort to take care of themselves physically as well as emotionally by engaging in regular exercise, eating healthy, and establishing healthy sleep patterns.

It is important to note that there are effective treatments available for those with PTSD, should people decide to avail themselves of such treatment. Medical doctors and psychiatrists can prescribe antidepressants or other psychotropic medications in order to help alleviate the symptoms of this disorder. There are numerous different types of talk therapy, including **cognitive processing therapy**, which involves twelve sessions of psychotherapy in which the client learns to identify traumatic thoughts and then to evaluate, challenge, and change those thoughts. It is hoped that changing the negative nature of those thoughts will then alter the emotions and the behaviors associated with those thoughts. **Exposure therapy** involves teaching the client a relaxation/deep breathing technique and then gradually exposing them to what it is that traumatized them, gradually allowing them to become more comfortable with the stimuli that they had previously found to be upsetting and traumatic.

Eye movement desensitization reprocessing (EMDR) is a technique originally developed in the late 1980s specifically for the treatment of PTSD. With EMDR, clients recount and remember traumatic experiences while also engaging in bilateral (back and forth) eye movements or alternately tapping their fingers on one side of their body and then the other. This technique produced greater benefit to subjects that received it than to control groups who did not receive treatment. However, there is controversy in regard to the specific mechanism of action of EMDR. The APA (2017) suggests that the mechanism of change may be simple exposure and that the bilateral eye movement or tapping may be unnecessary. More research into this is clearly warranted. Most importantly, though, effective treatment for PTSD is available for those who seek it out.

CONCLUSION

First responders operate at the front lines of crises and disasters, attempting to ensure the safety and well-being of those who may be impacted by such events. By definition, these first responders are being exposed to potentially traumatic situations that pose a risk of harm to themselves and to the people they are attempting to protect. The stresses of normal daily life, combined with the trauma and stresses of their occupations, constitutes a great risk for the behavioral health of first responders and puts them at risk for stress, depression, substance use, suicide ideation, suicide attempts, and PTSD. Both natural and man-made disasters were found to be associated with increased risk of these conditions. Given the significant and unique stresses of first responder occupations, it is important that candidates for such jobs be carefully screened and that they be evaluated if and when they demonstrate any impairment in functioning. It is also important for forensic psychologists and first responders to be aware not only of the great emotional rewards of being able to help others who are in need but also the cumulative trauma that may occur over the course of a career of responding to crises and emergencies. Of at least equal importance is for us to recognize the importance of self-care, resilience, and the availability of effective treatment; the helpers can be helped!

Exercises and Discussion Questions

1. As a forensic psychologist, you are tasked with coming up with a program to help first responders decrease and manage stress in a safe and healthy manner. What would you suggest that they and/or their agency do to help them manage stress? Be specific about your plan.

2. The head of a statewide police agency is appalled at the number of suicides in that agency every year. They ask you to develop a program to educate police officers about this issue and to hopefully reduce the number of suicides that occur. What information would you present and what changes might you suggest to help decrease the suicide rate in police officers? Again, be specific.

3. This chapter discussed a number of incidents involving the police and the public that led to accusations of the police being biased against minorities. Do you think this is the case? Explain your answer. What, if anything, do you think could be done to promote diversity, equity, and inclusion by police and other first responders?

4. Some might argue that requiring first responders to undergo regular psychological evaluation as part of their job duties would be an invasion of their privacy. Others might argue that it is a necessary component of making sure that they are taking care of themselves and able to interact appropriately in their job duties. Do you believe that first responders should receive such evaluations on a routine basis? Explain your rationale.

KEY TERMS

Cognitive processing therapy

Critical incident stress debriefing (CISD)

Diagnostic and Statistical Manual (DSM)

Diversity, equity, and inclusion

Exposure therapy

Eye movement desensitization reprocessing (EMDR)

Fitness for duty evaluation (FFDE)

Long-term stress

Major depressive disorder (MDD)

Minnesota Multiphasic Personality Inventory (MMPI)

Occupational stress

Organizational stress

Personal stress

Post-traumatic stress disorder (PTSD)

Psychological first aid (PFA)

Short-term stress

Stress

Substance use disorder (SUD)

Suicide

PSYCHOLOGY OF INVESTIGATIONS

1. Define normal and abnormal human behavior and research related to influences on human behavior.

2. Describe the polygraph and the manner in which it may be used to detect deception.

3. Discuss the challenges of eyewitness testimony and the role of own-race bias (ORB) in such testimony.

4. Compare and contrast the Reid technique and PEACE model for interview and interrogation.

5. Distinguish between voluntary, compliant, and persuaded false confessions and discuss the consequences for those who are falsely convicted.

Scenario #1: The local bank has been robbed at gunpoint. This has been reported to the police, who have viewed the videotapes of the offense and interviewed everyone who was in the vicinity who may have witnessed this event. Based on security cameras outside the bank, a description of the getaway vehicle was obtained. During a routine traffic stop several days later, a man matching the description of the robber is stopped while driving a car that is similar to the getaway vehicle. You are the detective tasked with interviewing this man, who has been detained. During the interview, you ask him for his name and address as well as other demographic information. You also ask him where he was on the day and time that the offense occurred and whether he has anyone who can verify that claim. You ask about his employment and whether he is having any financial difficulties. You also ask him if he owns the car that he was driving when he was stopped or whether he borrowed it from a friend. While interviewing him, you are closely observing his voice and facial expressions and determining whether he seems nervous and how open and honest he seems to be in his responses.

Scenario #2: Your 6-year-old son has just finished his soccer game. He and his teammate, Tommy, come running up to you after the game. "Mommy, mommy!" your son yells. "Tommy wants me to come to his house now! We are going to play and swim in his pool! It might even be a sleepover! Can I go, can I go?! Pleeeeease, Mommy!" Tommy's mother then approaches you. You have seen her at the games before, but you don't really know her or anything about her. She introduces herself, as do you. After making small talk about the weather, you ask her where she lives and whether or not Tommy has brothers or sisters. You share a little bit about your own family and then ask her what she does for a living and how long they have lived in their neighborhood. The whole time you are conversing with her, you are noticing how she is dressed and her facial expressions and are getting some ideas about her personality.

If we were to ask a roomful of people to describe Scenario #1 in a single word, it seems likely that many of them would use the word investigation *or some similar term. But what if we asked those same people to describe Scenario #2 in a single word? Would they be as likely to use the word* investigation? *Or might they simply describe it by using the word* conversation *or something similar? Scenario #1 seems easy to recognize as an investigation; the detective is clearly asking questions and obtaining information to be able to make an important decision: whether to charge the person being interviewed with having committed the bank robbery. However, people may not be so quick to recognize Scenario #2 as an investigation. After all, no crime has been committed; this is simply two parents discussing whether their children will have a play date. However, if we take a closer look at Scenario #2, we will find that it bears considerable similarity to the first scenario; you are obtaining information from Tommy's mother so that you can make an important decision about the welfare of your own child. That is, do you trust that she is a caring and capable parent who you can trust to properly supervise your child in the swimming pool and to care for the well-being of your child over the next 24 hours?*

In both scenarios, we are obtaining information and making an evaluation so that we can ultimately decide what happens next. In both of these situations, we are making some comparison of what we might expect and what we actually see. If we see that the person being interviewed for the bank robbery is calm and open, we might expect that perhaps he is not responsible for the robbery after all. If, while talking to Tommy's mother, we notice something unexpected—perhaps we smell alcohol on her breath—then we might decide that our child visiting Tommy's house today is not a good idea.

NORMAL VERSUS ABNORMAL

Police officers, detectives, forensic psychologists, Federal Bureau of Investigation agents, and many other officials conduct investigations of one type or another. But so do people during the course of their daily lives, often in situations such as Scenario #2 above. An **investigation** may be thought of as the systematic examination or research of a topic or a person. During the course of an investigation, people seek to gather evidence and information (formally or informally) by talking to those involved and by making observations. Often, they do so to reach a conclusion or to make a decision about what to do next. As it relates to Scenario #2, it might be a conclusion about whether to let our child go to a friend's house or to make an excuse about why he cannot if we are uncomfortable with what we find. As it relates to Scenario #1, the investigation may include deciding whether an individual should now be considered a suspect.

Although investigations vary widely in scope and type, they typically involve deciding whether the circumstances warrant the time and effort of an investigation. If it is decided that investigation is indicated, the next steps include planning the investigation, conducting interviews, and gathering evidence. Ultimately, there will be an evaluation of that evidence and a decision as to what action (if any) needs to be taken next. In the cases of a formal or official investigation of any type, all of the steps involved in the process must be documented.

As we will see in future chapters, forensic practitioners may be involved in a wide variety of investigations. When tasked to complete a child custody evaluation, for example, the clinician is essentially conducting an investigation of the home, the parents, and the child. This is not done for law enforcement purposes but so the clinician can make a meaningful report to the court about what parent and living situation might be in the best interest of that child. In the event of a psychologist in a correctional setting, that practitioner may be conducting an investigation of the inmate's background and interviewing that inmate as part of formulating a report to the parole board that will help to determine if the inmate should be released into the community. A psychologist constructing a criminal profile would conduct an investigation by looking at records and evidence at the scene as part of an attempt to reach some conclusions about the type of person that would commit such an offense. In the experience of the present author, these and other investigations must include knowledge of what is and is not considered normal human behavior. It is easy to assume that one knows what normal human behavior is, but as we will see throughout this text, a competent forensic psychologist does not base their practice on assumptions but on research and clinical experience.

Normal may be thought of as conforming to a standard, the quality of being average or typical. Thus, we might think of driving on the right side of the road as normal. It conforms to the standard of the law in the United States (U. S.) and is what we and others do every day. **Abnormal**, then, would be defined as deviating from a standard, the quality of deviating from average or usual. As discussed in the last chapter in regard to diversity, equity, and inclusion, it is vitally important in the context of human behavior for the forensic practitioner to remember that differences do *not* mean that a particular quality or behavior is bad or wrong. For example, while driving on the left side of the road would deviate from what is normal in the U. S., doing so *is* normal in other countries such as Ireland and New Zealand. To those who live in those countries, driving on the *right* side of the road would be considered abnormal.

According to the U.S. Census Bureau (2022), the average annual real wage in the U. S. in 2019 was approximately $65,000. Thus, we might consider that a normal income. On the other hand, basketball superstar LeBron James made a staggering $89 million in 2019 (Badenhausen, 2019)! Although his salary would certainly be considered abnormal in that it is not average or typical of anyone else in the country, we would not consider this abnormal salary to be bad or wrong if someone wanted to pay it to us. Similarly, we could state that Albert Einstein's estimated IQ of 160 is abnormal in that it is much higher than the average person's or we could state that quarterback Tom Brady won an abnormal number of Super Bowls (in that no one else has won seven). It is important to remember that in this context, abnormal carries no moral value; it simply indicates that a particular behavior is different (higher or lower) than the average.

Influences on Human Behavior

As noted above, distinguishing normal from abnormal behavior requires context; what is normal in one place, time, or condition may be anything but normal under different circumstances. It is important for the budding forensic psychologist to understand some of the factors that play a role in determining what behavior is normal in a given situation.

Helping Behavior

When it comes to the assumptions we make regarding human behavior, it would be easy to believe that helping others is a common and normal behavior. It would also be easy to assume that in an emergency situation, the more people who are present and who witness that situation, the more likely it is that someone (or multiple people) will intervene and help. However, as mentioned above, a competent forensic psychologist should not make assumptions, including the assumption that helping behavior is normal, frequent, and to be expected.

Late at night on March 13, 1964, Catherine "Kitty" Genovese left work and was returning to her apartment in Queens, New York. As she exited her car and walked to her building, a man by the name of Winston Moseley quickly approached her, stabbing her with a knife. She screamed loudly and pleaded for help. Moseley then left the scene, only to return shortly thereafter, at which point he stabbed her again, raped her, and eventually killed her. *The New York Times* reported that 37 people had heard her cries for help, but no one had called the police or intervened in any way (Gansberg, 1964). As might be expected, the article stunned many of those who read it—how could people be so callous and uncaring? How is it possible that no one would come to the aid of Ms. Genovese or even pick up the phone to call the police? It was later discovered that *The New York Times* report was inaccurate; in fact, some of the witnesses of this offense did indeed contact the police and the *Times* admitted the error (McFadden, 2016). However, the event and subsequent article served as a catalyst for a great deal of research on helping behavior. A study by Darley and Latane (1968) was one that underscored the notion that the more people who are present during an emergency, the less likely it is that they will intervene and help an individual whom they believe to be in distress. Darley and Latane referred to this finding as a **diffusion of responsibility**, meaning that the more people who are present during an emergency situation, the less responsibility each of them feels to intervene.

Diffusion of responsibility is not limited to the laboratory setting, though, and can have very real consequences. More recent than the research of Darley and Latane is the case of George Floyd, mentioned in the previous chapter. As you will recall, Floyd was handcuffed, and for a lengthy period of time, Officer Chauvin knelt on Floyd's neck. While Chauvin did so, three other officers (Alex Kueng, Thomas Lane, and Tou Thao) formed a loose perimeter around Chauvin and Floyd but took no action to intervene on Floyd's behalf (Chappell, 2020). Due to their inaction, Officers Kueng, Lane, and Thao were found guilty of depriving Floyd of his constitutional right to be free from unreasonable force and were each sentenced to between two and half years and three and a half years of incarceration as a result. Their inaction may be yet another example of the diffusion of responsibility; in no way does that excuse their inaction (after all, regardless of diffusion of responsibility, anyone who chooses to act is certainly free to do so) but it does underscore that when others are present, people may choose to take no action at all, having convinced themselves that others will do so if necessary.

The findings of Darley and Latane are not limited to the laboratory but apply to our everyday lives. Reflect on your own experience: How many times have you passed a stranded motorist and not offered to help—not even called for help without stopping—because you have told yourself that they must have already called for assistance or that someone else driving by surely must have already done so. Helping behavior is not to be taken for granted as normal in every situation.

Obedience to Authority

Later in this chapter, we will discuss false confessions. At first, it might be quite difficult for us to understand why anyone would admit guilt to a crime that they did not commit (espe-

The shock machine used in Milgram's study of obedience to authority. Although it was perhaps frightening in appearance, it did not actually deliver shocks to the Learner.

Cinematic Collection/Alamy Stock Photo

cially when the consequences of doing so could be quite severe) simply because someone in authority is telling them that they must confess. However, research by psychologist Stanley Milgram demonstrated how profoundly the orders of an authority figure can influence human behavior.

Milgram's research on **obedience to authority** was conducted at Yale University in 1961. Two subjects came into the lab setting and were greeted by a rather stern-looking experimenter with a white lab coat and a clipboard. The subjects were told that the experiment had to do with learning and memory and that one of them would be the Teacher and the other would be the Learner. Unbeknownst to the subject who became the Teacher, the Learner was actually a confederate who was working with the experimenter. The

Teacher was shown a rather ominous-looking shock machine that would allow them to (supposedly) deliver an electric shock to the Learner any time the Learner provided an incorrect answer. The Teacher and Learner were in different rooms and could communicate by intercom. Early in the experiment, the Learner began to make errors and the Teacher was to administer shocks. The Teacher could hear the Learner express discomfort, then pain, then agony as the shocks increased in severity. When the Teacher expressed concern or reluctance to administer the next shock, the experimenter would give one of a set of prompts, such as "The experiment requires that you continue." To the surprise of almost everyone, 65% of Teachers delivered the maximum 450-volt shock to the poor Learner simply because the experimenter, a person in authority, told them to do so. It is important to note that the Learner, a confederate, was not actually harmed at all during the experiment; the shock machine was fake, and the Learner was only acting as if they were being shocked.

As with the Darley and Latane study, Milgram's findings apply not only to the laboratory but to real life as well. After all, if people are willing to deliver painful shocks to others under the pressure of an authority figure, should we not believe that under similar pressure, they might confess to a crime they did not commit?

DETECTION OF DECEPTION

While working in the prison, the present author was told a joke that he found to be neither funny nor true: "How do you know if an inmate is lying?" The response was, "Their lips are moving." It is certainly true that people lie at times, and those who are incarcerated are no exception to this. However, as has been mentioned several times already, blind assumptions about human behavior are to be avoided at all costs. It would be a terrible mistake to believe that we are being lied to at all times. It is important to first review all available records and evidence and then to listen carefully before deciding if the person we are interacting with is attempting to deceive us.

It is not uncommon for people to lie. There have been many studies of the rates at which people lie (DePaulo et al., 1996). Such studies vary greatly in their results. In his 1977 book, psychologist Jerald Jellison reported that on average, people tell about 200 lies per day(!). On the other end of the spectrum, self-report studies of lying suggest that the average person admits to lying 1.65 times per day (Saad, 2011), although the author points out the irony that when we ask people about how often they lie, they may also lie about how often they engage in such behavior. In any event, it seems safe to say that lying may be a common behavior for some people.

People lie for a wide variety of reasons. In some cases, perhaps they are slightly embellishing their story for the amusement of those listening. In other cases, they may be attempting to be socially appropriate. For example, maybe a friend has asked them how they look in their new outfit. The truth is that the person they are asking thinks the new outfit looks rather silly; however, rather than offending their friend, who is clearly quite pleased with the outfit, they decide to tell a white lie and state that they think it looks terrific. Other people may lie if they feel it might benefit them to do so; if a person believes that lying to the police officer who has pulled them over for speeding might get them out of an expensive ticket, they may decide to give it a try. There are also those individuals who will lie even when there is no clear reason to do so. Perhaps they are excited at the prospect of getting away with a lie or succeeding in misleading the listener. This pleasure in lying has sometimes been referred to as **duping delight** (Ekman, 2009).

People often believe that they are capable of determining when they are being lied to. Perhaps we feel nervous when we are lying, so we believe that other people also feel that way when they lie. Therefore, we may believe that when we are interviewing them if they are lying, they will appear to be nervous. Again, such assumptions are *not* something that a good forensic psychologist or anyone in the legal system should make. Research does not support the belief that we can accurately assess when others are lying to us. On our own, we are no better than a coin toss when it comes to detecting lies. Bond and DePaulo (2006) found that people can only distinguish between being told the truth or a lie 54% of the time.

It is commonly believed that one way of determining whether someone is lying to you is based on the amount of eye contact they make while talking. We believe that if someone is making extended eye contact with us, they are likely telling the truth; if they fail to do so, they are likely being deceptive. Again, research does not support this belief. In fact, liars (knowing that eye contact is believed to be an indicator of truthfulness) tend to overcompensate by maintaining eye contact for *longer* periods of time than those who are telling the truth (Schafer, 2014). The present author can recall what one inmate told him before the inmate went to see the parole board as part of his effort to be released to the community. He said, "Hell, Doc, I'll tell them whatever they want to hear. I'll tell them I shot JFK [John Fitzgerald Kennedy] if I think that will get them to let me go. And I'll look 'em straight in the eyes while I'm saying it."

Cognitive Load Approach

Cognitive load refers to the amount of information that a person is able to process and retain in working memory at any one time. Much like gasoline in a car, cognitive load is limited. The car will run only as long as there is gas in the tank. Once the tank is empty, the car will go no further. Cognitive load is similar in that it is finite in amount. We have to pay attention and concentrate if we are to process information in a meaningful manner.

Let's say that you are learning to play the piano. This requires a considerable number of cognitive resources: remembering what each printed note means, which fingers to use to press each key of the piano, which pedal to depress, and so forth. But you are a dedicated student, and with time and practice, it is likely that you will be able to acquire this skill to some level of proficiency. Learning to speak French would be much the same, requiring a dedicated number of cognitive resources for you to remember how to pronounce different words, how to conjugate verbs, and the meaning of each word. Again, with time and regular practice, you will be able to learn the language. However, now let us imagine that you are trying to learn to play the piano and to speak French *at the same time*. We realize that this would likely be impossible (even for a brilliant and hardworking student like you!). Learning both at the same time is simply too much for anyone's brain to process. When cognitive load is exceeded, you can no longer function as you would like to in order to learn these skills.

Cognitive Load Approach to Detection of Deception

The **cognitive load approach** to detecting deception is based upon the notion that lying places a greater cognitive load upon the individual than does telling the truth. After all, telling the truth requires relatively few cognitive resources; we are merely recalling events that occurred. Lying, on the other hand, would require a considerably higher cognitive load, as the liar must craft their story, remember the details, make the story seem believable, and (if questioned) be able to weave their answers into that story in a manner that seems consistent and believable. The cognitive load approach is based on the idea that if an investigator purposefully increases the cognitive load on a person who is lying, that cognitive load may exceed their capacity and the investigator will be able to see what might be considered "leakage." That is, the person being deceptive may begin to express uncertainty or be overly vague in their responses. Under increased cognitive load, a person who is lying may demonstrate increased response latency, meaning that the length of time it takes them to respond to questions will increase, presumably as they are trying to think of how they should respond. The use of filler words such as "Um," "uh," or others may also increase (Schafer, 2020). In the experience of the present writer, it is common for such individuals to repeat the question they have just been asked verbatim. Of course, if they are able to repeat the question word-for-word, it is clear that they heard it and it may be speculated that they are repeating it in order to buy time to formulate a response.

   Indeed, research in the area of cognitive load approach has shown promise. In a study by Vrij et al. (2008), researchers increased cognitive load on both truth tellers and liars by asking them to repeat their stories in reverse chronological order. That is, they were asked to start at the end of their story and tell the order in which events occurred until they got to the beginning. Such a task requires an increased cognitive load for both groups, but more so for those who are being deceptive, as the events did not actually happen to them. These same researchers found that police officers were better able to discriminate between truth tellers and liars when those subjects were asked to tell their stories in reverse. Schafer (2020) suggests that in addition to asking subjects to tell their story in reverse chronological order, interviewers can increase cognitive load and better detect deception by asking people unexpected questions or asking for more information or details, both of which increase cognitive load.

The Polygraph

I took a course in biofeedback in graduate school. Biofeedback involves the electronic monitoring of various bodily functions as part of teaching a person to control those functions. For example, the monitoring of heart rate and respiration can be useful in teaching a person to decrease anxiety (Brauer, 1999). The monitoring of muscle tension by means of a device known as an electromyograph can be helpful in teaching a person to prevent headaches or to decrease the severity or intensity of those headaches (Lipchik, 2008). The professor for the course had a variety of biofeedback devices in his office. One day at the beginning of class, he asked, "Who thinks they can beat a lie detector?" I was working off some of my tuition by running subjects in the social psychology lab, and at that time, deception (basically, lying to the subjects about what the experiment was about) was a common practice. Subjects were, of course, debriefed about that deception and the reasons for it before they left the lab. However, as a result of this practice at deceiving others, I thought I could tell a pretty convincing lie, so I volunteered. The professor first had me secretly write down a number from 1 to 10 on a slip of paper. I wrote the number 7. The professor put a band around my chest to measure respiration, a blood pressure cuff around my arm, and several pads from a galvanic skin response device on the fingers of one hand. "OK," he announced. "I'm going to count off the numbers from one to ten and ask you if each one is your number. Whether it is your number or not, I want you to say 'No.'" I expressed understanding and told myself that I was going to beat the machines. I was going to stay calm, control my breathing, and emerge victorious. He started: "Is the number you picked one?" No. "Is the number you picked two?" No. As he started to get closer to the number seven, I could feel myself getting nervous, but I was determined to keep my breathing steady. "Is your number seven?" No. He went all the way up to ten. Then he immediately went back to "Is your number 7?" "No," I responded. He laughed and said, "Yes, it is, liar!" I was caught!

As the name implies, the **polygraph**—often referred to as a "lie detector"—measures and records a number of physiological functions simultaneously. Typically, a polygraph will measure and record at a minimum the subject's blood pressure, pulse, respiration, skin conductivity, and any movement on the part of the subject that might affect these other results (American Polygraph Association, 2019). The broad theory of the polygraph in detecting deception is that people will feel nervous or excited when they are lying, and those emotions can and will lead to measurable changes in physiological functioning. Thus, it is thought that when an individual's answers are accompanied by deviations from the baseline on the polygraph, it is likely that the individual is being deceptive. However, we must be wary of assuming that a change from baseline physiological functions indicates the presence of deception. There is no specific physiological factor that is reliably associated with lying (American Psychological Association, 2004a, 2004b). A physiological reaction during a polygraph examination might indicate that the subject is so vehement in their denial of the offense that the polygraph detects changes in their blood pressure and respiration. In such a case, these changes do not necessarily indicate that the subject is being deceptive.

Polygraphs are often used to assist in the screening of potential law enforcement officers at the local or state level or for some federal agencies. The military may use a polygraph to screen those who are being considered for high-security clearances. Law enforcement agencies will, at times, use the polygraph to help them with investigations. We would hope that in such cases, the polygraph would be an infallible tool in helping us select only the best employees and in helping us to bring guilty individuals to justice. However, as we will see below, although the polygraph appears to be a useful device in limited circumstances, it is far from infallible.

The Control (or Comparison) Question Test

The **control question test** (CQT) is sometimes also referred to as the **comparison question test**. The CQT was developed by Cleve Baxter, who was an expert on interrogations for the Central Intelligence Agency. The CQT involves asking subjects nonthreatening questions as well as questions in which the subject is likely to be lying but about a relatively unimportant matter (the "probable lie"). The subject is also asked questions relevant to the offense in question (the "relevant event"). If the subject produces a greater response to the question about the probable lie than about the relevant event, then it seems more likely that they are truthfully denying the relevant event. If they are guilty of the relevant event, then they would be expected to produce relatively little change for the probable lie but a much larger one for the relevant event. This procedure is typically repeated several times so that results can be compared for consistency.

A meta-analysis (a single study that combines the results of multiple other studies on the same topic) of 50 studies of the CQT on the polygraph concluded that CQT "discriminates truth tellers from liars with a large magnitude of effect" (Honts et al., 2020, p. 422). However, at no point do the authors suggest this technique is perfect, adding, "However, our results should not be interpreted as including that all CQT polygraph tests have high accuracy" (p. 422).

There continues to be considerable debate about the polygraph's effectiveness in detecting deception.

Myron Standret / Alamy Stock Photo

The Relevant–Irrelevant Technique

The **relevant–irrelevant** polygraph examination technique was pioneered by Leonard

Keeler, one of the two inventors of the polygraph. This technique involves interspersing questions relevant to the offense ("Did you murder John Smith?") to questions that have no relevance to the offense ("Is your birthday in May?"). It is expected that a guilty individual will demonstrate greater changes in physiological functions to the relevant questions than to the irrelevant ones.

The Guilty Knowledge Test (GKT)

The **guilty knowledge test (GKT)** is often used in Japan. In this procedure, the person administering the polygraph asks the subject multiple-choice questions about the crime that only the guilty party would be able to answer correctly. Physiological responses to each question are measured. If a subject demonstrates consistently greater physiological responses to the correct answers, then it is inferred that they have some knowledge of the crime and may indeed have been involved in that offense. One advantage of this procedure is that the person administering the polygraph does not know the correct answer to the questions they are asking, which may help to eliminate any conscious or unconscious bias in the way that the test is being administered.

A meta-analysis conducted by the American Polygraph Association (2011) included 38 studies on the validity of the polygraph and examined 14 different psychophysiological detection of deception (PDD) techniques. including the CQT, GKT, and others. This study found no significant differences between techniques and therefore did not rank them according to effectiveness. It also found that in terms of accuracy, the polygraph "significantly exceeded chance expectations" (p. 259). This study found accuracy rates of between 0.798 and 0.94 where 0 = no accuracy and 1.00 = perfect accuracy.

How Accurate Is the Polygraph?

The debate between clinicians and practitioners about the validity and accuracy of the polygraph in detecting deception has raged on for many years. As a general rule, polygraphers and those who utilize the results of that instrument hold that the polygraph is extremely accurate in detecting deception. Clinicians, however, often argue that laboratory evidence does not back up this claim; those who use the polygraph often fire back that this device is not appropriately tested in a laboratory environment but is quite accurate in the real-world environment.

There is a tremendous body of research on the utility and accuracy of the polygraph. This research, although helpful, does little to settle the debate on the utility and accuracy of the polygraph, as there are numerous studies supporting each side of the issue and many studies by each side contradicting the opinions of their detractors. For example, the American Polygraph Association (2004a, p. 1) states that "scientific evidence supports the validity of polygraph examinations" as long as they are conducted and interpreted with validated procedures. The Association points to a meta-analysis of all peer-reviewed studies on polygraph testing that found an accuracy rate of 87%. However, a lengthy review by the National Academy of Sciences in 2003 suggested that there was "little basis for the expectation that a polygraph test could have extremely high accuracy" (National Research Council, 2003) and the American Psychological Association (2004b, p. 1) stated that "most psychologists agree that there is little evidence that polygraph tests can accurately detect lies." Needless to say, this debate is unlikely to be resolved any time soon. For the purposes of this text, it is important for the budding forensic psychologist to be aware of the fact that the polygraph, while useful in some situations, is far from infallible.

Given the above debate on the validity and accuracy of polygraph results, it will perhaps come as little surprise that the courts are divided on the use of polygraphs' admissibility in court. Some states do not permit any reference to polygraph results in court. In other states, polygraph results may be entered into court as long as both sides stipulate that this is acceptable to them.

In Chapter 7, we will discuss individuals who have antisocial personality disorder and who, by definition, are lacking in (or, in some cases, completely devoid of) feelings of guilt or remorse for any of their actions, no matter how heinous. We might think that such individuals would have little difficulty in defeating a polygraph. After all, it would seem that a lack of remorse would mean that such individuals would not be nervous while lying; therefore, their responses to any question on the polygraph should elicit few (if any) physiological changes.

Stern and Krapohl (2004) looked at a number of studies comparing the polygraph results of those with antisocial personality disorder to the results of those without this disorder. Their conclusion in looking at these studies was that those with antisocial personality disorder had no more success in being deceptive on the polygraph than were folks who did not have this disorder. Why would that be? The belief of these researchers was that those with antisocial personality disorder are still concerned with those things that affect them immediately. They are not happy in an environment where the polygrapher and equipment are in control. Stern and Krapohl go on to state that feelings of guilt are "not a necessary precondition for polygraph detection efficacy" (p. 211).

Verschuere et al. (2007) reached a conclusion similar to that of Stern and Krapohl. They compared 48 male prisoners with antisocial personality disorder to 31 volunteers from the community. Subjects were instructed to be deceptive during the polygraph and were promised a financial reward if they were able to do so successfully. They found that the ability to detect deception in the prisoners using the polygraph was significantly higher than chance, with an accuracy of 79% and not significantly different than the ability to detect deception in the community sample at 87%. Thus, it appears that the polygraph can be used in a valid and useful manner with those with antisocial personality disorder.

EYEWITNESS TESTIMONY

In many courtroom dramas, there is an exciting moment when the person on the witness stand is asked if they can identify the individual who committed the crime in question. The witness points a finger at the accused and loudly and confidently exclaims, "It was him! I saw him! He did it!" For those of us watching, there seems to be little reason for the court to proceed further. A reliable-appearing witness has provided compelling proof that the accused is guilty. Indeed, witnesses truly believe their memories are accurate, so it is not surprising that they sound convincing (Chew, 2018).

But how accurate are eyewitness reports? In some of the courtroom dramas mentioned above (and in actual courtrooms as well!), upon cross-examination, that confident, reliable-appearing witness may admit that it was dark out when they witnessed the offense . . . and that they didn't have their prescription glasses on at the time . . . and that the person they saw had their face obscured by the hood of their sweatshirt, and so forth. Suddenly, the proof provided by the eyewitness seems much less than certain.

Staff writers for the Innocence Project (2020) report that 69% of people who were exonerated of crimes based on newfound DNA evidence were incorrectly identified by witnesses. Thus, eyewitness misidentification was at least partially responsible for their wrongful conviction and is "the leading contributing cause of these wrongful convictions." Although the total number of people wrongly convicted on the basis of eyewitness errors in identification is impossible to know, it can certainly be said that the wrongful conviction of even a single person represents a serious miscarriage of justice.

Fallibility in Eyewitness Reports

People may believe that their memories are like that of a computer or a video—what they saw or heard is *exactly* what happened and is not subject to any distortion, outside influence, or change over time. However, evidence does not at all support such a belief. In 1973, psychologist Elizabeth Loftus and her colleague John Palmer conducted seminal research on the effect of language (in fact, a single word) on memory. In their first study, they had subjects watch a film of a traffic accident. The subjects were then asked, "About how fast were the cars going when they _____ into each other?" In the first condition, the word *smashed* was used in place of the blank. In following conditions, the blank was filled in with other words, including *collided, bumped, hit*, and *contacted*. Reliably, subjects with the *smashed* word condition rated the cars as moving faster than did subjects in the other conditions, pointing out how even a single word can influence recall. In a follow-up study, a week after the initial experiment concluded, subjects were asked to fill out another questionnaire in which one of the questions was whether they observed broken glass at the accident scene. Nearly one-third of the students with the *smashed* word condition reported that they had observed broken glass. In fact, there was no such glass at the scene and subjects in the other conditions did not recall broken glass nearly as often as in those with the *smashed* word condition.

In 1979, Loftus continued to expand upon her work on the fallibility of eyewitness reports. In her book (1996), she noted that in addition to factors such as poor viewing conditions and stress, factors such as bias and expectation can play an important role in what is recalled and how accurately (or inaccurately) it is recalled. There has been a great deal of research into the reliability of eyewitness testimony since the 1970s. Since then, there has been a "large body of published experimental research showing that eyewitness testimony can be highly unreliable under certain conditions" (Wells, 2002, p. 663).

THE FALLIBILITY OF EYEWITNESS TESTIMONY— EVEN IN THE CLASSROOM

My daughter has always been an actor, and she is quite talented in this regard (not that I am biased, of course!). Some weeks after talking to my cognitive psychology class about the fallibility of memory and the unreliability of eyewitness testimony, I was lecturing in that class when a student barged in. She angrily waved a test in my face and yelled at me, saying that I had promised her a B as her midterm grade and that, given the 90 she got on the test that she was waving in my face, she deserved at least a B! I told her that I would talk to her about it after class, but she continued to tell me what a lousy teacher I was, then crumpled the test into a ball, threw it in my face, yelled a few more unkind words, and stormed out, slamming the door loudly behind her. I instructed my class not to talk, merely to write down exactly what had transpired so that I could make an official report to security. The students were instructed to write a detailed description of everything that had transpired: her physical appearance, what she was wearing, and what each of us had said in as much detail as they could possibly recall.

As you may have already guessed, when they were done, I went and got the student and introduced her to the class as my daughter. This was all an exercise to see how accurate and consistent their reports were of an event they had seen mere minutes ago. Descriptions of what was said and her clothing varied greatly. Estimates of her height ranged from 5'3" to 5'10" (she is actually 5'7"). In scripted scenarios, as in real life, it is important for forensic practitioners and all criminal justice professionals to remember that eyewitness reports can be accurate, error prone, or some combination of the two.

Can Race Play a Factor in Eyewitness Misidentification?

As noted above, the accuracy of eyewitness identification leaves a great deal to be desired. Many factors may play a role: visibility, expectation, and the physical and emotional state of the witness, to name a few. Is it possible that race is another one of these factors? That is, is it possible that an individual has greater difficulty in identifying a person of another race as opposed to someone of their own race? Can the already-mistake-prone process of eyewitness identification become even less reliable when it is a person of another race that one is attempting to identify? As we will see below, it would appear that the answer is yes.

Meissner and Brigham (2001) conducted a meta-analysis of 39 research articles including nearly 5,000 participants and found that subjects were consistently better at identifying members of their own race and made fewer mistakes doing so compared to when they were attempting to identify members of other races. They referred to this phenomenon as an **own-race bias (ORB)**. Subjects were consistently worse at identifying members of races other than their own and they made more mistakes when attempting to do so. Their study further suggested that these errors have a significant impact on eyewitness testimony. The Innocence Project goes on to point out that of the 358 people sentenced to death since 1989, 71% were convicted largely based on eyewitness evidence. Of those, 41% involved cross-race misidentification (221 of 358 were African American). A later study by Wong et al. (2020) suggested that living in a multiracial society does not necessarily eliminate or reduce this bias.

There are a number of theories about why people are more accurate in recognizing others of their own race. Aracena (2017) suggests that humans process faces of their own race more holistically, as a single unit. However, when looking at the faces of people of other races, people do not process the face in a holistic manner; instead, they attend to the features and details of a person's face rather than to the face as a whole. These researchers also suggested that motivation and ability to pay attention may also play a role. It is important for us to recognize that the already-mistake-prone process of eyewitness identification may be further confounded by this bias, meaning that cross-race eyewitness reports have an even greater probability of being inaccurate.

INTERVIEW AND INTERROGATION TECHNIQUES

The terms *interview* and *interrogation* are often used together, but it would be a mistake to think they are interchangeable. An interview may be thought of as a meeting during which there is an exchange of information or in which one person is trying to elicit information from another. There are, of course, many different types and styles of interview, each with its own purpose. A forensic psychologist conducting an interview so that they can help the court make a decision regarding child custody will proceed very differently than a police officer interviewing the witness of a violent crime.

For forensic psychologists, before beginning any interview, it is important to conduct thorough background research. Depending on the setting they are in, they may have more or less information, but there are always some records that they can examine. When the forensic psychologist is interviewing candidates for police jobs, they will be provided with background information on the candidate. For example, they will have access to an application, test scores, previous job references, and so forth. In corrections, the forensic psychologist will have files containing an abundance of information on each and every person in the institution. If they are conducting an evaluation to determine competency to stand trial, the practitioner will have records from the court process. All this background information must be read thoroughly before beginning any interview.

Earlier in this chapter, we discussed detection of deception. Depending on the setting in which the forensic psychologist is practicing, it may be advisable for them during the course of the interview to ask questions to which they already know the answer (since they have read the available records). This is merely one technique of attempting to detect deception: Are the answers given by the person being interviewed consistent with what was seen in the records? If their answers and their record don't match up, this is worth noting and documenting in whatever report is being written. One might write, for example, "On at least four occasions, the replies given to me by the applicant were inconsistent with replies they have given in the past."

During an interview, police officers (or in some cases, other first responders such as firefighters) are asking questions because they are seeking facts about a given situation. This could include a police officer asking an eyewitness, "How fast would you say the truck was going when it struck the telephone pole?" Such interviews are typically informal in format and use open-ended questions—"In regard to the fight that you witnessed, can you tell me what happened?"—before drilling down in an effort to obtain more specific information. In interviews, the interviewer is looking for answers, and while they might be attempting to determine who is responsible for an offense, they are not accusing anyone; they are merely gathering information. In many law enforcement–related scenarios, there may be an attempt by the interviewer to make the subject comfortable (offering them a bottle of water) or to get away from the scene of a brutal accident.

An **interrogation** is typically only utilized when law enforcement is confident that they have identified the perpetrator of a given offense. An interrogation is similar to an interview in that some information is still being sought, but it is different in almost every other way. In the interrogation, police tell the individual in a very direct manner that they are confident that this person is responsible for that offense. Interrogations occur in a much more formal setting and typically include making the person being interrogated less comfortable rather than more comfortable. This can mean leaving them in a small, windowless room for an extended period of time before the process commences. It can mean using a small room and crowding them into a corner to violate their sense of personal space.

The Reid Technique

There are a number of different police interrogation techniques. The one most often used in the U. S. is the **Reid technique**, named after John Reid, who was a police officer, a polygraph expert, and a psychologist. It would appear that Reid may have used his knowledge of psychology to create a technique that would exert a calculated pressure toward an individual admitting guilt. It is important to know that the Reid interrogation technique (and others) are only intended for use when law enforcement has clear evidence and good reason to believe that they have identified the person responsible for a given offense. Typically, that person is brought into a small and rather stark room. They are often made to wait for an extended period of time before the interrogation begins. The interrogation starts with the officer or detective informing the accused that they have more than enough evidence to prove that they are guilty of the offense, perhaps dropping a thick file of paperwork on the desk to bolster this claim and stating something along the lines of "All the evidence is right here. I know you did it. I just want to know why."

During interrogation, any attempts by the accused to deny responsibility or blame others are quickly contradicted or minimized ("I've already heard your story, and you know and I know that isn't what happened."). Later in the interrogation, the interrogator may purposefully shift the blame for the offense (but not the guilt) in some fashion. The interrogator at this point may be doing a bit of acting; they don't really believe what they are saying but instead may be finding a way to blame the victim, allowing the accused individual to save face while still admitting guilt. For example, if attempting to obtain a confession in regard to a burglary, it's possible that an interrogator would say, "Hey look, you tried the door and it was unlocked, right? If the homeowner really cared about their stuff, they would have locked the door, wouldn't they? So you just went in and took stuff they clearly didn't really care about, isn't that right?"

If necessary, the person conducting an interrogation may offer an alternative question, with one of those alternatives more socially acceptable than another. An example of an alternative question would be, "You know you killed your wife, and I know it. Here's the thing, there are two kinds of people who kill in this world. First, there are cold-blooded murderers. They are evil, worse than animals. Then there's people who've had a hell of a bad day, then they come home and maybe the wife is running her mouth at her husband and she won't give him a minute to relax. [Remember the officer does *not* believe this; they are simply saying it in the hopes of obtaining a confession.] And she just keeps on him and on him, and in a moment of stress, he just snaps. Bob, I know you. You aren't a cold-blooded murderer, are you? You just had a bad day and snapped, right?" Thus, the alternative question seeks to make the admission of guilt more palatable to the accused.

The Reid technique of interrogation involves the following steps:

1. Confrontation: Tell the accused, in confident terms, that the evidence indicates that they are the guilty party. ("I have a file full of evidence, all of which clearly shows that you committed this offense. Now I want to talk about why you did it.")

2. Develop a theme for shifting blame from the offender, allowing them to excuse or justify their offense. ("You don't seem like the type of guy that would do this if he was sober. You were drunk; is that why you did it?")

3. Handle denial by the accused. ("You did it. You know it and I know it.")

4. Overcome objections and further develop a theme.

5. Maintain the accused individual's attention. Close distance. Focus on the theme, not the consequences.

6. Continue to move toward the theme; justify the offense and appear understanding.

7. Ask the alternative question. ("You're not a cold-blooded murderer. You just had a bad day and snapped, right?")

8. Have the individual repeat their admission of guilt in clear terms.

9. Document/record the admission of guilt.

With the Reid interrogation technique, the accused is often placed in a small room, with the officers who are conducting the interrogation sitting very close to the accused.

Anna Kosolapova/Alamy Stock Photo

Although the Reid technique is still widely used in the U. S., it is of concern that putting so much psychological pressure on someone can produce false confessions, as people are under a great deal of emotional strain to obey the authority figure. As we discussed with the Milgram experiment, people are loathe to disobey authority figures. With the Reid technique, the accused person's denials are met with increased confrontation and anxiety. Meanwhile, the interrogator offers ways to decrease anxiety by confessing and offers alternative questions and confession as a way to save face. This would seem to be a recipe for false confessions. Indeed, the Reid technique has been found to lead to a significant number of false confessions, especially among the young, the mentally impaired, and those of lower intelligence (Kozinski, 2018). Scheck et al. (2000) found that more than 20% of the cases they examined in which the accused was exonerated by DNA evidence included a false confession on the part of the accused.

The PEACE Model

The **PEACE model** was developed in Great Britain in response to concerns about false confessions being obtained with more high-pressure interrogation tactics. The PEACE model is a five-stage model of interrogation. In this model, those conducting the interrogation encourage and allow the suspect to tell their entire story without any interruption. It is not until the suspect has finished doing so that the investigator(s) discusses inconsistencies in the suspect's story or confronts them with contradictory evidence. As you may surmise, the PEACE model is inherently less confrontative and accusatory in nature than is the Reid technique.

1. **Preparation and planning**: This stage involves obtaining all the evidence and deciding who to interview for more information.

2. **Engage and explain**: This stage involves establishing rapport with the person being interviewed. They are made comfortable, allowed ample time, and offered reassurance if they appear to be anxious or distraught.

3. **Account**: The person being interviewed is encouraged to give a full account of what they saw or did related to the incident in question. They are not to be interrupted as they give their version of events. After they have done so, the officer will ask them to clarify their story as needed and will ask follow-up questions to make sure all the necessary information is obtained. If there are inconsistencies in the account, the officer will seek to clarify those or may challenge those parts of the account.

4. **Closure**: This stage includes summarizing the account that has been given and the information that has been obtained. It also includes letting the person being interviewed know what is likely to happen next.

5. **Evaluate:** In the final stage of the process, those involved in conducting the interview evaluate the information they obtained and the process by which they did so, identifying any mistakes or areas that could be improved upon in the future.

False Confessions

As the term implies, a **false confession** can be said to have occurred when a person who is not guilty of an offense inaccurately reports that they are guilty. It may be difficult for us to understand why someone would confess to a crime they did not commit; however, such cases can and do occur. It is vitally important that we acknowledge the possibility of false confessions, as they can lead to the punishment and incarceration of people who are not truly guilty of the offense they are confessing to. Kassin and Wrightsman (1985) initially divided these cases into *voluntary, coerced–compliant*, and *coerced–internalized*. Ofshe and Leo (1997) extended this work, adding *coerced–persuaded* and *non-coerced–persuaded*. For the present purposes, it may be simplest to refer to the false confessions that occur as *voluntary, compliant*, and *persuaded*.

Voluntary False Confessions

Voluntary false confessions are confessions given by an individual who is not under police investigation for a particular offense. Individuals who give voluntary false confessions are clearly aware of the fact that they have not committed an offense but, without prompting, they claim that they committed the crime. In 2006, John Karr was a teacher in Thailand who was under investigation for an entirely different crime when he informed police that he was responsible for the death of JonBenet Ramsey in 2006. DNA evidence quickly demonstrated that this was not the case at all (Borger, 2006). According to Kassin and Wrightsman (1985), those who give voluntary false confessions often have some type of mental illness or are seeking notoriety for some reason. They know that they have not committed the offense but falsely report that they have in order to satisfy a psychological urge or to gain fame.

Compliant False Confessions

As noted above, interrogation techniques such as the Reid technique exert a calculated and often significant psychological pressure on the accused to produce a confession. Such interrogations may involve lengthy and intense accusations, occasionally sprinkled with promises of ending the interrogation, leniency in sentencing, or some other reward if the accused confesses. A **compliant false confession**, then, occurs when a person who knows that they are not guilty reports guilt anyway in the hopes of receiving some type of relief or reward for doing so. According to Kassin and Wrightsman (1985), such compliant false confessions are often recanted soon after the person is released from the pressure of the interrogation process. It should be noted, however, that once a confession has been made on paper or recorded in some fashion, withdrawing that confession or changing a guilty plea in court can be extremely difficult.

Persuaded False Confessions

We are aware of the mental strain and psychological pressure involved in interrogations. As discussed above, our memories can be faulty and are malleable. Under the pressure of interrogation, it is possible for some people who are not guilty of the offense to, at some point, believe that they are actually guilty. In some cases, they may believe it's merely possible; in other cases, they may become quite convinced of their guilt. In such cases, they may begin to doubt their own memory or, with police repeatedly telling them of events, they may come to believe that version of events. Such cases may also involve people who do not specifically recall the events surrounding the incident itself (due, for example, to extreme intoxication at the time of the event) and who then believe that perhaps they did indeed commit the offense.

False Confessions by Those With Intellectual Deficiency

If we acknowledge that an adult of average intelligence can make a false confession under the pressures of interrogation, then it is important for us to take a closer look at the possibility (or perhaps probability) that a person with intellectual limitations and/or a juvenile is even more vulnerable to doing so.

Of the 245 people on the National Record of Exonerations in 2018, Schatz (2018) noted that more than 25% displayed some evidence of intellectual deficiency. We can readily imagine that when given a complex order by a law enforcement officer, such as "Turn around, place your hands on top of your head, interlock your fingers and walk slowly backward toward the sound of my voice," it is entirely possible that their lack of understanding is interpreted as refusal and could lead to an escalation in the situation, maybe even resulting in a use of force by the police.

Schatz (2018) notes that of the 245 people on the National Record of Exonerations in 2018, more than 25% displayed some evidence of intellectual deficiency. Given what we have learned about the pressures of interrogation techniques and compliance with authority figures, it should come as little surprise to us that people with an intellectual deficiency are likely to be at heightened risk of making a false confession. Schatz notes that the pressures of interrogation "weigh disproportionately . . . on individuals with intellectual deficiency" (p. 643). It is important for forensic clinicians in the courtroom and other settings to realize that these individuals are particularly prone to confessing to crimes that they did not commit.

Lauren Rogal, a clinical teaching Fellow at Georgetown University Law Center, states:

Individuals with mental disabilities are uniquely vulnerable to making false confessions under police interrogation, prompting a cavalcade of devastating consequences for both the individual confessors and the cause of justice. A growing body of evidence shows that mental disabilities impair the ability of sufferers to withstand the pressures of interrogation, as well as understand and invoke their Constitutional rights during questioning. (Rogal, p. 64)

She suggests that there is already a framework for protecting these individuals from interrogation tactics that make them especially vulnerable to false confessions: Title II of the Americans with Disabilities Act. This act requires public agencies to provide reasonable accommodation for those with disabilities, and Rogal suggests that this must also apply to interrogations of those with intellectual and mental disabilities. New and improved interrogation techniques will be vitally important in providing a reasonable accommodation to such individuals and protecting them from being pressured into false confessions.

It is incredibly important that individuals with intellectual challenges receive such accommodation and protection from being pressured into false confessions. In my experience, the prison setting is an especially poor one for individuals with such challenges. In the community, some may feel sympathy or empathy for such people and provide them with assistance in one way or another. In the jail and prison setting, this is not the case and these already vulnerable people may be further exploited or harmed by those around them.

False Confessions by Juveniles

As we will see in the next chapter, juveniles face many challenges during their formative teenage years. During these years, their hormones and bodies are changing rapidly. Although some may begin to resemble adults physically, the brains of juveniles are still developing. Given changes in hormone levels and parts of the brain that are still not fully developed, young people tend to be impulsive and, at times, make poor decisions. Arndorfer and Malloy (2013) note that young people are especially suggestible and are highly susceptible to being influenced by others. Thus, there is every reason to believe that juveniles would be especially prone to making false confessions under the pressure of an interrogation that is typically used with adults. The aforementioned researchers suggest that other interview protocols be used for young people. An example of such a case of the interrogation of juveniles leading to false confessions may be seen in the box below.

There are no policies or regulations that prevent police from using the Reid interrogation technique or other high-pressure interrogation techniques with adolescents. Indeed, research suggests that police tend to use the same interrogation strategies with adolescents as they do with adults (Redlich et al., 2004). Such techniques have been shown to produce false confessions, and children and adolescents are especially vulnerable to them (Mandelbaum & Crossman, 2014).

THE CENTRAL PARK FIVE

In April of 1989, a large group of juveniles went to Central Park in the middle of New York City. At least some members of this group were reported to be harassing and assaulting people in the park. Some people reported being verbally taunted, while several joggers and bike riders claimed to have been assaulted. At 1:30 a.m., a female jogger was discovered in the park. She was tied up and showed evidence of having been beaten. It was later discovered that she had also been raped. Police rounded up and interviewed a large group of young men, including five juveniles who were Black and Latino; these youths claimed they were not part of the larger group and denied that they were involved in any of the assaults, including the assault of the female jogger. These five young people, who became known as the Central Park Five, underwent lengthy interrogations without parents or a lawyer present. There was considerable debate about what happened during those interrogations (Drizin & Leo, 2004). The juveniles claimed that they were yelled at, cursed at, and even slapped. The police denied that such actions had occurred. After lengthy interrogations, confessions were obtained from the youths, who ended up serving sentences of between 6 and 12 years. Ultimately, another individual confessed to having committed the rape and the sentences of the Central Park Five were vacated. The Central Park Five sued the city of New York and settled for $41 million. That settlement, while substantial in terms of dollars, obviously can do nothing to replace the years lost to incarceration. The case of the Central Park Five underscores the dangers of using high-pressure interrogation techniques on young people.

THROUGH THE EYES OF THE VICTIM

As we have discussed above, eyewitness reports are fallible. Despite the protections of due process and the best efforts of juries, it is unfortunately inevitable that some people who have not committed a crime will, at times, wrongly be found guilty and therefore suffer legal consequences for a crime that they did not commit. It is difficult enough to imagine spending years of one's life in a prison cell. It is impossible for us to fully comprehend what it would be like to spend many years in prison for a crime we didn't commit. Some of those who are wrongly convicted may be released early if their case is overturned or for other reasons, but such people have still suffered the indignities of incarceration for an offense they did not commit and the loss of their freedom, perhaps for years.

Some states provide financial compensation to those who were wrongly convicted when those convictions are later overturned. But what price could compensate for years of life lost, lost opportunities to celebrate children's birthdays, missed vacations with loved ones, or the inability to care for one's parents as they age? It is worth noting that other states guarantee no such compensation for those who were wrongly convicted, so the individual must file a lawsuit in hopes of receiving financial restitution for their years of incarceration. Such individuals are clearly victims of a miscarriage of justice, and the potential adverse impact of being so victimized cannot be overstated. Still others who are wrongly convicted will serve lengthy sentences with no early release for a crime they did not commit. Again, the emotional and psychological damage to them and to their families and loved ones cannot be overestimated.

Horrifically, some of those who are wrongfully convicted may even be executed for a crime they did not commit. The Death Penalty Information Center (n. d.) notes on its website that there is no way of telling how many of the 1,540 people executed since the death penalty was reinstated in 1976 are innocent, but it lists at least 20 people who it considers to be "executed but possibly innocent." As the Death Penalty Information Center notes, once a person is executed, the courts rarely consider claims of innocence, and the lawyers involved in the defense tend to shift their energies to those whose lives they may still be able to save. In addition to those who may have been executed despite their innocence, we must also realize that there are likely those who were innocent and died of natural causes or suicide while awaiting execution.

ANDRE DAVIS: WRONGLY CONVICTED

Andre Davis was 19 years old when he was accused of the brutal kidnapping, rape, and murder of 3-year-old Brianna Stickel in Rantoul, Illinois. When approached by police, Davis was reported to be calm and cooperative. He was taken to the local hospital for a forensic examination, and it was determined that there was no blood or semen on his legs or groin (Possley, 2021). It was later determined that hairs removed from the genitals of the victim did not match Davis's hair (Possley & Warden, n. d.). Nevertheless, Davis was tried and ultimately sentenced to serve 80 years of incarceration.

In 2012, Davis was eventually able to obtain a court order for DNA testing, which, of course, was much more advanced than it had been at the time of his conviction. The results of this testing did indeed verify that Davis was not guilty of the rape and murder of Brianna Stickel. He was released from incarceration after nearly 32 years. He then brought a lawsuit against the city of Rantoul, including several public officials and the police, alleging their misconduct in his case (The News-Gazette, 2013).

CONCLUSION

Law enforcement officials are tasked with the very difficult mission of protecting the community and bringing those who commit offenses to justice. Forensic psychologists seek to assist in this process in a number of ways. Very often, people assume that they know what to expect from others, how they will behave or what they might do. However, as we have seen in this chapter, it is vitally important for a forensic psychologist to resist the urge to make such assumptions; instead, they must rely on clinical practice and scientific research. The behaviors that some might expect others to demonstrate when someone needs help or when someone is being pressured by a person in authority are not always the behaviors that actually occur; research and real-life examples show us that.

For those working in the field of forensics, it is vitally important to seek the truth. At times, this may be challenging. Often, those accused of offenses are reluctant to admit guilt and may attempt to avoid legal consequences by lying about the events in question. Distinguishing those who are telling the truth from those who are lying can be challenging, but there are techniques for doing so that provide us with better-than-chance results. Increasing the cognitive load on a person may help us distinguish truth tellers from liars. The polygraph is another means of doing so, but it is not without its own challenges in terms of accuracy. Similarly, we must be cautious about how much weight we give eyewitness reports during the court process. Such reports may also be fraught with difficulties and inaccuracies, especially when those eyewitness reports involve cross-race identification.

Ultimately, law enforcement officials hope to keep the community safe by obtaining confessions from the accused so that they may face the legal consequences they deserve. However, caution must be used during the interrogation process; it is a difficult process for anyone to undergo, and false confessions can and do sometimes result, especially for vulnerable populations such as people with limited intellectual functioning and young people. Forensic psychologists must seek to balance the importance of keeping the community safe with making those involved in the process aware of the pitfalls that may be involved so that innocent people do not suffer from a miscarriage of justice.

Exercises and Discussion Questions

1. We have seen that the Reid technique of interrogation can produce false confessions. If you were to design an interrogation technique that would still obtain confessions from the guilty but would be less prone to false confessions, what would you suggest? Be specific.

2. There is a great deal of research on the polygraph; some find it to be very accurate, while other studies find the opposite. Do you think the polygraph is useful in investigations? Do you think it should be admissible in court? Explain your answers.

3. Given what we have learned about the fallibility of eyewitness testimony, especially in cross-race identification, do you think any special instructions should be given to a jury when they are presented with such testimony? If not, why not? If so, what instructions would you suggest be given to the jury? Be specific.

4. In this chapter, we discussed studies of helping behavior (diffusion of responsibility) and obedience to authority. Do you believe such studies have real-life applications or not? Explain your answer.

KEY TERMS

Abnormal

Cognitive load approach

Cognitive load

Compliant false confession

Control question test/comparison question test (CQT)

Diffusion of responsibility

Duping delight

False confession

Guilty knowledge test (GKT)

Interrogation

Investigation

Normal

Obedience to authority

Own-race bias (ORB)

PEACE model

Polygraph

Reid technique

Relevant–irrelevant

4 THE JUVENILE JUSTICE PROCESS

LEARNING OBJECTIVES

1. List and describe the steps involved in the juvenile justice process, beginning with a juvenile petition and ending with an adjudicative hearing.

2. Describe the function of juvenile detention centers and the potential benefits and risks of the placement of juveniles in such a setting.

3. Compare and contrast static and dynamic risk factors and protective factors in influencing juvenile behavior.

4. Compare and contrast punishment and rehabilitation in terms of changing juvenile behavior.

5. Summarize social learning theory and describe the impact of the social environment on young people.

6. Discuss statistics related to homicides committed by juveniles and the imposition of life sentences and the death penalty for such offenders.

Two very different paths can lead to the same place. "You had to be a villain where I grew up," said one offender from a part of Philadelphia he called the Badlands. "That's how it was. You had to hustle to survive. Sling dope, join a clique [gang], carry a gat [gun]. Just to get across the street you had to be willing to do those things. If you didn't, you were soft, a sucker, a vic [victim]. It was a jungle. It was survival. Other way?" He smirked, laughed, and shook his head. "There wasn't no other way."

Another offender took a very different path but ended up in the same place. "Man, I had everything I wanted growing up. And then some. Dirt bikes, nice clothes, cash in my pocket. I grew up in a nice house, nice neighborhood. My parents both worked. I had it all. In a way, that's kind of the problem. I learned growing up I could do what I wanted. I didn't really have any rules, anybody telling me what I could and couldn't do, so I knew I could do whatever I wanted to whoever I wanted. No one was gonna stop me or tell me no."

INTRODUCTION AND DEFINITIONS

In both the juvenile and adult criminal justice system, there are at least two equally important components of a crime. First, there must be a criminal *act*, a behavior that is contrary to established laws. We can think about whatever we want—assaulting a coworker, robbing a bank, or stealing a car—but, of course, thinking about it alone violates no laws. In order to commit a crime, there must be some type of criminal act typically referred to as an **actus reus**, Latin for "guilty act." The guilty act in and of itself is not all that is needed to establish that a criminal offense has occurred. In addition to the guilty act, the accused typically knows that what they are doing is wrong. This is referred to as "guilty mind" or in Latin, **mens rea**. In order for a criminal offense to be established, the accused must have acted in violation of the law despite knowing (or should have known) that their behavior was against the law.

Let's say that you have flown back home after a vacation. You walk to the airport baggage carousel and see a suitcase you believe to be yours. In fact, it so obviously appears to be your exact suitcase that you feel no need to check the luggage tag. You take the suitcase home with you. You get home, open it up, and are shocked to find that the contents are not yours after all. You check the luggage tag and verify that it is in fact not your suitcase. You call the number on the luggage tag, explain to the owner that you took their bag by mistake, apologize profusely, and begin to arrange to take the bag to them. In such a case, it could be argued that you committed a guilty act—after all, you *did* take a suitcase that did not belong to you. However, it would be much more difficult to prove that you had a guilty mind, that you meant to take it knowing that it did not belong to you, given that you quickly contacted the owner and made arrangements to return all their belongings to them as soon as possible. It seems extremely unlikely that you would be prosecuted for this. There might be a very different result, however, if you saw what appeared to be an expensive suitcase, concluded that the contents must be valuable as well, and purposefully took it knowing that it wasn't yours with the intention of keeping the valuables for yourself. Typically, neither the thought alone nor the act alone is enough to establish that a criminal offense has occurred; both the guilty act and the guilty mind need to be established for an offense to be charged.

The idea of a guilty mind can be especially challenging when it comes to young people. Think back to when you were 12 or 13 years old; some children at that age still believe in the existence of Santa Claus and the Tooth Fairy. At 14 or 15 years old, perhaps you felt like you were old enough to think clearly and make all of your own decisions and that you knew so much more than your parents did. Looking back on it now, do you think this was true? Perhaps you now realize that some of the decisions you made and actions you took at that age may have been impulsive, selfish, or risky. Does a 15-year-old fully comprehend the physical and emotional impact that assaulting an elderly person will have on that victim? Can a young person think past the attraction of the easy money obtained in a robbery and truly comprehend that their actions could result in a long time spent in a juvenile (or even adult) detention facility? As we will explore in this chapter, the juvenile brain and body are still developing in a number of important ways, and all of this must be taken into account in the decisions made by a forensic psychologist and by the criminal justice system when it comes to the juvenile justice process.

Juvenile delinquency is also known as *juvenile offending*, and while the exact definition and the legal system for dealing with juvenile offenders varies by state, it is usually thought of as the participation of a minor (a person less than 18 years old) in criminal activities.

The term **self-fulfilling prophecy** was first coined by Robert Merton, an American sociologist often considered to be the Father of Sociology. Merton believed that when people make a prediction about themselves or hear a prediction made about them by others, they will often then act in such a manner as to increase the probability that that prediction comes true. Let's say that you have an important presentation that you must stand up and deliver in front of your class. You are very nervous, having little confidence in your abilities as a public speaker and believing that it is unlikely to go well. Such beliefs add to your anxiety, and given your level of trepidation, we would not be surprised to find out that you were so nervous that you forgot some of the things you were supposed to say and sweated profusely during the presentation. Your belief that you would do poorly led you to be more anxious than you would have been otherwise, which consequently led you to struggle. Naturally, the fact that you struggled will then reinforce your belief that you are not a very good public speaker and may even make your next presentation that much more difficult.

What does the self-fulfilling prophecy have to do with juvenile offending? When the court system adjudicates a young person to be a juvenile delinquent, we may be concerned that this label may create a self-fulfilling prophecy. That young person may decide, "Well, if I'm really a bad guy and a criminal and that's how others are going to treat me, I might as well go ahead and act that way. That's all anyone thinks I am anyway." Thus, the belief that they are a delinquent may transform them into exactly that (Siegel, 2002). It is important for us to be careful of how we label others, as such labels may influence not only how we treat them but also how they perceive themselves and act toward others in the future. However, a clear link between labeling a young person as a delinquent and future criminal behavior is not clear and remains a topic of considerable debate. After all, it is entirely possible that a rebellious young person will reject and not believe the label given to them by an authority figure (Fernald & Gettys, 1980).

When we think of juvenile offending, we may first think of **status offenses:** actions that are prohibited to only a particular class of people, most often juveniles. In such a case, a status offense is an offense simply because the person in question is too young to legally engage in a particular action that would be legal if they were older. For example, possession and consumption of alcohol or tobacco by an underage person, truancy from school, running away from home, and driving late at night are all things that are only illegal if the person in question is too young to legally perform them.

In addition to status offenses, minors can, of course, commit and be charged with the same crimes that adults commit. It is entirely possible for young people to commit robberies, sex offenses, homicides, and other serious offenses. The manner in which juvenile charges are pursued and prosecuted varies according to the state that the juvenile is charged in. In some states, certain serious offenses are automatically tried as adult offenses. In others, the prosecution has discretion in this regard, and in still other states, the prosecution can petition the court to try the juvenile as an adult. If a juvenile is tried as an adult and convicted, their sentence may be more lenient than would be imposed on an adult who had been convicted of that same offense.

Juvenile Proceedings

Juvenile hearings are separate and different in many ways from adult courts, with the courtroom work group of the former typically specializing in juvenile justice administration. Juvenile offenses are generally handled quite differently than adult offenses. Accused juveniles are referred to as *respondents* rather than *defendants*, and their actions are referred to as *delinquent acts* rather than *crimes*. Instead of *court*, the juvenile typically attends a *hearing* overseen by a *master* rather than a *judge*. This different nomenclature distinguishes the juvenile process from adult court and also helps to avoid labeling and self-fulfilling prophecies, as discussed above.

Prior to a juvenile case hearing, a probation officer will conduct a **pre-sentence investigation (PSI)**. The PSI is a written report that includes a thorough review of the background of the accused juvenile and should also include a personal interview of the accused by the probation officer. A good PSI will include an overview of the accused's school performance, home life, living environment, whether they have been subject to any form of abuse, drug and alcohol history, mental health issues, criminal background (if any), socioeconomic status, peer influences, and other relevant issues (Bartol & Bartol, 2008). A risk assessment conducted by a forensic psychologist or mental health specialist may also be included in the PSI. The risk assessment should directly address factors that may increase the accused's risk of harm to others in the community as well as factors that mitigate (decrease) the risk of harm to those in the community. The purpose of the PSI is to provide the master with a thorough background on the accused so that the court can come to a fair sentencing decision if there is a finding of guilt.

Masters do have some latitude to decide if a case will be prosecuted in juvenile or adult court. A **waiver** means that a master has decided that, given the totality of the circumstances, they will waive the protections of the juvenile court system for a particular defendant and therefore that defendant will go to adult court. When the PSI and/or the forensic psychologist's risk analysis demonstrates that the accused is a clear and present danger to those in the community, when the charges are sufficiently serious, or when the accused does not appear to be amenable to diversion or treatment, the master may decide to waive the hearing to adult court (Bartol & Bartol, 2008).

A **juvenile petition** is the legal document that is used to initiate an adjudicative action against a juvenile. At the **arraignment hearing**, the juvenile is informed of the charges against them. At this same time, the master of the court will determine whether to release them or to keep them detained. This hearing, as with all juvenile hearings, is closed to the public. Attorneys for the prosecution and defense will each get to make their case and the master will decide whether to keep the case in juvenile court or waive it to adult court. If it is decided to maintain the case in juvenile court, the court may seek some type of **diversion**, meaning that the juvenile will be diverted from juvenile detention and instead will be mandated to receive treatment, counseling, community service, school attendance, or some other combination of treatments instead of incarceration. If the juvenile in question complies with these requirements for a given period of time, they may then be released from supervision. However, if they fail to comply with any or all of the required programs, formal charges may then be pursued. If and when formal charges are pursued, an **adjudicative hearing** will be scheduled. At this hearing, the master hears both sides and renders a decision. Typically, this decision is made by a master, with no jury trial for juveniles. In such a case, the burden of proof is the same as that for a jury trial. That is, the master must believe that the prosecution's case has been established beyond a reasonable doubt. If there is a finding of guilt, the juvenile is ruled a delinquent minor and becomes the responsibility of the court until they are 18 (or, in some cases, 21) years old.

Statistics

Beginning in the mid-1980s, it became socially and politically expedient for politicians and lawmakers to express the belief that our society needed to get tough on crime, including (but certainly not limited to) drug offenses. It was believed that lengthy, mandatory sentences for drug use, drug sales, and other offenses would be the answer that would help the United States to win the so-called War on Drugs and War on Crime. In 1986, President Ronald Reagan signed the Anti-Drug Abuse Act of 1986 into effect. The Act created mandatory minimum sentences for many drug-related offenses. As part of the Act, minimum sentences were much harsher for crack cocaine than they were for the powdered version of the same drug, leading to Senator Cory Booker (D-NJ) later telling Meet the Press in a 2016 interview that the War on Drugs led to a "five hundred percent increase in incarceration in our country, disproportionately affecting poor minorities" because at that time, crack cocaine was more popular in low-socioeconomic regions, while powdered cocaine was more often the drug of choice for those in middle- and upper-socioeconomic areas (Carol, 2016).

Indeed, in 1980, there were only 329,000 individuals incarcerated in the United States, but by 1993, this number had risen to 949,000 and skyrocketed to more than 1.5 million by 1995 (Lynch & Sabol, 1997). Juveniles made up part of this increase, with juvenile arrests peaking in 1996 at a staggering 2.7 million (Harp, 2020). Strict sentencing policies remained in place until 2004, when President George W. Bush passed the Second Chance Act to help assist with the reentry of incarcerated persons into the community and the mentoring of such individuals. In 2010, President Obama signed the Fair Sentencing Act as part of an effort to reduce the great disparity in sentencing for crack as opposed to powdered cocaine and to reduce the number of people incarcerated for nonviolent drug-related offenses.

By 2018, arrests of juveniles had dropped by 73%; for adults in that same time frame, arrests dropped by 22%. There were 696,620 arrests of people under 18 years of age in 2019. This is down markedly from 2010 (Office of Juvenile Justice and Delinquency Prevention, 2020). Juvenile arrests reached a new low in 2019 (Harp, 2020), and the number of status offenses like liquor law violations dropped 72% to only 26,650 in 2019. Robbery and aggravated assault by juveniles reached all-time lows in 2018 (Puzzachera, 2018). Although these numbers are promising, we should not lose sight of the fact that there were still 192,000 serious crimes committed by juveniles ages 12–17 in 2018 (Statista Research Department, 2018). In 2019, there were 44,010 juveniles arrested for violent crimes (Puzzachera, 2018), including (but not limited to) sex offenses. Juveniles account for 20% of all sex offenses that are committed (Barbaree & Marshall, 2006).

There are currently 200,000 people in 38 states who are on the National Sex Offender Registry for crimes they committed as juveniles. Even though the recidivism rate for juvenile sex offenders is low, being on this registry can label them for quite some time, making finding employment or housing very difficult (Juvenile Law Center, 2020). The average recidivism for juvenile sex offenders is 12.2%, so it is not accurate to believe that a juvenile sex offender is likely to continue offending throughout their lifetime (McCann & Lussier, 2008). However, such stigma, once attached, is difficult to remove, and it could be argued that such stigma results in continued punishment in terms of difficulty finding employment and housing long after one's sentence has been fully served.

JUVENILE DETENTION CENTERS

The number and rate of juveniles in locked detention facilities have shown steady declines since 1999, when the rate was 355 per 100,000 and when a total of more than 107,000 juveniles were incarcerated (Sickmund et al., 2019). In 2017, the rate of incarcerated juveniles had dropped 138 per 100,000, and the number of juveniles incarcerated was down to 43,000. It should not be surprising, given the decrease in many areas of juvenile offending described above, that the number of juveniles in confinement has also decreased markedly. The number of young people in confinement dropped by 60% between 2000 and 2017, according to the 2019 Prison Policy Initiative (2020). According to this same study, of those juveniles incarcerated, approximately 8,300 are incarcerated for the most minor offenses: status offenses and technical violations of probation. A *violation of probation* simply means that a juvenile has violated one of the conditions imposed on them by the court but has not committed a new illegal act of any kind. Examples of a violation of probation might be staying out past the court-imposed curfew, sending a text message to someone that they have been ordered to have no contact with, or even simply being late for an appointment with their probation officer. In short, both status offenses and violations of probation are typically nonviolent and are considered to be very minor infractions, hardly justifying or requiring a period of locked detention as a consequence.

There are slightly more than 1,500 juvenile corrections facilities at the present time in the U. S. (Office of Juvenile Justice and Delinquency Prevention, 2020). In 2019, there were 48,000 youth confined in "facilities far away from home" (Sawyer, 2019, p. 1). Since 2000, the number has dropped by 60%, but that also likely means fewer facilities. Of those who are in juvenile facilities, 92% are in locked facilities.

There are fewer juvenile detention facilities than adult jails or prisons in each state. Thus, there is a great likelihood that families who wish to see their incarcerated child or sibling will have to travel a significant distance in order to do so. For example, there is one state juvenile facility in Pennsylvania: the State Correctional Institution at Pine Grove. If someone from Philadelphia is incarcerated there, it would take four and a half hours one way for their family to come to visit them. If the family does not have a reliable means of transportation and instead takes a commercial bus, the trip would cost more than $100 per person and would take more than 14 hours one way. Having traveled for so long to get to see their loved one, we would also have to expect that those family members would need to be able to afford a hotel for a night or two before the return trip home. Needless to say, many of the family members of those in juvenile detention do not have the time or financial means to make this possible, meaning that many juveniles in detention go for lengthy periods of time—or perhaps their entire incarceration—without a visit from family members.

The monetary costs of juvenile detention are staggering. According to the Justice Policy Institute (2020), the cost of incarcerating young people is a mind-boggling $588 per person per day, with an average cost of $214,620 per juvenile per year, a 44% increase from 2014. These costs vary widely by state. For example, in Pennsylvania, the yearly cost of incarcerating a juvenile is $210,605 per year, whereas tuition at state university for a resident is $14,940. In Texas, juvenile detention costs $175,039 per person per year versus $10,470 per person per year for college tuition for residents. In California, it costs taxpayers $304,259 to incarcerate a single juvenile for a year and only $9,970 for in-state college tuition. In New York, it costs a mind-bending $892,206 to incarcerate one juvenile for a year as compared to a mere $8,430 for in-state college tuition—it costs close to *one hundred times* as much to lock up a juvenile as to send them to college. By comparison, Harvard University tuition is about $54,000 per year; for the price of incarcerating one juvenile in New York for a year, we could pay the tuition of eight students at Harvard University for that same year.

Extreme caution must be taken before placing a young person in juvenile detention, as it is quite possible that such a setting will do more harm than good.

Ken Hawkins/Alamy Stock Photo

It is extremely important to be cautious about placing young people in juvenile detention centers. Although it may seem that this would teach them a lesson and frighten them into law-abiding behavior in the future, it could also do quite the opposite. Indeed, a study by McCord (1997) suggested that grouping antisocial individuals together may promote antisocial alliances and intensify delinquent behavior. It should be noted that this study was in the relatively benign environment of a summer camp; we can only imagine that the effect would be amplified in a locked disciplinary unit. Juvenile detention centers are sometimes referred to as "gladiator schools," where those incarcerated learn the tricks of the trade and have to become even more violent to survive. The possibility that a young person will come out of a juvenile detention center worse than they went in should not be discounted. For this reason, diversion of youth to treatment programs and the use of probation and other intermediate sanctions instead of incarceration for juvenile offenders makes a great deal of sense.

From time to time, juvenile offenders are housed in the same facilities and institutions as adult offenders. According to the Juvenile Justice and Delinquency Prevention Act and the Prison Rape

Elimination Act, juveniles charged or convicted as adults should be held in juvenile facilities if possible and placed in an adult facility only if absolutely necessary. When there is no alternative to placing juveniles in the same facility as adults, those juveniles should be out of sight and hearing of adults at all times and should never be placed in isolation/segregation. Even the toughest and strongest juvenile is typically no physical or mental match for an adult convict, so such separation is vitally important for the physical, mental, and emotional safety of those young offenders.

Juvenile Gangs

When we hear the word *gang*, we may think of an unruly and chaotic mob; however, this is rarely the case. **Gangs** are groups of people that have a strictly defined leadership, hierarchy, and organization. Gangs have initiation rituals, regular meetings, and strict rules that members are expected to follow. Punishment for failing to do so is often swift and severe and is administered by other members of that gang. Gang members may identify themselves through hand signs, certain articles or colors of clothing, symbols, code words, and other means. Many gangs are formed according to the race of gang members, but affiliations based on geographic location, family of origin, and other factors are also possible. Gangs typically have a territory or region that they consider to be theirs and that they are willing to defend through violence. Many gangs are heavily involved in illegal activities in order to obtain cash and must be willing to defend these activities and impose their will on competing gangs through violence (Howell, 1997). Behaviors that may be frowned upon by larger society, such as dealing drugs and engaging in drive-by shootings, are strongly rewarded by the gang, with members who are willing to follow such orders rising quickly up the ranks of that gang.

Gang membership may be especially common in urban areas, with between 14% and 30% of urban youth joining a gang at some point (Miller, 1982). There has been an extremely rapid proliferation in youth gangs; in 1980, there were about 2,000 youth gangs with a total of 100,000 members. By 2000, there were approximately 3,000 youth gangs with nearly 800,000 members (Howell, 2000).

When youth enter a juvenile detention facility, they are far from home and may realistically fear for their safety. It is a common practice for gangs that formed on the street to reorganize and to recruit or pressure new inmates to join the gang upon their placement in locked detention. Indeed, the administrators of juvenile detention facilities estimated that 40% of their population is gang affiliated (Leiter, 1993); "Gangs clearly present significant problems in juvenile detention facilities" (Howell, 1998, p. 4).

Gangs will often approach newly admitted juveniles and recruit them into the gang. Such an invitation may leave the juvenile with little choice: If they decline to join the gang, they have now made enemies with that gang, who may seek revenge on them; they also leave themselves to be preyed upon by competing gangs. If they do choose to join a gang, they now have the protection of that gang, but they must also follow all the rules and orders of that gang or be subject to discipline from within that organization; a new member may be ordered to assault an opposing gang

Juvenile gangs often identify themselves with gang signs or clothing and will defend their territory with violence.

NataliaCatalina/iStockPhoto

member in order to test their loyalty. Failure to follow such an order typically results in swift and severe punishment from one's own gang. Furthermore, by joining a gang, they have instantly become the enemy of every member of a different gang in that institution. In short, it is not at all certain that incarcerating young people will lead to improvements in their behavior; the criminal associations they may form while incarcerated may lead to behavior that is less adaptive and law-abiding rather than more so.

MOFFITT'S DEVELOPMENTAL THEORY

In the early 1990s, psychologist Terrie Moffitt (1993) proposed that there were two primary developmental paths to deviant and antisocial behavior in young people. On the one hand were what she referred to as adolescent-limited (AL) offenders. The AL offenders comprise the majority of young offenders. AL offenders don't begin to demonstrate antisocial or violent behavior until their teenage years. Most often, their offenses are vandalism, minor thefts, and drug- and alcohol-related offenses. Violent offenses, if they occur, tend to be relatively rare and minor. AL offenders may engage in crimes for profit or social rewards but tend to cease engaging in these activities on their own as their teenage years come to an end, even if they have not been punished or rehabilitated in any fashion. Rather, it seems that as they get older, they realize on their own that they have more to lose than they have to gain by these behaviors and that money or social rewards can be obtained in other, more adaptive ways. AL offenders may be thought of as your average teenager who gets into a little bit of trouble—a fight or two or some minor offenses—but then seems to grow up and get their act together as they get into their late teens and early 20s.

On the other hand, according to Moffitt (1993), are the life course–persistent (LCP) offenders. These individuals start with maladaptive behaviors much earlier than do AL offenders. In fact, some LCP offenders will start to engage in such behavior as early as 3 years old. They may show some difficulties in school, even very early on. As they age, they tend to engage in a wide variety of illegal and violent offenses. Perhaps as a result, they tend to be rejected by other children and therefore have continued difficulty in developing adequate social skills. According to Moffitt, LCP offenders make up 5%–10% of the juvenile offender population in males and about 2% in females. These are the folks who demonstrate antisocial behavior early and maintain it at a high level well into adulthood rather than growing out of it.

RISK FACTORS AND PROTECTIVE FACTORS

Before discussing factors that may increase or decrease the probability of a juvenile engaging in a criminal act, it is important to mention a concept that will be discussed in greater detail in the next chapter: It is important for us to recognize how unlikely it is that any single factor is 100% responsible or identifiable as the sole cause of an individual's behavior. Statisticians often use the phrase "correlation does not imply causation": a fancy way of reminding us that just because two factors are associated with one another does not mean that either one of those factors causes the other. For example, if we were to track the number of hats and the number of gloves sold in a particular store, we might find that these numbers both increase markedly in the winter months. However, that does not mean that buying gloves causes a person to also buy a hat (or vice versa). We will discuss this in greater detail in the next chapter, but for the present, it is sufficient to realize that although the factors we are about to discuss increase or decrease the probability of offending by a juvenile, it is highly unlikely that any single factor will cause or prevent such offending in and of itself.

Risk factors are variables that, when present, increase the probability that a particular individual will develop a given behavior or disorder. It is important to keep in mind that there is not a 1:1 relationship between risk factors and delinquency. That is, there is no single path to delinquency (Shader, 2003). It is possible for an individual to have many risk factors and not demonstrate delinquent behavior and it is possible for them to have very few risk factors and still demonstrate such behavior. Risk factors simply increase the probability of such behavior. There are a number of risk factors in regard to delinquency, and we should keep in mind that those factors can have an additive (or perhaps even multiplicative) effect when several are present, which may markedly increase the risk of delinquency (Osher et al., 2003).

Protective factors are those factors that serve to decrease the impact of risk factors and/or promote engagement in prosocial, adaptive behavior. As with risk factors, there is no single protective factor that guarantees that a young person will overcome adversities. The benefits of multiple protective factors would appear to be cumulative. Furthermore, it should be noted that protective factors are not necessarily always the opposite of risk factors.

Static versus Dynamic Risk Factors

Some risk factors are more amenable to change than others. For example, age is a risk factor, with adolescent males being at greater risk than adult males for maladaptive or illegal behavior (Moffitt, 2018). Although age changes over time, it isn't something anyone can choose to change; we can't suddenly decide to be 30 instead of 19 years old. Age, then, is a **static risk factor**. Substance abuse, on the other hand, is also a risk factor but one that can change if the person in question desires to do so and has the necessary resources. Substance abuse, then, is a **dynamic risk factor**.

It has long been known that among the strongest predictors of later violent offenses are poor parental support and supervision, conflict between the parents, parental aggression, and punitive punishment/abuse of the child by the parent(s) (McCord, 1979). This likely comes as little surprise since children learn from what they see in their home environment, and if they are witness to parental conflict, violence, and abuse, it would certainly seem to follow that they may well grow up emulating such behaviors.

The primary characteristic before age 13 that predicts later delinquency is aggression (Haapasolo & Tremblay, 1994). As we will discuss later in this text, an individual's past behavior may, in some cases, allow us to predict their future behavior. That being the case, it is no surprise that when a juvenile has already demonstrated physical aggression by age 13, we may expect this trend to continue, especially once the juvenile reaches the age of puberty and even more if that juvenile is male and testosterone levels begin to rise (Tremblay & LeMarquand, 2001).

Young people who demonstrate poor academic performance, who have low educational goals, and who demonstrate poor commitment to school are at greater risk for delinquency (Herrenkohl et al., 2001). Furthermore, it seems entirely likely that such delinquency would only serve to further undermine their belief in the importance of education and adaptive behavior. When a young person misbehaves in school, the school district may respond by suspending or expelling that student from school. The supposed logic of such a consequence is presumably to both prevent that student from causing further harm to the other students and also to teach a lesson to the guilty party so that they do not engage in such behavior again. However, suspensions and expulsions from school do not reduce delinquent behavior and have not been shown to reduce maladaptive behavior on the part of the suspended student (McCord, 1997). Instead, these appear to be linked to *increased* delinquent behavior. Perhaps this should come as no surprise; why would we expect a young person who may not like school and who is therefore acting up to see a suspension as punishment? Instead, might they not view it as a reward? Furthermore, if we are talking about a young person who may have little or no parental support or supervision at home, can we not expect that their time out of school will be spent in a less-than-productive manner?

A study by McCord (McCord et al., 2001) showed that growing up in an impoverished, high-crime neighborhood increased the probability of a juvenile becoming involved in criminal behavior. Again, this comes as no surprise. A young person growing up in such a neighborhood may not see on a day-to-day basis the people who have succeeded in spite of the odds: people who joined the military, went to college, or learned trades and left that neighborhood. Instead, that young person sees the people who are still there—perhaps a drug dealer wearing expensive jewelry and driving a fancy car, flashing a wad of money and surrounded by lackeys. The evidence that crime pays may be right in front of that young person, and the idea of learning a trade, entering the military, or going to college may seem very remote.

Abuse

The U.S. Department of Health and Human Services (2015) tells us that in 2013, there were more than 3 million reports of child abuse involving more than 6 million and that 30% of abused and neglected kids will eventually go on to abuse or neglect their own children. Lansford et al. (2009) found that children who were physically abused in their first five years of life were more likely to be arrested as juveniles for violent, nonviolent, and status offenses than those who were not so abused. This does not mean that every child who is abused will repeat this cycle with their own children or will go on to commit criminal offenses, but it is certainly safe to say that being the victim of abuse has the potential to harm the individual in a number of different ways.

Children who are abused are far more likely to engage in crime and deviance than those who are not abused and are more likely to be arrested as both juveniles and adults compared to children who have not been abused (Currie & Tekin, 2007). Being abused as a child has been linked to the development of alcohol and substance abuse disorders (Galaif et al., 2001), perhaps as part of an attempt to numb or avoid the physical and emotional pain of that mistreatment. There are those who are abused or neglected who do not go on to do the same to their children, and there are those who never go on to abuse substances; it is not a foregone conclusion that abuse necessarily leads to such behaviors, but it certainly does appear to influence the probability of doing so.

Sexual abuse can, of course, have a devastating impact on those who are so victimized. Ogloff et al. (2012) studied nearly 2,800 Australian children who had been sexually abused. They found that when these children grew into adults, they were almost five times as likely to be charged with a criminal act as those in the general population and this was especially true for sexual and other violent offenses.

Mothers' alcohol consumption can be related to a condition known as **fetal alcohol syndrome (FAS)** in her child. FAS can lead to damage to the unborn child, including decreased birth weight, cognitive impairment, increased probability of mental illness and drug/alcohol addiction in later life, and impulsivity issues (Ethen et al., 2008). Abel and Sokol (1987) found that in a sample of 415 people with FAS, 60% had had legal problems and criminal problems and 50% had been incarcerated at some point. More than one-third eventually required inpatient treatment for drug and alcohol addiction at some point during their life.

Disorders of Childhood According to the DSM-5

It certainly is not the case that all criminals are mentally ill or that all mentally ill folks become criminals—far from it. However, it does appear to be the case that having a mental illness increases the probability that a person will come into contact with the criminal justice system. Katsiyannis et al. (2004) found that untreated mental illness increases the risk of substance abuse, suicide, aggression, and contact with the police and/or juvenile justice system.

Oppositional defiant disorder (ODD) and **conduct disorder (CD)** are two of the disorders of childhood described in the *Diagnostic and Statistical Manual of Mental Disorders* (5th edition; DSM-5). ODD is characterized by a period of six months or more of irritability, angry mood, and defiant behavior. Deliberate provocation of others and blaming others for their own misbehavior are common traits. With CD, we see more serious violation of the rights of others, with children who demonstrate this disorder bullying, starting fights, using weapons, and demonstrating cruelty to animals and people, among other aggressive behaviors. The DSM-5 goes on to note that CD may be diagnosed in approximately 4% of children but that few children with this disorder receive any treatment for it. The importance of recognizing these conditions as early as possible so that some type of intervention can be made cannot be overstated, given that CD is a robust predictor of future antisocial behavior and ODD predicts later criminal charges in males (Pardini & Fite, 2010).

A **personality disorder** involves stable and enduring traits that are either bothersome to the individual or are maladaptive and potentially harmful to that individual and/or others around them. Although the DSM-5 discourages diagnosis of personality disorders in those younger than 18 years of age, we can begin to see traits of such personality disorders begin to emerge in adolescence. Johnson et al. (2000) found that adolescents with a greater number of symptoms of a personality disorder are more likely to commit violent acts than adolescents with fewer such symptoms.

"Monkey See, Monkey Do!" Modeling and Social Learning Theory

We have all seen young people learn by imitating others: a boy pushing his toy lawnmower and following behind his father who is pushing the real version or a little girl with a white lab coat and toy stethoscope stating that she wants to be a doctor like her mother. Imitation is perhaps the sincerest form of flattery. Albert Bandura is a Canadian American psychologist who conducted one of the classic experiments examining whether viewing an adult engaging in verbal and physical aggression might lead young children to imitate that behavior. It was 1961, and at Stanford University, Bandura was permitted to conduct research using preschool children at the Stanford nursery school. The children were seated in a room that had a variety of games and activities and were allowed to play briefly. Then, an adult entered the room. In one condition of the experiment, the adult engaged in aggressive behavior toward one of the toys in the room, a so-called Bobo doll. The Bobo doll was a three-foot tall inflatable clown, roughly the shape of a large bowling pin. The bottom of the Bobo doll was weighted so that when punched or kicked, the doll would briefly tip over before coming back upright. In the aggressive condition, the adult demonstrated aggressive language ("Pow!" "Sock him in the nose!") and repeatedly punched and kicked the doll. In the nonaggressive condition, the adult sat quietly and played with a construction set. In the control condition, no adult entered the room.

The children were then taken to another room that contained various toys and activities; some of these toys were considered aggressive in nature (the Bobo doll, a dart gun, a mallet with pegs) and others were considered nonaggressive (crayons and paper, a ball, toy animals). Experimenters observed and rated the aggressiveness of the children's play during the course of the next 20 minutes and found that the children who observed the adult engaging in aggressive behavior toward the Bobo doll were significantly more aggressive in their own play activities than were children who observed the nonaggressive adult and children in the control group.

Bandura found that males were more likely to imitate physical aggression than females were but that there were no differences between males and females in regard to verbal aggression.

A later study by Bandura underscored these results and demonstrated that even children who watched similar aggressive behavior toward the Bobo doll on television (as opposed to live) demonstrated increased aggressive behavior compared to those who watched nonaggressive behavior on television. Specifically, Bandura found that 90% of those who watched the adult engaging in aggressive behavior on television imitated this behavior and 40% of such subjects continued to do so even eight months after the conclusion of the experiment. There are multiple likely explanations for such a finding; one possible explanation is socialization. While gender roles continue to evolve, the argument can still be made that young males are socialized and encouraged to be aggressive, while young females are discouraged from engaging in this same behavior.

Bandura developed what is referred to as **social learning theory**. He believed that humans often learn by observing what others around them do and by observing the consequences of those actions, be they positive or negative. Let's say young Johnny is told *not* to take a cookie out of the cookie jar but observes his friend doing just that, gobbling it down, smiling at how wonderful it tasted, and suffering no consequences (due to the fact that dad has left the room); Johnny might very well decide to imitate his friend's behavior. Unlike the behaviorists before him, Bandura believed there was more going on than simple stimulus and response; he believed that between the stimulus and the response was a mediating process in which the individual consciously decides which action they wish to take.

In one way or another, young people are exposed to both simulated and real acts of violence every day in their homes, schools, and communities. They watch television programs with graphic depictions of violence, they play video games in which violent acts are portrayed, and they can observe violent acts on a wide variety of social media platforms. Of course, they may also be personally witnessing acts of interpersonal violence in the home, seeing fights at school, and be subject to physical or sexual abuse. Such exposure may lead to significant physical, mental, and/or emotional harm, with long-term effects that can last well into adulthood (Finkelhor & Turner, 2016).

Anatomy, Biology, and Genetics

As a general rule, 17- and 18-year-old males have the highest naturally occurring levels of testosterone (Sissons, 2018), the primary sex hormone and anabolic steroid in males. Testosterone is responsible for the development of secondary sexual characteristics, such as the growth of muscles and facial hair. Testosterone has also been found to play a significant and causal role in physical aggression and violence, and it has been noted that testosterone levels are higher in prisoners who have committed violent offenses than in prisoners who committed nonviolent offenses (Batrinos, 2012).

Testosterone levels decrease with advancing age and decrease substantially after age 30 or so (Sissons, 2018). Perhaps not coincidentally, given the association of testosterone with aggressive behavior, the rate of violent crime typically diminishes as offenders age past 30 or 35 years. However, even testosterone is not the be-all and end-all in terms of aggression; if it was, we could simply sample testosterone levels and lock up those with high levels of that hormone, knowing that they would inevitably engage in some violent act. Indeed, in a review of studies on the topic, Mims (2007) suggested that testosterone does lead males to seek social dominance, but when it comes to violent behavior, this hormone is only one of a variety of factors that plays a role.

In addition to his research on the impact of testosterone on aggression, Batrinos (2012) notes that the prefrontal cognitive areas of the brain play an important role as well. The **prefrontal** cortex is a thin layer of brain tissue on the outer portion of the frontal lobe of the brain. This portion of the brain plays a significant role in what are referred to as *executive functions*. In imagining a person who is an important executive at a large company, we would likely think of someone who makes important decisions, who is required to use good judgment, and who must plan and problem solve for the company they work for. This is quite similar to the executive functions executed by the prefrontal cortex: decision making, problem solving, planning, and judgment (Miller & Wallis, 2009).

There is one more very important function of the prefrontal cortex: to suppress urges. At some time in each person's life, it will occur to them to engage in some type of impulsive or irrational behavior—a thought that they would like to punch an inconsiderate boss that they want to see exactly how fast their car will go with the accelerator all the way down, or professing their undying love for someone who has already rejected them on numerous occasions. At such times, it is the prefrontal cortex that (hopefully) will suppress that urge, essentially telling us, "Let's not do that . . . it really isn't likely to turn out well." Of course, that presupposes that the prefrontal cortex is fully developed, is functioning well, and is not being impaired by drugs, alcohol, or injury. Those can be very big conditions, especially given the fact that this area of the brain is not fully developed until age 25 (Arain et al., 2013).

The study of genetics involves the manner in which the genes and traits of parents are passed on to their offspring. For example, the genetic material of the parents determines the eye color of the children (Sturm & Larsson, 2009). The field of behavioral genetics is shedding light on the relationship and interaction of genetics and the environment. Kvalevaag and colleagues (2014) found that when the mother experiences repeated adverse life events, there is an increased probability that the child will later engage in aggressive behavior and is at increased risk of being diagnosed with CD. Maternal experiences of adverse events during pregnancy can lead to "lasting epigenetic marks in genes that affect maturational processes in the brain . . . including exaggerated aggression in adulthood" (Palumbo et al., 2018, p. 1). Research related to hormones, brain function, and genetics has provided tremendous insight into human development and juvenile functioning, but there is still a great deal for us to learn in each of these fields.

PROTECTIVE FACTORS

Protective factors are those factors that help to mitigate the risk of juvenile offending or recidivism (Jessor et al., 1998). The more protective factors one has, the less at risk one is of offending or re-offending (Werner, 2000). Protective factors, then, are the flip side of risk factors. That is, protective factors are those that, when present, help to decrease the probability that a particular behavior or disorder will be demonstrated. Again, this is a simple matter of probability; there is no single protective factor that guarantees that a young person won't offend.

The Office of Juvenile Justice and Delinquency Prevention has its Model Programs Guide of evidence-based programs to promote prevention, intervention, and reentry. The Prev@cib Program in Spain has been rated as "Promising." This is an anti-bullying and anti-cyberbullying program with ten 1-hour sessions. Sessions focus on providing information about these topics, awareness modules about the harm such behaviors can do, and a description of how students can go about preventing and intervening in such situations as well as promoting self-respect and respect for others (Ortega-Barón et al., 2019).

More recently, there have been increasing numbers of studies of strength-based factors. Rather than unfairly viewing the young person as the sum total of their deficits while neglecting their attributes, such studies emphasize that every individual has unique strengths that may enhance their ability to rise above challenges and risk factors (Kenziora & Osher, 2004). For example, a panel of experts associated with the Office of Juvenile Justice and Delinquency Prevention (Wasserman et al., 2003) suggested that protective factors as well as risk factors can generally be divided into one of four categories: individual, family, peers, and school/community. For example, among individual protective factors are those such as high IQ and positive social skill development. In regard to family protective factors, the presence of a positive adult influence and ally to mentor and support the juvenile is another important protective factor. Avoiding or minimizing contact with antisocial peers is yet another protective factor and reinforces the notion that placement in juvenile detention, close to antisocial peers, may do more harm than good. Lastly, an important protective factor is attendance in a safe and supportive school environment.

One study of the judges, district attorneys, probation officers, and others who work with juvenile offenders demonstrated that those professionals make many of their decisions about young offenders based more on risk factors than on protective factors (Reilly, 2012). Such findings may suggest that either we need to find a way to add to or bolster the number of protective factors that young people have or we need to assist those professionals who work with them to recognize that there may be more strengths and protective factors than they realize and that these protective factors may help decrease risk.

Bullying and Cyberbullying

Bullying is defined by Gladden et al. (2014) as any unwanted and aggressive behavior (verbal or physical) by an individual or group toward someone who is not a sibling or romantic/sexual partner that involves a power imbalance and that is repeated or likely to be repeated. Finkelhor and Turner (2016) found that two in five children (41.2%) were physically assaulted in the year preceding their study, and 10.1% were injured.

Cyberbullying is any type of threatening, harassing, or demeaning language that is communicated through social media, text messages, phone calls, emails, online gaming, or other electronic means. On his late-night talk show *Jimmy Kimmel Live!* the host occasionally presents a segment where celebrities read "Mean Tweets" about themselves. In this segment, the celebrity looks straight into the camera and reads from their phone an extremely unpleasant message that someone has written to them on the social media platform, Twitter. The celebrity then reacts to that tweet in some way and the audience laughs. Although entertaining on television, and perhaps of no great emotional consequence to the rich and famous celebrity who is reading the tweet from an anonymous stranger, we should not underestimate the power of insulting, disrespectful, and sometimes overtly threatening social media messages on young people (or those of any age, for that matter). As we will see below, cyberbullying is extremely common and can have a devastating impact on those who are victimized in this manner.

Fifty-nine percent of U.S. teens report having been subjected to online bullying, including (but not limited to) name-calling, having false rumors spread about them, and threats of physical violence (Anderson, 2018). This same study found that while boys and girls were subject to online bullying at the same rate, girls reported more frequently being victimized by false rumors and receiving unwanted explicit images.

Cyberbullies can be extremely difficult to track and identify. Even those in their early teenage years are often capable of developing alternate and false names/profiles on social media. Inexpensive burner phones and activation cards can be bought at most big-box stores. Such phones may be purchased with cash and are not associated with anyone's name and are therefore nearly impossible to track back to a source. Using public Wi-Fi or a Virtual Peripheral Network

(VPN) are only a few of the ways that a person can use online media to harass another person while making themselves difficult to track or trace.

CYBERBULLIED TO DEATH: THE TRAGEDY OF GABRIELLA GREENE

Gabriella Greene was 12 years old and attending the idyllically named Surfside Middle School in Panama City Beach, Florida, when she was found dead, having hanged herself in a closet in her home on January 10 of 2018. It was later discovered that two other 12-year-olds from the same school had been cyberbullying her, calling her cruel names and spreading the rumor that she had a sexually transmitted disease. A subsequent investigation did lead to the arrest of the two minors and charges of cyberbullying. More serious charges were not made by the police, as it was determined that although the cyberbullying and name-calling had occurred prior to Gabriella's death, there was not enough evidence to support the notion that her death was a direct result of that cyberbullying, despite the fact that when Gabriella had informed one of the bullies that she had attempted to hang herself, he reportedly responded, "If you're going to do it, just do it." Her case is unfortunately not unique, and the physical, emotional, and psychological damage inflicted by cyberbullying should never be underestimated.

PUNISHMENT VERSUS REHABILITATION

A central and ongoing debate in the field of forensics, for both juvenile and adult populations, is the question of whether it is best to punish those who commit illegal acts or whether it makes more sense to attempt to rehabilitate them. Like a pendulum, the United States (and other countries as well) has swung back and forth at times in terms of a philosophy of how the country should treat offenders. Each of these stances—punishment and rehabilitation—has perceived advantages and disadvantages.

On the surface, the argument for punishing wrongdoing seems to make sense. If young Johnny who was told not to take the cookie does so and we catch him and make him stand in the corner for 15 minutes, it seems reasonable that Johnny will not take another cookie without permission. But, if Johnny re-offends by taking another cookie even after having to stand in the corner, the punishment argument would suggest that we simply need to administer longer or more severe punishment. Sooner or later, when the punishment becomes unpleasant enough, Johnny is going to stop taking cookies without permission. At least, that is the theory, and on the surface, this seems like a logical approach to decreasing maladaptive behavior.

Punishment seems to satisfy our thirst for revenge or retribution. We feel that if someone has broken the law and has been made to suffer as a result, this is moral (and social) justice, which may feel satisfying to us. Someone beat up an elderly woman and is now serving 10 years in prison? Many in the public sector may think, "Good, that's what they deserve!" Furthermore, as long as that offender is incarcerated, we may be satisfied that they are no longer a threat to others in the community.

Although the argument that punishment discourages criminal behavior seems valid on the surface, when we look a little more closely, things might not be as simple as they seem. For example, what *is* punishment anyway? One person's punishment ("Go to your room!") may be another person's reward ("Now everyone will leave me alone!"). Prison would be perceived as a severe punishment to those who grew up in a middle-class neighborhood, but to a homeless individual, the idea of three meals a day, a roof over one's head, and heat in the winter and air conditioning in the summer might instead be perceived as luxurious rather than punishing. Furthermore, how much punishment is the right amount? The type and amount of punishment that discourages one person may not at all be the same for the next person. During class discussions of what constitutes punishment versus abuse, it is not uncommon that one student will declare any sort of punishment as cruel and unnecessary while others will brand such measures as insufficient. During class one day, a student vigorously argued that spanking a child was abuse while another declared spanking to be a normal, everyday occurrence in his household. Experiences and opinions vary greatly.

Is it logical to believe that punishment makes a person better in some way? If there was a vicious dog that the owner (who is equally aggressive) decided to hit every time the dog demonstrated aggressive behavior, would we believe that the end result would be a kind, gentle dog? It would seem illogical to do so. One would think the most likely outcome from physically punishing an already aggressive animal would be an even more angry and aggressive animal. Should we expect that punishing humans would have a different result?

The argument may also be made that punishment doesn't necessarily teach anyone to stop what they are doing but instead may teach them that they have to be more careful so that they don't get caught. That is, punishment could have the unintended effect of making people better criminals by making them think and act in such a way so as not to be detected and caught. The teenager caught for retail theft after being seen on store video may not decide to stop stealing but instead might learn to be more careful about wearing a hat and hooded sweatshirt to obscure their face and avoid recognition.

Scared Straight

The original Scared Straight program began at Rahway Prison (now East Jersey State Prison) in 1978. The idea of a group of inmates who called themselves The Lifers at that institution was to speak to those with juvenile offenses and teach them the stark reality of what prison life was like. The Lifers hoped to be able to convince these at-risk young people to change their ways and avoid a life of incarceration. The intentions of The Lifers and the prison administrators who allowed this project may have been good, but their actions were not based on any empirical data or scientific research. The program did win an Academy Award, perhaps legitimizing this as a valid method of juvenile intervention despite the complete and utter lack of any scientific rigor.

In Scared Straight, juvenile offenders were brought into the maximum-security prison and were essentially treated as convicted felons for several hours. As the youth were processed into the institution, the guards were purposefully gruff and rude with them. The juveniles then met with The Lifers, all of whom were serving lengthy sentences for a violent offense. The Lifers took the juveniles' shoes from them, briefly put them in cells, and told them in graphic terms the grim reality of what life is like in prison. The Lifers were extremely intimidating, yelling at the juveniles, invading their personal space, and even making overt physical and sexual threats, such as "I'll bite your nose off and spit it in your damn face!" and "I'll make you my [sexual victim], fool," and "You're going to get knocked out." The juveniles were clearly overmatched and intimidated, as anyone would be in that circumstance.

It might seem that such an approach could be effective. The juvenile offenders were clearly nervous and scared. Some cried, others were shaking noticeably; none of them appear to be unaffected. However, Finckenauer and Gavin (1999) found that despite the obvious discomfort of the juveniles during their experience with The Lifers, there did not appear to be any long-term benefit to this program in terms of reducing the probability that these young people would go on to commit further offenses. After all, as scared as they may be when a convicted murderer is yelling at them, after they return home and weeks or months go by, the experience may be no more than a distant memory. In fact, it may have done more harm than good and may have increased the probability of future offending. Indeed, "controlled studies show that boot camp and 'Scared Straight' interventions are ineffective, and even potentially harmful, for delinquents" (Lilienfeld et al., 2010, p. 225).

Petrosino and colleagues (2002) decided to investigate the effectiveness of programs such as Scared Straight, in which juvenile delinquents and predelinquents (children in trouble but not officially adjudicated to be delinquents) were taken on prison visits with the goal of deterring them from any future criminal activity. Nine trials met the criteria for the study. The researchers' results indicated that there was "no evidence that Scared Straight and other juvenile awareness programs have crime control effects. In fact, all analyses showed that involvement in these programs *increased* measures of crime and delinquency" (p. 18, emphasis added). In other words, Scared Straight not only doesn't work, but it may be more harmful than doing nothing.

With the clarity of hindsight, we have to question the ethics of such a program. The film itself begins with a warning that it is "not intended for children's viewing" and that "parental guidance is advised." The irony seems unnoticed by the producers, who are allowing children ages 15–17 to not only view the film but to be right in there with the convicts who are threatening them. Should we really be subjecting teenagers to verbal abuse and threats and sexual threats—especially when those young people may be coming from that background already—in an untested program in the hope that it might help a few of them? Threats, even well-meaning threats intended to keep them out of prison, are threats nonetheless. It would no longer be considered ethical or even legal to threaten someone with physical or sexual harm.

Rehabilitation may be thought of as restoring an individual to a normal or healthy lifestyle through training, education, therapy, or other positive approaches. Rehabilitation teaches people the skills they need to engage in more adaptive and legal behavior in the future. That might mean providing the individual with drug and alcohol treatment or instruction in anger and stress management; it could even mean teaching them some job skills and how to complete a job application so that they can obtain legal employment in the future. Rehabilitation could involve providing education and allowing people the opportunity to complete their graduate equivalency diploma, as getting a legal job without such a diploma is difficult at best. As we discussed earlier in this chapter, it should not be assumed that rehabilitation is more expensive than punishment when punishment means incarceration.

Rehabilitation does not always meet people's desire for revenge or retribution, however. Many times, we will hear people complain that those incarcerated are getting an education or vocational skills that people who are not incarcerated would never have access to or would have to pay for, such as a barber's license.

Rehabilitation

Just as there is no single identifiable cause of juvenile offending, there is also no single cure for this issue. It has been suggested that the earlier an intervention occurs, the better the chances of disrupting the cradle-to-incarceration pipeline that some youths find themselves in. Osher et al. (2003) suggested that early intervention can prevent the onset of delinquent behavior and support a juvenile's individual strengths and their ability to rebound from difficult circumstances.

The positive youth development model (Butts et al., 2010) proposes a 2 x 6 matrix in which young people both learn/do and attach/belong in six separate domains: work, education, relationships, community, health, and creativity. This strength-based program has shown promise in terms of demonstrating that young people can overcome challenges and develop positively if they are connected to the right opportunities and positive role models and are given support.

The U.S. Department of Justice, Office of Justice Programs reports high rates of drug use and abuse among juvenile offenders. McClelland et al. (2004) found that 77% of juvenile offenders admitted to substance use in the past six months. It is important for forensic professionals to realize that placing a juvenile in a locked detention center in and of itself does not cure or even necessarily treat substance use and abuse issues. Despite efforts on the part of security staff at these institutions, incarcerated youth can and do obtain (and, in some cases, manufacture) drugs and alcohol in these settings, so it would be a mistake to believe that locking them up makes it impossible for them to maintain their addiction. Furthermore, even if forced abstinence may be maintained by making it impossible for young offenders to obtain alcohol or other drugs, they can immediately resume such use when they are released from detention.

In a study conducted in Louisiana, Phillippi et al. (2020) found that drug treatment court guidelines requiring monitored treatment of young offenders showed considerable promise in terms of increasing positive outcomes, increasing community service, and decreasing the rate of juveniles in detention. The goal of drug treatment court is to divert some young, nonviolent offenders from the harsh environment of juvenile detention and instead provide them with a monitored and supervised program for alcohol and other drug treatment, counseling, and other conditions that will help them resume adaptive functioning.

In the past, it was often believed that juveniles were simply physically smaller versions of adults. Thus, juvenile sex offenders were often believed to be experimenting or beginning to practice and develop the traits of adult sex offenders and that their development into adult sex offenders was a near-foregone conclusion. However, such an assumption was not evidence based; in fact, at least one meta-analysis suggested that the rate of sexual recidivism for juvenile sex offenders averages only 12.2%; that is, an average of 87.8% of juvenile sex offenders do not go on to commit another sex offense (McCann & Lussier, 2008). For nearly 30 years, research has supported the idea that juvenile sex offenders are a heterogenous group rather than being cut from the same cloth (Barbaree et al., 1993).

Little is known about juvenile sex offenders and the treatment that is effective for them, relative to what is known in regard to adult sex offenders. A review by Dopp, Borduin, and Brown (2015) of more than 1,600 juvenile sex offender treatment programs yielded only 10 that fit their criteria as evidence based. Much treatment is cognitive behavioral in nature but not necessarily empirically sound, while another form of therapy referred to as *multisystemic therapy* shows promise empirically but is not widely used. Given the potentially devastating impact of sexual abuse and child molestation, this area is deserving of considerably more research, time, and energy.

LIFE SENTENCES, DEATH SENTENCES, AND JUVENILES

It was 2003 and Evan Miller was 14 years old when he badly beat his neighbor with a baseball bat before setting his house on fire, resulting in the neighbor's death. He was found to be guilty and sentenced to serve life without parole. In 2012, the U.S. Supreme Court (Kagan & Supreme Court of the United States, 2011) reviewed the case and found that the imposition of mandatory minimum sentences of life for any offense committed as a juvenile violated the 8th Amendment of the Constitution against cruel and unusual punishment.

Justice Elena Kagan, writing for the majority, stated:

Mandatory life without parole for a juvenile precludes consideration of his chronological age and its hallmark features—among them, immaturity, impetuosity, and failure to appreciate risks and consequences. It prevents taking into account the family and home environment that surrounds him—and from which he cannot usually extricate himself—no matter how brutal or dysfunctional. (Liptak & Bronner, 2012)

That being said, minors (those under age 18 in some states and under age 16 in others) can still be sentenced to life, but such sentencing cannot be mandatory and must balance all factors, including the upbringing of the accused offender (Schaffer, 2018).

Death Penalty

Prior to 2005, there were American states that permitted capital punishment (also known as *the death penalty*) to be levied upon those who committed serious offenses prior to their 18th birthday. Indeed, 365 people in the history of the United States have been executed for crimes that they committed as juveniles (Death Penalty Information Center, 2023). However, the imposition of the death penalty for crimes committed as a juvenile changed upon a decision by the U.S. Supreme Court in the matter of *Roper v. Simmons* (Kennedy & Supreme Court of the United States, 2004). In this case, the court recognized the qualitative differences between juveniles and adults and, citing evolving standards of decency, ruled that it was unconstitutional and a violation of the 8th Amendment against cruel and unusual punishment to sentence someone to execution for a crime they committed as a juvenile.

Dalton Prejean was a 17-year-old African American male with a history of conflict with the law, mental illness, and borderline intellectual functioning and had been abandoned by parents; his tested IQ was 76 (what would have been referred to at that time as *borderline mental retardation*). He and some friends had been out drinking when their car was pulled over. Dalton was later convicted of shooting and killing the Louisiana State Policeman who pulled them over. Prejean was sentenced to death and was executed by the electric chair in 1990 at age 30. At the time that he committed the offense, Prejean wasn't considered old enough by society to be allowed to drink, smoke, or buy a lottery ticket but he was considered by the court and jury to have known exactly what he was doing in this offense.

KIDS WHO KILL—JUVENILE HOMICIDE OFFENDERS

It is relatively rare for juveniles to commit homicides. Between 2010 and 2014, only 7%–8% of all homicides that occur are committed by those under the age of 18 (Baglivio & Wolf, 2017). Despite the relative infrequency of such offenses, cases in which juveniles do commit homicide attract a great deal of public attention—and with good reason. In cases in which a juvenile kills, it seems natural to wonder why they did so, what factors may have led to this offense, and what (if anything) could have been done to predict or prevent the offense.

Although only a fraction of those homicides that occur are committed by juveniles, it is still worth noting that this small fraction adds up to approximately 1,000 homicides per year (Gest, 2020). The rate of such homicides by juveniles increased between 2012 and 2017 and then leveled off in 2018. Juvenile homicide cases jumped 35% between 2014 and 2018, which is especially notable given that most other juvenile offenses declined during that same period (Hockenberry & Puzzachera, 2020). Part of the increase in juvenile homicides might be attributable to the fact that between 2016 and 2019, four states increased the age of who is considered a juvenile from 16 to 17, so when a 17-year-old commits a homicide, they are considered a juvenile (Gest, 2020) Thus, the increase in juvenile homicide statistics may reflect the fact that more people are being included in this statistic. More states appear to be getting ready to increase the age at which people are considered to be juveniles, so further increases in this statistic may be expected.

At least one study (Heide, 2020) interviewed offenders 35 years after they had committed homicides as juveniles. It was hoped that this might allow these offenders to reflect on their offense and provide some insight into why they had committed their offense. This study suggested that these individuals tended to externalize blame for their actions. That is, the men interviewed in the study tended to state that peer pressure played a role in their offense and that being under the influence of alcohol and/or other drugs was a factor. Furthermore, many of those interviewed reported that homicide and other serious offenses were routine in the neighborhood that they grew up in. Statistics related to how many juvenile offenders there are and how often they commit homicide are relatively easy to come by. It will be important for future research to continue to search for the reasons that young people commit these offenses in the first place.

Juvenile Homicide—School Shootings

Although homicide is the second leading cause of death among those 5–18 years old, only 2% of homicides occur on school grounds (Centers for Disease Control and Prevention, 2021). With 98% of homicides of young people occurring anywhere but school property, we might say that our schools are a relatively safe place to be. However, school shootings generate a tremendous amount of media coverage and public interest. The number of books and articles written about school shootings and the number of social media postings and news programs focusing on such events would likely be impossible to count. Many of these incidents are committed by juveniles.

On April 20, 1999, Eric Harris (a juvenile at 17 years old) and Dylan Klebold (who had turned 18 only six months earlier) entered Columbine High School with the intention of killing hundreds of students. When their improvised explosive devices failed to detonate, they walked through the school, killing 12 students and a teacher before committing suicide. It was later learned that they had become obsessed with the violent first-person shooter video game Doom and had made multiple entries in their journals related to violent behavior.

On March 21, 2005, Jeff Weise, who was 16 years old, murdered his grandfather and his grandfather's girlfriend. He then entered Red Lake High School, where he had been a student. He shot and killed five students and two staff members and wounded several others before taking his own life. Investigation later showed that Jeff was "homebound," having been asked not to return to the school after some disciplinary problems and had created violent images and animations online.

On November 30, 2021, Ethan Crumbley, who was only 15 years old at the time, brought a handgun to Oxford High School in Michigan. He shot and killed four students and wounded seven more. He later pled guilty to multiple counts of homicide, and at the time of the publication of this book, his parents were being charged with involuntary manslaughter for allowing the gun to be easily accessible to Ethan. Prior to the murders, was found to have drawn some upsetting images with the words "Help me" and "Blood everywhere." These images were reported and his parents were notified, but it appears no further action was taken at that time.

In each of these cases (and other similar incidents), people across the United States wondered what, if anything, could have been done to predict and prevent these tragedies and why these young people committed these awful acts. In hindsight, it is easy to say that Klebold and Harris's obsession with a violent video game, Weise's violent animations, or Crumbley's "Help me" note should have been red flags, alerting us that they needed intervention. However, many young people play violent video games or draw graphic pictures or upsetting notes. Others listen to music with violent lyrics or write papers about serial killers or punch holes in the wall. However, the vast majority of those who demonstrate such red flags never go on to commit acts of homicide. Efforts by those in the schools and community to identify those who may be at risk of engaging in violent behavior and provide intervention are well-intended but are far from a perfect science at present.

It seems as though those who ask why a young person would commit an act as atrocious as a school shooting want a single simple answer as to why they did so; after all, if there were a single simple reason, then it stands that there would be a single simple answer. Some people might blame these shootings on the easy access to firearms in the United States, in which case, the single simple answer would be to restrict access to firearms. Others might argue that school shootings have nothing to do with firearms but instead are a symptom of mental health problems in young people, in which case, the single simple answer would be to provide better mental health diagnosis and treatment. However, as we have seen in this chapter, the factors that may contribute to maladaptive and violent behavior in young people are as complex as the individuals themselves. The budding forensic psychologist should know that there is still a great deal of important work to be done in this area.

THROUGH THE EYES OF THE VICTIM: THE IMPORTANCE OF BREAKING THE CYCLE

As we learned earlier in this chapter, children who have been abused are more likely to go on to abuse their own children than are children who have not been abused. The impact of being physically, sexually, or emotionally abused or neglected cannot possibly be overstated. In all too many cases, the effects of such abuse or neglect may be compounded by growing up in poverty with food insecurity, a lack of positive role models, and exposure to a high-crime environment starting at an early age. It likely comes as no surprise to us that children raised with a host of such risk factors are prone to develop in a very different manner than those that did not encounter these same challenges.

It is well-documented that such abuse and neglect increases the risk of multiple physical ailments, including (but not limited to) brain damage, visual impairment, difficulties with balance, cancer, and stroke (Widom et al., 2012). Adverse psychological reactions to such abuse have also been noted, with increased incidence of depression, anxiety, and other mental health concerns, in addition to poorer response by such individuals to antidepressant medication (Williams, 2016).

Sadly, those who have been abused as children may grow up mistakenly believing that such abuse is a part of normal parenting and may therefore repeat this cycle when they have children of their own. Furthermore, such maltreatment impacts not only the family but larger society as well. The costs of physical or psychiatric hospitalization, the costs of incarceration, and the emotional impact on those in the community are difficult or impossible to adequately estimate. The importance of providing support and assistance early on to those who need it cannot be overestimated.

CONCLUSION

The development of an individual from infancy through adulthood is a long and incredibly complicated process. Young people face innumerable challenges as they grow up. Some have the benefits of a stable upbringing in a home in which supportive parents and others provide all the basic necessities of daily life and more. However, many others are not so fortunate. Many young people grow up in an environment in which they may be abused or neglected or forced to struggle to survive.

In any of the above cases, at some point during their lives, many young people test the boundaries of society and the limits set by the adults around them by engaging in behaviors that are maladaptive and/or illegal. Some juveniles, left to their own devices, will return to adaptive, legal behavior on their own as their brain and body mature into adulthood. Others, however, may continue down the path of increasingly maladaptive and harmful behavior unless some type of outside intervention or redirection occurs. It is here that we as a society must be incredibly careful. It is vitally important to remember that juveniles are not simply miniature adults. Rather, young people see, think, and respond to the world around them much differently than do adults.

Early intervention and the provision of supportive services are extremely important for our youth. Counseling, training, and education may help that young person avoid a future in which they harm others and themselves. Juvenile detention, including a punishing environment and exposure to other young offenders and/or violent individuals may only serve to reinforce and even strengthen maladaptive behavior. Harsh, lengthy sentences for offenses committed prior to the full development of the brain and body are likely to do far more harm than good. If our young people are our future, we must guard and guide this precious resource with care and compassion.

Exercises and Discussion Questions

1. You are the superintendent in charge of a large juvenile detention center and have received a significant government grant to study the impact of various types of programming in reducing juvenile offending. What types of education, vocational, rehabilitation, or other programming would you institute? Be specific. Explain your rationale for each type of program that you would implement.

2. In reference to the scenario in Exercise #1, there are those who would say that spending money on such programs is being soft on crime and that juvenile offenders should be punished and should not have the privilege of receiving such supportive services. How would you respond to such objections? Do you agree or disagree that the provision of such services to offenders is soft on crime? Why or why not?

3. As discussed in this chapter, the Scared Straight program in which young offenders were brought into a maximum-security prison in the hopes that the inmates could scare and intimidate the juveniles out of a life of crime was not effective and may have resulted in worse rather than better outcomes. Why do you think this was the case? Be specific. If you could design a different, more effective program to convince young people not to continue engaging in criminal behavior, describe what that program would look like.

4. School administrators might suggest that by suspending young people who are misbehaving in schools, we are protecting other students from being influenced or harmed by those who are suspended. Others might state that suspending students for

misbehaving does nothing to correct their behavior and even reinforces their maladaptive behavior by giving them a vacation from school. What would you propose should be done with young people who are being disruptive in school? What kind of program would you implement to keep other students safe while also encouraging the disruptive individual to behave in a more adaptive manner?

KEY TERMS

Actus reus

Adjudicative hearing

Arraignment hearing

Bullying

Conduct disorder (CD)

Cyberbullying

Diversion

Dynamic risk factors

Fetal alcohol syndrome (FAS)

Gangs

Juvenile delinquency

Juvenile petition

Mens rea

Oppositional defiant disorder (ODD)

Personality disorder

Prefrontal cortex

Pre-sentence investigation

Protective factors

Risk factors

Self-fulfilling prophecy

Social learning theory

Static risk factors

Status offense

Waiver

5 AGGRESSION AND VIOLENT BEHAVIOR

LEARNING OBJECTIVES

1. Define the key terms associated with aggression and violence in modern society.

2. Describe the meaning and importance of the phrase "correlation does not imply causation."

3. Define intimate partner violence (IPV) and discuss its impact on victims.

4. Differentiate between child abuse and neglect.

5. Compare and contrast clinical prediction versus actuarial prediction of violence and the role of the VRAG–R in assisting with such a prediction.

6. Compare the tendency toward violence between people with mental illness and those without mental illness.

7. Explain the concept of personality disorder and which personality disorder is most often associated with aggressive and violent behavior toward others.

"I wasn't going to shoot her, but I had to. I didn't have a choice," said the offender sitting on the other side of my desk. From his record, I knew that in the course of committing an armed robbery, he shot and killed his victim, a 42-year-old married woman and mother of three children. "How do you mean?" I asked. He responded without hesitation, "She wouldn't give up her purse." "What?" I asked, barely hiding my astonishment. "Yeah, I pulled my nine [millimeter handgun] on her and told her to give up her money. She didn't want to, so I had no choice but to put a bullet in her." He shrugged and added, "If she'd have known how to get robbed, she'd still be alive today." I sat there, almost too stunned to write down what he had told me.

INTRODUCTION

Unfortunately, the above offense is hardly uncommon in today's society. The World Health Organization World Report on Violence and Health Abstract (Krug et al., 2002) indicates that worldwide, 1.6 million people lose their lives to violence every year and that violence is among the leading causes of death for people 15–44 years of age. Cities including St. Louis, Baltimore, San Juan, and Detroit have murder rates among the highest in the world (USA Today, 2019). Aggravated assault is the most common violent crime, occurring at an average rate of about 247 instances for every 100,000 residents, and contributes greatly to the overall violent crime rate of 383 instances per 100,000 residents and 1.21 million violent crimes in the United States (U. S.) in 2018 alone. However, there is considerable variability based on location, with cities such as

Washington DC showing a rate of about 996 instances of aggravated assault for every 100,000 residents (Statista Research Department, 2020).

Make no mistake, we live in a society that publicizes and often even glorifies violent behavior. When we look at the news or social media, very often the leading stories pertain to a crime spree, homicide, or terrorist attack. The feel-good stories about a child collecting money for the homeless are left until the end of the program, but the headlines more often carry news of the latest active shooter or a mother and child who cannot be found and who are presumed to have met an untimely end.

Violence in our society is not only publicized, but even glamorized. Dylan Klebold and Eric Harris, the Columbine High School shooters, were the first two teenagers to ever make the cover of *TIME*, and they were featured on the cover of that magazine not once but twice (first on 5/3/99 and again on 12/20/99). Since then, there have been teens who made the cover for positive contributions, such as Greta Thunberg for her advocacy for environmental causes, but the emphasis on violent behavior is frequent and obvious, as demonstrated by *TIME* covers related to "How to Spot a Troubled Kid" (5/31/99) "The Aftermath of Columbine" (10/25/99), and "What Happens If We Try to Leave Afghanistan" (8/6/2010, featuring a graphic image of a young girl whose nose was cut off because she tried to escape her abusive husband). Yet another cover (4/2/18) featured the survivors of the Marjory Stoneman Douglas High School shooting in Parkland, Florida.

Further evidence of the glamorization of violence can be seen in the numerous video games that include graphic, detailed, and extremely realistic depictions of person-on-person violence. The Call of Duty series features up-close, graphic first-person battle scenes. As opposed to a game in which the player sees their character engaged in violence, in a first-person game, the player *is* the character and points the sights of their weapon toward the enemy, pulls the trigger, and sees the result, often in graphic detail and sometimes even in slow-motion. An experienced player can easily engage in 100–150 acts of violence per hour in such a game. The video game Payday depicts the player as a bank robber who is shooting and killing police and SWAT team members. In 2015, the aptly named Destructive Creations released Hatred, a game in which the player was a serial killer whose only goal was to engage in a genocide crusade. Needless to say, the game generated a great deal of controversy (although such controversy did not do anything to discourage sales, and it could be speculated that such notoriety may actually have increased sales).

There has been and continues to be considerable debate about the impact of video games in regard to violent behavior. While there are studies that suggest that increased exposure to violent games leads to an increase in violent behavior (Sifferlin, 2015), there are also studies that suggest the effect is nonexistent (Ferguson & Wang, 2019). Other studies find a positive correlation between playing such games and increased aggression, and further studies find that family factors moderate this effect; in other words, those who play violent video games but have positive family relationships don't demonstrate as great an increase in aggression as those who play these games and have poor family relationships (Shao & Wang, 2019). Simply put, it is difficult to prove that playing such games is the one and only cause of any particular violent act. Video game companies, naturally, are quick to deny that their games are intended to glamorize or promote violence in any way (perhaps to absolve themselves of any legal or financial responsibility in this regard). However, what seems undeniable is that such games normalize violent behavior.

The glamorization of violence would be impossible without a willing audience. Not only do many people voluntarily seek out and watch violent acts for free on social media, YouTube, and numerous other sources, but many go a step further in the fact that they are willing to pay for the privilege of viewing violent behavior. Songs with lyrics advocating violence and movies showing images of sexual assault, homicide, and even torture are easily (and frequently) purchased by a willing public; so too are real (as opposed to simulated) acts such as those seen on television or in the movies. The Ultimate Fighting Championship (UFC) involves an (almost) no-holds-barred competition between two fighters in a steel cage. In 2001, the UFC was financially struggling and faced opposition from Senator John McCain, who referred to the sport as "human cock-fighting" (Szczerba, 2014). After a (very) few rules were put in place and weight classes implemented, the UFC gained incredible traction and was sold only 16 years later for the phenomenal sum of 4.2 *billion* dollars, having acquired a global fanbase of 278 million people and having pay-per-view matches reaching 1.1 billion households in 163 countries.

A single match in 2017 (the largest grossing match to date) generated $600 million in revenue as more than 2 million people paid nearly $100 dollars apiece to do so (Rafael, 2017). Not only does violence sell, it sells quickly and it sells for top dollar.

Aggression

Aggression is a behavior that intends to inflict some type of harm on another person. *Verbal aggression* is the use of words or gestures to inflict psychological or emotional pain on another person. As such, verbal aggression can include name-calling, profanity, insults, and threats. Keep in mind that not all verbal aggression is illegal; "I hate you and wish you were never born" is certainly verbal aggression intended to cause emotional pain to another person, but it is not illegal as it contains no threat. "I hate you and I'm going to burn your house down with you in it" is also verbal aggression but is illegal, as it contains a direct threat of harm.

Physical aggression involves an act that attempts to or does inflict physical/bodily harm upon another person. Kicking, biting, stabbing, slapping, shooting, and numerous other such acts are examples of physical aggression. With very limited exceptions (we will address self-defense later in this chapter), such acts of physical aggression are illegal.

Generally, we can distinguish between two different motivations for physical aggression: instrumental aggression and emotional aggression. **Instrumental aggression** is typically planned ahead of time and occurs for a reason, with a specific goal in mind. The drug user who pulls a knife on a passerby and demands money so that they can buy more of their drug is engaging in instrumental aggression. They are not angry at their victim; the goal is simply to get money to supply their habit. The Mafia hitman we see in the movies who says, "It's just business, nothing personal," before killing is engaging in instrumental aggression; the hitman is not angry at the victim. In the hitman's mind, they are simply carrying out an order that was given to them by someone in authority.

Emotional aggression (sometimes also referred to as *expressive aggression* or *expressive violence*) is qualitatively different than instrumental aggression. Emotional aggression often occurs impulsively, with little or no planning. The only goal of emotional aggression is to express anger (or jealousy, rage, or a variety of other emotions) toward the victim by inflicting some type of physical damage or pain onto them. The husband who walks in on his wife having sex with another man, becomes enraged, and physically assaults the other man is engaging in emotional aggression; his intent in doing so is to express his rage and inflict some damage over this act of betrayal. Incidents of road rage, where a driver becomes so enraged at someone who cut them off in traffic that they ram into the other car, are also examples of emotional aggression.

It is possible for there to be some overlap between instrumental and emotional aggression. Perhaps you and your family are sound asleep one night when you hear the front door being kicked open. Grabbing the nearest heavy object you can find, you peer down the stairs to see that a stranger is indeed coming in the front door. Angered that he is doing so and determined to protect your family, you advance quietly down the stairs, determined to do whatever you need to in order to preserve your safety. This combination of factors—you are angry at this unknown person *and* you have the goal of protecting yourself and your family—is an example of aggression that is both emotional and instrumental at the same time. A soldier engaged in combat might experience the same overlap between instrumental and emotional aggression; it is certainly possible to be angry at the enemy combatant who is trying to kill them (emotional aggression) and at the same time know that completion of a successful mission requires that soldier to demonstrate violence toward their opponent (instrumental aggression).

CORRELATION DOES NOT IMPLY CAUSATION

In assessing factors contributing to violence (or nearly any human behavior), it is vitally important to understand and remember the phrase, *Correlation does not imply causation*. This rather impressive-sounding phrase simply means that two factors being related does not necessarily mean that one of those factors is the *cause* of the other. Imagine that you are in the market for a car. Your friend tells you, "Whatever you do, don't get a red car. Everybody knows that red cars get more speeding tickets than cars that are other colors." Being a good scientist, you decide to research this. It can't possibly be true, can it? To your surprise, you find that there is indeed a mathematical correlation between the color of a car and how often the driver is ticketed for speeding (Cooley, 2018). That is, red cars *do* in fact get ticketed for speeding more often than cars of other colors. If you make the mistake of believing that driving a red car *causes* the driver to get ticketed for speeding, you have made the error of mistaking correlation for causation; you mistakenly believe that because color and tickets are related, the color of the car must be the cause of those tickets. With a little more thought, you might realize that it doesn't make sense that the mere color of a car would cause the driver to get more tickets. After all, if we observe a police officer monitoring a driver's speed, we will see that the officer is aiming the radar gun at every single car that passes them. Furthermore, the radar gun can monitor speed but does not perceive color.

So, there *is* a correlation between the color of the car and the number of speeding tickets the drivers receive, but if the color of the car isn't the cause of the tickets, then what is? In this circumstance, there is what is referred to as a "lurking variable"; that is, another factor that isn't immediately obvious to us that plays a role in this matter. In this case, that variable is the fact that people who drive red cars tend to drive *faster* than those who drive cars of other colors. It certainly stands to reason that people who drive faster are going to get more speeding tickets than those who obey the speed limit.

Similarly, when we look for causes of violent behavior, we must be careful not to confuse correlation with causation. For example, the Centers for Disease Control and Prevention (CDC; n. d.) tells us that being a victim of violence, being in a state of emotional distress, and witnessing violence among family members while growing up (sometimes referred to as *intergenerational transmission of violence*) can all increase the risk of an individual being aggressive themselves. Associating with delinquent peers (as was discussed in Chapter 4) can also increase the probability of an individual being violent, as can being raised in a low-income, high-crime environment. All of these factors (and others) are correlated with violence to a greater or lesser extent and can combine to raise or lower the risk of such behavior. Still, as much as we would like to find a singular cause for violent behavior, it is important that scientists and researchers resist the impulse to oversimplify.

Dylan Klebold and Eric Harris, who murdered 11 students and a teacher at Columbine High School in 1999, were reportedly members of a cadre of Columbine students known as the "Trench Coat Mafia" because they wore such coats to school from time to time. After the shooting, many schools changed their dress code and prohibited the wearing of such coats in school, with some schools going as far as to ban students from wearing all-black clothing (Nyce, 2016). There seemed to be a belief that by banning trench coats, students would not be able to smuggle weapons into the school and this type of tragedy would be avoided in the future—an understandable goal, to be certain, but likely a case of mistaking correlation for causation. The trench coats were certainly associated with these violent acts, but to believe that an item of clothing caused such acts (or that forbidding such clothing would protect against such acts in the future) seems absurd. It is worth noting that Klebold and Harris were not in fact members of the Trench Coat Mafia and did not have any association with that group (Brockell, 2019).

Violent Offenses

Violent offenses involve an intent to inflict or the actual infliction of physical or sexual harm on another person. Although definitions vary by jurisdiction, violent offenses generally include assault, robbery, homicide, forcible rape, and domestic violence (now referred to as **intimate partner violence [IPV]**), the latter of which will be discussed shortly.

Simple assault is generally defined as an offender putting another individual in reasonable fear of being harmed or injured. Actual physical injury may be inflicted but is often not required for the definition of simple assault to be met. Punching, kicking, or choking another person would qualify as examples of simple assault. **Aggravated assault**, on the other hand, is typically defined as knowingly, intentionally, or recklessly attempting to or actually inflicting serious bodily harm on another person. In many cases, aggravated assault will involve the use of a weapon. Shooting someone, stabbing them, or hitting them with a baseball bat would all qualify as acts of aggravated assault.

In the U. S. in 2018, aggravated assault was the most commonly reported violent crime with more than 800,000 such offenses being reported, a rate of 246.8 cases per 100,000 U.S. inhabitants; such offenses contribute greatly to an overall violent crime rate of 382.9 violent offenses per 100,000 inhabitants (Statista Research Department, 2020). It is important to keep in mind that many offenses, including violent offenses, go unreported. There are many reasons why a person might choose not to report being the victim of a violent offense. Perhaps the victim is afraid that if they report the offense, the offender will seek revenge and harm them further. Perhaps they fear retaliation from the offenders' associates, or perhaps the victim is simply too embarrassed or ashamed to report being victimized. In some cases, the victim may have been engaged in an illegal act when they were assaulted; it may not be in the victim's best interest to report to the police that they were assaulted by a drug dealer while they were in the act of purchasing methamphetamine. Thus, the actual number of assaults, robberies, and rapes that occur is likely to be far higher than the numbers reported.

Robbery is usually defined as the unlawful taking of another person's property through force or through threat of force. More than 267,000 robberies were reported in 2019, a rate of 82 robberies for every 100,000 U.S. inhabitants.

Broadly defined, *homicide* is the act of one person killing another. In our legal system, the intent of the offender is important when it comes to determining guilt and/or the penalty for an individual accused of homicide. **Mens rea** is Latin for "guilty mind" and refers to the criminal intent of the accused at the time the crime was committed. Simply put, a homicide is typically considered more serious if the offender planned it out ahead of time and carried it out in a calculated fashion. **First-degree homicide** may occur when the offender has planned out the crime ahead of time and has engaged in an act that was clearly intended to cause the death of the victim. A disgruntled employee obtains a firearm, sneaks it into the workplace in their briefcase, and at the time of the weekly meeting with their supervisor, shoots and kills the supervisor. Such a case would be prosecuted as first-degree homicide, as it was planned ahead of time and there was clear criminal intent. In such a case, a guilty ruling would typically involve a very lengthy sentence of incarceration or, in some states, the offender could be sentenced to death.

In another case, a man and a woman become involved in a road-rage incident. From their individual vehicles, they begin yelling at one another. Enraged, they pull over to the side of the road, get out of their respective vehicles, and continue to yell at each other. As the argument escalates, the man pulls a knife out of his pocket and stabs the woman in the chest. She dies on her way to the hospital. This offense involved no planning or premeditation; the man did not set out that day to kill her. In fact, he didn't know the victim until a few minutes before he stabbed her. However, although there was no premeditation, his act was clearly intended to harm or kill her. Such a case would in all likelihood be prosecuted as **second-degree homicide** and often would involve a lengthy period of incarceration, albeit not as long as a finding of first-degree homicide.

Two high school students are in the bathroom arguing about which of them is the better basketball player. As the argument escalates, they begin pushing and shoving each other. Chad pushes Brian hard, and Brian slips and falls, hitting his head hard on the tile floor. Several days later, Brian dies of his injuries. Chad did not premeditate this offense, and his actions, while certainly reckless and ill-advised, were not clearly intended to kill Brian. Thus, this case would likely be prosecuted as **third-degree homicide**, referred to as *manslaughter* in many jurisdictions. A finding of guilt in such a case would typically involve a much shorter sentence of incarceration than would a finding of guilt for first- or second-degree homicide.

Any crime committed toward an individual or group on the basis of another person's hostility or hatred for that group is considered a **hate crime/bias crime**. Such offenses may include vandalizing property, assault, arson, homicide, and other acts of violence based on the offender's hostility toward the victim's race, gender, sexual orientation, national origin, disability, or a variety of other factors. The Federal Bureau of Investigation (FBI) Uniform Crime Report indicates that in 2018, more than 7,000 such offenses were reported to law enforcement authorities.

Of these offenses, 57.5% were based on race, ethnicity, and ancestry, with nearly half of these being committed against African Americans. Approximately 20% of such offenses were committed against those with certain religious beliefs, with more than half of those offenses being committed against those of the Jewish faith. Seventeen percent of hate or bias crimes were committed against people based on their sexual orientation, with most of these being committed against homosexual males. It should be noted that it can be difficult to prove that a crime was motivated by hate or bias. For example, perhaps a group of three men assault an individual who is homosexual. The fact that they assaulted this individual may not be difficult to prove, but proving that the assault was hate- or bias-related can be difficult if the offenders did not use verbal slurs or other evidence of prejudice and hatred.

Forcible rape is defined by the FBI as sexual penetration, no matter how slight, without the consent of the victim. Ninety-eight thousand such offenses and attempted offenses were reported in the U. S. in 2019, for an overall rate of 30 such offenses for every 100,000 inhabitants. Statutory rape and other sexual offenses are categorized separately. It is especially important to realize that these numbers may significantly underestimate the actual rate of forcible rape, as such offenses often go unreported. We will discuss such offenses, and the reasons why victims are often reluctant to report them, in greater detail in Chapter 6.

When Is Homicide Not Homicide?

U.S. law does recognize that potential victims are allowed to engage in self-defense and to take action to prevent themselves from being victimized. Of course, such laws vary by state and (especially) by the circumstances of the specific events that transpire. Generally, it is recognized that if an individual has a reasonable belief, given the totality of the circumstances, that they are in imminent and unavoidable danger of death or serious injury from another person, that individual is allowed to act to defend themselves (or other innocent parties) up to and including the use of deadly force against the assailant.

Some states require the individual to retreat before engaging in a use of force; that is, the individual must attempt to leave the area or at least back up and attempt to avoid the use of force, if possible. Other states have "stand your ground" laws that state that if an individual is in a place they are legally permitted to be, there is no requirement that they attempt to retreat or leave the area; they may retreat if they wish to, but in states with stand your ground laws, such retreat is not required before self-defense. Still other states have "castle doctrine" laws that state that individuals in their home have no duty to attempt to retreat or avoid a use of force in that setting. If the circumstances do indeed suggest that self-defense was justifiable, the case may not be prosecuted; if prosecuted, this defense may be used by the defendant and the jury might (or might not!) decide to find the defendant not guilty in such a case. The concept of self-defense and justifiable homicide may appear rather simple by definition, but in reality, such cases are often complex and open to considerable legal wrangling.

CLEAR AS MUD

On October 8, 1981, Israel Grove came home drunk. According to his wife, Jessie, Israel had physically abused her for the past 22 years, and before going to sleep that night, he had threatened to kill her the next day. Jessie got a 12-gauge shotgun and killed him while he slept. At trial, she argued that she had done so in self-defense. The jury found her guilty of first-degree murder and sentenced her to life in prison.

In a New York case that would appear very similar, Madelyn Diaz had been physically abused by her husband for five years. He reportedly threatened to kill her and then when to sleep. Madelyn then shot and killed him. The jury was allowed to consider self-defense and acquitted Madelyn of any wrongdoing; she received no sentence for her actions.

Obviously, there may be numerous details of these cases that we are not privy to; however, it is important to recognize that self-defense and justifiable homicide are subject to a great deal of argument and interpretation. Before engaging in any type of physical altercation, it is important to know the laws that apply to self-defense in that state. What one person considers to be self-defense, a jury just might consider to be homicide.

INTIMATE PARTNER VIOLENCE (IPV)

With some frequency, we see ads on television for home security and alarm systems that show a masked burglar prowling around the house and attempting to break in. The ad implies that if the homeowner had such-and-such security system, the police would be on the way momentarily and all would be well. That same ad also suggests that if they did not have that security device in place, the outcome would be much worse. Such fear-based attempts to sell a product can be effective but often play upon our fears rather than being based in reality.

Intimate partner violence (IPV) involves violence between any two people who are or were domestic partners.
lolostock/Alamy Stock Photo

The unfortunate reality is that the danger we face in our own homes is very often not from the masked stranger who is attempting to break in but instead from a family member who already resides in the home or others who are well-known to us. In fact, more than 10 million people are physically abused by an intimate partner every year (Black et al., 2011). One in four women and one in nine men are victims of physical abuse, sexual abuse, or stalking during the course of their lives, and IPV constitutes 15% of all violent crimes (Truman & Morgan, 2014).

The term *domestic violence*, which was thought to encompass the violence by one married partner (most often the husband) toward the other, has now been replaced by the more inclusive term *intimate partner violence* (*IPV*). IPV refers to physical, sexual, or psychological aggression and/or stalking carried out by one domestic partner/spouse toward another. IPV is inclusive of couples of any and all genders and applies regardless of age and whether the couple is married or unmarried and current or former partners.

IPV is a serious and unfortunately all-too-common problem. Throughout the course of their lives, 43 million women and 38 million men will report being victimized in such a manner, with 41% of these women and 14% of these men sustaining physical injuries as a result (Smith et al., 2018). It is important to note that such victimization often begins early in life; 11 million women reported being a victim of IPV before age 18, and 5 million men reported being victimized in such a way prior to age 18.

The CDC (n. d.) states that IPV can include emotional abuse, threats of physical or sexual abuse, and actual physical or sexual abuse. In theory (and sometimes in practice), such definitions are quite clear and easily understood. In reality, however, things are not always so simple; as we discussed in the previous chapter in regard to child abuse, there can be ambiguity in terms of what people perceive as abuse. For example, some people might express the belief that one partner pushing another against the wall (without any physical injury) would constitute abuse. Others might express the belief that while such behavior should obviously not occur, it does not fit their personal definition of abuse. Therefore, some people would report such a behavior to the local authorities, while others might not believe there is any reason to do so.

It is important to keep in mind that not all abuse is illegal; this is perhaps most often true in regard to emotional abuse. Although emotional abuse can have a very real and lasting impact on the abused individual, it is frequently not illegal. "I hate you and hope you die a long, slow death" would certainly fit the definition of emotional abuse, but it is likely legal, as it does not constitute a threat of harm. "I hate you and one of these days I'm going to put you six feet under the ground" is also emotionally abusive but is very likely illegal as it constitutes a threat to that person's safety and life.

The question often asked about IPV is why the victimized individual doesn't simply leave and remove themselves from that situation. To answer this question, it is helpful to take a look at who is most often at risk of being a victim of IPV. According to the CDC (n.

d.), victims of IPV are often young women who have a low level of education, are unemployed or have a low income, have heavy drug and alcohol use/abuse, have few social connections or friends, or who may have been removed from their social support networks and are isolated by their abuser. In short, victims of IPV are often ill-prepared in terms of being able to extricate themselves from the abusive environment. Even in those cases when the abused partner has their own income and has the support of friends or family, the answer to IPV is rarely as simple as "leave." A victim of IPV may fear the consequences to themselves or their children if they attempt to remove themselves from the situation. Indeed, 40% of female murder victims are slain by a current or former intimate partner (Niolan et al., 2017), so their fear is based in reality. If and when the abused partner does leave, the abuser may feel they have nothing to lose by seeking revenge.

It is perhaps not surprising to see who is most likely to be a perpetrator of IPV. As we discussed in Chapter 4, and will discuss further in this chapter, young males consistently demonstrate more violent and impulsive behavior than other groups. It should come as no surprise to find that males in the 18–30 age range are most likely to be perpetrators of IPV. Such individuals also tend to use/abuse alcohol and other drugs, have a history of impulsivity in a variety of contexts, and have been victims of or witnesses of familial violence while they were growing up. It is also important to keep in mind that while victims of IPV tend to be young and unemployed with a low level of education and perpetrators tend to be young males who are abusing substances, IPV can and does occur across all demographics and levels of income; no one is immune to the impact of IPV.

Responding to Intimate Partner Violence

Police officers readily acknowledge that one of their least favorite duties is responding to domestic disturbance calls, for a wide variety of reasons. By definition, the scene is likely to be emotionally charged and volatile when they arrive. Furthermore, the responding officers have little or no knowledge of whether there are weapons, an aggressive dog, or other dangers in the household. They often find that by the time they reach the scene, the report they got from the dispatcher ("Victim reports that the offender attempted to strangle them") has now changed, with the victim in some cases now denying that they ever said such a thing. It is commonplace for one or both of the individuals to be under the influence of alcohol and other drugs, and each one tells a very different story about who is the protagonist and what exactly has transpired. In the past, police responded to incidents of IPV by telling the aggressor (most often the male) to leave the house and cool off for a couple hours. However, such advice was of little use (and likely only made matters worse!) if the perpetrator went to a bar or a friend's house to continue to consume alcohol prior to returning to the scene of the crime.

Intimate partner disagreements and violence may leave the responding officers in a very difficult situation. If there is no probable cause for arrest, they may temporarily de-escalate the situation, but they are also well aware that they may be called back to that same house later in the night or the next day when things again escalate out of control. However, police are also familiar with the fact that if they do make an arrest, the perpetrator will likely only be held in jail briefly before being bailed out (in some cases, by the victim themselves!) to return to the same situation. The hopelessness and frustration of the police in such a situation is understandable.

A 1984 study by Sherman and Berk demonstrated that arrests can and do decrease the probability of an aggressor being violent again toward the same victim in the future. Their study found that when an arrest is made, there is only a 10% chance that the aggressor will again demonstrate violence toward the same victim, whereas if the police advised the perpetrator to not become violent again (but did not actually make an arrest), there was a 19% probability of future violence against the same victim, and if the police merely told the aggressor to leave the scene for some time, there was a 24% probability of repeated violence against the same victim. It should be noted, however, that there did seem to be some erosion of this effect after six months. That is, the aggressor learns their lesson for some time after being arrested, but the impact of this arrest may fade over time.

Fortunately, progress is being made in recognizing the plight of victims of IPV and providing them with the support and services that they so desperately need and deserve. Some states have enacted mandatory arrest statutes. While these vary somewhat by state, such statutes essentially require police to make an arrest in cases in which there is probable cause to determine who the primary aggressor is in a given case. Such mandatory arrest laws do not necessarily require there to be any visible injuries to either party. Although mandatory arrest when there is probable cause to identify an aggressor may appear to be helpful, at least one study suggests that such an approach can backfire. Peralta and Novisky (2015) found that mandatory arrest statutes may decrease the probability of the abused partner reporting this incident. That is, if the abused knows that the aggressor will be arrested, they may fear that the revenge sought by that aggressor will be even worse than the initial abuse and therefore may not report the incident at all.

Instead of mandatory arrest statutes, some states have enacted preferred arrest statutes. Preferred arrest statutes make it known to the responding officers that arrest is the preferred outcome in such cases but is not necessarily required. Thus, officers have discretion in such cases in terms of whether they feel arrest is warranted.

CHILD ABUSE AND NEGLECT

Of all the crimes that we find difficult to understand and comprehend, crimes of violence against children must be one of the foremost. Even among hardened criminals, who may think nothing of murder and assault, crimes against children are still considered taboo and those who are known to have committed such offenses are frequent objects of scorn and anger.

The U.S. Department of Health and Human Services and childwelfare.org generally define child abuse as falling into one of four categories: physical abuse, sexual abuse, emotional abuse, and neglect. *Physical abuse* includes the use of physical force or excessive physical force or forced restraint or confinement. *Sexual abuse* includes inappropriate touching of private areas, sexual acts, and exposure to pornography or forced compliance with pornography. *Emotional abuse* can include verbal threats, insults, intimidation, or any statement or action intended to cause the child emotional or psychological pain or trauma.

Neglect differs from abuse in that abuse generally involves the commission of an act that will cause physical, sexual, or emotional pain or trauma. Neglect, on the other hand, generally involves the failure to provide for the basic needs of a child. For example, a parent may neglect to provide for a child's medical needs by failing to take them to regular medical check-ups or for routine dental care. Failure to provide the child with adequate nutrition, not aiding the child with hygiene, or not providing them with adequate clothes for winter temperatures would all be examples of neglect.

The impact of childhood abuse and neglect may be significant and long-lasting. This is not to say that every abused child is destined to suffer greatly and will be unable to overcome such treatment. However, there is no question that abuse and neglect can and does play an important role in the later life of that individual. At least 700,000 children per year (between 1 and 2% of all children) are subject to some form of abuse or neglect (National Children's Alliance, 2018). Unfortunately, this is likely an underestimate, as such cases are not always reported. Such abuse and neglect can be (and at times, is) deadly, with 1,770 children dying from abuse and neglect in 2018 alone (U.S. Department of Health & Human Services, 2018).

Being abused or neglected as a child can have a lifelong and significant emotional impact.

Birute/iStockPhoto

In 2020 alone, more than 600,000 cases of child abuse were reported in the United States (Statista Research Department, 2022). Sadly, it appears that the youngest children are at greatest risk, with more than 136,000 of these cases occurring in children one year old and younger and another 150,000 of these cases being reported in children ages 2–5 (Statista Research Department, 2020).

Those children who survive the abuse still suffer significant and potentially long-lasting consequences. Eighty percent of 21-year-olds who reported suffering from childhood abuse met the criteria for at least one mental health diagnosis (Silverman et al., 1996). Another study (Harlow, 1999) suggested that children who have been subjected to abuse and/or neglect are nine times more likely to become involved in criminal activity than those who have not suffered from such maltreatment. Obviously, becoming involved in such activity increases the probability of contact with the criminal justice system and incarceration, which may only make matters worse.

As with IPV, a significant issue in regard to the issue of abuse and neglect is one of definition. Some cases are very clear-cut: Not providing a child with adequate nutrition so that the child is severely underweight or shaking an infant so vigorously that they will have permanent damage are definite examples of abuse. However, many cases are less clear-cut. During classes, the present author often polls his students as to what they believe are examples of abuse. Without fail, some students will agree that sending a child to bed without dinner constitutes abuse while others will argue that it is an appropriate form of discipline for certain types of misbehavior. Similarly, some students believe that spanking constitutes physical abuse while others believe it is perfectly appropriate under some circumstances. Opinions vary widely, as does reporting of such incidents. After all, if one does not consider a particular act to be abuse, one has no reason to report it.

Many schools and other organizations offer lectures and workshops on "stranger danger." While there is likely no harm to be done by such education, such workshops fail to address the fact that statistically, children are more likely to come to harm in the home from a parent than outside the home from a stranger. In 2018, 76% of perpetrators of child abuse or neglect were parents (U.S. Department of Health and Human Services, 2018). Table 5.1 is a sampling of the data from the aforementioned Department of Health and Human Services report and underscores that it is more often relatives and/or their partners that are likely to harm children than are strangers.

Although abuse or neglect of a child can occur in any household, the CDC does suggest that there are factors that increase the probability of an individual perpetrating such an offense. Those who do so tend to have been abused or neglected themselves when they were young; as

TABLE 5.1 ■ Sampling of Data: Perpetrators of Child Abuse and Their Relationship to Their Victim				
State	Relative	Unmarried Partner of Parent	Other	Unknown
California	2,784	3,556	2	7
Illinois	1,317	1,065	570	293
Kentucky	935	832	155	130
Michigan	1,038	77	276	12
Texas	5,349	3,302	1,165	103

Source: Adapted from U.S. Department of Health & Human Services. (2020). *Child Maltreatment 2018.* https://www.acf.hhs.gov/cb/research-data-technology/statistics-research/child-maltreatment

parents or caregivers, they tend to be young, uneducated, and have a low income and a history of alcohol or other drug use/abuse and/or mental health concerns.

Child Abduction and Kidnapping

It's every parent's nightmare. Your 12-year-old has told you that she is going to play with a neighbor down the street. It's only a few blocks away, and she is a responsible child, careful about looking before crossing the street and aware of her surroundings, so you give her permission to walk there, and off she goes, promising to stay in touch by text. You get caught up in routine household chores and don't give it much thought for an hour or so. Then you text her and get no response. "OK, no big deal," you think to yourself. "She is probably playing with her friend and not paying attention to her phone." A little while later, you text again, and again there is no response. Now you are starting to get concerned, so you call her; the call goes to voice mail. No need to panic though; you are friends with her friend's mother, so you call her. She sounds surprised: "No, they're not here. In fact, my daughter told me that she was going to walk to your house to play with your daughter." Panic starts to rise in both of you. Maybe they are at another friend's house, maybe they are doing something they know they are not supposed to do, or maybe—just maybe—something worse has happened. Every parent dreads this scenario, and while abductions and kidnappings are uncommon, they can and do occur.

Abduction and **kidnapping** both involve the unlawful taking of a person against their will and holding them captive, whether by means of persuasion, force, or fraud. Abduction and kidnapping are similar in that either one can occur by deception or by force. The difference is that with an abduction, obtaining possession of the child *is* the goal of the act. The abductor typically does not ask for any type of ransom or demand for the child; the child is what the abductor wants. Furthermore, in an abduction, the perpetrator is not seeking attention—and is typically seeking to *avoid* attention at all costs, perhaps disguising themselves and/or the victim. Often, the abductor may be a noncustodial parent who has decided that they must regain their child or children. According to the National Crime Information Center (2018) in 2017, there were 2,359 cases of abduction by a noncustodial parent—many times higher than the number of children who were abducted or kidnapped by a stranger.

Kidnapping is distinguished from abduction by the fact that the kidnapper has typically taken the child in order to have leverage to make a monetary or other demand. In this regard, kidnappers do not mind attention to the offense, as it may provide pressure for the parents or community to meet the kidnapper's demands. Abduction or kidnapping by stranger is far less common than such offenses committed by noncustodial parents, with the National Crime

Information Center (2021) reporting less than 350 stranger abductions or kidnappings (0.1%) in 2021 per year. Kidnapping leading to homicide is rare but not unheard of, and such incidents generate tremendous attention and concern. Indeed, a report for the Office of the Inspector General (2009) suggested that 99.8% of children reported to be missing were later found alive.

Inveiglement is a term that means using trickery or deception in order to commit an abduction or kidnapping. Offenders who plan to engage in such offenses can be extremely clever when it comes to luring their victim to their home, into a car, and so on. Such offenders are well aware of the fact that children are told to beware of strangers. Thus, the potential offender may go out of their way to make sure that they are *not* considered a stranger by the victim. That is, the offender may "accidentally" cross paths with the intended victim as that victim gets off the school bus or may find a way to introduce themselves to the intended victim at some point. After all, if you know my name and we see each other from time to time, we aren't strangers, are we? Such interactions will often include the offender praising the child or promising them some gift or special treatment in order to ingratiate themselves to the child.

Such offenders may make use of props, such as a dog collar and leash, with a story along the lines of "Oh, hey, can you help me? My dog, Fluffy, got off his leash, that little rascal! He is *so* cute and I am *so* worried about him. I think he went over here somewhere. Will you help me look for him? Please? I'll give you a $20 reward if you can help me find him!" Despite parental warnings to beware of strangers, many children can and do want to help others and can indeed be persuaded to help the supposedly heartbroken dog owner.

The National Center for Missing and Exploited Children (2022) conducted a study of 29,000 cases of missing children and found that 91% of them had not been abducted or kidnapped but had run away. This is still of great concern, however, as such children may be vulnerable to human trafficking, sex trafficking, and other forms of abuse.

Anatomy and Biology

In Chapter 4, we discussed the influence of anatomy, biology, and genetics on the development of young people. The influence of such factors does not end, of course, on their 18th birthday but continues throughout the lifespan.

As we discuss in Chapter 4, and as noted by Copping (2017, p. 1), "Perhaps the most ubiquitous finding across multiple research disciplines regarding aggression and violence is that of consistent gender differences, with the male of the species exhibiting greater levels of these behaviors than the female." Batrinos (2012, p. 563) goes on to note, "Testosterone plays a significant role . . . in aggression" and "Testosterone levels are higher in individuals with aggressive behavior, such as prisoners who have committed violent crimes."

In Chapter 4, we noted that **testosterone** levels are quite high in 17- and 18-year-old males. As the 17- and 18-year-olds we discussed in Chapter 4 become adults, testosterone levels continue to be relatively high through their 20s and don't begin to level off and decrease until about age 35 (McAvennie, 2023). Thus, the link between testosterone and social dominance (and in some cases, aggression) that exists for juvenile males continues to exist for males as they age into their 20s and mid-30s. The rate at which offenders commit violent offenses drops off significantly after age 35, leading Marc Mauer of the Sentencing Project and others to suggest a 20-year limit on incarceration, as this would be a sufficient amount of time for violent offenders to "age out" of committing such offenses (Goldstein, 2015).

Just as the role of testosterone does not cease playing a role in impulsive and aggressive behavior as a juvenile becomes fully adult, neither does the role of the prefrontal cortex cease to be important in this regard. As described in the previous chapter, the prefrontal cortex plays an important role in decision making, problem solving, and suppressing impulsive, possibly violent behavior. Yet this area of the brain is not fully developed in many cases until age 25, so it should come as no surprise that even as teenagers become adults, they may continue to display impulsive behavior and poor decisions well into their 20s (Arain et al., 2013). Furthermore, a study by Arnstein, Mazure, and Sinha (2012) suggested that even under mild stress, the prefrontal cortex can essentially shut down and allow impulsive and maladaptive urges to go unchecked.

Thus, the combination of high levels of testosterone and a not-yet-fully developed prefrontal cortex that exists in juveniles may serve to increase the probability of impulsive, maladaptive, and illegal behavior that continues on into young adulthood and may well have the same consequences for those in their 20s and even early 30s as they do for those in their late teens.

Furthermore, increased impulsivity and aggressiveness are not uncommon after an individual has sustained a head injury or traumatic brain injury (TBI), especially if that injury is to the frontal lobes of the brain (Floden et al., 2008). Such individuals show diminished concern for the risks and consequences of their actions and may become rude, irritable, and tactless when interacting with others. We may speculate that an individual who suffers such

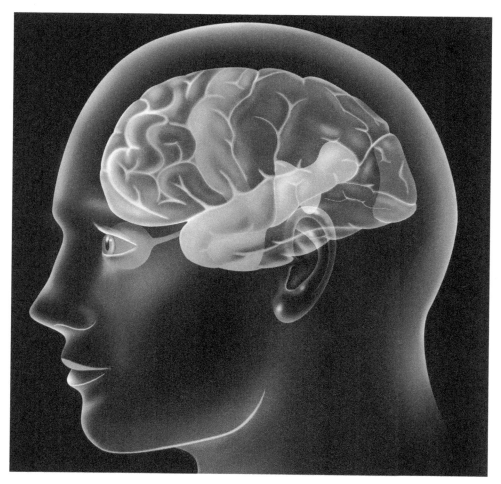

The human brain is gray in color, but for illustration purposes in the above photo, the prefrontal cortex is the blue portion of the brain in the forehead area.

BSIP SA/Alamy Stock Photo

an injury and consequently becomes more impulsive and less concerned about the risks they take then puts themselves at increased risk of yet another such injury. Aggression, both verbal and physical, is one of the most common consequences of an individual who suffers a TBI (Rao et al., 2009).

CHRIS BENOIT: THE IMPERFECT STORM

On July 25, 2007, World Wrestling Entertainment (WWE) was preparing for its weekly taping of Monday Night RAW. One of the night's star attractions was wrestler Chris Benoit, also known as "The Rabid Wolverine," a powerfully built and energetic star. Management and other wrestlers became concerned when Benoit was late reporting for the show. The police were called to make a welfare check to his home and found a devastating scene. Investigations later determined that Benoit had murdered his wife and 7-year-old son and had then committed suicide.

In the face of such tragedy, it is human nature to wonder how this could have happened, what may have led Benoit to engage in such unthinkable acts. Indeed, an autopsy did indicate that his urine contained ten times the amount of testosterone that would normally be expected, indicating that he had injected steroids not long before committing his offense (Donaldson-Evans, 2015). However, while testosterone has been linked to impulsive and aggressive behavior, no firm conclusion could be reached in this regard as other factors were also present that may have contributed or played a role; there was speculation that Benoit was depressed, perhaps in relation to marital difficulties. Furthermore, an examination of Benoit's brain did suggest that he had suffered multiple concussions and demonstrated symptoms of chronic traumatic encephalopathy, a serious brain disorder also found in many National Football League players (ABC News, 2009). Any of these factors, or perhaps a combination of all of them (and perhaps even some unidentified variables), may have played a role in this tragic event.

Modeling and Social Learning in Adults

In Chapter 4, we learned that children in Albert Bandura's "Bobo doll" study who viewed aggressive adult behavior tended to imitate that behavior. It should not be assumed that the tendency to be influenced by the objects and people around us ends in childhood. Indeed, even the mere presence of a weapon in our sight increases the frequency of aggressive thoughts and behaviors; Berkowitz (1967) found that subjects who saw firearms nearby were more likely to deliver electric shocks to another subject than those who did not see such firearms.

A meta-analysis conducted by Bushman and Huesmann (2006) sought to determine the short-term and long-term effects of viewing violent media and aggression on children and on adults. They found that observing violence can indeed lead to a short-term increase in aggressive and violent behavior in adults, and the impact of viewing such aggression and violence on adults was significant. Huesmann went on to state, "If you're exposed to violence, you're more likely to catch it," (as quoted in Swanson, 2015). Exposure to violence, either by viewing it on various forms of media or by up-close-and-personal observation, does appear to be an important risk factor in terms of increasing violent behavior. Thus, some researchers have compared violence to a contagious disease that can be spread from one person to another. These studies seem to suggest that what we see in the environment around us plays a role in the behavior we demonstrate not only as children but also as adults, and if we are frequently exposed to violent acts and images, this may increase the probability of aggressive behavior in ourselves.

Mental Illness

Very often, when we hear of an act of particular cruelty or a mass shooting, we may see or hear people responding that the perpetrator must have been "sick" or "crazy," suggesting that person must have had some type of mental health issue as the explanation for that act. Monahan et al. (2005) suggest that the public perception that mental illness predisposes an individual to acts of violence may have increased in the past several decades. The MacArthur Violence Risk Assessment Study they conducted sought to identify whether there was any evidence for such a belief and what factors show evidence of increasing the probability of violent offending. The researchers found that although 31% of individuals with both mental health and substance abuse issues committed at least one act of violence during the year, when substance abuse was factored out, the rate of those with mental health issues engaging in at least one act of violence fell to 18%, and when compared to other individuals living in the same geographic area, those with mental illness were no more likely to engage in an act of violence than those without mental health concerns.

Though we might consider them to be among the most seriously mentally ill, individuals diagnosed with schizophrenia (a thought disorder in which individuals often experience hallucinations and bizarre beliefs) are actually *less* likely to engage in an act of violence than people without such a mental health diagnosis. The exception to this rule, as noted in a study by Fazel et al. in 2009, was for those with schizophrenia who also had a substance abuse disorder, who did indeed show increased rates of violence compared to those with schizophrenia and no substance abuse disorder. The present author spent a considerable amount of time working in special needs units in the Pennsylvania prison system. These are specialized units that house those offenders with schizophrenia, intellectual limitations, and other similar concerns. He found that there were rarely disciplinary problems or acts of violence in these units, as the inhabitants were sometimes hard-pressed to get through their normal daily routine and had neither the time nor the desire to harm others.

Individuals *not* diagnosed with schizophrenia but still experiencing hallucinations or delusions were no more likely to engage in acts of violence than individuals not experiencing such episodes (Fazel et al., 2009). The only exception that the study found was for individuals experiencing command hallucinations. Command hallucinations occur when a person is not only hearing non-existent voices but those voices are repeatedly telling them/ordering them to engage in a certain behavior. For example, an ordinary auditory hallucination might be describing to the person what they are doing or might be derogatory but not an order (i.e., "You smell so bad!"). A command hallucination occurs when the effected individual repeatedly hears, for instance, "You have to get her before she gets you. Get her. Hurt her." It is for this reason that the experienced forensic psychologist, when interacting with a client who admits hearing voices, responds with "What is the voice telling you?" as part of making a determination about their own safety and the safety of others.

Personality and Personality Disorders

In everyday life, we use the word **personality** with some frequency. Maybe we say that our roommate has an outgoing personality or perhaps that a coworker has an abrasive or annoying personality. Although we may use this term frequently, when asked to define it, we may find it rather difficult. Psychologists often think of personality as who we are, a set of enduring traits that starts rather early in life and that remains relatively stable over time. Personality encompasses how we perceive the world around us and how we interact with others. Personality is not our mood of the day, which obviously changes with circumstance, but is more stable and enduring.

The 5th edition of the Diagnostic and Statistical Manual of Mental Disorders (DSM-5) is the manual used today by psychiatrists and psychologists to diagnose mental health disorders. Previous versions (such as the DSM-IV-TR) distinguished between Axis I and Axis II disorders. Simply put, an Axis I disorder was thought of as a disorder a person *had* whereas an Axis II disorder was thought of as a disorder of who that person *was*. The current DSM-5 has eliminated that distinction, but it is still the case that personality disorders (which used to be Axis II disorders) refer to who a person *is*, something that is a part of them.

As briefly discussed in Chapter 4, a personality disorder refers to an enduring pattern of thinking, interacting with others, and behavior that leads to distress on the part of that same individual (which is not common) or which is harmful or potentially harmful to that individual or the individuals around them (which is more common). In this context, *harm* can mean physical harm or may mean harmful in terms of occupation, social interactions, finances, and so forth. The DSM-5 distinguishes between ten different personality disorders, but for the purpose of the current chapter, we will focus on antisocial personality disorder, as this is the personality disorder most closely associated with violent and impulsive behavior toward others.

It could be argued that laws don't really prevent most people from engaging in criminal behavior. In all likelihood, a person with no criminal record could walk out of the grocery store with a cart full of food and, if caught, would likely receive little or no real legal consequences. Yet those of us with clean records seldom engage in such activities not because it is against the law but simply because we have been raised to believe that stealing (or assault, homicide, etc.) is wrong. But imagine if you didn't feel that way. Imagine if, for whatever reason, you did not feel there was anything wrong with taking the groceries without paying for them. Imagine if you felt no hesitation in harming others and no guilt after doing so. If you were truly unconcerned about anything other than what was best for you at that moment, it might lead you to behave in a very different (and less law-abiding!) manner.

Such is the individual with **antisocial personality disorder**. Such individuals are motivated by doing what they believe will serve them best, regardless of the impact it may have on others. To them, the world is a dog-eat-dog one and if they do not take advantage of others, it means that others must be taking advantage of them—an unacceptable option as far as they are concerned. Such individuals have a markedly diminished (or in some cases, completely absent) sense of guilt and/or remorse. They may be convincing liars and their motivation in interacting with others is frequently to obtain whatever they believe is in their own best interest. Not surprisingly, such individuals come into contact with the legal system with some frequency. Fazel and Danesh (2002) found 47% of those incarcerated to be diagnosed with antisocial personality disorder, but such contacts (and even harsh penalties and incarceration) often appear to make little difference in terms of changing their behavior. When individuals with antisocial personality disorder are caught and punished for their misdeeds, they may not think, "I made a mistake by committing that crime, and I'm not going to commit another crime in the future." Instead, such individuals may instead think, "I made a mistake that led me to get caught. In the future, when I commit a crime, I have to be more careful so that I don't get caught."

Alcohol and Other Drugs

Seldom does one watch an action movie in which there is not a bar scene where the main character/hero of the story is accosted and forced to fight a drunken and obnoxious bar patron; the perceived connection between being intoxicated on alcohol or drugs and physical violence is well-established. Unlike many other Hollywood stories, however, this one does have evidence to back it up.

The Bureau of Justice Statistics tells us that in 2005, there were more than 750,000 crimes that were tied to drug or alcohol intoxication. A study of numerous other studies (referred to as a *meta-meta-analysis*) showed a consistent and significant relationship between drug and alcohol use and intoxication and the commission of violent offenses (Duke et al., 2018). In fact, they found that 48% of all homicide offenders had alcohol in their systems at the time they committed an offense, and this finding was especially true for men. Such a finding supports an earlier claim by Fagan (1990) that alcohol may be the substance that is most likely to be associated with violent behavior; whether this is due to the unique chemical effects of alcohol or merely the fact that alcohol is more readily available than many illegal substances is not clear.

As with factors mentioned already (and with those yet to come!), it cannot be said that the use of alcohol and other substances directly and invariably leads to violent behavior. There are people who use such substances and refrain from engaging in violence or other criminal acts, but the increased probability of such behaviors when an individual is under the influence seems clear. It is worth noting that not only drug use but even buying and selling drugs is often associated with violent acts. In the mid-1980s, for example, crack cocaine became extremely popular among drug users, and homicide rates increased dramatically during this time (Goldstein et al., 1989). Such incidents are not unique to crack cocaine or any particular drug. During periods of addiction, heroin users demonstrate markedly increased rates of assault, robbery, and burglary as they attempt to obtain money to fuel their addiction and stave off the physical misery of withdrawal from this substance (Ball, 1982).

CLINICAL VERSUS ACTUARIAL PREDICTION OF VIOLENCE

Imagine you are a 17-year-old high school student and you've saved up enough money to buy a car (maybe even a red one!). You call up an insurance company so that you will be covered in the event of an accident only to find out that the insurance is going to cost you as much per year (or more!) than the car itself. Frustrated, you ask your parents how much they are paying for insurance, but this only adds to your frustration, as you find out that they are paying a tiny fraction of the amount that you would be charged. Naturally, you wonder why—does the insurance company not like you or is there some reason that they are charging you so much more?

The above is an example of clinical versus actuarial prediction: Does the insurance company have a subjectively bad feeling that you are going to wreck your car (clinical prediction) or do they actually have a reason to believe that you are at high risk of doing so (actuarial prediction)? As it turns out, the insurance company has an excellent reason for charging a 17-year-old more than their parent; the data is clear that 16- and 17-year-olds are 4.5 times more likely to be involved in an accident than their 40- to 49-year-old parents are (Tefft, 2017).

Examples of clinical versus actuarial prediction occur frequently in forensic settings: A judge must set bail for a man accused of a violent offense. The judge wonders where they should set the defendant's bail; if this individual is able to bail themself out of jail pending trial, what are the odds that they will commit another violent offense? The parole board is reviewing an incarcerated person for release into the community. This person has a history of an extremely violent offense but has been a model inmate for nearly 20 years; if released, what is the likelihood that they will live peaceably in the community? These are important questions and highlight the difficulty and importance of predicting future violent acts.

It is not uncommon for forensic psychologists and psychiatrists to be asked to assist in making such predictions. Unfortunately, such professionals do not have the crystal ball that others sometimes expect them to have in terms of being able to predict the future. How then can such judgments be made?

Although the individuals mentioned above may state that such a prediction is based on their professional opinion, the key word in such a statement is *opinion*. Clinical prediction of violence is based on that clinician's experience, belief, and even intuition (often a "gut feeling" based on however many years of experience they have). Of course, they believe (and would have us do the same) that given the hundreds of books that they have read, the numerous classes they have taken, the multiple diplomas hanging on their office wall, and their years of experience, that their judgments will be reasonably (or extremely) accurate. Unfortunately, as we will see below, clinical predictions are less accurate than we might hope them to be. Furthermore, there is no reason to believe that clinical judgment improves over time. After all, opinion is still opinion.

Actuarial predictions rely not on opinion but rather on evidence-based research, using factors that have been mathematically determined to be the best predictors of future behavior. Numerous studies suggest that actuarial prediction of violence is more accurate than clinical prediction. Grove et al. (2000) found statistical prediction of violence to be 10% more accurate than clinical prediction. This was later underscored by another study that suggested that in 1,000 such predictions, actuarial prediction accurately predicts 90 more violent clients than does clinical prediction (Ægisdóttir et al., 2006) and clinicians who ignore actuarial scores do so to their detriment. Unlike clinical judgment, which does not necessarily improve over time, actuarial approaches (based on research and evidence) can and do improve over time as research continues and new evidence is obtained.

One of the most frequent and most difficult tasks faced by some forensic psychologists is the prediction of future violent behavior. The question may be asked by a judge, the parole board, or many other officials, but the question is always the same: "If we let this person out into the community, are they going to be safe or are they going to hurt someone else?" This is obviously an incredibly difficult question to answer, and the price for being wrong is high indeed; if the psychologist determines that the person in question will be violent when released but that is not accurate, we have someone locked up who does not need to be. On the other hand, if the psychologist assures the referring agency that the individual is no threat to the community and is wrong, someone may be harmed.

The Violence Risk Assessment Guide–Revised (VRAG–R) is a well-documented and empirically supported example of an actuarial instrument for assessing the risk of future violence among males who have previously engaged in a violent act. The VRAG–R is a 12-item actuarial measure that takes into account factors such as the individual's score on the revised psychopathy checklist (more about that in Chapter 7), a history of early school maladjustment, the diagnosis of a personality disorder, age, a history of early separation from parents, and failures on prior releases, among other factors, in order to provide an actuarial prediction of that person engaging in future violent behavior. While there is unfortunately no crystal ball that will allow clinicians to predict future violence with 100% accuracy, actuarial measures such as the VRAG–R are extremely useful and show great promise in helping to improve clinician accuracy in this regard.

THROUGH THE EYES OF THE VICTIM

It is vitally important for forensic psychologists and law enforcement to understand and appreciate the significant emotional impact on the victim of being physically, sexually, or emotionally abused. The author has listened to numerous offenders state that they "just pointed a gun at [their victim]; no one got hurt" or that the victim "was fine [and] didn't need to go to the hospital or anything." Such statements demonstrate a callous indifference toward the victim. It is difficult to imagine the emotions experienced by an individual who has a loaded gun pointed in their face or who has been choked and unable to breathe. Although no lasting physical injury may have transpired, it is likely that the victim and their family may suffer significant and lasting trauma after such an episode.

The impact of being a victim of violent crime is difficult to predict; people's responses to such unfortunate circumstances are highly individual and variable (Wasserman & Ellis, 2010). The consequences may be quantifiable, such as losses of property or income, lost wages due to missing work, or medical bills associated with injuries that were sustained as a result of being victimized. In some cases, the consequences are much more difficult to quantify. Many of those who have been directly or indirectly affected by violent crime experience emotional changes; feelings of sadness and anxiety are common and may last long enough or become pronounced enough to warrant a clinical diagnosis. Some victims experience changes in cognition after being victimized. That is, some no longer trust other people or may blame themselves for being victimized; others may experience racing thoughts, difficulty concentrating, or impairment in memory. Still others may experience behavioral changes and may isolate themselves, increase their use of alcohol and other drugs, or find themselves struggling to go to school or work or even to perform the basic activities of everyday living.

It is vitally important for forensic practitioners to recognize that each victim will respond differently to their circumstances and that there is no right or wrong way for them to respond. Similarly, there is no specific period of time for which we can expect the symptoms of their victimization to last. Some people appear to return to their baseline level of functioning fairly quickly, though it is important to remember that though they *appear* to be back to normal, this may not actually be the case internally for them. Other people's recovery process after being victimized may be lengthy indeed. All victims should be treated with the utmost respect and dignity, understanding that their journey after having been victimized is a unique one and one that must be treated with great compassion and empathy by those around them.

CONCLUSION

In all likelihood, acts of aggression and violence by humans have occurred for as long as the race itself has existed. From the times of Cesare Lombroso and Phineas Gage, we have speculated about and attempted to explain and predict such behavior: Who becomes violent and when and why? The answers, as we have seen in this chapter, are more complicated than many would like to believe. Physical factors such as hormone levels and brain structure play a role, but so do social factors such as observing and imitating what is seen on television and movies and in real life. Environmental factors such as upbringing and substance abuse play contributing roles, as do personality factors. As with other human behaviors, violence and aggression remain a complex puzzle deserving of continued study.

Exercises and Discussion Questions

1. Some people would argue that violent video games desensitize the player to acts of violence, making them more prone to engage in actual violent behavior themselves. Others would argue that such games have no such influence and might contend that violent video games are a healthy way of expressing anger and might even decrease the probability of the player engaging in acts of violence. Do you believe such video games increase, decrease, or have no impact on actual violence? Explain your position.

2. IPV is an all-too-common and very serious problem. What specific actions do you think could be taken by society, law enforcement, support agencies, and others to protect victims and decrease the frequency and severity of such instances?

3. Child abuse and neglect is another very difficult topic discussed in this chapter. In your opinion, what can schools, parents, and society do to attempt to reduce the frequency and impact of child abuse and neglect?

4. Both biological factors (such as testosterone and the development of the prefrontal cortex) and social factors (such as modeling) may contribute to violent behavior. Given that we likely cannot alter the biological factors, what steps do you think we could take in terms of social factors or programs to help decrease the frequency of violent behavior, especially in young men?

5. The mentally ill are often unfairly characterized by the public as being especially unpredictable and dangerous to others. What do you think could be done by individuals, groups, or society to help change this stereotype, advocate for those with mental illness, and provide the public with more accurate information?

KEY TERMS

Abduction

Aggravated assault

Aggression

Antisocial personality disorder

Child abuse

Emotional aggression

First-degree homicide

Forcible rape

Hate crimes/bias crimes

Instrumental aggression

Intimate partner violence (IPV)

Inveiglement

Kidnapping

Neglect

Personality

Robbery

Second-degree homicide

Simple assault

Testosterone

Third-degree homicide

6 SEXUAL ASSAULT, RAPE, AND CHILD MOLESTATION

LEARNING OBJECTIVES

1. Define sexual assault and rape and be able to discuss the frequency of such offenses as well as the reasons that such offenses are often not reported.

2. Define and distinguish between paraphilias and paraphilic disorders.

3. Discuss the procedures for psychological assessment of sex offenders and the treatments available to such offenders.

4. Explain Megan's Law and the Adam Walsh Act and discuss whether they are effective in deterring further offending.

5. Review the symptoms of post-traumatic stress disorder and discuss the manner in which victims of sex offenses may experience and (hopefully) overcome such symptoms over time.

"No was not an acceptable word to say to me at that point in my life. Man, woman, or child, I didn't want to hear that word coming out of your mouth. If you said that word to me, something bad was going to happen to you. That's just how it was back then, and the people who knew me knew not to say that word to me. She did say, 'No' so, well . . ." He then shrugged his shoulders, his face displaying not a hint of remorse or regret. He said nothing about the fact that he later pled guilty to aggravated assault and aggravated indecent assault after brutally raping and beating his victim, a single mother in her mid-20s.

INTRODUCTION AND DEFINITIONS

The word *rape* comes from the Latin "rapere" meaning "to take away by force." In regard to sexual behavior, **consent** means that a person is of age and capable of making an informed, voluntary, and willing decision to engage in sexual activity. Consent should never be assumed, even if one has consented to sexual activity on past occasions with that same partner. If an individual is coerced, manipulated, threatened, intimidated, or physically forced to engage in sexual behavior, that is *not* consent. Silence does not equal consent, so a lack of resistance or the fact that a partner did not say "No" does not equal consent. A person who is under the influence of drugs or alcohol to such an extent that they cannot make informed decisions cannot consent to sex. An individual who is unconscious for any reason (for example, sleeping or unconscious due to a medical condition) or impaired for any reason including, but not limited to, the use of alcohol or other drugs is not legally able to give consent.

Although definitions vary by state, **rape** is generally defined as sexual intercourse by force or by forcible compulsion; that is, by force or by threat of force that would cause a reasonable person to believe that their life or the life of a loved one would be in danger if they were to resist. **Indecent assault** is generally thought of as the touching of a private area of a non-consenting and/or underage individual's body, either over their clothes or under their clothes. **Aggravated indecent assault** involves penetration, no matter how slight, of a non-consenting and/or underage individual's mouth, vagina, or anus with any part of the perpetrator's body or a with a foreign object that is not part of a medical procedure or good-faith hygienic procedure. A gynecologist performing a legitimate vaginal examination is not engaged in a sexual offense. A parent cleaning their infant's genitals after they have soiled their diaper is not engaged in a sexual offense. A man forcing a woman to engage in sexual intercourse is engaging in a sexual offense.

Nearly one in five women (18.3%) and almost one in 71 men (1.4%) report having been raped during their lifetime (Black et al., 2011). This glaring discrepancy—1 in 5 versus 1 in 71—is referred to as a **differential risk**: an area in which one group (in this case, women) is at distinctly greater risk than another (men). Thus, the total number of women in the United States (U. S.) who report having been raped in their lifetime is a staggering 22 million.

Additionally, nearly one in three women and more than one in six men have experienced sexual violence other than rape, totaling approximately 53 million females and 25 million males in the U. S. (Smith et al., 2017). In addition to rape, 13% of women and 6% of men report having experienced unforced sexual coercion. That is, they were not physically forced but were coerced to engage in sexual activity that they did not consent to. Sex offenses are perpetrated far more often by males than females. The Bureau of Justice Statistics (1997) found that 99% of forcible rapes were committed by male offenders, and fully 92% of other sexual offenses were committed by males, leaving only 1% of forcible rapes and 8% of other offenses being committed by female offenders. When males are raped, the perpetrators are most often male as well (Centers for Disease Control and Prevention, 2021).

Despite the incredibly serious nature and the profound physical and emotional consequences that sexual assaults inflict, many victims are reluctant to report having been assaulted in such a manner. Indeed, a 2016 report from the U.S. Department of Justice indicated that nearly 80% of sexual assaults go unreported (Morgan & Kena, 2016). There are likely numerous explanations for such reluctance. As we shall see in this chapter, the vast majority of sexual assault victims know their assailant (Koss & Burkhart, 1989) and they may be concerned that if they report the offense, the offender will seek revenge, perhaps in the form of another offense and/or additional violence. It is common for those who have been sexually assaulted to be emotionally traumatized by their experience (Chivers-Wilson, 2006). Such individuals cannot be blamed for not wanting to think about, talk about, or report their victimization to others; such a choice is a highly personal one. Victims may be embarrassed to talk to police, hospital staff, or others about such a personal and traumatic experience. They may wish to avoid at all costs the public spectacle of having to sit on the witness stand and speak in detail about their experience to a room full of strangers and in front of the accused themselves. Some victims may experience feelings of guilt or may worry that in court, the defense will imply that they were in some way at fault or contributed to the offense that occurred. Concern that cross-examination will imply that their consumption of alcohol, their choice of clothing, or other factors played a role in their victimization may make many victims choose to decide not to report or pursue charges after having been sexually assaulted. For all of these reasons (and more), victims may choose not to report having been sexually abused, and it is important that the forensic practitioner be aware that for every sexual assault that is reported, an untold number occur but are not reported.

It is often believed that most sex offenders were victims of sexual abuse themselves, leading to a cycle of victim-to-victimizer. However, the evidence does not support this as a widespread pattern. Glasser et al. (2001) studied nearly 750 males and found that 35% of those who perpetrated sex offenses reported having been victims of sexual abuse themselves, while 11% of those who had not perpetrated sex offenses reported having been so victimized. Thus, they concluded that the cycle of victim-to-victimizer is only present in a minority of male offenders, and they found no evidence of such a cycle in female offenders. Plummer and Cossins (2016) found no evidence for a cycle of abuse among females who had been abused but did find this to be the tendency for males who had been abused. The common theme among males who had been abused and later became abusers themselves, they argued, is the feeling of power experienced by the abuser and the powerlessness of the abused. Similarly, Milaniak and Widom (2016) found that males who had been neglected and abused were abused were more likely to become sexual abusers than were a control group who had not been neglected or abused. Remember that being sexually abused is only a risk factor for becoming a sex offender; that is, it may increase the probability of one becoming an offender but by no means is it the sole determining factor.

Fight, Flight, or Freeze

Physical force is not required for a finding of rape. The present author interviewed one offender who stated that he had never raped anyone, claiming that his victims were always consenting. He said, "I just asked them to take their clothes off. Then I asked them to perform a sex act on me. That's not rape. They could have said no." If his version is true (and it is certainly not clear that it is!), what this offender failed to realize or mention was the fact that he was 6'6" tall and weighed 350 pounds. His mere physical presence, even in the absence of threats, was extremely intimidating. When someone that size tells another person to do something, they may well feel compelled to do so even though they do not wish to. Such lack of resistance should not be interpreted as consent.

Many of us have heard of the "fight or flight" response (also referred to as the *acute stress response*) in which the brain sends a signal to the body to release massive amounts of adrenaline to activate the body by increasing heart rate, respiration, and blood pressure as well as mobilizing other bodily functions as part of preparing the individual to fight or to run in a life-threatening situation. However, there is one additional option available to the body: to freeze or hold absolutely still. As noted by Seltzer (2015), there are situations in which we are confident that neither fighting nor running will allow us to survive. Perhaps we are being attacked by a large, vicious dog. Our chances of fighting off or outrunning the dog are equally slim. In such a case, our body may respond by freezing. According to Seltzer, when we freeze, the assailant may lose interest in attacking us, and perhaps more importantly, we are doing everything we can to dissociate ourselves from the trauma of the experience. If we can't make the attacker go away, perhaps we can make ourselves go away by withdrawing into oneself as part of an effort to reduce or emotionally distance ourselves from the trauma. There are undoubtedly cases in which sexual assault victims freeze rather than fighting or fleeing, for the very reason that Seltzer notes. Such freezing is a survival mechanism and should not be interpreted as consent; it is anything but that. Furthermore, attempts by a defense attorney to suggest that a victim could have walked or run away or screamed for help have no merit and do a terrible injustice to the victim of such an offense.

THE DIFFERENCE BETWEEN NICE AND GOOD

When we hear the term *sex offender, rapist, child molester,* or *sexually violent predator,* some vivid image is likely to leap to mind. It's not unusual for us to equate such phrases with *monster, animal,* or some other word with the strongest possible negative connotations. Even among incarcerated offenders, who bear no grudge against murderers or drug dealers, rapists and child molesters are often looked down on and may have to seek protective custody in the institution to avoid the verbal taunts and possible victimization they might receive at the hands of other inmates. However, sex offenders are not animals or monsters, and equating them with monsters may be a mistake. We imagine monsters having green skin or three eyes or alien tentacles; they are clearly and obviously recognizable as something other than human. That would be a mistake when it comes to sex offenders. If those who commit sex offenses were so easy to recognize, doing so and reducing the frequency of sex offenses would be relatively easy. Many of those who commit sex offenders present as normal in many ways. Those who commit sex offenses come from all walks of life; they may work in the business world, wear nice clothes, have good hygiene, and go home to their family every night (Arizona Coalition to End Sexual and Domestic Violence, 2022).

In an alternate version of the popular fable "Little Red Riding Hood," Little Red is indeed fooled into thinking that the Big Bad Wolf is really her grandmother. Despite the abnormally large teeth and ears, Little Red gets too close to the Big Bad Wolf, who gobbles her up. A Woodsman, passing by, hears the commotion. Using his axe, he splits open the belly of the Wolf and Little Red emerges unscathed. The Woodsman asks Little Red, "Why would you get so close to the Wolf?" Little Red replies, "He seemed so nice!" The Woodsman sagely replies to her, "Little Red, *nice* is not the same as *good*." To a forensic psychologist (or a person trying to maintain their own safety), this statement is invaluable. Nice is *not* the same as good. Those who commit sex offenses can (and do) often act nice . . . and *act* is the key word. Sex offenses may be preceded by luring the victim away from others to an isolated location. Such manipulation is easier if the potential victim feels at ease and comfortable with the perpetrator. Behaviors such as smiling, laughing, and making eye contact are easily learned and purposefully demonstrated by many sex offenders in order to allow them an opportunity to commit their offenses. But neither these nor other seemingly friendly, engaging behaviors mean that the individual has good intentions. Niceness can be a choice rather than a quality of personality. Nice is not always the same as good.

In movies and on television, a rapist is often portrayed as a scary stranger, lurking in the shadows waiting to attack an unsuspecting victim as they pass by. As with many characterizations in the media, such an attack *can* happen, but sexual attacks by strangers are the exception rather than the rule. In fact, 51% of women who are raped are raped by a current or former intimate partner and an additional 41% are raped by an acquaintance (Black et al., 2011). That means that only 8% are raped by a stranger. Once again, we see that stranger danger can be a misnomer. Sadly, those we know are more likely to victimize us than a stranger is.

Noncontact sex offenses are those in which the offender demonstrates sexually inappropriate behavior without actually touching the victim. Examples of such offenses include the offender exposing their genitals to an unsuspecting victim ("flashing"), viewing a non-consenting person in various stages of undress ("peeping"), or giving unwanted sexual comments or harassing the victim. It is estimated that 1 in 10 Americans will be the victim of such offenses in their lifetime (Gold & Jeglic, 2017). It should be noted that such offenses may be reported even less frequently than contact sex offenses, as noncontact offenses may be considered less serious, nuisance offenses. However, some research suggests that such noncontact offenses can and do have a lasting impact on the victims (Clark et al., 2016).

Noncontact offenders tend to be highly recidivist (MacPherson, 2003). There are several possible explanations for the persistence of this behavior. First, because it is considered even by some victims to be a nuisance crime, noncontact offenses may often go unreported. Even when they are reported, incarceration for such offenses may be the exception rather than the rule.

Thus, many such offenders may receive little or no punishment (or treatment for that matter) and therefore continue to engage in such behaviors. In the experience of the present author, noncontact offenders such as exhibitionists are often looking for a reaction from their victims. When they do not get the reaction they are hoping for, they offend again, hoping that the next time they do so they will get the desired reaction. However, when they *do* get the reaction they are looking for, this reinforces their behavior and they repeat the offense. Thus, their maladaptive behavior seems to be reinforced regardless of whether the victim responds in the manner the offender intended.

SEX OFFENDER TYPOLOGIES

Many classifications and typologies of sex offenders have been proposed over the years. Nicholas Groth (1979, pp. 44–45), whose work focused exclusively on male sex offenders, proposed a typology of four varieties of rapists: power-reassurance, power-assertive, anger-retaliatory, and sadistic. According to this typology, the power-reassurance rapist had poor social skills and hoped through his offense to obtain some type of reassurance that he was a "real man." According to Groth, although such offenders typically do use force to commit the sexual act, they use only enough force to complete that act and no more. The power-assertive rapist, on the other hand, is more aggressive than required to overcome the resistance of the victim. Such an offender commits the offense impulsively and often has a weapon in order to obtain compliance and/or inflict additional damage on his victim. The anger-retaliatory rapist in this typology wants to assert his power and dominance over his victim and often attempts to achieve this goal by degrading or humiliating his victim in some way. The rarest of Groth's typology was the sadistic rapist. Such an individual is aroused by inflicting pain and damage on others and may inflict extensive damage or kill his victim in the course of the offense. That such individuals can be incredibly dangerous is likely no surprise.

A common thread that we see in the Groth typologies is that of power and control. It is tremendously important for the student studying forensic psychology to not get so caught up in the labels *sex offense* and *sex offender* that they believe that such offenses are committed primarily for the sexual satisfaction of the offender. In fact, a desire for power and control appears to be primary in the commission of this type of offense (Beesley, 2017). Offenders' motivation in committing these offenses is much more closely tied to inflicting emotional and physical pain on their victim and often involves degrading and/or humiliating the victim in some way as an expression of that desire for power and control (Arizona Coalition to End Sexual and Domestic Violence, 2022). In this chapter, we will see that regardless of typology, the desire of offenders to feel powerful and in control is near-universal in the commission of these offenses.

Lanyon (1986) distinguished between preference molesters (pedophiles) and situational offenders. The former have a strong sexual attraction to children and offend against them based on that attraction. As the name implies, such offenders prefer sexual activity with minors to such activity with adults. Situational offenders, on the other hand, prefer a consenting adult partner, but if/when the opportunity presents itself to have sex with a child, they may very well do so. Lanyon's classification of preference molesters/pedophiles versus situational offenders makes a great deal of sense. During his time treating those who had committed sex offenses against children, it was often the present author's experience to hear them describe in graphic detail what they perceived as the sexually attractive elements of a small child. As difficult as such descriptions may be for others to hear and comprehend, these individuals clearly find children to be sexually attractive. This is typically referred to as a **deviant arousal pattern**, meaning that for that offender, they are sexually aroused by stimuli that are highly unusual compared to the prevailing social norms, that are illegal, and that will cause harm to others if/when these urges are acted upon (Hanson & Morton-Bourgon, 2005).

Lanyon's conceptualizations of preferential and situational offenders are consistent with the experience of the present author. For some offenders, sexual acts with a child or non-consenting adult are their preference. Quite simply, they are sexually attracted to children or to the idea of a non-consenting adult partner. With such individuals, it should come as no surprise that they often have multiple convictions for such offenses and very few or minor offenses for nonsexual crimes. Given that this is their preferred means of offending, they may plan such offenses ahead of time and may take with them the "tools of the trade" that they use to commit such offenses: duct tape, zip ties, weapons, or other such implements.

Situational offenders, on the other hand, can and do at times have sex with consenting adult partners. However, when the opportunity to have sex with a child or with a non-consenting partner presents itself, they may take advantage of that opportunity. The present author has spoken to a number of offenders who spoke convincingly of intending to burglarize a residence, but when they found the residence to be occupied, they decided to sexually assault the occupant as well. Such offenders are likely to have a wide variety of offenses as part of their criminal record, with sexual offenses sprinkled in among the others. As opportunistic offenders commit sexual assaults impulsively, they seldom bring weapons or implements of restraint with them to the scene of the crime but rather will use weapons or improvise means of restraint from what is available to them at the scene.

Acquaintance Rape

Acquaintance rape is a relatively broad category, encompassing all forms of rape and sexual assault committed by a perpetrator who is known to the victim. The offender can be a coworker, a neighbor, a counselor, or a (supposed) friend. One in four female college students have reported being the victim of a rape, attempted rape, or other sexual assault (Cullen et al., 2000). In 84% of these cases, the victim and offender knew each other (Koss & Burkhart, 1989). As previously discussed, rapes occur far more often than they are reported, and this appears to be especially the case when the victim and offender know each other; according to the U.S. Department of Justice (1993), acquaintance rapes make up less than 2% of all rapes that are reported to the police. The victim may be concerned that the offender, who knows them, will seek out revenge if reported to police by the victim. It is also possible that the victim is concerned that they will not be believed, especially if the offender has some status in the community, or that the victim themselves may be blamed in part or even in whole for the offense that was committed against them.

Date Rape

Date rape is a subcategory of acquaintance rape in which the individuals are involved in some sort of romantic or potentially sexual relationship, whether it be a first date, a long-term relationship, or something in between the two. Date rapes are thought to be among the most common forms of rape (Hammond et al., 2011), with at least one study suggesting that nearly 17% of all rapes are date rapes (Jenkins & Petherick, 2014). Such rapes may involve psychological manipulation, intimidation, and/or physical coercion or force. It is important to understand that date rapes may involve knowing or unknowing consumption of alcohol or other drugs by the victim. It is vitally important for the forensic psychologist to understand that in either of these cases, such consumption does not mean that the victim was in any way to blame or responsible for the offense committed against them. For example, the offender may be giving the victim a greater quantity or potency of alcohol than the victim expects or may be adding drugs to that alcohol without the knowledge or consent of the victim (Smith, 2004, p. 54). Medications such as fluni-trazepam (brand name Rohypnol, sometimes referred to as "roofies") and other sedative drugs may result in the victim being semiconscious or unconscious and therefore unable to consent to sex or to resist being sexually assaulted. Such medications may also make it difficult or impossible for the victim to recall the offense. Generally, date rapes are thought to be motivated by sexual desire on the part of the offender, and the offender (but not the victim) often views their own actions as seduction rather than rape (Chancellor, 2012, p. 167).

Although we may think of rape as a crime committed by a stranger, many rapes are committed in the context of a dating relationship.

istock/ Anton Novikov

Prison Rape

In television series such as HBO's *Oz* or in movies such as *Shawshank Redemption*, it is portrayed as fairly commonplace for one inmate (or a group of inmates) to rape another inmate, and it seems to be a common belief that such offenses occur on a near-daily basis. Perhaps due to this belief, the Prison Rape Elimination Act was signed into law in 2003. The purpose of this law was to require federal, state, and local jails and prisons to collect and report data related to sexual offenses committed within these correctional systems. The ultimate goal, of course, was the reduction of (and ideally, the elimination of) sex offenses perpetrated in the correctional system and to enhance the safety of those who are incarcerated from being victimized themselves. A survey conducted by the Bureau of Justice Statistics in 2013 demonstrated that approximately 4% of prison inmates and 3% of jail inmates reported having been the victim of a sexual assault while they were incarcerated.

CHILD SEXUAL ABUSE AND MOLESTATION

"I had no idea how old she was, Doc. You know how kids are these days. You know how they dress. Hell, she told me she was 19. How was I supposed to know that she was 12? She looked 19 to me, the way she dressed, the way her body was developed."

Regardless of the above statement made by a convicted sex offender, a claim not to know the age of the victim is of little or no use in a legal defense, except in very rare circumstances. For example, if the offender met the underage victim while both were drinking in a bar, it is conceivable that this could serve as a defense in terms of believing the victim was older. Otherwise, such a defense is no more likely to be successful than telling a police officer that you were speeding because you didn't know what the speed limit is. When engaging in sexual acts, it is the responsibility of both individuals to be certain that each is of the age of consent as well as fully consenting.

Statutory rape is generally defined as an adult having sexual intercourse or other sexual contact with a person who is under the age of consent. The age of consent does vary by state in the U. S. and varies considerably in other countries. In the U. S., the youngest age of consent is 16 years old, while some states set the age of consent at 17 or 18 years of age. While force may be considered, the primary consideration in statutory rape is the age of the perpetrator and the victim. Thus, in states with an age of consent of 16 years old, someone who is 16 or older may legally consent to sex with someone of any age. One exception to this is that even if they are of the age of consent, there can be no consent when the other partner is in a position of power over them. For example, in a state where the age of consent is 16, it would still be considered a sex offense if that 16-year-old was having sex with a high school teacher where they were attending school, as that teacher is in a position of power and influence over the student.

Someone under the age of consent cannot ordinarily consent to sex with anyone, and an individual who has sex with someone who is under the age of consent would be charged with statutory rape. As noted above, force (if used) can be considered, but even if there is no resistance on the part of the underage individual, the person who had sexual contact with that young person would be charged with statutory rape.

It should be noted that some states have a close in age exemption, also known as a "Romeo and Juliet law," that states if one (or both) of the two people engaged in sexual contact are within a designated number of years in age, and neither is being forced or coerced, statutory rape will not be charged. For example, in Pennsylvania, the age of sexual consent is 16 years old and the close in age exemption states that if the two participants are within four years of age, then no statutory rape charges will be filed. In such a state, a 17-year-old (of legal age of consent) and a 15-year-old (under the legal age of consent) who are having sex would not be charged with statutory rape, as long as neither of them was being forced or coerced, given that their ages are within four years of each other. That same 17-year-old having sex with a 12-year-old, however, would be charged with statutory rape, given the age difference of more than four years. These statutes vary by state; for example, Oregon has 18 years as the age of consent and a three-year close in age exemption, and Idaho has 18 years as the age of consent with no close in age exemption (Guideline Law, 2022).

Child sexual abuse is defined by David Finkelhor (1984) as involving the use of force or coercion in order to engage in sexual activity with a victim younger than 13 years old when the perpetrator was at least five years older or with a victim 13–16 years old when the offender is at least 10 years older than the victim. The perpetrators of such acts are overwhelmingly male, with fully 96% of such crimes committed by males (National Sexual Violence Resource Center, 2011).

Child pornography is defined by the U.S. Department of Justice (2015) as any sexually provocative depiction of a minor (less than 18 years of age). The age of consent in a particular state is not relevant, and the minor does not need to be engaged in sexual activity for the depiction to be considered pornography, as long as that depiction is sexually suggestive.

Grooming refers to actions taken by a sex offender to maximize their chances of being able to commit a sex offense against a child. Often this involves special favors, treatment, or gifts. Taking the child to a special event, letting them out of school early, or buying them their favorite toy are all common means of currying favor with a potential victim. Furthermore, such actions purposefully take advantage of a social rule that predators are very much familiar with: the so-called norm of reciprocity. Quite simply, when someone extends us a favor or gift, we feel a strong desire to repay their kindness in one way or another (Whatley et al., 1999). We see this on a daily basis: It comes as little surprise that after complimenting a friend's outfit, they respond by telling us that they love our hairstyle. It is a simple but powerful social rule; we don't like to be in someone's debt. We want to return favors. Grooming takes advantage of this tendency. The offender realizes that doing favors for their victim creates a debt in the mind of the victim—a debt that the victim may later feel compelled to repay by compliance with the offender's request for sexual favors or for secrecy on the behalf of the victim.

Those who offend against children may be careful and well-planned in setting up their offense. They may "coincidentally" walk their dog across the path the child takes coming home from the school bus stop to provide an excuse to talk. Some children have their name or initials stitched on their backpack; if they do, the offender will notice and perhaps call the child by name. Others may wear a shirt with their favorite superhero or pop star on it; again, the offender will notice, and this may give them grounds for striking up an "innocent" conversation. In one case in the experience of the author, the offender who made sure to introduce his victim to his dog one day showed up with an empty collar and leash, asking his victim to help him search for the dog, who he claimed had run away. Unfortunately, this ruse worked and the child was victimized.

Grooming may include a conscious effort on the part of the offender to acclimatize the victim to being touched by the offender. Brief episodes of tickling, wrestling, or hugging may be used by the offender in order to allow the victim to become gradually accustomed to being touched by the offender. Planned involvement in activities that allow one to be unclothed or partially clothed such as swimming, bathing, or showering may also be part of a conscious effort by the offender to manipulate the victim into being comfortable in such a state with the offender.

MEGAN'S LAW AND THE ADAM WALSH ACT

Jesse Timmendequas was already a convicted sex offender when he lured 7-year-old Megan Kanka into his house in Hamilton Township, New Jersey. He subsequently assaulted her, raped her, and strangled her to death, confessing to this crime the very next day. The public shock and outrage that such a thing could happen was both predictable and understandable. In 1994, soon after the murder, **Megan's Law** became federal law, requiring that sex offenders register their address with local law enforcement agencies and that the community be provided with information about that offender. Although it varies a bit by state, Megan's Law typically requires that the offender provide (and the community must have access to) their name, the address at which they reside, their photograph, their place of employment, the type of offense that they have committed, and (in some cases) the make and model of the car they drive. The manner in which this information is made available to the public also varies; sometimes it is posted on social media, the state police website, or in newspapers or pamphlets.

Adam Walsh was also seven years old in 1981 and was standing in front of a Sears department store in Hollywood, Florida, when he was lured into a car, assaulted, and eventually decapitated. Serial killer Ottis Elwood Toole eventually confessed to the murder but later recanted and was never convicted in this offense. John Walsh, Adam's father, went on to host the television program *America's Most Wanted*, which provided viewers with details of unsolved offenses and encouraged them to report anything they might know that would aid in the apprehension of a particular offender. In 2006, the Adam Walsh Child Protection and Safety Act was passed, supplementing Megan's Law sex offender registration requirements and implementing a three-tier system for classifying sex offenders in which the offenders considered most dangerous (Tier 3) must update their address with local law enforcement every 90 days and must continue to do so for life.

Public outrage at the sexual abuse and murder of these and other children is entirely understandable, as is the fact that the laws were subsequently passed with the goal of preventing such tragedies from happening again. But do Megan's Law and the **Adam Walsh Act** actually achieve those goals? It is not entirely clear that they do. Both the Office of Justice Programs and the Association for the Treatment of Sexual Abusers note that research on the effectiveness of such laws in decreasing the incidence of sexual abuse and violence is mixed (Association for the Treatment of Sexual Abusers, 2010; Office of Justice Programs, 2012). Common sense would tell us that knowing the address of such an offender, their place of employment, or the type of car they drive will not necessarily have any role in preventing them from committing another offense. Furthermore, it could be argued that community notification will make it more difficult for such an offender to obtain housing and employment and therefore might increase rather than decrease the recidivism rate of such offenders. Although many Megan's Law websites require users to click on a button indicating that they agree not to harm or harass anyone listed on that site, the possibility of people seeking vigilante justice cannot be ruled out. Lastly, those who are convicted of homicide (even multiple homicides) in the absence of a sex offense are not required to register their whereabouts with law enforcement and no notification is made to the community that a convicted murderer has moved in, so it could be deemed unfair or excessive that this is required of sex offenders.

PARAPHILIAS AND PARAPHILIC DISORDERS

People find a wide variety of qualities and characteristics to be sexually arousing. Some may prefer a partner with a certain color of hair or body type. Others may be physically attracted to someone with a good sense of humor or a charismatic smile. Still others may desire a partner who cares deeply for them and shares similar interests. We may (or may not) know why we find such qualities attractive, but we do, and it seems likely that it would be difficult to change such attractions. One can certainly fall in love with someone whose hair color is not the color they are attracted to, but it seems unlikely that they would lose their attraction to people with that color of hair.

The term **paraphilia** refers to an intense and persistent sexual interest other than sexual activity with a consenting adult partner. A paraphilia may involve sexual arousal to nonsexual activities (such as vomiting or eating) or it may involve sexual arousal to nonsexual objects (such as shoes or cars). Indeed, the line between paraphilia and simple sexual preference for a particular activity or object can be blurry. Most importantly, what distinguishes a *paraphilia* from a *paraphilic disorder* is that the paraphilia does not cause distress to the individual and is not harming them or anyone else in any way. Becoming sexually aroused by watching someone eat or by rubbing a shoe on oneself is simply a paraphilia as long as it is practiced with a consenting, adult partner (or no partner) and/or it is clearly not disruptive, harmful, or upsetting to anyone in any way.

A paraphilia crosses the line into a **paraphilic disorder** in one of two cases: First, when it causes significant distress to the individual with that persistent sexual desire. If it greatly bothers the individual that they are sexually aroused by watching others eating—if they wish to stop finding it arousing and they are trying to stop but cannot do so—then this would qualify as a paraphilic disorder because it causes that individual emotional distress. Alternatively, if the persistent sexual attraction is causing some type of harm (or risk of harm) to that individual or to others, then it has reached the clinical threshold of a paraphilic disorder. It is important to know that such harm includes (but is not limited to) physical harm, harm to relationships, financial harm, loss of job, and so forth. For example, if an individual goes to public places and stares at others who are eating and clearly becomes sexually aroused by doing so, scaring and upsetting those nearby, then this would qualify as a paraphilic disorder. It is upsetting to others and has the potential for harm (that individual getting arrested). Similarly, if an individual's partner decides to terminate their relationship because the individual seems to gain greater sexual satisfaction from items of clothing then they do from their partner, this would again qualify as a paraphilic disorder, as some discernible harm to that relationship has come from it.

The *Diagnostic and Statistical Manual of Mental Disorders* (5th edition; DSM-5) recognizes a number of paraphilic disorders. *Voyeuristic disorder* involves a recurrent and intense sexual desire to observe others in various stages of undress. Again, if practiced with an adult, consenting partner, then this is merely a paraphilia or perhaps even a simple preference. However, when it involves observing a non-consenting partner, it is by definition harmful to the victim. Furthermore, such acts can result in the arrest of the offender and therefore have potential for harm to the offender as well as to the victim, so this behavior rises to the level of a paraphilic disorder.

Exhibitionistic disorder involves the recurrent and intense sexual desire to expose oneself to others. Again, if this is practiced with a consenting adult partner, it is a simple preference or paraphilia. It is only when the individual is distressed by their own actions or when they are exposing themselves to a non-consenting individual that this would rise to the level of exhibitionistic disorder. Such self-exposure may be done overtly (dropping one's pants as a jogger goes by in the park) or the offender may claim it to be accidental. For example, they may claim that they happened to be naked when the mail delivery person came to the door or that their old gym shorts must have had a hole in them that they weren't aware of.

Frotteuristic disorder includes the recurrent and intense sexual desire to touch or rub up against a non-consenting partner. Once again, this is not problematic if practiced with a consenting adult partner. However, it does rise to the level of a disorder and is illegal when enacted upon a non-consenting individual. Often offenders do so by "accidentally" touching or rubbing up against someone in a crowded public place.

Sexual sadism disorder is demonstrated by a recurrent and intense desire to cause significant pain, and this desire is inflicted on a non-consenting partner or in some way is potentially harmful to that person or others. The individual with sexual sadism disorder derives sexual arousal from the infliction of significant pain or harm on a non-consenting partner. *Sexual masochism disorder* is the flip side of sexual sadism: With sexual masochism, the individual finds it sexually arousing to have pain or humiliation inflicted upon them, and this leads to distress on their behalf or is potentially harmful. Remember, two adult consenting partners who decide they wish to engage in bondage or spanking each other would not be considered to have either sexual sadism disorder or sexual masochism disorder as long as both were consenting and neither one was being harmed.

Pedophilic disorder involves a persistent and intense sexual attraction to children (generally 13 years of age or younger). As with the other paraphilias, pedophilic disorder would be diagnosed when it is distressing to the individual or when it is acted upon in any way. Of course, when sexual urges toward children are acted upon, these actions necessarily involve harm to the children who are victimized. Any sexual act with a child is non-consenting and is clearly harmful to that child in a wide variety of ways.

Sexually Violent Predators (SVPs)

A **sexually violent predator** (SVP) is generally defined as a person who has a mental or personality disorder that makes it likely that they will commit repeated sex offenses. Specifically, as defined by Section 6600 of the California Welfare and Institution Code, Article 4, an SVP is

> a person who has been convicted of a sexually violent offense against one or more victims and who has a diagnosed mental disorder that makes the person a danger to the health and safety of others in that it is likely that he or she will engage in sexually violent criminal behavior. (California Legislating Information, 1998)

It should be noted that this definition is not a clinical one but a legal one. During (or after) a trial, the court may request an evaluation of the offender in question for the purpose of determining whether they should be adjudicated as meeting criteria as an SVP. Such an evaluation is generally performed by one or more psychologists, psychiatrists, or other mental health professionals who are specifically trained in such assessment. These assessments will generally include an interview, use of measures including but not limited to the Static 99-R (which we will discuss a bit later in this chapter), and a careful review of any and all available records for that offender. Ultimately, the assessment will recommend for or against designation as an SVP, and a judge will make their decision based at least in part on that recommendation. Many factors may be taken into account when making such a recommendation, but prime among them are the details of the offense, the number of sex offenses, and prior adult and juvenile sex offenses.

At present, twenty states do allow SVPs who have been released from incarceration to be civilly committed to a psychiatric and/or sex offender treatment facility after their release from incarceration. While there has been some controversy in regard to this (after all, the offender has served their sentence of incarceration), it has been upheld as constitutional by the U.S. Supreme Court on multiple occasions, including *Kansas v. Hendricks* (1997). Objections have come from those who argue that it is impossible to predict with accuracy who will and who will not commit another sex offense after being released from incarceration in addition to the fact that once civilly committed, there are no specific criteria for if, when, and how that individual should eventually be released into the community.

SEX OFFENDER ASSESSMENT AND TREATMENT

In the movie *Minority Report*, it is the year 2054 and crime has been virtually eliminated thanks to the ability of three people who are able to see the future and predict crimes with incredible accuracy before those offenses occur. The "Precrime" unit then arrests the individuals before they can commit the crime, thus preventing the offense before it can happen. As implausible as this is, we would certainly like to be able to do so: to predict who is going to re-offend and to provide them with treatment or sufficient supervision to prevent such offenses from occurring. All too often, it seems that politicians, parole boards, and police hope that the forensic psychologist has a crystal ball that will allow them to predict who will re-offend and when. Certainly, prediction of future violence and/or sexual recidivism is an important but extremely difficult endeavor and, as we saw in Chapter 5 in our comparison of clinical versus actuarial prediction of violence, the subjective prediction of the clinician often comes up short compared to the actuarial prediction of an objective measure. With that in mind, let us take a look at the **Static-2002R**.

Assessment

The Static-99 was developed in 1999 by R. Karl Hanson and David Thornton as an actuarial measure of violent and sexual recidivism risk in adult male offenders who had already been charged with or convicted of a sex offense. The original version of this measure included ten static (unchanging) factors found to be correlated with sexual recidivism in adult males who had committed a sex offense. These factors included the age of the offender, whether they had ever lived with an intimate partner for two years or more, any history of noncontact sex offenses, and other factors (including several victim variables). The Static-99 was further developed and evolved into the Static-99R and then into the Static-2002R (Hanson & Thornton, 2003). The purpose of the most recent measure remains the same: to provide actuarial prediction of the risk of sexual recidivism in adult males who already have committed a sex offense. The Static-2002R now contains 14 items comprising five subcategories: age at release, persistence of sex offending, sexual deviance, relationship to victim, and general criminality. This measure should only be administered by a trained and certified practitioner and yields a score that places the offender in one of five risk categories for re-offending, from Level I (very low risk) to Level IVB (well above average risk) and allows the prediction of the likelihood of sexual recidivism over five-year and ten-year periods. Such actuarial prediction is invaluable in assisting with the assessment of future risk. It should be noted that the Static-2002R is only one such actuarial measure. Measures such as the Minnesota Sex Offender Screening Tool–Revised (MnSOST–R; Epperson et al., 1998) and the Sex Offender Risk Appraisal Guide (Quinsey et al., 2006) provide other options for actuarial prediction of sexual recidivism.

As discussed in Chapter 5, the Violence Risk Appraisal Guide–Revised (VRAG–R) is an actuarial instrument that may be used to aid in the prediction of future violence, including sexual violence in males who have already been convicted of violent acts. The VRAG–R consists of 12 items determined by statistical multiple regression to be the most effective in such a prediction. Those items include the offender's score on the revised psychopathy checklist, whether there is a history of early school maladjustment, the presence (or absence) of a personality disorder, and early separation from a parent or both parents. Also included on this measure are failures on prior conditional release, any history of nonviolent offenses, history of being married, history of (or absence of) schizophrenia, victim injury, history of alcohol abuse, and whether the offender committed violent acts against female victims. Similar to the Static-2002R, a thorough record review is needed when scoring the VRAG–R (Harris et al., 1993). Actuarial measures such as these are vitally important in sex offender assessment, as the following example illustrates.

I recall interviewing a sex offender who was soon to be seen by the parole board. I remembered him from being in my sex offender treatment group. He had done extremely well: His written assignments were timely, thorough, and insightful. He appeared to understand the impact of his offense on his victims, and he had a solid, detailed relapse prevention plan in the event that he was released. I reviewed his record and interviewed him. He had a thorough recall of everything he had learned in the group and appeared genuinely remorseful for his offense. After he left my office, I reviewed his file one more time, just to be sure, when I noticed something that I had not noticed before. His tested IQ was 144. This means that his IQ was in the Very Superior range; only about 2% of people in the world score that high. It is worth noting that this IQ test is administered days after their entry into the state prison system and they are certainly not at their best that day, so his true IQ could be even higher. That presented me with a very unique dilemma: Was this man so intelligent that he was truly able to incorporate and understand all that we had taught him during the nearly two years of sex offender treatment he had undergone, or was he simply brilliant enough to portray that image, despite having not benefited from treatment at all? It is a very difficult and important distinction indeed.

As we discussed in Chapter 5, it is important that the forensic psychologist not rely exclusively on clinical prediction but that they also make use of the actuarial tools that are available to them. Such measures can be especially helpful in challenging cases such as this.

Treatment

McGrath et al. (2010) found that more than 1,300 different sex offender groups were being run in the U. S. in 2008. Obviously, this makes room for innumerable approaches in clinical intervention, setting, and clientele. Given the devastating impact of being the victim of a sexual offense, the primary goal of any type of sex offender treatment is to reduce the probability of the offender committing another such act in the future. However, there are many different paths in the pursuit of this same goal, as we will see below.

Cognitive Behavioral Therapy

It was an average workday for me. Once a week, I conducted group therapy with about 10 sex offenders. Each and every member of the group had admitted to and been found guilty of at least one sex offense. The program that I was leading them in consisted of seven different phases or modules and lasted between 18 and 24 months. We hoped to help these offenders gain some insight into why they had committed their offenses and provide them with the skills necessary to avoid doing so again in the future. The point wasn't to change their attraction to young children or non-consenting partners into an attraction to consenting adults but rather to help them identify maladaptive thoughts and urges early and to provide them with coping skills so that they would not commit further such offenses. We were only a couple weeks into the year-and-a-half to two-year-long group when I said to them, "OK, if you are a sex offender, please raise your hand." All ten guys sat there with their hands folded . . . not a single hand went up. I waited. Then I pointed to one of them. "You're not a sex offender?" "No," he replied. "I only have one offense. A sex offender is somebody who has lots of offenses." I pointed to another group member. "How about you?" "Not me," he responded. "Sex offenders are child molesters. I can't stand them. My victim was an adult." I tried again. "How about you over there?" He didn't hesitate: "Man, I was so drunk I didn't know what I was doing. I mean, I did it, but I'm a drunk, not a pervert." This pattern repeated for the rest of the group, with each member providing some rationale or excuse for why the label sex offender *should not apply to them, despite the fact they had pled or been found guilty of such an offense. Such excuses or defenses are often referred to as* cognitive distortions, *meaning that the individual is bending their reality by thinking in an irrational manner.*

Yates (2013) notes the importance of following evidence-based practices and the use of cognitive behavioral therapy in this regard. **Cognitive behavioral therapy** is based upon the premise that our thoughts play a significant role in our emotions (Figure 6.1). For example, if you cut in line in front of me at the grocery store and I think you did it by accident, I may only be mildly put off by your actions. However, if my thought in regard to this event is that you did it on purpose and have taken advantage of me, I may feel far angrier. Our emotions, in turn, play an important role in our subsequent actions. Thus, if the thought that you cut in line by accident leads me to be only mildly irritated, I might calmly inform you that you cut in front of me or I might choose to do nothing. However, if the thought I have is that your actions were purposeful and intolerable and I therefore become angry, I might express myself loudly or even push my way back in front of you. Simply put, the premise of cognitive behavioral theory is that our thoughts influence our emotions, which in turn influence our actions. Cognitive behavioral therapy, then, hopes to help us to change our thinking to be more adaptive so that we experience different emotions and respond in a more adaptive manner. Indeed, Hanson et al. (2009) conducted a meta-analysis that demonstrated cognitive behavioral therapy to be more effective than other types of sex offender treatment and superior to criminal sanctions in terms of changing behavior.

FIGURE 6.1   ■   In cognitive behavioral therapy, it is believed that an individual's thoughts influence their emotions, which in turn play a role in determining that person's behavior. Their behavior then plays a role in future thoughts.

THOUGHTS
create Feelings

FEELINGS
create Behaviour

HELPS to CRACK the VICIOUS CYCLE of Negative Thinking and Feeling

Cognitive
Behavioral
Therapy

BEHAVIOUR
creates Thoughts

Artellia / Alamy Stock Vector

Sex offenders use a wide variety of cognitive distortions to justify (in their own minds) their actions. They may express the belief that they are "teaching the child about love," that exposing themselves to an unwilling other "isn't bad because I'm not even touching them," that a rape "didn't count because she was a stripper and a prostitute," or a wide variety of other excuses, rationalizations, or justifications. Cognitive behavioral therapy strives to teach offenders to recognize these cognitive distortions when they occur, to challenge such distortions, and to substitute more adaptive thoughts, with the hoped-for outcome being that they will then act in a more adaptive (and law-abiding) fashion and will not commit any further offenses.

Good Lives Model (GLM)

The Good Lives Model (GLM; Ward & Stewart, 2003) has been incorporated into some cognitive behavioral models. The GLM is a strength-based program tailored to a particular offender's needs. This strength-based approach recognizes that the individual has relative strengths: some quality or ability that is relatively well-developed in that individual. Rather than focusing on the sex offender as an evil person or a monster comprised only of deficits and defects of character, the GLM focuses on what person is good at and at how that strength can be used to help them meet their own needs in some sort of adaptive, prosocial manner. For example, we may find that one offender has very limited intellect and social skills but has a relative abundance of empathy. In such a case, we may focus treatment on helping that individual to understand the true emotional impact of sex offenses on the victim, thereby using that offender's strength (empathy and compassion) to motivate them to not harm anyone else in such a manner in the future.

Relapse Prevention Model

The Relapse Prevention Model of sex offender treatment was derived from the field of alcohol and drug treatment. It was hoped that strategies similar to those employed in drug and alcohol treatment to reduce the risk of relapse into substance abuse could be utilized to reduce the risk of sex offenders committing future sex offenses. Relapse prevention measures typically involve identifying high-risk situations and learning how to avoid such situations, extricate oneself from them, or mitigate risk in such situations. We may have heard those addicted to drugs and alcohol state that they need to avoid the people, places and things associated with their addictions. Sitting at a bar to have a soft drink would generally be considered a very high-risk situation for a recovering alcoholic, one to be avoided at all cost. Similarly, sex offenders in a relapse prevention program learn to identify high-risk situations—such as being unsupervised in the presence of minors, having access to pornography, or fantasizing about rape—with the goal of learning to avoid or mitigate risk in such situations.

One important note in regard to conducting any treatment with incarcerated sex offenders (or conducting treatment of any kind with incarcerated offenders) is the issue of leveraged treatment. Undoubtedly some of those who are incarcerated truly wish to change their behavior, either for the good of society or, at the very least, so that they are not incarcerated again in the future. However, there are also offenders who merely wish to be released from prison as soon as possible and who are aware that if they comply with treatment (or *appear* to be doing so!), they may be released from prison earlier. Thus, some may be going through the motions and learning to write or say what they are supposed to in order to please the clinician, prison authorities, and/or parole board in the hopes of an early release rather than due to a desire on their behalf for any real change. It seems likely that offenders who are merely going through the motions of a therapeutic group but have no inherent desire to change are unlikely to obtain any meaningful or lasting benefit from that treatment.

Sex Offender Recidivism

Any analysis of sex offender rearrest rates must be looked at with the same caution that original offense rates are looked at. Given how often such offenses are not reported or prosecuted, we can only assume that the actual rates of re-offending are higher than the documented rates; how much higher is impossible to know with certainty. That being said, Harris and Hanson (2004) found that at a five-year follow-up, 9.2% of those convicted of a sex offense against a child had gone on to commit another sexual assault. At ten years, this number rose to 13.1%, and after fifteen years, the probability exceeded 16%. Perhaps these numbers seem low, but remember that they are underestimates and that one re-offense is one too many. These same researchers found the rates of recidivism for rapists (adult victims as opposed to child victims) as measured by the commission of a new sex offense to be 14% at five years, 21% at ten years, and 24% at the fifteen-year mark. The recidivism rate for female sex offenders is lower than for male offenders. Cortoni et al. (2010) found that at a six-and-a-half–year follow-up, only 3% of females had re-offended.

Stalking

Stalking is generally defined as an offender putting another person in fear that their movements and activities are being monitored and that the offender may harm them or kill them at some point. That is, stalking involves those actions that would put a reasonable person in fear of death or bodily injury. It is worth noting that it is not always easy to prove that one is being stalked. When one partner notices that their former intimate partner keeps "accidentally" seeing them in public places and giving them creepy looks, it would be very difficult to prove in court that they are being stalked or that they have legitimate reason to fear being harmed. However, if the former intimate partner is texting threats, having a friend convey threats on social media, or is observed slashing the tires of the former partner's car, that is a very different matter indeed.

Similar to sexual assault, with stalking, we may imagine that the stalker is typically a stranger. Again, as we have seen with various types of assault, it is seldom the case that the stalker is a stranger. Approximately 15% of women and nearly 6% of men report having been a victim of stalking during their lifetimes (Centers for Disease Control and Prevention, 2014). Of those women who have been stalked, 66% report that the stalker was a current or former intimate partner and 24% report that the stalker was someone they were acquainted with. This means that only 10% of those who are stalked are stalked by a stranger. Strangers can be a danger, but as noted in other chapters, this is by far the exception rather than the rule. In cases when men are stalked, there is an equal chance they are stalked by a current or former intimate partner (40%) or by an acquaintance (40%). As with women, men being stalked by a stranger is the exception rather than the rule. In the vast majority of cases, women are stalked by men (89%). According to this same study, when men are stalked, the numbers are close to equal, with 47% of men reporting that they are stalked by women and 44% of men being stalked by other men.

With advances in technology and social media, stalking and cyberstalking is becoming easier and likely more prevalent. When we post on social media that we are "having a great time in Ocean City," a stalker now knows where we are (and where we are not). Similarly, if we check in on social media to a certain gym, restaurant, or place of worship, our stalker now knows exactly where we are and likely has a good idea of how long we will be there. The locations of cell phones can be tracked in a variety of ways. Some cars are equipped with a GPS as a theft deterrent but

Stalking often involves physically following a victim but may also include the use of electronic devices, social media, text messages, and other means of tracking and intimidating a victim.

Alessandro de Leo / Alamy Stock Photo

such a device can potentially be used by a stalker to locate where someone is. Small, easily hidden tracking devices are readily available online and can be purchased by a stalker and hidden on the victim's car so that the stalker can monitor their whereabouts. Spy cams disguised as wall outlets, clocks, and other devices can be readily purchased online. Even monitoring a victim's whereabouts and activities by drone or other means is entirely possible and becoming increasingly easy, given advancements in such technologies.

Cyberstalking and cyber-harassment can be especially difficult to track and prove. Small police departments often do not have the training and resources to do so. Inexpensive burner phones and data plans can be easily purchased at most electronic stores and even in gas stations and can be used to make harassing calls and send threatening text messages. Since they are not associated with a name, tracking them to their source is often impossible. Public libraries and numerous other locations have local networks over which a stalker could monitor or send messages to their victim under a false profile. Adept computer users can use Virtual Peripheral Networks (VPNs) and various other means to make it next to impossible for most police departments to determine where a message, email, or image is truly coming from. Truly, the only limits are the imagination and technical know-how of the offender.

THROUGH THE EYES OF THE VICTIM: THE DIFFICULT JOURNEY OF VICTIMS OF SEXUAL ASSAULT

Psychologists learn not to compare one person's trauma to another's. It is not up to the clinician (or anyone else, for that matter) to decide that one type of trauma is better or worse than another or that one individual's trauma exceeds that of another person or exceeds that of what is to be expected. The experience of trauma is a profoundly personal one. That being said, few would argue that the trauma of having been sexually abused can be an incredibly difficult one. Indeed, more than 30% of people who are sexually assaulted go on to develop post-traumatic stress disorder (PTSD) as a consequence (Koenen, 2015).

There can be stigma associated with having been sexually abused, and that stigma may be imposed by others or self-imposed by the victim. Unfortunately, it is not uncommon for others to blame the victim for what happened to them by implying that they precipitated or provoked the offense in some way—for example, by how they were acting or how they were dressed. There is, of course, no objective reality to this. No one wants to be sexually assaulted. However, there are persistent attempts to blame the victim by defense attorneys, the media, the public, and (in some cases) even those who know the victim.

It is important for the forensic practitioner to understand why victim blaming is so commonplace. One possible explanation for this comes from the work of Lerner and Montado (1998). These researchers discussed what they referred to as the "Just World Hypothesis." They contend that humans have a desire to see the world around them as fair or just. That is, people desperately want to believe that the world around them is fair and that everyone gets what they deserve, with good things happening to good people and bad things being reserved for bad people. Such a belief can help us to feel safe: If I am a good person (and we typically believe that we are; Myers, 2015), then we can feel safe because bad things only happen to bad people; that group (we believe) does *not* include us!

And yet there is no objective evidence that life is fair, no matter how much we want it to be. Good things do sometimes happen to bad people—a scoundrel can win the lottery—and (unfortunately) bad things can and do happen to good people. Innocent children get terminal diseases. Law-abiding, hardworking citizens can be permanently injured in a car accident. These things do happen, but that is not what we want to believe. We want to believe that bad things happen to bad people, good things happen to good people, and (most importantly!) since I am a good person, good things (never bad ones!) will happen to me. Such a belief, as unrealistic as it is, makes us feel safe.

The Just World Hypothesis can provide some explanation for the tendency of people to blame victims for the misfortune that has befallen them. If a person can convince themselves that a victim of sexual assault (or any crime, for that matter) did something wrong that led to their victimization, then it is a short leap for that person to convince themselves that they (and their loved ones) would never act in that manner and therefore will never be victimized. If we can convince ourselves that an individual was sexually assaulted because of what they were wearing, then we can also convince ourselves that since neither we nor our family members dress that way, we are all safe; it could never happen to us. Unfortunately, people's desire to feel safe and secure leads them to blame others for being victimized when this is objectively not the case. It is vitally important for the forensic psychologist to recognize the all-too-common tendency to blame the victim and for them to educate others and reassure victims that nothing could be further from the truth.

PTSD is more common in rape victims than in victims of trauma unrelated to crime. Resnick et al. (1993) suggested that approximately 9% of non–crime-related traumas may result in the development of PTSD, whereas 30%–32% of rape and sexual assault victims go on to develop this disorder. According to the DSM-5, PTSD occurs in some individuals who have experienced (or witnessed) traumatic events. Typical symptoms include recurrent, intrusive, disturbing thoughts; recurrent nightmares; flashbacks in which the individual feels they are reliving the traumatic experience; and feelings of psychological distress. Those who suffer from PTSD after being sexually assaulted often attempt to ignore these intrusive thoughts with little success. Attempts to avoid people, places, or objects that remind them of the trauma are also common. For example, we can certainly understand that a rape victim would go out of their way to avoid passing by the parking garage in which they had been assaulted.

Smell can be a very powerful memory trigger, with smell, emotion, and memory being closely intertwined (Walsh, 2020). Perhaps when you smell crayons, it brings back vivid and pleasant recollections of first grade art class or when you smell of the ocean, it reminds you of a wonderful beach vacation you had when you were young. However, smell can be just as strong a trigger for negative events and dysphoric emotions. The present author had a victim of sexual assault inform him that when she was out in public, if she happened to smell the scent of Brut cologne on a passerby, it would trigger a flashback and panic attack on her part, as that was the cologne worn by her offender at the time that she was assaulted.

As with other types of victimization, the effects of being the victim of a sex offense are highly variable and individual and depend on numerous factors. It is important to remember that no particular reaction to being so victimized is wrong or abnormal. Rather, any reaction should be treated with dignity and profound respect as a normal reaction to a (very) abnormal experience. Fortunately, there are many types of treatment and help for those who have been sexually assaulted, whether or not they suffer from PTSD as a result. The National Center for PTSD notes that there are some medications known as selective serotonin reuptake inhibitors (SSRIs) that are recommended for the treatment of PTSD. The medications named by this organization as beneficial for PTSD include Prozac, Paxil, Zoloft, and Effexor (U.S. Department of Veterans Affairs, 2023). Cognitive behavioral therapy has also been found to be useful in assisting those who have been assaulted. Such therapy generally begins by identifying unpleasant or maladaptive thoughts that the victim may be experiencing. Such thoughts may lead to dysphoric emotions such as anxiety or depression, with those feelings triggering maladaptive behaviors such as drug use, isolation, or poor sleeping and eating habits, among many others. It is hoped that by helping victims learn to identify and challenge maladaptive thoughts, they will be able to experience less dysphoria over time and will be able to gradually resume more adaptive functioning (Monson & Shnaider, 2014). It is vitally important for victims of sexual abuse to know that help is available and recovery is possible.

CONCLUSION

Few topics elicit stronger emotions than the topic of sexual assault in our society. During the course of a career in forensic psychology, the odds are great that the clinician will come into contact with both perpetrators and victims of such offenses. It is important to understand that as often as such offenses are reported, official statistics are underrepresented. Victims often choose not to report the offense for a variety of reasons. It is also important to recognize that sex offenders are a heterogeneous group; most offenders know their victims, but some are strangers. Some offenders prefer sexual assault to consensual intercourse, while for others, such an offense is a crime of opportunity. Some offenders with pedophilia are sexually attracted to children and act out on these urges, while other offenders seek adult victims. A variety of treatment strategies are available for such offenders, with the hope of decreasing their risk of harm in the future. It is vitally important for both forensic psychologists and victims of sexual assault to know that although the process of recovery from such a traumatic event may be difficult, there is real hope for survivors and their loved ones.

Exercises and Discussion Questions

1. In this chapter, we learned that sex offenders who target children are aware that children may have been warned of stranger danger and told not to talk to strangers, so the offenders go out of their way to become familiar to their victims. What advice might you give to parents that they could pass along to their children to decrease the probability of their child being victimized in this way?

2. Do you think that Megan's Law and the Adam Walsh Act actually serve to protect children and families? If so, how? If you had the power to enact further laws or changes to protect those in the community from sex offenders, what would you change? Why?

3. Some would argue that civil commitment of an SVP after release from incarceration is important in protecting the community. Others might counter that the SVP has served their sentence as dictated by the court and should be released back into the community, as there is no sure way of knowing that they will ever commit another offense. Which of these do you believe is appropriate? Explain your position.

4. In this chapter, we discussed sex offender assessment and treatment modalities. Do you think that convicted sex offenders should be offered such treatment or should we simply manage sex offenders by incarcerating them and thereby keeping society safe? Do you believe that the time and effort spent on treating sex offenders is well spent in that it may reduce the chances of future offenses or do you believe it is a waste of taxpayer money, as such offenders are unlikely to change? Please explain your position.

KEY TERMS

Acquaintance rape

Adam Walsh Act

Aggravated indecent assault

Child pornography

Child sexual abuse

Cognitive behavioral therapy

Consent

Date rape

Deviant arousal pattern

Differential risk

Grooming

Indecent assault

Megan's Law

Paraphilia

Paraphilic disorder

Rape

Sexually violent predator (SVP)

Static-2002R

Statutory rape

EXTREME VIOLENCE

Mass Murder, Spree Killing, and Serial Killing

I knew that the inmate in Cell #4 had pled guilty to murdering a young boy and a girl. I had talked to him occasionally in the course of my usual monthly rounds of the housing unit, but I didn't know him very well and had never had occasion to ask him about his offense. I hadn't even planned on stopping at his cell that particular day, though I did notice his face at the window as I walked past. Then, out of nowhere, he said, "Hey, Doc!" I paused. He added, "The little girl . . . she was a lot more fun." Caught off guard, I could only stammer, "Huh?" He smiled at me. "Yeah, she lasted a lot longer." His smile broadened, and he chuckled a little, looking directly into my eyes and watching my expression. I'll never forget that smile . . . or those eyes.

INTRODUCTION: ANTISOCIAL PERSONALITY DISORDER, PSYCHOPATHY, AND PSYCHOSIS

It is a capital mistake to theorize before one has data. Insensibly, one begins to twist facts to suit theories, instead of theories to suit facts.

Sherlock Holmes in Arthur Conan Doyle's A Scandal in Bohemia

Sir Arthur Conan Doyle (1859–1930) began writing the Sherlock Holmes novels and short stories in 1887. These stories captured the imagination of the public and foreshadowed the notion of criminal profiling. Indeed, in *A Scandal in Bohemia*, Holmes informs his assistant Watson that it is obvious that Watson has been out in bad weather lately, that Watson's housekeeper is rather clumsy, and that Watson himself has recently returned to the practice of medicine. Watson, stunned, agrees that all this is true but asks Holmes for an explanation. Holmes responds with an exceedingly logical explanation of the manner in which the mud and scrapes on Watson's boots and the smell of iodoform have led him to these conclusions. Holmes tells Watson that, like most people, "you see but you do not observe."

In the 1940s, psychiatrist Hervey Cleckley took the advice of Holmes to heart, not only seeing but also *observing*. Cleckley was interviewing institutionalized psychiatric patients when he noticed a stark contradiction. It became apparent to him that some of the individuals he was interviewing, who appeared to look and act as normal, relatively well-functioning adults, did not appear to experience emotions in the same way that most other people did. From his observation and research, he wrote his seminal book, *The Mask of Sanity* (1955, p. 7), suggesting that such individuals are able to put on a "mask," purposefully *acting* like others but internally having a very different and extremely deficient experience of human emotions. Cleckley described such **psychopathy** as a "confusing and paradoxical disorder," going on to say that the "biological organism is outwardly intact . . . but centrally deficient or disabled in such a way that abilities . . . cannot be prevented from regularly working toward self-destruction and other seriously pathological results."

The *Diagnostic and Statistical Manual of Mental Disorders* (5th edition; DSM-5) states that the diagnosis of antisocial personality disorder "has also been referred to as psychopathy, sociopathy, or dissocial personality disorder" (p. 659). As discussed in Chapter 5, among other symptoms, antisocial personality disorder is distinguished by unlawful behavior, lying, impulsivity, irritability, and a lack of remorse, as demonstrated by *indifference* to having hurt others.

The present author has tremendous respect for the DSM-5. After all, it is *the* authoritative classification of mental health disorders, developed over the course of ten years by hundreds of experts from countries all over the world. However, over the course of thousands upon thousands of interviews with convicted felons, the author began to notice a discrepancy. Some inmates demonstrated what appeared to be genuine remorse and regret for their actions. Many more demonstrated a callous indifference to their actions, either outright denying guilt ("Yeah, everyone says I did it but I didn't."), minimizing guilt ("I'm not hurting anyone by selling them drugs. If I don't sell it to them, someone else will."), or even placing blame on the victim ("Hey, you disrespect me and I have no choice but to hurt you."). Over time, such statements and denial of fault became sadly commonplace. But there were a few offenders that stood out not for their callous indifference to the suffering that they had caused but because of the clear joy they expressed at the suffering they had inflicted on others. Pleasure or arousal at the suffering of others is very different indeed than mere indifference to such suffering. Those like Cleckley, Robert Hare (author of the **Hare Psychopathy Checklist–Revised**), and others who have extensive real-world experience with assaultive and murderous offenders often seem to view this issue differently than those whose primary experience is in reading the literature pertaining to the topic. In the opinion of the present author, the DSM-5 fails to appreciate the difference between being *unmoved* by the suffering of others and *enjoying* such suffering; the difference between these two is important.

As noted by Kent Kiehl in *The Psychopath Whisperer*, the DSM is a "good starting point" (2014, p. 48) but should not necessarily be interpreted as the last word in diagnosis. After all, there existed diagnoses in previous versions of that book that have been eliminated in the current edition, and it seems likely that some of the diagnoses that are contained in the present version will be changed or eliminated when the next version is published. In short, the DSM-5, like all good works of science, is a work in progress and is subject to healthy debate and consideration.

At times, the psychopath may understand their own disorder better than the professional who is interviewing them. Robert Hare, in *Without Conscience* (1993), details an interaction between a graduate student of his and an offender. The offender states that he would rather be a psychopath than a sociopath; the graduate student responds by asking, "Aren't they the same thing?" The offender insightfully replies,

> No, they're not. You see, a sociopath misbehaves because he's been brought up wrong. Maybe he's got a beef with society. I've got no beef with society. I'm not harboring hostility. It's just the way I am. Yeah, I guess I'd be a psychopath. (p. 24)

It is important to keep in mind that not every psychopath is a serial killer or even a criminal. Psychopathy is far more common than many of us would like to realize. Robert Hare (1993) estimates that there are two *million* psychopaths in North America and perhaps as many as 100,000 in New York City alone! Obviously, if each and every psychopath was a violent criminal, the world would be a very different place than it is now. Some psychopaths are able to maintain or even excel in a career (after all, "glib and superficially charming" may well be an asset to someone in sales, politics, and other professions!) and do not commit violent offenses (Chester, 2020). Such individuals demonstrate conscientiousness and an ability to restrain impulsive urges (Mullins-Sweat et al., 2010). However, their lack of empathy and concern for others will still leave them prone to sabotaging relationships, making impulsive decisions, and ignoring the wants and needs of others. Their lifestyle, while not criminal, is still likely to be harmful to those around them in one way or another, whether that be in terms of relationships, finances, employment, or other areas of daily living. As psychopaths are easily bored and require near-constant stimulation, we would not expect them to take a routine, boring job working in a cubicle—or if they did, it is not difficult to imagine that they would create some drama in order to keep their life interesting and exciting.

Before proceeding further, it is important to distinguish between two similar-appearing terms: psychopath and **psychosis/psychotic**. These two terms bear little relation other than grammatical similarity. As previously discussed, *psychopathy* refers to a pronounced disregard for the emotions of others, a callous indifference to what others want or need and a complete and utter lack of remorse. The DSM-5 includes psychopathy along with other personality disorders, including antisocial personality disorder. *Psychosis*, on the other hand, is an acute psychiatric disorder, often characterized by schizophrenia, a thought disorder. Individuals with such disorders typically demonstrate delusions (irrational thoughts), experience hallucinations (hearing or seeing things that do not actually exist), disorganized speech and behavior, and (as a result of the aforementioned) an impaired ability to function in daily life. Thus, although both psychopaths and those with psychosis may demonstrate a restricted range of affect, the primary (and very significant) difference between the two is that the thinking of the psychopath is not impaired, while the thinking of the individual with psychosis is often significantly impacted.

The Hare Psychopathy Checklist–Revised (PCL–R)

Originally developed in the 1970s by Robert Hare and revised since that time, the Hare Psychopathy Checklist–Revised (PCL–R) remains a widely utilized instrument in assessing psychopathy and predicting the risk of criminal re-offending. This measure consists of 20 items, each rated by a trained mental health clinician as absent (zero points), somewhat present (1 point), or markedly present (2 points). The PCL–R is conducted on the basis of a semi-structured interview concerning that individual's upbringing, schooling, work history, criminal history, drug and alcohol use, and other important life events. A thorough and careful review of all available records is also critical. Given the nature of the interview, the clinician must carefully evaluate statements made by the individual being assessed, comparing them against records whenever possible; the possibility of an individual lying while being assessed for psychopathy certainly cannot (and should not!) be ruled out. Indeed, the quality of ratings on the PCL–R can depend on how forthright the interviewee is (Huchzermeier et al., 2007). It is vitally important for the forensic psychologist to understand that while they are evaluating the (potential) psychopath, that individual may very well be conducting their own evaluation of the clinician. It is also important for the psychologist to realize that the person they are interviewing may be every bit as adept in doing so as the psychologist. After all, an ability to effectively evaluate the intentions and behavior of others is what allows the psychopath to protect themselves and manipulate others to do their bidding.

Included among the items scored on the PCL–R are factors including glib and superficial charm. In other words, does the individual in question tell amusing (though perhaps improbable) stories but upon further examination seem superficial and shallow? Also examined and rated is whether the individual demonstrates a grandiose and inflated sense of self-worth; despite a lack of accomplishments, does this person hold themselves in great esteem, blaming any (perhaps all) failures on bad luck while claiming (or exaggerating) responsibility for those things that they do accomplish? Another important factor in the PCL–R is callousness and lack of empathy; does this individual look out only for their own self-interest while disregarding the wants/needs of others and viewing emotions generally as a sign of weakness? With each of 20 items rated as 0, 1, or 2 points, a total score of 30 or greater is interpreted as indicative of psychopathy.

Factor analysis is a statistical method that allows a researcher to determine which of numerous variables are correlated into a smaller, more meaningful number of unobserved variables referred to as *factors*. For example, if we were studying the factors that influence how many widgets an assembly line worker can produce in an hour, we might enter quite a few variables into our statistical model: age of the worker, number of mistakes made, number of hours worked, downtime, years of experience, and so forth. Our factor analysis may tell us that statistically, the factor that is most important in terms of the many variables that we are looking at is the total amount of time that a worker has spent performing that particular task.

Using a factor analysis, the PCL–R demonstrates two primary factors: The first is a selfish, remorseless, and callous use of others for their own best interest. Individuals scoring high on this factor tend to demonstrate relatively low anxiety (Hare et al., 1989) and high achievement and are at low risk of suicidality (Verona et al., 2001). It should be noted that while such traits may be harmful to those around such an individual, they can be and often are adaptive in the self-interest of that individual. This first factor is correlated with **narcissistic personality disorder,** and of course, people low in anxiety and high in achievement can be persuasive and even charming at times. Furthermore, we should not be surprised if a person with narcissistic traits and a lack of remorse is unlikely to commit suicide; after all, why would a person with no regrets who holds himself in high regard contemplate (much less attempt) suicide?

The second factor of the PCL–R is more highly correlated with antisocial personality disorder and **borderline personality disorder**. Individuals scoring high on this factor tend to demonstrate criminal behavior and react to being challenged with anger and impulsive violence. Such individuals tend to be sensation-seeking and are concerned with what will be best for them or feel best to them in the very near future. They are concerned with having their own needs and desires met and met right away, regardless of the cost to others or even of the long-term costs to themselves: "I want what I want and I want it now!" At one prison that the present author worked at, an inmate was drinking from a water fountain in the hallway when another inmate, who had no previous grudge against the first, came up behind him, grabbed him by the hair, lifted his head up and back, and then violently and repeatedly smashed the inmate's face into the water fountain and spigot, fracturing both of the first inmate's orbital bones and cheeks and breaking a number of his teeth. As the assaulter was being processed into the restricted housing unit, it was the author's duty to evaluate him for suicidality or further potential violence as well as any mental health concerns. Upon interview, this inmate was completely calm and devoid of remorse. When asked why he had committed such a violent act, he simply shrugged and said, "He was at the water fountain. I was thirsty," as if this was a rational and understandable reason for nearly killing another human being.

Smashing another person's face into a water fountain rather than waiting a few seconds for them to finish is as different from normal human behavior as night is from day. But is it simply the actions of the psychopath that are different or is there an underlying cause? Is something different about their brains than the brains of those who are not psychopaths? Kent Kiehl, in his fascinating book, *Psychopath Whisperer: The Science of Those Without Conscience*, describes a series of experiments he conducted in a Canadian maximum-security prison. Utilizing an electroencephalograph (EEG) and functional MRI (fMRI), he examined the brainwaves and brain function of psychopaths and compared them to the brainwaves of non-psychopaths. What he found was fascinating: a reliable difference in an evoked response potential known as P3. Simply put, P3 is a brainwave that is normally activated when there is some new, unexpected stimulus in our world—for example, the tractor-trailer driving behind you suddenly sounding its horn or your roommate suddenly turning on all the lights while you are sleeping. You would be startled, and your P3 would jump, tracing a steep, near-vertical line . . . unless you are a psychopath. Compared to non-psychopaths, psychopaths in Kiehls's study demonstrated a markedly diminished P3. Simply put, psychopaths in his study didn't startle nearly as much as non-psychopaths did. Such a diminished emotional reactivity should come as no surprise to us; psychopaths simply don't experience emotion in the same manner or with nearly the same intensity that other people do.

The Mark of the Criminal: Modus Operandi, Ritual, and Signature

Modus operandi is Latin for "mode of operating" and refers to one's characteristic way of doing something. Often abbreviated *M.O.* when referring to criminal offenses, it refers to the offender's typical way of committing the offense and of attempting to get away with that offense. For a burglar, their modus operandi might be to identify a house that is likely to be vacant by noticing excessive mail in the mailbox and multiple newspapers in the front yard. They might then dress in dark clothing, pry open a window in the back of the house, and make certain to wear gloves so as to not leave fingerprints. Modus operandi can and does change and evolve over time; if the burglar cuts themselves going through a broken window, they may decide that it is best to pry the back door open in the future so that they don't cut themselves again. Crimes such as burglary that involve modus operandi typically tell us very little about the offender's personality. We might guess that an individual who grabbed a jar of change and some DVDs before leaving without taking more valuable items from the house was startled or nervous, but such a guess provides us with little valuable or unique information.

However, some offenders unwittingly provide the forensic psychologist with additional information. **Ritualistic behavior** is behavior that is not necessary to commit or get away with the crime but that the offender engages in anyway and does so on repeated occasions. For example, post-mortem mutilation of a corpse when not disposing of it as part of an effort to avoid capture but instead for their own enjoyment would be an example of ritualistic behavior. There is no point to mutilating a corpse, other than whatever personal motivation the offender has for doing so. Some offenders (such as Ted Bundy or Edmund Kemper) were known to take personal items that had no monetary value from their victims: hairbrushes, driver's licenses, a scarf (Bourgoin, 2020). Such petty thefts are neither the point of the offense nor are they a necessary part of getting away with the crime. However, given that they occur repeatedly, it is safe to assume that they serve some purpose to the offender and thus tell us something about that offender—perhaps that they intend to use such trophies to remember or relive the offense.

A *signature* is a ritualistic behavior that is unique to a particular offender. As with ritualistic behavior, this behavior is not necessary to commit or get away with an offense, but the offender engages in it anyway on repeated occasions. A signature, however, is a ritual the likes of which has never exactly been seen in another offender. Post-mortem mutilation of a corpse, not as part of an attempt to dispose of the body, is ritualistic behavior. However, if we find that a particular offender is mutilating the body by carving the letter M into the torso of his victims and we are not aware that any other offender has engaged in this particular ritual, this behavior rises to the level of a signature. A signature can be helpful in establishing a linkage analysis; that is, if a body is found in Florida to be mutilated in such a way and a similar mutilation is seen later on a corpse in Alabama, we may believe with some confidence that these offenses have been committed by the same individual (as long as this behavior is not common knowledge to the public and therefore not the work of a copycat).

The Zodiac killer and BTK killer Dennis Rader wrote letters to the media and law enforcement authorities. Such communications serve no purpose in the commission of the offense and may be counterproductive in terms of getting away with committing the crime (just ask Dennis Rader, whose computer disk mailed to authorities helped lead to his capture; Girard, 2013, p. 417). The Zodiac killer signed his letters with a symbol of a circle with a + sign in the middle, reminiscent of what it looks like to look through the scope of a rifle. Rader signed his letters with the letters B, T, and K intertwined, with the B specifically designed to look like a woman's breasts. Such literal signatures are in fact also signature behaviors.

Rituals and signatures can allow the forensic psychologist to make inferences about the offender's personality and thus are valuable in terms of behavioral analysis. Serial killer Jeffrey Dahmer was known to drug his victims and to go so far as to drill into their skulls, pouring a combination of acids into their brains (Masters, 1993). Ultimately, he killed them, but he obviously could have killed them much more quickly without having done so. Given that we are not aware of any other offender drilling holes into their victim's heads, such a behavior then is a signature. We could certainly speculate here a need to be in complete control of his victims. Indeed, at Dahmer's trial, psychiatrist Dr. Fredrick Fosdal testified that a zombie love-slave would be a "solution to [Dahmer's] dilemma" (Walsh, 1992). In this way, behavior reflects personality and is immensely helpful from the standpoint of behavioral analysis.

KNOW THEIR ROLE: MASS MURDERER VERSUS SPREE KILLER VERSUS SERIAL KILLER

Media reports can and sometimes do confuse descriptions of criminal activities, perhaps stating, "There is a serial killer walking through the mall shooting people!" Although it is certainly a newsworthy incident, and important for people to be aware of, the terminology *serial killer* would not be correct in such a case. It is important to note that there still exists some debate as to the exact definition of these terms, and there are some exceptions to the definitions that are in place.

According to the Behavioral Analysis Unit of the Federal Bureau of Investigation (FBI), after their multidisciplinary symposium in 2005, it was decided that a mass murderer would be defined as an individual who kills four or more people in one location at one time (Morton & Hilts, 2005). These same editors note in their report that there was considerable debate at that symposium about whether a spree killing should be defined as separate and distinct from mass murder. In the past, a *spree killer* has been defined as an individual who kills three or more people in different places at different times but all as part of a single, angry episode; there is no cooling-off period between the killings. Therefore, the individual often referred to as an *active shooter* as they shoot and move throughout a school or office building is a spree killer. A spree killer may be thought of as a mass murderer on the move. The FBI originally defined a *serial killer* as someone who killed four or more people but later lowered that number, defining a *serial killer* as someone who kills three or more people in different places at different times with a cooling-off period between kills. That is, a serial killer kills someone (or more than one person) and then ceases doing so for some period of time, perhaps months or even years before striking again (Morton & Hilts, 2005).

It should be noted that these categories serve as a guide but are not absolute and exceptions can and do exist. Take, for example, the case of a military sniper. Such an individual may indeed have killed three or more enemy combatants. In all likelihood, such kills occurred in different places at different times with a cooling-off period of time passing between each kill. Technically, such actions fit the definition of a serial killer. However, as we shall see, the motivation and dynamics of serial killing are quite different than those of military combat.

Mass Murderer: Timothy McVeigh (1968–2001)

Timothy McVeigh was reportedly raised under relatively normal circumstances in Lockport, New York (Russakoff & Kovaleski, 1995). There is no evidence to suggest that he was abused in any way. He claimed to have been bullied during his school years, but there is no firm evidence of this being the case. Early in life, he became interested in the Second Amendment and firearms (Chase, 2004), but this interest did not seem to be problematic in any way. After graduating from high school, he joined the Army, where he rose to the rank of Sergeant and fought in the Gulf War. Although his service was not entirely without incident (he was reprimanded for purchasing a "White Power" shirt at a Ku Klux Klan rally), he received a number of service awards and received an Honorable Discharge from the service in 1991 (Michel & Herbeck, 2001).

McVeigh was often angry, disgruntled with the government in regard to taxes and what he perceived as governmental control of the populace (CNN, 2008). His pro–Second Amendment stance was so extreme that he disassociated himself with the National Rifle Association after deciding that their stance on gun rights was not as strong as it should be (Michel & Herbeck, 2001, p.111).

The event that appears to have brought McVeigh's anger to the boiling point was the U.S. government forces, including the Bureau of Alcohol, Tobacco, and Firearms (ATF) and the FBI surrounding the Branch Davidian Compound in Waco, Texas. Some might say that David Koresh, the leader of this group, was a cult leader; his followers appeared to think of him as a religious prophet. In any case, the U.S. government believed that he and his followers had illegally modified a number of firearms to be fully automatic and that this group represented a significant threat to the safety of the public. The ATF and FBI surrounded the compound, and a 51-day standoff ensued. The siege ended on April 19, 1993, when authorities used an armored vehicle to pump tear gas into the compound. In the ensuing fire, 76 Branch Davidians died. For McVeigh, this event appeared to crystallize his anger at the U.S. government; he decided that something must be done to protest this perceived injustice and governmental control.

On April 19, 1995, exactly two years to the day of the raid on the Branch Davidian compound, McVeigh parked a rented Ryder moving truck in front of the Murrah Federal Building in Oklahoma City, Oklahoma. At 9:02 a. m., his improvised explosive device, comprised of approximately 4,000 pounds of ammonium nitrate (ordinarily used as a farm fertilizer) exploded. One hundred and sixty-eight people in the building were killed, most instantaneously. Nearly 700 more were seriously wounded.

There is no evidence to suggest that McVeigh ever verbalized any remorse or regret for this offense, not even after learning that children had been killed in the blast. In his handwritten eight-page manifesto, McVeigh stated, "Based on observations of the policies of my own government, I viewed this action as an acceptable option" (McVeigh, 2001). Indeed, it is reported that instead of last words expressing any remorse or even acknowledgment of his actions, McVeigh instead chose to hand a copy of the poem "Invictus" by William Ernest Henley to the prison warden. This poem alludes to the brave and unconquerable spirit of the author; perhaps McVeigh was suggesting that he did not regret his actions or their consequences.

In examining the facts and research around McVeigh's bombing of the Murrah Federal Building, there does not appear to be evidence to suggest that he was psychotic. As discussed earlier in this chapter, psychosis typically means that a person is experiencing hallucinations, bizarre beliefs, and impaired thought processes. That does not appear to have been the case for McVeigh; his thinking up to and including the explosion appears to have been logical and coherent. That may sound strange; how can it be said that a person who blew up a building full of people was thinking clearly? But solid logic and clear thinking would appear to be necessary in order to build a bomb and survive doing so. For those people who are unintelligent, psychotic, agitated, and/or impulsive, bomb building generally ends suddenly and violently in an unintended explosion. McVeigh not only built a bomb, but he also managed to rent a Ryder truck without attracting any undue attention to himself. It is also reported that after parking the truck in front of the Murrah building, he inserted into his ears the hearing protection he had brought with him that day for that exact purpose. McVeigh's offense was the furthest thing from impulsive; it was carefully planned and methodically thought out for a period of precisely two years.

Spree Killers aka "Active Shooters": Eric Harris and Dylan Klebold, the Columbine Shooters

With a father who was in the Air Force and a mother who was a homemaker, Eric Harris and his family moved frequently, as his father's military service required. The family settled in the Littleton area of Colorado in 1993. There is no evidence to suggest that Eric was subject to any form of abuse during his lifetime. He played soccer in school, and despite some suggestion in his online accounts, there is no firm evidence to suggest that he was socially rejected or bullied during his school years (Brooks, 2004). Eric had an account on America Online (AOL) in the early days of the internet. He used his account to talk about the first-person shooter game, Doom, and to complain about school and other students. As time went on, the account took on a markedly more sinister tone, with him threating others and alluding to white supremacist beliefs (Wright & Millar, 1999).

Harris's anger was clear and long-standing. Nearly a year before the massacre, he wrote in his blog that all he wanted to do is to "kill and injure as many of you as I can" (Brown, 1999, pp. 72–73). Similarly, long before their murderous actions, Dylan Klebold wrote in Harris's yearbook that he looked forward to "killing enemies, blowing stuff up, killing cops" (Jefferson County Colorado Sheriff's Report, 1999).

Dylan Klebold, 17 years old at the time of the shooting, was born and raised in Colorado. His family attended church on a regular basis. Dylan played baseball and soccer while growing up, and like Eric Harris, there is no evidence that he was abused in any way during his formative years. Similar to Harris, there is no evidence to suggest that he was at the bottom of Columbine High School's social ladder or that he was especially bullied or ostracized by his peers (Brooks, 2004).

As noted in Chapter 5, much was made of the supposed fact that Harris and Klebold were members of a group of Columbine students who dressed in black clothes and trench coats, referring to themselves as the "Trench Coat Mafia." However, extensive investigation yields no evidence that either of the shooters associated themselves with this group (Cullen, 1999).

On April 20, 1999, Harris and Klebold first planted a number of propane bombs and other improvised explosive devices in the cafeteria at Columbine High School, planning for these to explode during the busy lunch hour. When they realized that the bombs were not going to detonate, they pulled out their guns and shot students outside the school before proceeding inside. Once inside, they walked the hallways, shooting and moving, eventually killing 10 more students and a teacher and wounding 21 more before turning their guns on themselves.

As with McVeigh's bombing of the Murrah building, Harris and Klebold's attack upon the students of Columbine High School was carefully and methodically planned out. They were not of age to legally purchase firearms, so they convinced two older men to do so for them (Pankratz & Simpson, 1999) and they practiced with these weapons. They wrote plans and drew maps. They made at least eight improvised propane bombs and acquired a carbine, several handguns, two shotguns, and numerous rounds of ammunition. Such planning and acquisition do not happen overnight. They even made several videotapes detailing their homicidal plans and intent, and one final tape immediately before their rampage began (Cullen, 2010). It is incredibly fortunate that none of the bombs in the school detonated or the casualty count undoubtedly would have been even worse than it was.

On the day of the shootings, Harris wore a shirt with the words "Natural Selection" on it, an apparent reference to his white supremacist beliefs and perhaps his own narcissism, his idea that he should determine who lived and who died. Klebold's shirt simply contained the word "Wrath" (Cullen, 2010, p. 41). In the case of Harris and Klebold, a forensic psychologist might say that there are small clues that can carry a great deal of meaning. For example, Harris and Klebold fired enough shots that each must have reloaded multiple times during the course of their offense. This tells a forensic practitioner something important: In a rage, an individual can pull the trigger of a gun enough times to empty the magazine. Doing so requires little effort or thought. Reloading is very different, though. Reloading a firearm takes time, thought, and fine motor skills. Reloading would appear to be difficult or impossible when one is in a rage. This suggests that although Harris and Klebold were undoubtedly angry and wanted the world to know their anger, they were not in a blind rage while carrying out their actions.

A memorial for the victims of the Columbine High School shooting.

istock/ BanksPhotos

Indeed, not only were the shooters not in a blind rage, but they also seemed to be enjoying what they were doing. It is reported that at one point, Eric Harris rapped his fist on top of a desk to get the attention of Cassie Bernall, who was hiding under it. When she looked at him, he said, "Peek-a-boo!" and proceeded to shoot her with the 12-gauge shotgun he was holding (Jefferson County Sheriff's Office, 2018); for Harris, murder appeared to have become a game.

Klebold, for his part, demonstrated a similar level of enjoyment in carrying out the atrocities of the day. Student Lance Kirkland, already seriously wounded, was pleading for help. Klebold responded, "Sure, I'll help you," and then shot him in the head with a 12-gauge shotgun. Miraculously, Kirklin survived (Kirklin, 2019).

Commonalities: What Mass Murderers and Spree Killers Share

As we have seen, it is *movement* that separates a mass murderer from a spree killer. If the offender opens fire in the school gymnasium, killing ten people, they are a mass murderer. If they then walk down the hallway and shoot several more people in a classroom, they would now be considered a spree killer. They are cut of the same cloth: A spree killer is simply a mass murderer on the move (and again, it has been argued that the distinction between mass murder and spree killing is not necessarily important).

Mass murderers and spree killers are similar in many ways. As was the case with McVeigh and with Harris and Klebold, we do not often see evidence that they have been subjected to physical, emotional, or sexual abuse. This is not to say it could not have happened, but firm evidence for such abuse is absent in these particular cases.

Anger on the part of the offender appears to be universal with mass murderers and spree killers. It would seem that they feel that such anger at the world is justified, but in many cases, their perceived injustices and victimization may be just that—perceived rather than actual. With McVeigh, Harris, Klebold and others, we do not have clear evidence that they were bullied, ostracized, or rejected in any objective way. A chronic, underlying anger leaking out through statements, websites, and so on is noted in many such individuals.

In the face of a violent event such as a mass murder or spree killing, people often wish to know what triggered this event or why the perpetrator snapped. Why did this "nice, normal" person suddenly engage in such a horrendous act? In fact, such events may not be as impulsive as they appear to be on the surface. It takes considerable time, effort, and planning to carry out such an offense. McVeigh took most of two years to plan his offense and learn how to build a bomb and then patiently waited for the anniversary date to wreak his revenge on people he believed represented the U.S. government. Harris and Klebold acquired weapons and ammunition over time, built their own improvised explosive devices, practiced shooting, and developed their plan of attack. All of these things take time and effort. It is difficult to kill large numbers of people impulsively; doing so is almost always a planned, methodical event.

Mass murderers and spree killers often engage in violent acts as a form of protest or revenge. However, their revenge appears to be targeted at humanity and the world in general rather than at specific individuals. McVeigh, after all, did not kill a member of the ATF or the FBI but random federal employees who had nothing to do with the raid on the Branch Davidian compound. Harris and Klebold were not noted to specifically target any particular students in their rampage at Columbine High School but did so randomly. In fact, it is noted that prior to the shooting, Harris encountered Brooks Brown, with whom he had had some disputes. Not only did Harris not shoot Brown, but he told him to leave the school grounds, thus going out of his way to spare Brown's life (Brown & Merritt, 2002, pp. 13–15).

Mass murderers and spree killers tend to be concerned with the number of people they kill; the more the better as far as they are concerned. After all, if such killings are an expression of rage against the world and a reaction to perceived injustice, then does it not stand to reason that the more people that are killed, the greater the protest and expression of rage? Eric Harris and Dylan Klebold's written plans suggested that they intended to kill between 500 and 600 students (BBC News, 1999). Given their desire to kill as many people as possible, mass murderers and spree killers make use of what might be referred to as "weapons of mass destruction": weapons that kill quickly and efficiently. It would certainly be difficult for such an offender to kill numerous people with a knife or by strangulation. However, the bomb employed by McVeigh and the firearms employed by Klebold and Harris are certainly capable of killing many people in a short amount of time. Such weapons are typical of these offenders.

Mass murderers and spree killers both typically seem unconcerned with being caught. After all, if an individual is so angry at the world and the perceived injustices that they have suffered that they choose to express their dissatisfaction with murder, then it seems likely that they would want the world to know who they are. Mass murderers and spree killers often make no special effort to avoid being captured. They either know that they will commit suicide when their protest is finished or are unconcerned with incarceration and/or the death penalty as long as they make society pay the price first so that the world becomes aware of their rage at the injustices they believe they have suffered.

Lastly, mass murderers and spree killers both demonstrate little remorse or regret for their actions. After all, their actions were carefully planned and carried out to achieve their intended goal. It hardly seems likely that they would later decide their actions were wrong or that they would experience compassion for their victims or regret for their offenses.

Terrorism

It should be noted that some of those who commit mass murders or spree killings do so with a specific agenda in mind: to strike fear into the hearts of a group of people, often with a particular agenda in mind. Although definitions of terrorism vary a bit from one source to the next, a common thread is that terrorism involves the unlawful use of intimidation, force, and/or violence in the pursuit of a political, religious, social, ideological, or other objective. Terrorism is considered to be a form of asymmetric warfare in that it is not one organized military force fighting against another but a single person or small group perpetrating violence, often against unarmed civilians. The FBI distinguishes between international terrorism, in which violent criminal acts are committed by an individual or group inspired by or representing foreign groups or nations, and domestic terrorism. According to the FBI, domestic terrorism stems from the desire of an individual or group to use violence to achieve some change in domestic political, social, religious, or other laws and policies or to protest such domestic policies. The FBI goes on to state that the primary mission of their organization is to protect the country against foreign and domestic terrorist acts (Federal Bureau of Investigation, n. d.).

The act of Timothy McVeigh (discussed above) is considered to be an act of domestic terrorism; as we noted, he was angered at what he considered to be the U.S. government's intrusion on the Second Amendment rights of the Branch Davidians. Our country became very much more aware of the threat of international terrorism on September 11, 2001, when al-Qaeda terrorists carried out the coordinated suicide bombings with planes at the Pentagon and the World Trade Centers and had one other plane that ultimately crashed in Pennsylvania (Moghadam 2008, p. 48). Although the attacks of the al-Qaeda terrorists have been characterized as "suicide attacks" because they resulted in the death of the terrorists themselves, it could also be argued that these terrorist acts were instead "homicide attacks" in that the goal of these attacks appeared to be the killing of American civilians rather than the self-inflicted death of the terrorists. Such acts, in addition to being terrorist in nature, also represent mass murders.

Serial Killer: Jeffrey Dahmer, "The Milwaukee Cannibal" (1960–1994)

Born in Milwaukee, Wisconsin, in 1960, reports concerning the early life of Jeffrey Dahmer are unclear; although he did not grow up in an ideal situation (his mother may have suffered from mental illness, and his parents did eventually divorce), there is no clear evidence that he was subject to any physical, emotional, or sexual abuse (Campbell & Denevi, 2004). However, it is clear that early on, he became fascinated with the morbid and grotesque: examining dead animals, picking up roadkill, and playing with the bones of those animals (Norris, 1992). Eventually, he killed a neighborhood dog and nailed its decapitated head to a post (Masters, 1993). He is reported to have had a few friends in school but often acted oddly, faking seizures and drinking alcohol heavily before and even during school hours (Norris, 1992). How such behavior did not come to the attention of school officials and then to the attention of his parents is difficult to understand. With increasing frequency, he began to experience fantasies and images of death, dismemberment, and preservation of bodies and body parts; perhaps the alcohol abuse was an attempt to bury, erase, or lessen the intensity of such thoughts.

Dahmer committed his first murder in 1978, shortly after graduating from high school. He picked up a hitchhiker and took him back to his house, where they drank heavily. Dahmer then assaulted him, choked him until he was unconscious, and strangled him. Sexually aroused, he later masturbated on the corpse of the deceased prior to dismembering and disposing of the body (Norris, 1992).

After a failed attempt at college and a largely unsuccessful stint in the Army, Dahmer returned to civilian life and did not commit another murder until nine years later. He quickly established a modus operandi: He would go to a bar, get intoxicated, and attempt to talk men into leaving with him to have sex or to take nude photos. If they agreed, once back at his apartment, he would drug them and sexually assault them (Masters, 1993). It was not uncommon for him to drill a hole into his victim's skull, pouring acid into this opening in an attempt to have complete control over his victim. In 1987, he assaulted and murdered his second victim, then dissected the corpse into numerous pieces to dispose of it. He retained the victim's head, attempting to preserve it and using it for purposes of masturbation for several weeks before finally disposing of it.

This modus operandi and pattern occurred repeatedly from 1987–1991, with Dahmer sometimes cannibalizing parts of his victims' bodies and at other times engaging in sexual acts with the corpses of the deceased. But make no mistake—as bizarre as all of this is, Dahmer was able to put on what Cleckley referred to as the "mask of sanity" and appeared normal and even quite charming and charismatic. In 1991, in a case that defies the imagination, Dahmer convinced 14-year-old Konerak Sinthasomphone to come home with him. Naked, drugged, drunk, and beaten, the boy managed to escape and talked to several women who then called the police. Dahmer, seeing what had occurred, did not panic. In fact, he talked to the women and the police so calmly and convincingly that the police believed Sinthasomphone to be 19 years old and merely engaged in a "lovers' quarrel" with Dahmer! The police helped Dahmer take the boy back to his apartment, where Dahmer completed the murder (Masters, 1993). The point of this heartrending story is to highlight the fact that, as Dr. Cleckley pointed out more than 70 years ago, it is amazing how convincing the mask of the psychopath can be, even to trained police officers.

Dahmer was finally caught after a potential victim called the police, who responded to the call and noticed the awful odor permeating the apartment. After seeing the morbid evidence of his crimes, he was cuffed and arrested and sentenced to 16 consecutive life sentences. He was beaten to death by another inmate at the Columbia Correctional Facility in Wisconsin in 1994.

Serial Killers: Differences Between Mass Murderers and Spree Killers

Although the early life of Jeffrey Dahmer was less than ideal (but again, who among us has had an ideal upbringing?), there is no firm evidence that he was subjected to any significant physical, sexual, or emotional abuse. Such abuse is common in the history of serial killers; a study by Mitchell and Aamodt (2005) demonstrated that in a sample of fifty such killers, all types of abuse (other than neglect) were more common in serial killers than they were in the general population. Edmund Kemper ("The Co-Ed Killer") reported being severely abused by his mother; the (extremely) strained relationship between serial killer Eddie Gein ("The Plainfield Ghoul") and his mother was the basis for the movie *Psycho*; and John Wayne Gacy ("The Killer Clown") reported being subjected to severe physical and emotional abuse at the hands of his alcoholic father, to name a few examples. Again, it is important to keep in mind that a forensic psychologist must be careful in evaluating and interpreting any and all such statements made to them by such an offender.

Although mass murderers and spree killers are unconcerned with being caught, serial killers (with one notable exception) do not wish to be caught; they enjoy committing their offenses, wish to continue doing so, and are therefore careful to avoid detection. The lone exception to this may be Edmund Kemper, who, after murdering his mother and going on the run, decided that he had accomplished his life's mission and then called the police to confess. In fact, his call was first interpreted as a prank; the operator hung up on him. Edmund had to call back and speak to an officer he knew personally (Calhoun, 2016). Fortunately, the second time around, police did believe him and subsequently arrested him!

As opposed to mass murderers and spree killers, who are completely unbothered by killing others, serial killers are different in that they often take an admitted pleasure in doing so. Russian serial killer Andrel Chikatilo was noted to say of his victims, "The whole thing, the cries, the blood and the agony gave me relaxation and a certain pleasure . . . it brought me some peace of mind" (Cullen, 1994, p. 205). Similarly, Richard Ramirez ("The Night Stalker") stated that he "loved all that blood. I loved to watch them die" (Associated Press, 1986). It is again important to note that the lack of remorse demonstrated by most mass murderers and spree killers is qualitatively different than the enjoyment expressed by such serial killers.

Unlike mass murderers and spree killers, who appear to be concerned with the number of people they kill, serial killers are more

Jeffrey Dahmer being led into the courtroom.
REUTERS / Alamy Stock Photo

concerned with *how* their victims die than *how many* they kill. Gary Ridgeway ("The Green River Killer"), when asked how many victims he had, replied, "I killed so many, it's hard to keep track" (Seattle Post-Intelligencer, 2003). German serial killer Fritz Haarmann ("The Butcher of Hanover"), when asked the same question, replied, "Thirty or forty, I don't remember exactly" (Lane, 1993). If it was important to either of these offenders, they certainly could have and would have counted; it simply was not important to them. More important was the manner in which their victims died; the more slowly and painfully, the better as far as a serial killer is concerned.

Given their desire that their victims suffer slowly and to a great degree, it is not surprising that many serial killers choose very different methods of killing than do mass murderers or spree killers. Instead of the guns and bombs chosen by mass murderers and spree killers to kill as many people as quickly as possible, strangulation (either manually or using a ligature) is a common technique employed by serial killers (Pettigrew, 2019). John Wayne Gacy ("The Killer Clown") employed what he referred to as the "hammer trick": looping a rope around the neck of his victim and then inserting the handle of a hammer into this loop, so that he could tighten it and loosen it around the neck of his victim at will. Not surprisingly, at 6'9" tall and weighing over 300 pounds, Edmund Kemper had little difficulty overpowering and strangling his much smaller female victims. Strangulation is an up-close-and-personal crime and affords the killer a chilling degree of control over when and how the victim dies.

In fairness, it should be noted that there are exceptions to the pattern of serial killers not using firearms in the commission of their offenses. For example, David Berkowitz ("The Son of Sam") shot and killed eight people with a .44 caliber handgun, and Aileen Wuornos shot and killed seven men between 1989 and 1990. In the next chapter, we will discuss the Beltway Snipers, a pair of serial killers who also used firearms to kill. Similar to many other aspects of their offending, the notion that many serial killers use weapons that kill slowly is a tendency and is not carved in stone; there are always exceptions to the rule.

THROUGH THE EYES OF THE VICTIM: THE GLOBAL IMPACT OF SCHOOL SHOOTINGS

The impact of school shootings on both the immediate community and the country as a whole cannot possibly be overestimated. Although homicide is the second-leading cause of death among 5- to 18-year-olds, homicides in the school are quite rare, comprising only 2% of all youth homicides (Centers for Disease Control and Prevention, 2019). However, such tragedies appear to have an impact out of proportion to their frequency. Googling "Columbine High School Shooting" yields more than 14,100,000 results. At least 30 books have been written on the topic, and articles related to this incident are too numerous to count. People all over the United States and in other countries donated more than $6 million to more than 30 charities in the wake of Columbine (Liebelson, 2013). Similarly, Googling "Sandy Hook Elementary School Shooting" yields more than 4,300,000 results, at least 12 books, and (again) articles beyond counting. Donations to the school and victims totaled in the neighborhood of $15 million. The impact does not end with the emotional trauma caused to those directly and indirectly impacted by these and other tragedies.

In the wake of Columbine and other school shootings, many schools have implemented and maintained a system of requiring clear book bags and backpacks, passing through metal detectors at the entrance to the school, various uniform requirements and/or dress codes, and the hiring of school resource officers (armed or unarmed). Zero-tolerance policies for weapons and threats have been adopted by the vast majority of schools (91%, according to USA Today; Cauchon, 1999), with anecdotal reports of such policies going so far as prohibiting children who dress as firefighters and police for school Halloween events from including toy axes or guns as part of their costumes.

Along with changes in school policies, significant changes in police and SWAT team tactics in regard to school shooters/active shooters have been implemented nationwide. After an extremely slow response by police and SWAT teams at Columbine, tactics have changed to a much more dynamic and rapid approach (CNN, 1999). Many school districts and police collaborate by having active shooter drills on school grounds, sometimes during the school day. However, such procedures meant to enhance safety may have an (unintended) adverse effect; some studies suggest a 39% increase in depression, a 42% increase in stress and anxiety, and a 23% increase in physiological health concerns among students in schools where active shooter drills are practiced as opposed to schools that do not practice such drills (Everytown Research and Policy, 2020). The balance between protecting students from violence and maintaining an environment that is emotionally safe and supportive is vitally important and will deserve ongoing attention and effort.

What Can Be Done to Protect Our Schools and Our Children?

On December 14, 2012, for reasons that are still unclear, spree killer Adam Lanza perpetrated one of the most heinous acts ever committed on school grounds, shooting and killing six teachers and 20 first graders at Sandy Hook Elementary School before turning the gun on himself. To say that America (and other nations) was stunned by this tragedy would be an understatement. Along with the understandable anger, grief, and other emotions that accompanied this event was the question, "What can we do to make sure this doesn't happen again?" In an effort to find real answers to that question, Governor of Connecticut Dannel P. Malloy formed the Sandy Hook Advisory Commission (SHAC). The SHAC was comprised of 16 subject-matter experts in law enforcement, mental health, security, and facility safety engineering. These subject-matter experts, in consultation with numerous outside experts, spent two years studying the tragedy at Sandy Hook Elementary and other campuses where such shootings had occurred. The purpose of the SHAC was not to point fingers or place blame

A tribute to the teachers and children who lost their lives in the Sandy Hook Elementary School shooting.

iStock/ Eliyahu Parypa

but to determine what measures could be taken as part of an effort to prevent such tragedies in the future. The final report to Governor Malloy was a 277-page tour-de-force.

Ultimately, the SHAC recommended an all-hazards approach to school safety; that is, an approach not geared simply at school shootings but in making schools safer in every way possible—safer in the event of school shooters, natural disasters, fire, civil unrest, and so on. Interestingly, the #1 recommendation of the SHAC was this: All classroom and safe-area doors can be locked quickly and easily from the inside by the teacher or students. This recommendation was made with good reason: In investigating numerous school shootings, the SHAC found that "there has never been an event in which a shooter breached a locked classroom door" (Sandy Hook Advisory Commission, 2015, p. 24) Put simply, the ability to lock the classroom door quickly and easily from the inside saves lives. The SHAC also recommended that exterior doors be equipped to implement a full-perimeter lockdown; in other words, the press of a single button should close and lock all exterior doors. Entryways should have double sets of doors so that visitors enter one set of doors but cannot enter the next set of doors into the school until they have shown ID and made their purpose known to school officials. It was also recommended that heavily populated areas (such as classrooms) be placed as far away from the main entrance as possible. In such a manner, an active shooter who is able to breach the perimeter may find himself entering empty meeting or storage rooms, giving students, teachers, and law enforcement a longer time to react to this potential danger.

CONCLUSION

Although we may have been told to never judge a book by its cover, is it not the case that the cover tells us a great deal about the book? The cover should indeed tell us, at the very least, the name of the author, the title of the book, and (between the title and the picture on the cover) a reasonably good idea of what the book is about. Similarly, analysis of a crime scene may help the forensic psychologist to develop an idea of the type of individual who may have committed a particular offense; the crime can and does tell us about the criminal. Although mass murders, spree killings, and serial killings are relatively rare occurrences, their portrayal in the media has fueled a public fascination with such offenses and those who commit them. It is hoped that by understanding the pathology that underlies such offenses and the development of offender typologies, we will be better able to apprehend such criminals and to keep ourselves and our families safer in the future.

Exercises and Discussion Questions

1. It could be argued that Malvo and Muhammad (the Beltway Snipers) were serial killers: They killed more than three people in different places at different times with a cooling-off period between kills. However, it could also be argued that they do not fit the mold of serial killers in that they killed quickly with a rifle from a great distance. Would you categorize them as serial killers, spree killers, or something else? Explain your rationale.

2. As the superintendent of your local school district, you have decided that you want to make your schools as safe as possible in every way. What physical changes would you make to the structure of the building and what changes in policy and procedure might you make to keep the students as safe as possible? Remember, you do not have an unlimited budget to do so, so it is important to be realistic about the changes that you suggest.

3. In this chapter, we discussed Adam Lanza, the perpetrator of the Sandy Hook Elementary School shooting. Conduct your own research; do you believe that Lanza was mentally ill at the time he committed this offense? Was he psychotic, a psychopath, or did he exhibit signs of some other mental illness? Explain your position and rationale.

4. Some people would say that easy access to firearms in the United States has fueled the number of mass murderers and spree killings, as ready access to weapons makes it easier to perpetrate such offenses. Others would say that it is the person, not the weapon, that is responsible for such offenses and that allowing citizens to be armed makes society safer. Which of these positions do you support and why?

KEY TERMS

Borderline personality disorder
Hare Psychopathy Checklist–Revised
Modus operandi (M.O.)
Narcissistic personality disorder

Psychopathy
Psychosis/psychotic
Ritualistic behavior

8 BEHAVIORAL ANALYSIS

LEARNING OBJECTIVES

1. Explain the manner in which early unsolved cases led to the application of the scientific method in attempting to apprehend offenders.

2. Discuss the manner in which movies, television programs, and other forms of media have misled the public about the criminal profiling process.

3. Cite and explain important tenets of criminal profiling.

4. Discuss the accuracy of the notion that to catch a killer, you must think like a killer.

5. Identify and describe at least three different profiling methodologies.

6. Describe the purpose and process of victim–offender mediation.

On television and in the movies, the portrayal of the criminal profiler is often strikingly similar: A serial killer who the press has dubbed "The Jester" or something equally dramatic is on the loose, police are baffled, and the pressure is on to find the perpetrator before they strike again. For reasons never explained in the story, a young, inexperienced Federal Bureau of Investigation (FBI) agent is brought in from the Behavioral Assessment Unit to assist with the case. The agent begins by interviewing a captive serial killer, the rationale being that the best way to understand the strategy, tactics, and next target of the current threat is to talk to someone who has committed similar crimes in the past.

After several conversations with the imprisoned serial killer, the young agent visits the scene of one of The Jester's crimes. Ominous music plays while the agent (alone, of course!) walks through the dark, dusty crime scene, examining bloodstains, photographs, and personal effects of the victim. The tension builds as the music reaches a crescendo. Suddenly, as if by magic, an image flashes through the profiler's mind, perhaps too quick for us to make it out clearly. And then another—a flashback to the crime itself—a knife being thrust or perhaps the sound of a scream. Several more times this happens, as if the agent has been transported back to the time of the offense itself. These images lead the agent to find a strand of hair that the legion of police and detectives who had thoroughly searched the scene somehow missed. The angle of the shot makes us think that maybe the killer has returned to the scene of the crime! But no, the agent staggers back outside into the bright sunshine. After returning to headquarters, the young agent is able to inform their boss that the killer is a male in his mid-30s, was abused by his mother, and is committing his offenses according to the phase of the moon. The agent adds that the blood spatter clearly indicates that The Jester is left-handed. The agent then places the hair they found in a futuristic computer and a 3D hologram of the hair is projected into the air. From this, the agent is quickly able to confirm their profile and track the name, address, and license plate number of The Jester. The profiler then rushes to a private jet and lands in time to meet the SWAT team, puts on a bulletproof vest, draws their duty weapon, and leads the team down a dark passage, where (after a dramatic shoot-out), the agent subdues and captures The Jester.

Scenarios such as the above are both fascinating and thrilling. But as dramatic and engaging as such a scene may be, it is full of unanswered questions. Why would the FBI send their least experienced agent to interview a serial killer? Why should we believe that a serial killer would be motivated to be truthful to us or care if another serial killer is apprehended? Where do these magical visions experienced by the FBI agent come from? Are we really expected to believe that some type of psychic or supernatural event is occurring or that the agent has some type of hidden powers? Are we supposed to believe that the agent found a strand of hair that escaped the notice of everyone else? Are we also expected to believe that along with being a criminal profiler, the agent is a trained blood spatter expert and therefore able to deduce the handedness of the killer? What logical explanation is there for the agent's ability to announce confidently the killer's history of being abused? Other than in movies, when have we ever seen a computer project 3D holograms into the air while spitting out every fact we need to solve the case? In addition to the agent being a blood spatter expert and profiler, doesn't it seem to be a bit of a stretch to also believe that they are the leader of the SWAT team? Why do we never see the agent completing a mountain of paperwork, sitting in their cubicle trying to find their stapler or attending some boring training? If we stop suspending our disbelief and think about this scenario for a few moments, the (numerous) holes in it become quite obvious.

THE (VERY) EARLY DAYS OF CRIMINAL PROFILING

In 1888, the residents of London England were scared, and with good reason. In the London slums, the bodies of women were found to have been brutally murdered. In addition to having their throats cut, some of the bodies demonstrated evidence of post-mortem mutilation, with internal organs having been removed. The murderer was dubbed by the press the "Whitechapel Murderer" and sometimes referred to as "Jack the Ripper"; this case included an early attempt at behavioral analysis. Dr. George Phillips carefully examined the victims' wounds as part of an attempt to make deductions about and identify the perpetrator. Given the offender's propensity for removing some of the internal organs of the victims, it was speculated by some that the offender must be a surgeon or have some formal knowledge of surgical techniques. Though the cases were never conclusively solved, they certainly did spark human interest in terms of what the crime might tell us about the criminal themselves.

In the previous chapter, we saw Sherlock Holmes's amazing observational skills in Sir Arthur Conan Doyle's *A Scandal in Bohemia*. In that novel, Holmes notes, "It is a capital mistake to theorize before you have evidence. It biases the judgement." Though based on a fictional character in a book written more than a century ago, this statement still holds true and is wisely applied to criminal profiling.

The Scientific Revolution, starting in the mid-1500s and extending until the late 1700s, was a time of sweeping change in the manner in which people observed and studied the world around them. At this time, people began to apply the scientific method of observation, formulation of hypotheses, and experimentation to the fields of mathematics, biology, chemistry, astronomy, and other areas (Hannam, 2011). It was hoped that by doing so, humans could solve many of the world's great mysteries and improve people's quality of life in a wide variety of ways.

Hans Gustav Adolf Gross (1847–1915) was an Austrian criminal jurist and criminologist, considered by many to be the Founding Father of criminal profiling. He established the Institute of Criminology in Graz, Austria, and developed the idea of using the scientific method to study criminals and criminal behavior (Grassberger, 1957). Gross emphasized the importance of an objective examination of facts and evidence as opposed to intuition and personal opinion. Gross strongly believed in the importance of balancing emotion and judgment with logic, reasoning, and evidence (Burney & Pemberton, 2012).

Criminal Profiling: George Metesky, "The Mad Bomber"

Many years after the case of Jack the Ripper, New York City residents experienced a similar fear, again with good reason. Someone was planting bombs in the heart of that city—in Grand Central Station, Penn Station, the subway, Radio City Music Hall, and other popular attractions. At least 22 of the 33 bombs exploded, injuring more than 15 people. Despite the bomber calling in threats, writing letters to the local newspaper, and even leaving notes with some of the bombs, police were unable to determine the identity of the perpetrator. The only obvious item from the notes was that the bomber had a grudge against Con Edison, the supplier of electrical power in New York City at the time.

Despite the best efforts of the New York Police Department (NYPD), little progress was being made in terms of identifying the bomber. Captain Cronin of the NYPD was friends with Dr. Brussel, a psychiatrist who also had experience in working with criminals. Captain Cronin turned to him for help, allowing Dr. Brussel to examine evidence related to the case in hopes that the good doctor could shed some light on the identity of the offender. It is notable that a precedent set in this case remains in effect today: Behavioral analysis is not performed in cases that are actively being investigated and where evidence is still being collected. It is not until all evidence has been collected and the investigation is at an impasse that behavioral analysis should be utilized.

Dr. Brussel began his analysis with evidence: "Male, as historically most bombers are male" (Boysun, 2011). (Indeed, excluding those women who are suicide bombers, it is so rare for women to be bombers that it is nearly impossible to find data on this topic.) "Well-proportioned and of average build, based on studies of hospitalized mental patients." (Again, Dr. Brussel is referencing his studies and evidence.) "Forty to fifty years old, as paranoia develops slowly. . . . Precise, neat and tidy based on his letters and the workmanship of his bombs." Dr. Brussel continued to refer to objective data; in this case, evidence related to the offender himself: His letters and bombs show evidence of being precise and organized. Again, this is logically derived from the facts; people who are impulsive and fail to pay attention to detail would seem likely to come to a sudden and violent end when attempting to build a bomb.

"An exemplary employee, on-time and well behaved" (Boysun, 2011). Only here does Dr. Brussel begin to speculate, but while doing so, he does not stray far from the evidence and his ideas remain evidence based. After all, wouldn't an employee whose work was precise and neat likely be the ideal employee in many ways? Dr. Brussel goes on to say that the bomber is likely to be "courteous, but not friendly. A loner, no friends, little interest in women. Unmarried, perhaps living with an older female relative. He will be wearing a double-breasted suit, buttoned." In these last few sentences, we are not sure how Dr. Brussel is drawing these inferences. What is known is that police raided the home of George Metesky late at night, and before taking him into custody, they allowed him to change from his pajamas into clothing of his choice—and he chose a double-breasted suit, buttoned.

Perhaps Dr. Brussel's prediction in regard to Metesky's clothing was one of simple probability; double-breasted suits were common in that day and age. Or perhaps he got lucky on this prediction, or maybe Dr. Brussel was making use of some difficult-to-explain (but accurate!) intuition. In any case, his incredibly precise analysis of this case set the bar very high in terms of people's expectations related to behavioral analysis.

Federal Bureau of Investigation (FBI)

Federal Bureau of Investigation (FBI) Special Agent Howard Duane Teten is often credited as the first official profiler at FBI headquarters in Quantico, Virginia. As a police officer who studied both psychology and criminology, he began to see parallels between these two fields

George Metesky, "The Mad Bomber," under arrest; his suit was styled and buttoned exactly as predicted by Dr. Brussel.

Everett Collection Historical / Alamy Stock Photo

and became interested in what motivated some criminals to behave in the manner they did. In 1970, he started to teach about his theories, which he referred to as "applied criminology." Teten and Special Agent Jack Hirsch founded the **Behavioral Sciences Unit (BSU)** at the FBI headquarters in Quantico, Virginia, in 1972. Later, Roy Hazelwood, Robert Ressler, and John Douglas continued to expand on the idea that by interviewing offenders, one could identify common characteristics, develop typologies, and brainstorm how and why an offender had committed a crime. It is important to note that they were not proposing that agents use these techniques to identify specifically *who* the offender was but rather *how* and *why* the offender was committing such crimes. Their subsequent books further fueled public interest in profiling.

In 1994, the FBI established their **Critical Incident Response Group (CIRG)**. The purpose of this reorganization was to integrate tactical responses, negotiations, behavioral analysis, and other crisis management services into one cohesive structure. The **National Center for Analysis of Violent Crime (NCAVC)** and the Behavioral Sciences Units (now known as the **Behavioral Analysis Units or BAUs**) now fall under the umbrella of CIRG. There are currently five BAUs in addition to the **Violent Crime Apprehension Program(ViCap)**. ViCap is a computer-based program that allows the FBI to compile (and share with approved agencies) a plethora of data collected from violent offenses across the country. The information stored in ViCap includes (but is not limited to) crime scene photos, victim and offender data, crime scene descriptions, and court records. It is hoped that by collecting and sharing this information with other law enforcement organizations, ViCap will assist in the apprehension and conviction of serial violent offenders.

At the present time, the FBI has five BAUs dedicated to case support, analysis, and education. Each of the five BAUs is dedicated to a separate task. Some deal with crimes specifically committed against children; others with terrorism, counterterrorism, or threats of violence; and BAU 5, which is the descendant of the original BSU, focuses on teaching, research, and strategy. The task of BAU 5 is to use behavior analysis to provide operational support involving complex, typically violent crimes. The FBI website (https://www.fbi.gov) does not indicate how many people in the BAUs are considered full-time or part-time profilers. Law enforcement agencies can request the assistance of FBI BAU by reaching out to a coordinator in any of the FBI's 56 field offices located across the country (FBI, 2014). There is no charge for BAU assistance.

Although we may typically think of behavioral analysis as a process engaged in only by FBI agents and other highly trained professionals, it is important to keep in mind that all of us analyze and interpret the behaviors of those around us on a daily basis. This may or may not be done in any formal or systematic manner, but we still do so. You may notice that the student who sits two seats over from you consistently smiles when you look in their direction. You may analyze this behavior and ask yourself if they are simply a friendly person who tends to smile at everyone or is this a sign of potential romance? Perhaps the person driving ahead of you is weaving back and forth a bit in their lane. Is there reason to believe they are intoxicated or is it possible that they are attempting to text while driving? Perhaps your professor is getting ready to return last week's tests and looks rather glum. Does that mean the grades are poor or merely that the professor didn't sleep well last night? In our everyday lives, it is commonplace for us to observe others, analyze their behaviors, and try to come up with our own Sherlock Holmes–like deductions about what that behavior means. There are many clues that provide us with potentially valuable information about those around us. As we will see below, even the vehicle someone drives is fodder for analysis.

BEHAVIORAL ANALYSIS IN DAILY LIFE

Even seemingly mundane objects, such as the type of vehicle someone drives or the bumper stickers they put on it, can give us valuable clues about that person. Look at the two vehicles in Figure 8.1. You would likely be able to guess which political party each person supported. You would have little difficulty guessing which of the owners supported the Second Amendment. If asked which driver would be pro-choice and which would be pro-life, again, you would likely have little difficulty making an educated guess in this regard. Even making a prediction about which driver is vegan and which enjoys a juicy steak would likely be fairly simple. We can and do conduct behavioral analyses on the basis of what we see, hear, and experience every single day of our lives.

FIGURE 8.1 ■ Bumper Stickers

B Christopher / Alamy Stock Photo; Michael Dwyer / Alamy Stock Photo

THE ACCURACY OF PROFESSIONS AS PORTRAYED IN THE MEDIA

Released in 1986, *Top Gun* starring Tom Cruise as Lt. Pete "Maverick" Mitchell was a box-office smash, ultimately making more than $350 million. Moviegoers were in awe of fighter jets taking off and landing through the smoke and haze of the sunrise while set to the dramatic music of "Danger Zone" by Kenny Loggins. Just how accurately the movie portrays life as a naval aviator is perhaps best left to naval aviators to judge. However, there is no question as to the success of the movie, even as a recruiting tool. *Top Gun* was the highest-grossing film of 1986. It increased Navy recruitment by a staggering 400% (some sources even quote it at 500%; Sirota, 2011); 90% of Navy pilot hopefuls told recruiters they had seen the movie (Leidy, 2020). *Top Gun: Maverick*, released in 2022, has already grossed close to $1.5 billion (Thompson, 2022). Time will tell if this sequel will have the same impact on naval recruiting as its predecessor did.

The *Top Gun* franchise shows us that dramatic portrayals can convince many people to attempt to pursue a vocation even though only a few people will likely be qualified to do so, and even then, the job itself may be vastly different from what they expected. Things may not be so different when we discuss careers in criminal profiling; an exciting and immensely popular movie or television program is not necessarily an accurate portrayal of reality.

There are almost too many books to count on the subject of criminal offenders and profiling. Some novels are clearly fictional in nature, others purport to be true stories of criminal profiling but are penned by authors of dubious backgrounds, and others are written by experienced professionals, some of which include the pioneers of the FBI's original BSU. John Douglas, who served 25 years in the FBI's Investigative Support Unit, has written a number of popular books, including *Mindhunter: Inside the FBI's Elite Serial Crime Unit*. Robert Ressler, another FBI agent, wrote *Whoever Fights Monsters: My Twenty Years of Tracking Serial Killers for the FBI*, and Roy Hazelwood wrote *The Evil That Men Do: FBI Profiler Roy Hazelwood's Journey into the Minds of Sexual Predators*. Don DeNevi and John Campbell wrote *Into the Minds of Madmen: How the FBI's Behavioral Sciences Unit Revolutionized Crime Investigation*. All of these books and many others are quite popular. However, distinguishing between those that have some academic merit and those that are fiction masquerading as fact can be difficult at times.

The BSU/BAU and criminal profilers are also popularly portrayed in movies and on television. The 1981 book *Red Dragon* by Thomas Harris became a movie called *Manhunter* in 1986. Thomas Harris's 1988 *Silence of the Lambs* portrayed the early days of the BSU and became a top-grossing movie soon after it debuted in 1991. The movie generated considerable acclaim from critics and audiences alike, with Jody Foster winning one Academy Award for her role as FBI Agent Clarice Starling and Anthony Hopkins winning another for his portrayal of serial killer Dr. Hannibal Lecter. The CBS series *Criminal Minds* portrays the BAU, as does several episodes of *Law and Order: SVU*.

Profiler was a television series from 1996–2000, in which Ally Walker played Dr. Sam Walters, a profiler assisting a number of federal agencies in solving violent offenses. In addition to being a criminal profiler, Dr. Walters had the supernatural gift of being able to see through the eyes of other people, which helps her to see the crimes as if she was the offender that she is seeking. The combination of her profiling skills and supernatural ability allowed her to track down and apprehend offenders. Such a portrayal may certainly be dramatic and entertaining but is terribly inaccurate and should not be interpreted by those who watch the program as being representative of any type of reality.

The present author, in his role as an associate professor of criminal justice, has frequent occasion to talk to students who are considering a career in criminal justice. Too many to count reference one of the countless movies, television shows, or podcasts as their inspiration for wishing to pursue a career in criminal justice in general or as a criminal profiler specifically. It is vitally important for the budding forensic psychologist to remember that as fascinating as such portrayals may be, they do not necessarily paint an accurate picture of careers in the field and, in some cases, may badly mislead the public about the availability and requirements of such positions.

The "*CSI* Effect"

As we will see in the next chapter, a jury must be convinced beyond a reasonable doubt of a defendant's guilt to convict them for a given offense. However, Hedgepeth in the *Campbell Law Observer* (2012) notes that portrayals as seen on television shows such as *CSI: Crime Scene Investigations* have greatly raised the standards of what is considered to be beyond a reasonable doubt. The **CSI effect** refers to the notion that such programs have led many potential jurors to believe that numerous complex and involved scientific, investigative, and DNA tests can be quickly and easily performed and are expected and required for a finding of guilt.

Hedgepeth (2012) goes on to reference a case in which a teenage girl was raped in a local park in Peoria, Illinois, in 2004. The victim was able to identify the accused, his property was found at the scene, and it was demonstrated that his saliva was present on the breast of his victim. Despite this evidence, the jury found the accused to be not guilty, after which, one jury member commented that the jury had wanted proof that the dirt found on her body matched the dirt at the scene of the crime. Given that no such evidence had been provided, the juror reported that the jury did not feel the case was proven beyond a reasonable doubt. In this case, it might appear that the inaccurate portrayals often depicted on television and in the movies might have played a role in the jury's decision.

WHEN CRIMINAL PROFILING GOES WRONG

Those who seek to construct criminal profiles must be acutely aware of the very serious errors that have been made in the past when it comes to making overgeneralizations, false accusations, and (in some cases) punishing the innocent. In and around the town of Salem, Massachusetts, between 1692 and 1693, the townspeople were terrified that there were witches among them, conspiring with the Devil to do harm to the community. Thus began what became known as the **Salem Witch Trials**. Women, especially those whose physical appearance did not fit the image that was expected of them in that era, were regarded with suspicion (Reis, 1997). Those who were unmarried and had no children, especially those with a mole or blemish that was insensitive to touch (Roach, 2002) were often accused of practicing witchcraft.

Those who confessed to being witches were often spared punishment (which one would presume would lead to a certain number of false confessions!). Those who did not confess were prosecuted with little (if any attempt) at due process and were often convicted exclusively based on "spectral evidence." That is, a witness would testify that they saw a vision or "specter" of the accused, and this was often accepted as proof of the guilt of the accused (Craker, 1997). On the basis of such proof, "witches" were hung. Such hysterical accusations and lack of evidence are clearly a violation of any type of due process or fair trial and resulted in innocent people being put to death, often based on nothing more than their gender or physical appearance.

Early Sciences

In the early 1800s, German physician Dr. Franz Joseph Gall began to examine the idea that the shape of an individual's skull could provide us with meaningful and important information about their personality. This "science," which became known as **phrenology**, started with the idea that different parts of the brain have specific, localized functions. Gall believed that bumps, divots, or imperfections on the outside of a person's skull were correlated with the localized function of the brain underneath that part of the skull and that feeling or measuring those bumps or divots on the surface of the head would provide useful and reliable information about the individual's underlying brain. This idea was popular enough that the Edinburgh Phrenological Society was established in 1820, and phrenological theory played a significant role in psychiatric and psychological theory during this time. By the 1840s, there were more than 28 different phrenological societies in London, with more than 1,000 members (Staum, 2003). However, despite the popularity of this theory and the fact that there were official organizations dedicated to its study, the idea that the small bumps and imperfections in the skull were correlated with the underlying functioning of the brain ultimately had no merit. It is important for forensic (and all!) scientists to keep in mind that a theory can become popular and spawn organizations and conferences and later be found to have no scientific validity. Popularity does *not* necessarily indicate accuracy.

Cesare Lombroso (1835–1909) was an Italian physician and criminologist. He believed that criminality was an inherited trait, no different than the color of one's hair or eyes. In the ongoing debate of nature versus nurture, he decisively favored nature. That is, he believed that some people were born criminals and that it was possible to identify such individuals through physical characteristics, such as left-handedness, which he associated with criminal and "degenerate" behavior (Kushner, 2013). Lombroso became known as the Father of **positivist criminology**, the idea that criminals are born rather than made. He expressed the belief that criminals were **atavistic** or savages, essentially a different (and worse) type of person than noncriminals (Carra, 2004). While his attempts to recognize criminality may have been well intended, it is important for us to recognize that the notion that people are "savages" or that criminals can be recognized merely based upon physical appearance is dangerous territory indeed.

In hindsight, it is easy to criticize the Salem Witch Trials, the "science" of Gall's phrenology, or Lombroso's attempts to identify "born criminals." As we will see below, much more recent attempts at profiling have also missed the mark, as happened in the case of the Beltway Snipers. We must balance our desire to protect the community from harm against the harm done by jumping to conclusions and making accusations that are erroneous, misleading, or downright false.

THE DC SNIPERS: WHEN BEHAVIORAL ANALYSIS GOES WRONG

In October of 2002, the communities in and around Washington DC, Maryland, and Virginia were scared and those fears were certainly justified. A sniper (or as it would turn out, *snipers*) was terrorizing the area. Innocent people who were simply putting gas in their car, going to the grocery store, or walking from the mall to their car were being shot and killed from a distance. Unbeknownst to anyone at the time, this killing spree had actually begun in February in the states of Alabama, Arizona, Florida, Georgia, Louisiana, and Texas, where the perpetrators had, over the course of the last eight months, shot and killed seven people and seriously wounded seven more.

In October, the killings increased in frequency, with four people being killed in separate incidents on October 3 alone. The busy DC metropolitan area came to a near-standstill. Gas stations hung tarps around the pumps so that customers might feel safer. The discovery of a Tarot card with the scrawled phrase "Call me God" at the scene of one of the shootings and the discovery of a letter from the shooters stating, "Your children are not safe anywhere, at any time," only heightened tensions further.

Armchair behavior analysts—with little (or no) evidence—began to assume that this shooting was the work of a single white male, perhaps with military experience. Rumors of the shootings being connected to a white box truck spread rapidly, with drivers of such trucks (which are quite common as work trucks for various trades) being regarded with considerable suspicion and pulled over and searched frequently by police and SWAT teams (MacGillis et al., 2002).

In fact, the shooters in this case were John Allen Muhammad, who was 41 years old at the time, and Lee Boyd Malvo, 17 years old at the time. Both Muhammad and Malvo were Black and were not driving a white box truck but a blue Caprice Classic. They had converted the trunk of this vehicle into a "sniper's nest" so that a shot could be taken from a supine position out a narrow aperture in the rear of the trunk (Pedrini, 2007). In fact, the shooters and the vehicle were so different from what was expected that it appears they were stopped for a minor traffic violation in the Caprice on October 3 and were then allowed to leave. At the end of October, Muhammad and Malvo were discovered sleeping in the car and were arrested, ending the killing spree. Muhammad has since been executed, and Malvo remains incarcerated to this day. As useful as behavioral analysis can be, it must be remembered that incorrect analysis that leads investigators in the wrong direction can do more harm than good and can delay rather than expedite the process of bringing the offender to justice.

TENETS OF PROFILING/BEHAVIORAL ANALYSIS

It is a tenet of behavioral analysis that behavior reflects personality. Behavioral analysis holds that the way an individual *acts* is a function of who they *are*, and by studying how people act, the forensic psychologist can make inferences about that individual's personality. The more available data, the more likely it is that those inferences will be accurate. If I've only ever met Teddy once at a party and observed him to be rather loud and interacting with everyone there, I might believe him to be an outgoing person. However, based on a single observation, there is a decent chance I'm wrong; maybe Teddy was simply intoxicated or in an unusually upbeat mood that day. However, if I've known Teddy for years and on repeated occasions seen and heard him to be loud and boisterous, I may more accurately infer that he is indeed extroverted and outgoing. On this basis, if you were to ask me to predict his behavior if he were to attend the Super Bowl, I could make a better-than-chance guess that he would likely cheer loudly and be extroverted and energetic in that setting.

Cumulative evidence allows typologies to be developed (Turvey, 2012). Although it is important to guard against stereotyping, it is the case that cumulative evidence can provide important information and may at times be used to predict behavior. As discussed in Chapter 5, insurance companies use cumulative evidence regarding driver age and frequency of accidents to determine insurance rates. Doing so has allowed them to determine that 16- and 17-year-old drivers are at greater risk of having an accident than older drivers are (Tefft, 2017). This is a typology: Younger drivers are at greater risk than older drivers. This is not to say that every younger driver is at greater risk than every older driver, only that there is evidence for the typology in general.

For the forensic psychologist, cumulative evidence from the scene of a homicide might help to construct a typology. Careful investigation of the crime scene can provide important evidence about the offender. Perhaps a homicide victim is found to be bound with coarse rope and their mouth sealed shut with black duct tape. No fingerprints are found on the body or at the scene. If a search of the premises does not yield any similar coarse rope or black duct tape, we might well infer that the perpetrator brought these items with them. The lack of fingerprints might suggest that the offender was wearing gloves or carefully wiped the scene clean prior to leaving. In either case, a behavioral analyst will likely think of an offender who planned the assault ahead of time, bringing with them what they needed to commit the crime. Thus, there is reason to believe that the offender was able to think logically and methodically planned and organized the crime ahead of time. However, if it was determined that the victim was secured with the extension cord to the television and then stabbed with a knife from the kitchen drawer, it would appear more logical to conclude that the crime may have been a spur-of-the moment one, with the offender using items that were readily available to them at the moment.

The scientific method, used since the 1700s, is a method by which we attempt to acquire knowledge. Briefly described, the scientific method first involves observation of the world around us, followed by research on a particular topic. We then formulate a hypothesis (an educated guess) at what might be happening (or how or why). We then conduct experiments or seek to obtain some objective data. After doing so, we analyze that data and attempt to draw a logical, objective conclusion concerning the accuracy of our initial hypothesis. Whether or not our hypothesis is correct is not the point; either way, the scientific method allows us to learn something about the world around us. Even if we learn that our hypothesis was incorrect, we have still learned something. This scientific method has been used to help us understand more about astronomy, physics, human behavior, geology, and other fields too numerous to name.

Motive

Criminal profiling seeks to define motive, as motives affect behavior (Leonard, 2001). That is, *why* is an offender doing what they are doing? What material, emotional, psychological, or physical needs is the offense meeting? In prison, some staff would say that an inmate's motivation for engaging in a particular behavior (for example, self-injury) would be to manipulate others. However, on further reflection, what exactly does *manipulate* mean in this context? What is the inmate manipulating for and why? It is important that forensic analysts to be able to go beyond the obvious (and not necessarily correct) answers.

Motive may be difficult or impossible to know for certain, but it may be inferred with some degree of confidence from evidence at the scene. The burglar who took a large jar of change in the room with the broken window did not appear to look around the rest of the apartment and did not take other valuable items in other rooms. This might seem impulsive and certainly doesn't demonstrate much evidence of planning. Such an offense may seem rushed, with the offender grabbing the first item of any value they could find before making a quick retreat. So maybe they were an anxious, first-time offender. This certainly does not show evidence of being a skilled and practiced burglar.

In some cases, even the offender does not appear to know why they committed their offense. While working in the prison system, the present author was well acquainted with "William" (not his real name, and some of the details of the event have been altered to protect those involved). William had committed a brutal rape in a local park. He was sitting on a park bench enjoying the sunshine and claimed he had no intention of committing any crime when a young woman rode her bike past him and down a nearby trail. William got up from the bench, pursued her down the trail, knocked her off her bike, and raped her. William did demonstrate some intellectual limitations and a moderate level of mental health challenges, but overall, he was cooperative, coherent, and typically quite pleasant in social interactions. Every year, he met with the parole board, and every year, they asked him the same question: "William, why did you rape her?" His face would go blank, and he'd start by saying something like "I knew you were going to ask me that, so I've thought about it a lot this past year," only to conclude with "and I just don't have any idea of why I did it." Understandably, the parole board was concerned that if he didn't know why he committed this offense, what would prevent him from committing another? Year after year, the parole board gave William another year to think about it, but he was repeatedly unable to gain insight into his own motivation, despite that if he was able to do so, he might possibly gain his release from incarceration. In cases where the offender themselves is unable to determine the motivation for their offending, how difficult must it be for the profiler, on the outside looking in, to do so?

Practical Aspects of Profiling

It is vitally important for the scientist (forensic or otherwise) to remain open-minded and to be acutely aware of the fact that they may be wrong or may need to reconsider possibilities that they had previously ruled out. Scientists are not attempting to prove that their hypothesis is correct but rather are testing their hypothesis to see if it can be disproven (Popper, 1959). Objectivity is key, and emotion should be left outside the laboratory door. A skilled practitioner will look not only for evidence that supports their theories but also for evidence that refutes those theories. It is important to be able to recognize one's own limitations. It is advisable that a profiler uses words such as *likely, probably,* and other words that clearly indicate when they are uncertain or when they are speculating. It is ethical and appropriate to make the boundaries of one's knowledge abundantly clear.

Part of understanding the behavior and thought patterns of criminals can only be obtained by working with them on a regular basis. Research is certainly important and should never be discounted, but it is also important to consider real-life experience. The forensic psychologist must be careful in evaluating research on offenders, especially when that research is based on the self-report of those offenders. Being open-minded means that the practitioner recognizes and respects the unique nature of the people they are studying and is cognizant of the fact that individuals may be truthful, deceptive, or some combination of the two. During the course of his career, the present author read many reports that said (for example), "The inmate is a high school graduate." If such a statement is based on an objective examination of records or a call to an official at that school, then such a statement may well be valid. Unfortunately, such a statement often means, "I (the person writing the report) asked the inmate if he graduated from high school and he said yes." These two are obviously not equivalent. It would be more accurate to state, "The inmate reports graduating from high school, but there is no evidence to confirm or contradict this at the present time." Good scientists make it readily apparent when their knowledge is limited or incomplete.

In the experiences of the present author, interviewing offenders is often quite fascinating; some criminals are surprisingly willing to talk openly about their offenses, though the interviewer must be careful in attempting to separate truth from fiction. FBI behavior analysts are well aware of the fact that offenders are not always telling the truth, and they interview offenders hoping to learn from both the truth and the lies told by those offenders (FBI, 2011). Such agents conduct interviews with the full consent of the offender and the interviews are not confrontational; as they are being conducted with convicted criminals, there is no need to establish guilt as it has already been acknowledged. Instead, the purpose of such interviews is to understand more about *why* the offender did what they did so that if and when a similar case arises in the future, the profiler may have greater insight into the mindset, emotions, and/or behavior of that offender.

Unlike what we may see in movies and television, those who construct criminal profiles are not experts in multiple fields of study. Some forensics experts may spend an entire career studying the ballistics of various types of projectiles, the physics of traffic accidents, or the biology of a decomposing body. It is impossible for one person to be an expert in every field of forensics, so it is important for each professional to recognize and refer to the work of others and to make it abundantly clear when doing so. It would not be appropriate for a forensic psychologist to state, "The blood spatter pattern suggests that the gunshot occurred at close range." It is preferable to state, "The report of (name of analyst and date of report) states that the gunshot occurred at close range."

Forensic scientists are as susceptible as any other individuals are to engaging in **belief perseverance**, the human tendency to persist in a particular belief even in the face of directly contradictory evidence. The 1980s saw the emergence of "crop circles," areas where a farm crop such as corn or wheat was flattened down in a symmetrical and often complex design. Some people believed that alien life forms were responsible for constructing these designs. Remarkably, even after two men admitted to making the circles and demonstrated how they had done so, some people persisted in their belief that at least some of these phenomena were truly crafted by aliens. Forensic scientists and profilers must be extremely cautious about the human tendency to persist in a belief even in the face of markedly contradictory evidence. Scientists must maintain an open mind.

As discussed in Chapter 5, it is vitally important for forensic psychologists to remember that correlation does not imply causation. The fact that two variables are related does not necessarily indicate that one of those variables causes changes in the other. Just as the red car mentioned in earlier chapters does not cause the driver to get a speeding ticket, it should not be assumed that the fresh dent in the new car at the homicide scene caused the driver to assault and kill the victim. Forensic psychologists must keep an open mind, avoid assumptions, and be extremely careful in ascribing causality.

Police and other law enforcement professionals have extensive experience with criminals and crime scenes but may have little or no training in the behavioral sciences. Mental health professionals, on the other hand, may be quite familiar with research on human thought, emotion, and behavior but, in many cases, may have little practical experience with offenders or the workings of the criminal justice system. Forensic mental health professionals, who (ideally) have both training and practical experience, may be thought to have a foot on either side of the fence and be better at behavioral analysis. The importance of years of experience should never be underestimated. In the experience of the present author, many college students want to go directly from college or graduate school to the FBI's BAU and seem unaware that there are certain aspects of criminal thinking and behavior that can only be learned from firsthand experience.

Report Writing

In any report, it is important to establish exactly what sources of information were examined; the name, dates, and responsible persons or agencies for all files, photos, and pieces of evidence. Examining evidence may include hours of reading old files, looking at unpleasant photos, or contacting those who wrote the reports as part of an attempt to clarify something in that report. Good research includes attempting to make sense of information that appears contradictory or confusing. A visit to the crime scene may be helpful, if that is possible. Older records may include audio- or videotapes, which may require obtaining devices that are outdated or difficult to find in order to review them. This is an aspect of forensic investigation and criminal profiling that is distinctly missing from television shows and movies portraying profiling as being consistently exciting and fast-paced. It is important that the profiler conduct a thorough review of all evidence and reports, even when this means spending hours combing through dusty boxes of old records. The process is time-consuming, labor-intensive, often not terribly interesting, and never portrayed in movies. However, it is an essential part of the profiling process.

Along with a detailed explanation of what evidence and records were reviewed for a report, it is equally important to describe what information could *not* be accessed and why that was the case. If the scene of the crime has been demolished so that the analyst was able to view photographs but not visit the scene itself, it is important to note that explicitly. If there was someone who may have been helpful to talk to but they refused, this should also be made readily apparent in the report. Those reading the report will then be clear on the fact that due diligence was done in the research and writing of a profile.

It is important that reports and descriptions of criminal profiles should avoid using unnecessarily technical terminology or psychobabble. When writing a report, it is important to do so in such a manner that a person who is not a psychologist or forensic expert can understand and make use of it. "The schizophrenic patient demonstrated evidence of auditory and visual hallucinations and speech was characterized by echolalia" is likely to be confusing rather than helpful. It would be just as accurate (and much less confusing for the reader) to state, "Mr. Smith stated that he sometimes hears voices even when he is in a room alone and occasionally sees what he believes are fleeting images of a demon. His speech was at times repetitive and illogical." Clarity is an important part of any report.

It is essential that reports written by forensic practitioners be objective and unbiased. Although this may seem simple, when working with a forensic population, it may be more challenging than one would expect. It is entirely possible that the practitioner is working with offenders who are accused of or who are guilty of committing homicides, torture offenses, sex offenses, and other crimes that may be disturbing or offensive by their very nature. The author of this text had occasion to interview hundreds of people who had committed homicides and sex offenses, many of whom described their offenses in graphic detail. Such details may be included in reports, but the offenders themselves must be treated with respect and the writer of the report must be careful not to use judgmental or demeaning language in the body of the report. To say, "The offender has a history of committing two sex offenses" would be appropriate, but to state that the offender is a "monster" or to use other demeaning language would be unethical and highly inappropriate. Often, before submitting a report, it can be helpful to have a trusted colleague review it to make sure that there is no subtle (or obvious!) demeaning language included therein.

TO CATCH A KILLER, YOU HAVE TO THINK LIKE A KILLER—OR DO YOU?

"In order to catch a killer, we have to think like a killer." We have heard these words (or very similar ones) in the trailers for movies and television shows about criminal profiling. Such a phrase seems self-evident, but on further examination, is it valid? Would we be as ready to believe that to catch a fly, a spider must be able to think like a fly? Or are we instead able to understand that a spider instinctively weaves its web, never needing to think like a fly? Would we be as ready to believe that to catch a ball, one has to think like a ball? Or are we instead able to understand that to catch a ball, we simply have to think about the trajectory of the ball and how fast it is traveling? Although there may be situations in which it helps to think like an offender or to understand their motivation for offending, it should not be assumed this is a necessary or sufficient condition for catching the perpetrator of a homicide (or any other offense).

Furthermore, when it comes to thinking like a killer, how many of us are truly able to do that? The present author interviewed a man who killed his own brother in an argument over a forty-ounce bottle of beer. It seems unlikely that we can truly understand why anyone would do such a thing. Some serial killers have reported becoming sexually aroused by the act of killing another human being. Can most people truly understand such a horrific motivation and behavior? Hopefully not. So, not only is it unnecessary to think like a killer to catch a killer, but it also seems likely that it is beyond most people's ability to do so.

During his 20-year career as a psychologist in the Pennsylvania state prison system, the present author talked to offenders of every type imaginable: those who had committed robberies, sex offenses, murders, burglaries, drug offenses, and so on. Having done so, it seems fair to say that the explanations these offenders gave for committing their crimes were as varied as the individuals themselves. In the above case of the man who murdered his brother over a beer, he stated that he did so because his brother disrespected him by taking the beer. It is an oversimplification to believe that all criminals of a given type necessarily share many similarities any more than we would think that all lawyers, all bus drivers, or all chefs are cut of the same cloth and similar in many ways. We seem to know inherently that any two people of similar professions may be quite different in terms of gender, political beliefs, religion, personal habits, and an infinite variety of other factors. Should we assume that all offenders of a particular type share many other similarities as well? It appears that we should not, as we will see below.

Different As Night and Day

Eddie Gein, "The Plainfield Ghoul," was a murderer and grave robber in Wisconsin in the mid-1950s. He was diagnosed with schizophrenia, clearly demonstrated numerous signs of severe mental illness, and pled not guilty by reason of insanity (Stevens Point Daily Journal, 1957). In stark contrast to the overtly bizarre Gein was serial killer Ted Bundy, who murdered numerous women in the early 1970s. By all accounts, Bundy was handsome, charismatic, and generally quite charming, demonstrating no evidence of psychosis whatsoever. Serial killer Ottis Elwood Toole was noted to have an IQ of 75, generally considered to be borderline impaired intellectual functioning (Ramsland, 2015). At the other end of the intellectual spectrum is Ted Kaczynski, "The Unabomber," whose tested IQ in middle school was 167—in the "genius" range—and who went on to attend Harvard University (Elder, 2008).

Some killers commit their crimes in an impulsive manner. For example, there was Andrei Chikatilo, "The Rostov Ripper," whose blitz-style attacks on women from 1978–1990 in the Soviet Union appeared to occur with little or no planning on his part. On the other hand, Timothy McVeigh meticulously planned his attack, detonating a bomb two years to the day after the raid on the Branch Davidian compound. Some individuals engaged in post-mortem mutilation of the bodies of their victims, like "The Milwaukee Cannibal" Jeffrey Dahmer, while others show no evidence of having done so. Many murders occur in a violent fashion, such as those committed by the "Ice Man" Richard Kuklinski, who was known to use a gun and/or strangulation. Other homicides are committed in a nonviolent fashion by means of the incorrect or excessive but purposeful administration of medication, such as by former nurse Genene Jones. Still other murderers engaged in sexual acts with the victim prior to killing, while others, such as "The Co-Ed Killer" Ed Kemper engaged in sexual acts/necrophilia post-mortem. There are many kinds of doctors, teachers, engineers, and airplane pilots and we do not assume that they are all alike or share the same motivation for what they do. Similarly, we should not assume that all those who kill (or commit other offenses) are similar in terms of motivation, thinking, or behavior. The assumption that all killers are cut from the same cloth is likely terribly misguided.

PROFILING METHODOLOGIES

Having read about the FBI's development of criminal profiling and having been inundated by movies and television shows that claim to portray this method of profiling, we may erroneously believe that the FBI method of profiling is the only or the best method of doing so. This is not the case. The FBI method is not the only method of profiling and has been called into question by some critics (Bonn, 2020). Indeed, like other sciences, the science of profiling continues to evolve, and what is considered state-of-the-art today may be recognized as woefully inadequate or simply incorrect years from now. Indeed, debate regarding profiling and behavioral analysis continues. Central to that debate is the question of whether profiling is an art, a science, some combination of the two, or perhaps none of the above but rather a skill acquired through years of research, study, and practice.

Criminal Investigative Analysis (CIA)

Criminal investigative analysis (CIA) is the technique that was developed and used in the early days of the FBI's BSU. CIA involved the development of a body of research to systematically study those who commit violent crimes. This research often included interviews of violent criminals as part of an attempt to gain insight into their behaviors. This technique is still used by the FBI (Scherer & Jarvis, 2014). The FBI uses CIA to examine behavioral information and evidence and to provide advice and support to a requesting law enforcement agency. Even in the uncommon event where the FBI goes out into the field, it is not for the purpose of taking over for the local law enforcement agency that requested that assistance but instead to provide resources and support to that agency.

Investigative Psychology (IP)

Investigative psychology (IP) was developed by Professor David Canter, who is a fellow of the American Psychological Association and who has worked with numerous police agencies. IP is rooted in research and stresses the importance of examining the offender's actions and their behaviors rather than speculating about their motives in order to develop an understanding of crime and criminality, with a goal of managing and solving crimes (Canter & Youngs, 2009).

IP begins with the methodological review and study of closed police cases. For example, in 1996, Professor Canter conducted a study of 66 sexual assaults committed by 27 offenders to come up with a composite analysis of rapist behavior. IP is based on the notion that to construct a profile, we must have knowledge of identifiable consistencies in human behavior and the relationship of those behaviors to aspects of an offender. Thus, IP looks at what are referred to as "ideographic themes." For example, IP might be used to determine if a murder was expressive (because someone was emotionally upset) versus instrumental (in order to achieve some gain or get insurance money).

Behavioral Evidence Analysis (BEA)

Behavioral evidence analysis (BEA) is a fusion of past practices in which crimes are interpreted to generate profiles based on deductive reasoning. BEA warns against a one-size-fits-all solution and holds that profiles should be generated based on unique factors (Turvey, 2012). Deductive reasoning is the foundation of BEA and holds that it is important for the forensic clinician to approach the profiling process with an open mind and to consider all the evidence, including forensic evidence such as blood spatter, the crime scene itself, any victim/witness statements, and a thorough analysis of the victim.

Crime Action Profiling (CAP)

Crime action profiling (CAP) was developed by Dr. Richard Kocsis, a psychologist and leading profiler. CAP assumes that the practitioner has a thorough knowledge of human behavior and psychology and uses structured interviews to construct profiles. CAP stresses both the importance of studying the behavioral patterns involved in violent offenses and the skills related to constructing profiles. Profiling then, is seen as a skill acquired with time and experience. CAP involves "identifying personality traits, behavioral tendencies, and demographic variables of an offender based on the characteristics of the crime" (Kocsis, 2007, p. 167).

Criminal Profiling Today

According to the website for the **International Association of Forensic Criminologists (IAFC)**, the Academy of Behavioral Profiling was first established in 1998 with the goal of creating an "independent, nongovernment, interdisciplinary professional organization" and whose mission was (and is) "the development of investigative and forensic protocols related to evidence-based crime scene analysis, victimology, and criminal profiling" (IAFC, n. d.). In 2009–2010, the organization evolved into the IAFC and has a code of ethics for criminal profilers, written practice standards, and an exam to test knowledge of the subject. There is now also a professional certification act that provides credentialing and verification of some level of expertise. This is part of an attempt to continue to evolve forensic criminology as a coherent and respected professional body.

Criminal Profiling: Managing Expectations

Public belief and confidence in the ability of profilers appears to be quite high, but as mentioned earlier in the chapter, many people also believed that *Top Gun* was an accurate portrayal of the daily routine of Navy pilots and that anyone could become a Top Gun fighter pilot. The popularity of profiling in the media does not mean that such portrayals bear any resemblance to reality. In television and movies, criminal profilers appear to be experts in all facets of crime scene investigation and are often portrayed as having some type of special insight or psychic ability. Those instances in which profiling is useful and even amazingly accurate (such as Dr. Brussel's prediction about George Metesky's neatly buttoned suit) do not prove that profiling is consistently accurate or even helpful in every case.

Although psychological profiling has achieved some degree of acceptance in law enforcement investigations, empirical research into the skills needed for successful profiling is still lacking. Experience in law enforcement investigations is one factor that is often cited as essential for effective profiling. However, a study by Kocsis, Hayes, and Irwin (2002) compared the profiles for a closed criminal case that were generated by undergraduate chemistry students and police and detectives with varying levels of experience and training in criminal investigations. Ironically, the chemistry students were found to produce more accurate profiles than any of the groups of police, detectives, or a control group. As is the case with many studies, there has been some debate about the accuracy of the results of this study, but such research should be carefully considered, and it should not be automatically assumed that those with a law enforcement background are superior to others in terms of their ability to generate accurate profiles.

Louw (2015) points out that acceptance of profiling in the law enforcement community is far from unanimous, adding that the sensational and dramatic portrayals depicted in movies and on television are often in sharp contrast to reality. Indeed, the cases in which such analysis helps law enforcement to apprehend a criminal may represent the exception rather than the rule. Kocsis (2007) surveyed more than 30 authors, discussing the various uses and multiple limitations of profiling. Ribeiro and Soeiro (2021) noted that there is controversy in regard to the validity of profiling techniques. After a systematic review, they chose eight articles related to profiling validity and expressed the view that the technique of criminal profiling has yet to be statistically validated.

Behavior analysis/criminal profiling was originally developed as an investigative tool to assist law enforcement. There has been some discussion and debate as to whether an individual could testify in court as an expert witness in criminal profiling (Kocsis & Palmero, 2016). These authors also suggested that there might be a discrete form of behavior analysis that is supported by sufficient research to be considered admissible by an expert witness.

Many mental health professionals believe that profiling is valid and useful. An internet survey of more than 150 forensic psychologists and psychiatrists found that while only 10% had ever been involved in profiling, 25% considered themselves knowledgeable in the field. Approximately 40% felt profiling techniques were valid, reliable, and useful to law enforcement, while 25% did not feel such techniques were valid and reliable (Torres et al., 2006).

THROUGH THE EYES OF THE VICTIM: VICTIM–OFFENDER MEDIATION

After being found guilty or making a plea of guilty but before sentencing, the victim of an offense or their family may be given the opportunity to make a **victim impact statement** to the court. This will be described in greater detail in the Through the Eyes of the Victim section of the next chapter, but for now, it is enough to know that the victim impact statement is a chance for the victim or their loved ones to express the manner in which the offender harmed them physically or emotionally. In some cases, the victim may find that making such a statement brings emotional closure and helps them to cope with having been victimized.

In some instances, however, the victim may find that they still have unexpressed emotions about having been victimized or that they want answers from the offender about why they did what they did. In such cases, victims and/or their loved ones may decide to avail themselves of a process known as victim–offender mediation (VOM). VOM is a process by which a victim (or their family member) may request a supervised and safe meeting between themselves and the offender in the presence of a trained and experienced mediator. The mediation session typically occurs face-to-face and according to a prescribed format that allows both parties to express themselves and to ask and answer questions in a safe, structured, and supervised atmosphere. The process of VOM is described in considerable detail by Mark Umbreit in *The Handbook of Victim Mediation: An Essential Guide for Practice and Research*. This book is noted to be "victim sensitive," suggesting that it places the safety and comfort of the victim as a top priority.

VICTIM–OFFENDER MEDIATION IN THE CORRECTIONAL SETTING

If and when the VOM process is initiated by the victim, trained mediators preinterview both the victim and the offender in order to assess their stated reasons for meeting and to gain an impression of how those individuals will conduct and be able to control themselves within the mediation session. In one case that I was involved in, the offender had committed an especially brutal rape/homicide. The victim's surviving daughter, now an adult, had expressed a desire to meet with him in order to ask him why he had done what he had done. I knew from previous conversations with him that he lacked remorse for his offense and it seemed doubtful that he would offer an apology for it during a VOM session. With his consent, I furnished representatives from the Office of the Victim Advocate in Pennsylvania with my full assessment of him, including his lack of apparent remorse. The victim's daughter was informed of that and decided to proceed with the mediation. Although I was not privy to the details of what occurred during that session, it is my sincere hope that the victim's daughter found solace, comfort, and meaning in the mediation process.

The Office for the Victims of Crime is part of the U.S. Department of Justice. This Office states that as far back as 2000, there were already 300 communities in the United States making use of VOM and more than 700 in Europe. VOM sessions are conducted by various trained social service agencies, sometimes by a Victim's Services arm of the Attorney General's Office, and they may be facilitated or conducted within the Department of Corrections. A state-by-state list of where VOM is offered is available from the Office for the Victims of Crime (2000). The preface to this list notes that it is hoped that VOM will empower victims and their families, bring them some comfort, and help to impress upon offenders the reality and magnitude of the impact of their actions and promote restitution to the victim by the offender.

CONCLUSION

As long as violent crimes have been committed, there have been those who speculate about why somebody would commit such an offense: "What kind of person would do such a thing?" Social media, books, movies, and television programs frequently portray and even glamorize the process of criminal profiling and finding out what kind of person commits violent offenses. However, the popularity of such portrayals does not indicate that they are accurate or have any basis in reality. From the early days of Howard Teten and the FBI's original BSU, profiling has continued to adapt and grow as a technique and science. As with any science, mistakes have been made from time to time, and forensic scientists have hopefully learned and grown from these errors as the science of profiling continues to evolve. As we have seen in this chapter, it is vitally important for profilers to keep an open mind, to question themselves and others, and to remember that even offenders who commit very similar crimes may do so for very different reasons. Although it is not certain that those who are not killers can think like those who are (or that this is necessary), it is important that we attempt to understand their motivation and methods of operation. Hopefully, by doing so, we can assist law enforcement in keeping our communities and our families a little bit safer.

Exercises and Discussion Questions

1. Watch the television show or movie of your choice related to criminal profiling. Having read this chapter, what aspects of that show/movie do you think accurately portrayed the criminal profiling process? Why? What parts do you think were inaccurate? What leads you to this belief?

2. In this chapter, we discussed the notion that to catch a killer, you have to be able to think like a killer. Do you agree or disagree with this statement? Provide the rationale for your response.

3. In reference to the statement in Question #2, do you think that it is possible for someone who has never committed a homicide to truly understand the motivation and actions of someone who has done so? What would allow them to do so or prohibit them from being able to do so? Please explain.

4. In this chapter and throughout this text, there have been discussions about interviewing captive offenders to understand the motivation and actions of those who are currently committing similar offenses but have not yet been caught. Do you think this is a worthwhile endeavor? Why or why not? Explain your rationale and provide supporting evidence for your response.

5. It could be argued that the crime tells us about the criminal. However, others might argue that offenses are often committed impulsively and therefore may tell us a bit about the circumstances of the offense but very little about the motivation and personal qualities of the offender. Do you believe that the crime provides us with meaningful information about the criminal or is this not truly the case? Explain your answer.

6. In this chapter, we discussed various methods of profiling, such as CIA, IP, and BEA. If you had to pick one of these methods to create a criminal profile, which one would you choose and why? What are the advantages of the method that you have chosen?

KEY TERMS

Atavistic

Behavioral Analysis Unit (BAU)

Behavioral evidence analysis (BEA)

Behavioral Sciences Unit (BSU)

Belief perseverance

Crime action profiling (CAP)

Criminal investigative analysis (CIA)

Critical Incident Response Group (CIRG)

CSI effect

International Association of Forensic Criminologists (IAFC)

Investigative psychology (IP)

National Center for Analysis of Violent Crime (NCAVC)

Phrenology

Positivist criminology

Salem Witch Trials

Victim impact statement (VIS)

Violent Crime Apprehension Program (ViCap)

9 FORENSIC PSYCHOLOGY AND THE COURTROOM

The accused man had chosen to represent himself in court. His court-appointed attorney strongly urged him not to do so and remained available to him in the court, but the accused had insisted. It was his right to represent himself and that is exactly what he was going to do, despite the fact that he had no knowledge at all about how to do so. It was clear from watching him that he relished being the center of attention. He was dressed in a rather ill-fitting suit issued to him by the prison that normally housed him. He stood in the middle of the courtroom, gesturing widely and talking loudly, often completely off-topic, frequently using large words but doing so incorrectly.

On the witness stand was his alleged victim, the woman that he was accused of robbing at gunpoint. He said to her, "Do you see in this courtroom today the man who robbed you?" She appeared surprised at this question and responded, "Yes." He followed with, "And would you point to him, please?" Again looking surprised, she pointed right back at him and said, "You. You robbed me."

The accused turned to the judge, a look of smug satisfaction on his face and stated, "Your Honor, I call for a mistrial. She can't possibly have identified me as the robber. The day I robbed her, I was wearing a mask!" The courtroom erupted in both astonishment and laughter.

INTRODUCTION AND DEFINITIONS

Forensic psychologists, forensic psychiatrists, and other forensic mental health specialists typically spend many years learning about the complex workings of the human mind and, with experience, may become experts in the manner in which people think and act and the emotions they experience. A great deal of coursework and training goes into learning and developing an expertise in diagnosing and treating mental illnesses. Even the most competent forensic psychologist, however, may feel like a fish out of water upon their entry into the arena of legal work and the courtroom. It is hoped that the present chapter will provide a foundation for understanding courtroom policies and procedures, so that in the following chapter, we will be able to delve deeper into the intersection between psychology and the courtroom.

In Chapter 4, we discussed a crime as being composed of an *actus reus* or "guilty act" and *mens rea* or "guilty mind." Just as this is the case for juvenile offenses, these same standards apply to the courtroom in cases involving adults. It should be noted that for both juveniles and adults, there can be exceptions in regard to intent and the guilty mind, however. Some acts are considered criminal regardless of whether there was criminal intent. For example, statutory sexual assault is a crime regardless of whether the perpetrator knew the age of the victim at the time of the offense. Similarly, if you borrow a friend's car and are stopped by the police for a traffic violation, and the officer notices an open container of alcohol and drug residue in the car, you will be charged with criminal offenses, regardless of whether you knew of these items when you borrowed the car.

The Federal Court System

The U.S. Constitution allows for a federal government that oversees and frequently shares power with the states. Both federal and state governments are divided into executive, legislative, and judicial branches, each with its own powers and responsibilities. The federal government has the power and authority to manufacture currency, declare war, and conduct international relations as well as the authority to prosecute criminal activities. The state government, on the other hand, oversees those matters occurring within state borders including (but not limited to) state criminal codes, public health and safety issues, and maintenance of roads and other structures. Both the federal and state governments may establish laws and issue taxes. Parallel to this divided federal and state system of government, the United States has two separate federal and state court systems.

The federal court system consists of three levels: There are 94 total **district courts.** These district courts may also be referred to as *trial courts*, and they accept both civil and criminal cases, as we will discuss below. These federal courts have discretion in what cases they hear, meaning that such courts may choose which cases they will consider. For example, perhaps a driver from Ohio and one from Pennsylvania have a traffic accident in West Virginia. It appears that one of the drivers was exceeding the speed limit and the other was under the influence of narcotics. Given the interstate nature of this offense, charges could be pressed by the federal court or this court has the discretion to decide not to try the case and instead defer to the state courts involved. District courts also address conflicts between parties from different states or, in some cases, issues between the United States and another country.

Federal court cases are prosecuted by a United States attorney or assistant United States attorney. Once a verdict or ruling has been made by the district court, an appeal may be made to one of the 13 **U.S. circuit courts of appeal** if it is believed that some type of error occurred during the district court process. Being dissatisfied with the outcome of the case is not sufficient grounds for an appeal; there must be some belief that an error occurred during the case in order for an appeal to be filed. It is the job of the circuit courts of appeal to determine whether the trial court correctly interpreted or applied the laws and procedures relevant to the case being considered. A circuit court of appeal consists of three or more judges and does not make use of a jury. The circuit court of appeal may then decide to affirm the decision of the district court (in other words, stating that the district court followed the proper procedures) or reverse the decision of the district court (stating that the district court made some type of procedural error). The circuit court may also remand the case back to the district court (requiring the district court to take some specified further action on that case).

The highest court of appeal in the United States is the **U.S. Supreme Court**. This court consists of nine justices appointed by the president of the United States and then approved by the U.S. senate. The Supreme Court is not required to hear all appeals and actually hears less than 1% of all appeals presented to it (Office of the United States Attorneys, n. d.). The Supreme Court has the discretion to decide which cases it will review. Typically, the cases chosen for review by the Supreme Court are ones in which lower courts have demonstrated considerable disagreement, which include important Constitutional questions and cases in which a decision will likely have broad implications for the entire country.

The State Court System

As noted above, state governments regulate those activities and affairs occurring within the limits of that state. For example, state governments regulate state criminal codes, levy income taxes, regulate the functioning of schools and hospitals, and oversee the maintenance of roads and bridges, among many other responsibilities. State trial courts hear a wide variety of both criminal and civil cases involving minor to serious violations of state laws.

State courts have far more contact with the public than federal courts do and hear far more cases than the federal court system. According to FindLaw (Bui, 2022), approximately 30 *million* state court cases are filed per year in the United States, as opposed to "only" one million federal cases.

The state court system varies a bit by state but typically starts with magisterial or municipal courts, also referred to as *lower courts*. These are the courts that many citizens have some experience with, and such courts hear cases involving traffic violations, minor criminal violations, and civil cases involving relatively small amounts of money.

In a criminal court case, if and when there is a finding of not guilty, the defendant is free to go and the prosecution cannot appeal this verdict. However, if there is a finding of guilt and the defense believes that an error occurred during the legal process, the decision may be appealed to the appellate court. The appellate court will then review the case and decide if the decision of the lower court will be affirmed, reversed, or remanded (sent back to) the lower court. Ultimately, a case may be appealed to the state supreme court, which generally hears and decides important matters of state law. The state supreme court or "court of last resort" is the final arbiter of legal appeals. In regard to state laws, the decision of a state supreme court is final and binding.

Criminal versus Civil Courts

Criminal cases are considered to be crimes against the state—that is, against society as a whole. Although the accused may have robbed or assaulted an individual (or multiple people), the crime is considered to be against society as a whole and therefore is titled (for example) *State/Commonwealth of_____ v. J. Smith*. Because the penalty for criminal offenses is generally much harsher than for civil offenses and can include fines, imprisonment, and even execution, such cases have many more protections in place for the defendant. For this reason, as we discussed in Chapter 4, the burden of proof is beyond a reasonable doubt, meaning that the jury must be very close to certain of the defendant's guilt in order to render a guilty verdict. As we will see in this chapter, forensic and other psychologists can and do play important roles in both criminal and civil court cases.

The process for misdemeanors and felonies includes an extra step, that being a **preliminary hearing** (also referred to as a *grand jury hearing*). At the preliminary hearing, the district attorney/prosecution must demonstrate that there is sufficient evidence or probable cause that a crime occurred and that the crime was the responsibility of the defendant. If the lower court does not find sufficient probable cause, the case is dismissed. If there is probable cause, the case is bound over to trial court; it is in trial court that there can be a finding of guilty or not guilty.

The number of criminal cases heard in court has been declining slowly and steadily, at a rate of about −2% per year (National Center for State Courts, 2018). However, the number of such cases heard in court, including homicides, assault, robbery, drugs, driving under the influence, and other crimes is still staggering at more than 15 million such cases per year. As a result of such enormous court dockets, the courtroom work group, in cooperation with the accused, may decide to enter a plea bargain. In a **plea bargain**, the accused agrees to plead guilty to some or all of the charges against them. In return, the prosecution agrees to drop some of the charges or impose charges of a lesser severity, so that in return for their plea of guilty, the defendant will receive a less severe sentence than they might have if they pled not guilty and were later found to be guilty at trial.

A plea bargain assures the prosecution of a conviction and the imposition of some type of sentence and typically assures the defendant of a lesser sentence than they might have received otherwise. The vast majority of cases (90%–95% according to Devers, 2011) are resolved by means of a plea bargain. The plea bargain has the great advantage of requiring much less time and effort on the part of the court and the courtroom work group and helps to reduce judicial and court overload (Lesh, 2015).

Civil cases, as the name implies, involve almost all actions that are *not* criminal in nature. In a civil case, the plaintiff is not claiming that a law has been broken but that the actions (or lack of action) of the defendant have resulted in some type of harm (physical, financial, or emotional) to the plaintiff. The plaintiff is typically petitioning the court to make the defendant fulfill their duty or to order that the defendant be compensated in some manner for the harm that they claim has been done to them. For example, a civil case might stem from a person slipping on the newly mopped floor at the grocery store. The plaintiff may claim that there was no sign indicating that the floor was slippery, and as a result of the grocery store's negligence in posting such a sign, they fell and were injured, incurring both medical costs and lost wages. The plaintiff may be asking the court to order a change in store procedures or reimbursement for their hospital costs, lost wages, and perhaps pain and suffering. In such a case, it is not likely that a psychologist or other mental health professional would be involved, unless the plaintiff is alleging that they suffered emotional distress as well as physical injury.

In a civil case, there is no finding of guilty or not guilty. Rather, the jury seeks to determine whether the defendant is liable for the harm that the plaintiff claims to have suffered. Furthermore, the burden of proof is different and lower than it is in criminal court. In a civil case, the burden placed upon the plaintiff is usually a **preponderance of the evidence**. In other words, is it more likely than not that the events described did in fact occur in the manner alleged by the plaintiff? If this were put into numbers, a preponderance of the evidence means that if the jury is 51% or more sure that the defendant has been negligent, then there will be a finding that the defendant is indeed liable. On the other hand, if the jury is 49% or less sure that the defendant has been negligent, then there will be a finding that the defendant is *not* liable. The burden of proof is lower in civil cases because potential consequences to the defendant might involve a monetary payment to reimburse for damages and possibly for pain and suffering but do not involve incarceration. The punishment may also involve an injunction, meaning that the defendant is ordered to take a particular course of action or to cease a particular course of action (Bui, 2022).

The case of *Fitzgibbons v. Integrated Healthcare Holdings Incorporated (IHHI)* was a civil case in which Dr. Michael Fitzgibbons sued IHHI, the agency for which he once worked, claiming that the CEO of that company had Dr. Fitzgibbons arrested under false pretenses in order to embarrass him. According to Dr. Fitzgibbons, that arrest had caused him significant emotional distress. In a case such as this one, a psychologist or psychiatrist would likely play a significant role in testifying in regard to the claim of emotional distress. Although the legal wrangling of this case and its appeal are beyond the scope of this text, it is worth noting that a jury did indeed find IHHI to be liable in this case and Dr. Fitzgibbons was awarded $5.7 million as a result (*Fitzgibbons v. IHHI*, 2015).

Civil cases apply to business law rather than criminal law, though there can be some overlap when it comes to cases involving allegations of wrongful death. Wrongful death is said to have occurred when a person or persons die due to the alleged negligence or misconduct of an individual or an entity. For example, in cases of medical malpractice or negligent driving, the plaintiff (or their family) may sue in civil court as part of an attempt to receive compensation for injuries that were suffered and financial damages that were incurred as a result. There may (or may not be) a criminal prosecution for homicide as well, but in a wrongful death suit, the jury hears the case and renders a decision based on what it considers to be the preponderance of the evidence.

THE GEORGE ZIMMERMAN CASE: MURDER OR SELF-DEFENSE?

George Zimmerman was living in the Retreat at Twin Lakes, a gated community in Sanford Florida. He was in charge of the local community's neighborhood watch program, and homeowners in the neighborhood had been instructed to contact the police and Zimmerman if they had any safety or security concerns. On February 26, 2012, Zimmerman noticed Trayvon Martin, a 17-year-old Black teenager, walking through the community with his sweatshirt hood up. Zimmerman believed this to be suspicious, though no particular behavior was noted in that regard. Zimmerman contacted the police, who told him to wait and that they would respond. However, instead of waiting, Zimmerman continued to follow Martin. Zimmerman claimed that Martin then assaulted him, and he (Zimmerman) defended himself with his handgun. Zimmerman was charged with second-degree homicide but was later acquitted of these criminal charges. The Martin family pursued civil litigation for wrongful death against the Twin Lakes Homeowners Association and reached a settlement in that regard without an admission of fault or responsibility on the part of the Homeowners Association.

COURTROOM WORK GROUP

The term *courtroom work group* refers to those individuals who are paid to work in and for the court. The courtroom work group then includes the judge, attorneys for either side, the bailiff, the courtroom reporter, and anyone else who is tasked with and paid for their assistance to the court process. The aim of the courtroom work group is to process the case and to seek a just conclusion (Eisenstein & Jacob, 1977). That implies finding justice and does not necessarily mean a finding of guilt or innocence, merely that the case has been resolved. Although the process itself appears adversarial at times, with the opposing attorneys (and sometimes the judge) disagreeing with one another, the goal is still the same: to bring the case to a fair and just conclusion. Those who are not being paid for being in court are not a part of the courtroom work group. Thus, witnesses, members of the public in attendance, jurors, and the plaintiff and defendant are not part of the courtroom work group.

Judge

In state courts, most **judges** are elected officials, while the governor of that state appoints others. Federal judges are appointed by congress or by the president of the United States. Generally, being a judge requires a juris doctorate, though this is not required for some low-level magisterial district judges. The judge may be thought of as an impartial referee whose job it is to make certain that both the prosecution and the defense conduct their portion of the proceedings according to the rules of law. In lesser cases, a judge may grant a summary judgment, meaning that the judge may reach a decision without proceeding to a jury trial. More often, however, it is the jury that is tasked with making a finding of guilt or liability. In the case of a finding that the defendant is guilty or liable, the judge is then tasked with determining the sentence or sanction.

Defense Attorney

There is considerable debate as to whom should be attributed the notion, "He who represents himself has a fool for a client." This quote has been attributed to numerous people, including (but certainly not limited to) Abraham Lincoln and Benjamin Franklin. While we might not be able to determine the original source for certain, what is clear is that few (if any) untrained people would be able to defend themselves adequately in court. Hopefully, the story at the very beginning of this chapter served as an example of exactly why one should not attempt to represent oneself in court. Many lawyers accused of wrongdoing hire other lawyers to represent themselves in courts in matters where they are not experts or because they are too emotionally invested in the outcome to be able to represent themselves adequately. The odds of an untrained person being able to represent themselves adequately during the trial process are slim indeed.

The Sixth Amendment of the Constitution guarantees that those accused of a criminal offense have the right to a "speedy and public trial" and that the accused will "have the assistance of counsel for [their] defense" among other rights. It is this provision that allows defendants to hire a lawyer in their defense or to have the state assign them a public defender for that same purpose if they cannot afford one. When the defendant cannot afford a private attorney, the court will then appoint (and the state will pay for) a public defender to represent the defendant. Thus, the defendant will not be encumbered with having to pay for their defense. Public defenders are experienced attorneys whose job is to provide appropriate representation and defense in court. As they are contracted by the state, public defenders typically have very large caseloads and are not as well paid as private attorneys. Thus, many public defenders may not have the time or ability to communicate with the defendant until they actually see the defendant in the courtroom, and the defendant has little or no say in what attorney is assigned to them by the court.

Hiring a private **defense attorney** is an option for those who can afford it. Hourly fees vary considerably based on factors such as the complexity of the case, the seriousness of the charges, and the experience of the attorney. Fees range from as little as $50–$100 per hour to as much as $1,000 per hour or more for highly specialized legal work performed by a highly sought-after attorney (Bieber, 2023). According to the 2022 Legal Trends Report (Clio, 2022), the average hourly rate for an attorney at that time was $313 per hour. It is important to note that the client is not only paying for time spent in the courtroom but also time spent investigating the case, reviewing evidence and case law, interactions with the client, and so forth. It is easy to see how costs may quickly become significant.

There are potential advantages for those who are able to hire their own defense attorney. Such clients are able to choose their own attorney and are likely to have more communication with that attorney (at a price, of course!). Given that such attorneys only take as many cases as they want, they are generally less overwhelmed with cases than a public defender is. Furthermore, privately hired defense attorneys are highly motivated to seek the best possible outcome for their client, as doing so is part of establishing their reputation and generating new clients and referrals.

Prosecuting Attorney

District attorneys, also referred to as *prosecuting attorneys*, are the chief law enforcement officers representing the state. District attorneys are assisted in their efforts by deputy district attorneys. The district attorney and deputy district attorney may be in charge of guiding investigations, deciding what charges (if any) are to be pursued in regard to the defendant, and presenting the case against the accused. District attorneys are also involved in any negotiations with the defense in terms of offering the defendant a plea bargain.

Bailiff

The job requirements and duties of bailiffs vary considerably. Bailiffs are tasked with maintaining a safe and orderly courtroom environment. This can mean screening those in the courtroom for weapons, announcing the entrance of the judge, escorting jurors during lunch or other breaks so that they do not have contact with those they should not, and making sure the judge has their required records. Bailiffs are also in charge of escorting defendants in and out of the courtroom. Perhaps the most important duty of the bailiff is to maintain the safety and security of everyone in the courtroom. There are many cases in which the accused and the victim or the victim's family are in the courtroom together; in cases in which the victim has been seriously harmed, tempers in the courtroom can run high and occasionally escalate into threats or attempted assaults. In such cases, it is the job of the bailiff to maintain the safety and security of all concerned—using force, if necessary.

Court Reporter/Stenographer

The job of a court reporter is to be able to record and produce a verbatim (that is, word-for- word) transcript of everything that is said during the course of court proceedings. This becomes an official certified court transcript. Court reporters are trained and often state certified and/or licensed by the state in which they practice.

LAY WITNESSES AND EXPERT WITNESSES

In criminal or civil proceedings, each side may present and question witnesses. Witnesses are individuals who have seen or heard the crime or incident in question or who have information that may be useful in resolving the case. Lay witnesses can only testify as to facts: what they saw or heard at the time of the offense. Thus, a lay witness could testify that they saw the defendant pointing the gun at Ms. Smith or that they heard Mr. Jones making inappropriate sexual remarks to an employee. Lay witnesses cannot give their opinion about any aspect of the case. Thus, a lay witness stating, "He had to be crazy to point that gun at her" would not be allowed, as a lay witness has no basis for giving an opinion about the defendant's state of mind or mental health issues. If a psychologist happened to witness a motor vehicle accident and was called into court to testify as to what they saw, they would be testifying as a lay witness. However, as we will see below, when they are called to court to testify based on their expertise in the field, then they are doing so as an expert witness.

Courts will, at times, make use of **expert witnesses**. An expert witness, as the name implies, is an individual who has specialized knowledge or skills that are relevant to the case being considered and whose expertise in a particular area may help the jury to understand the facts of the case they are hearing. Expert witnesses typically have specific training, certification, or education in a field that is relevant to the case, and their knowledge is far greater than that of a layperson or the average jury member.

Based on the training, education, or experience of the individual, the presiding judge will decide whether to qualify an individual as an expert. This may include a review of the person's resume, training, licensing, and credentials. It is important to keep in mind that a high level of formal education is not necessarily required to qualify someone as an expert witness. For example, if a person has training in driving a particular type of truck, is licensed and trained to drive that type of truck, and has done so for many years, the judge may consider them to be an expert witness in regard to driving that truck, even if that person has a limited formal scholastic education.

Unlike lay witnesses, expert witnesses *are* allowed to offer their opinion about facts relevant to a criminal or civil case. The opinion of an expert witness will only be allowed for those areas in which they have been qualified as an expert. Thus, someone qualified as an expert in forensic psychology would be able to offer the opinion, "The defendant does suffer from posttraumatic stress disorder, and that likely contributed to his threatening behavior toward the defendant." However, this same expert witness would not be permitted to offer an opinion on an area in which they are not a qualified expert. Thus, this same expert would not be allowed to offer the opinion, "The trajectory at which the shot was fired indicated that he did not intend to shoot the victim, only to scare her." An expert witness may be presented by either the prosecution or the defense as part of an attempt to bolster their case. In some cases, each side may present an expert witness, and it is entirely possible that those experts express very different opinions. That is acceptable to the court (though perhaps confusing to the jury, which is tasked with determining which of the two professionals is more credible) as long as each expert is presenting their opinion and their rationale for that opinion based on accepted principles in their area of expertise.

Forensic psychologists, forensic psychiatrists, and other mental health clinicians may be utilized as expert witnesses in a wide variety of court cases. For example, in a case involving child custody, a judge may request a psychologist or other mental health professional to provide the court with a report concerning the child's living circumstances and to make a recommendation as to what custody arrangement would be in the best interest of the child. Forensic psychologists could be called upon to explain and discuss psychological testing that has been performed or the potential effects of abuse on a defendant or a victim involved in a particular case. A forensic psychiatrist might provide testimony in regard to the psychotropic medications being administered to the defendant and the potential effects and side effects of those medications. Psychologists and other mental health clinicians may be called upon by the court to testify as to what mental illnesses the defendant has been diagnosed with and what impact such diagnoses may have had on their functioning and behavior.

In the case of *Moreno v. Texas* (2019) Ricky Moreno was accused of committing aggravated kidnapping. As part of his defense, Moreno claimed that he was under duress at the time of this offense. Specifically, the defense suggested that such duress was related to Moreno suffering from post-traumatic stress disorder. In similar cases, the testimony of forensic psychologists and/or other expert witnesses can be vital in helping the jury to understand the full picture of the case so that they can take such evidence into account when making their decision.

As we will examine in depth in the next chapter, forensic psychologists and other mental health professionals may also serve as consultants to the court and as expert witnesses regarding mental health issues. Such practitioners may testify in regard to matters of competency to stand trial, not guilty by reason of insanity, guilty but mentally ill, and issues related to rehabilitation versus punishment of those who are convicted of offenses. There are many roles that mental health practitioners can and do play in the courtroom.

TRIAL CONSULTANT

A **trial consultant** will have a bachelor's degree, master's degree, or PhD, typically in a behavioral or social science field such as psychology, criminology, sociology, or a related field. Training or a degree in the legal field is also possible. Trial consultants may help to prepare a witness as to how to convey their testimony most effectively to the jury; such preparation should be tailored to the witness. With a witness who is intelligent and well-spoken, the consultant may advise asking the witness open-ended questions and allowing them to give their testimony at some length. With a witness who perhaps possesses a lower level of literacy or limited communication skills, the trial consultant might suggest that their lawyer primarily ask them a series of closed-ended questions, which can be answered with a simple yes or no.

A trial consultant might instruct the witness in deep breathing or relaxation techniques in order to decrease that witness's level of anxiety, which can be especially pronounced during the ordeal of cross-examination. In some cases, the trial consultant, in cooperation with the attorney, may help prepare the witness by asking them sample questions or conducting a simulated (practice) cross-examination. The present author, having no prior experience testifying in court, was briefed by a lawyer before doing so. The lawyer emphasized the importance of answering only the exact question that was asked and no more. Although that seems easy, it was trickier than it appeared. For example, the lawyer said, "If you are asked if you know what time it is, don't answer 11:30. That's not what they asked. If you are asked if you know what time it is, your answer should be 'Yes.' Keep it succinct."

The appearance and demeanor of the defendant may play a role in what the jury decides to believe about the defendant. In some cases, a trial consultant may make suggestions as to how the witness should dress and what mannerisms to use or avoid in order to have the desired impact on the jury. In many courtrooms, the defendant will not be dressed in prison clothes, even if they are currently incarcerated, as this could influence the jury into believing that they are guilty of the present charges. It is not difficult to imagine that a defendant appearing in court handcuffed, shackled, and wearing a prison jumpsuit would appear to be guilty of whatever they were being charged with. We would certainly imagine that a defendant who appears unmoved by the suffering of the victim or who appears uncaring when graphic images are shown in court could have a significant impact on the jury. Some accused persons have even been known to laugh or smile or appear to be bored during the course of the proceedings, and we can only imagine that such behavior is self-defeating when it comes to the jury. A trial consultant, then, may have a role in educating a defendant in how to conduct themselves in court, as may have been the case in the following example.

JODY ARIAS: QUIET AND SHY OR COLD-BLOODED MURDERER?

Jodi Arias began dating Travis Alexander in 2007. On June 4, 2008, he was discovered to have been brutally murdered. Investigators found that his throat had been slashed, that he had been stabbed between 27 and 29 times, and that he had sustained a gunshot wound to the head. Among other evidence, they found sexually explicit photos of him and Arias on a camera that he had recently purchased. Arias claimed that she had been forced to kill Alexander in self-defense. Perhaps at the advice of a trial consultant, she

Jodi Arias at the time of her trial; she was dressed in a demure and conservative fashion.

REUTERS / Alamy Stock Photo

appeared in court dressed quite conservatively, with little or no makeup or nail polish, in very plain clothing, and wearing large glasses. This may well have been a strategy on the part of a trial consultant or her defense team to present her in such a manner that the jury could not reconcile the demure-appearing defendant with the brutal offense that had been committed. If that is indeed the case, on this occasion, the strategy was ineffective; ultimately, she was incarcerated with a sentence of life without the possibility of parole.

JURY SELECTION

The Sixth Amendment of the Constitution affords everyone the right to trial by an impartial jury. District courts select the names of potential jurors randomly from lists of state residents who have driver's licenses or state IDs and from lists of registered voters in the state. The individuals selected are summoned to court, where they are given a questionnaire to complete and are interviewed by the lawyers for each side. Juries are typically comprised of 12 people who are sworn to make a verdict based on the evidence presented to them in a court of law.

Naturally, both the prosecutor and the defense attorney hope to select jurors who will be sympathetic to their side of the case. **Voir dire** is a French term meaning "to speak the truth." Once the prospective jurors appear in court, the voir dire takes place, which involves questioning by the judge and the attorneys to determine if a potential juror would be appropriate for inclusion in the jury. This is the preliminary examination of a witness or a juror by the judge or counsel for each side.

Both the defense and the prosecution have **challenges for cause**. After the voir dire, the prosecution and defense meet with the judge to decide which jurors have valid reason to be dismissed. For example, if during the voir dire, it is discovered that one of the potential jurors is the cousin of the defendant, that individual would be dismissed for cause, as it can be concluded that they would not be objective in this particular case. Similarly, if it was found that a potential jury member had been a victim of a crime similar to the crime that the defendant was accused of, this juror would be dismissed for cause as well, due to their likely inability to be objective in regard to this particular case. There is no set limit to the number of potential jurors who can be dismissed for cause.

Peremptory challenges mean that the lawyer for either side is able to dismiss a particular juror without providing a specific rationale for this dismissal. Typically, the prosecution and defense will each be allowed either five or seven such challenges. This allows each side to dismiss potential jurors that they feel may not support their case but for which they do not have sufficient evidence for a challenge for cause. Peremptory challenges should not be made based on race, ethnicity, gender, or other demographic factors. As both the prosecution and the defense have equal roles in voir dire, challenges for cause, and peremptory challenges, it is hoped that this process will result in a balanced and impartial jury.

Diversity, Equity, and Inclusion in Juries

Defendants are entitled to have a jury of their peers—in other words, their equals. This has been interpreted by the courts to mean that the jury pool and the jury itself should be diverse in respect to factors such as (but not limited to) gender, age, race, and ethnicity. In a precedent-setting case, the U.S. Supreme Court in *Hernandez v. Texas* (1954) upheld the importance of diversity and inclusion in the criminal justice system in finding that the defendant, a man of Mexican and American descent, did not receive a fair trial due to the fact that the trial was held in a county in which Mexican Americans were routinely prohibited from serving on a jury. The court held that the Fourteenth Amendment of the U.S. Constitution protects people beyond the Black/white racial binary and includes other racial and ethnic groups (Ogborn-Mihm, 2015).

Today's society is becoming increasingly aware of the tremendous importance of diversity, equity, and inclusion (DEI). This term—DEI—refers to the importance of establishing programs and policies that promote fair and equal treatment of many groups of individuals, including (but not limited to) those of different ages, religions, ethnicities, abilities, genders, sexual orientations, races, and beliefs. The importance of DEI in the selection of juries and the subsequent justice process cannot be overstated. Our emerging recognition of the importance of DEI has prompted some federal courts to reevaluate and modify the manner in which potential jurors are selected.

"The public's engagement and trust in the court system is dependent on jury diversity," said Chief Judge Juan R. Sánchez of the Eastern District of Pennsylvania, which covers nine counties and includes Philadelphia (United States Courts, 2019). "Jurors from a cross section of the community bring different life experiences and perspectives to jury deliberations, leading to more informed discussions and greater public confidence in the judicial process." This has led some courts to broaden the lists from which potential jurors are drawn as part of an effort to assemble a more diverse jury. Other programs include but are not limited to community outreach and education programs that educate and encourage those in the community to be more involved in this aspect of the justice system.

William Beaver was being tried in a federal district court of Chicago, Illinois, for criminal tax evasion. Despite this court including the racially and ethnically diverse Cook County, among other counties, there was not a single African American represented among the fifty people who showed up in court for the jury pool (Sweeney & Dizikes, 2013). Examples such as this highlight the importance of and the notable lack of diversity in some juries. It is vitally important that we recognize that the inclusion of minority group members on juries may help the group to understand and appreciate the different life experiences of that group and may help to lessen individual biases, preconceptions, or blatant misperceptions.

In order to afford defendants a jury of their peers, it is vitally important that juries are diverse, equitable, and inclusive.

Andor Bujdoso / Alamy Stock Photo

Scientific Jury Selection

Scientific jury selection means to use science and correlational techniques to assist in picking a jury that would be favorable to one's case. Scientific jury selection is sometimes employed in civil litigation when the stakes are quite high, and one side (or both) is seeking to gain a tactical advantage. In such cases, a lawyer may have a forensic psychologist or other individual versed in the social sciences attempt to determine what kind of demographic factors (income, age, occupation, or other factors) and what type of attitudes might correlate with the desired voting behavior in the jury room. For example, if the consultant for the defense finds reason to believe that those who have higher incomes are more likely to believe that the offenses allegedly committed by the defendant are insignificant, then the defense attorney will survey the jury pool in regard to income and intentionally select those with higher incomes.

However, studies in regard to the effectiveness of scientific jury selection are mixed in terms of whether they truly have an impact on the outcome of such cases. Kressel and Kressel (2004, pp. 79–81) suggest that the evidence presented at the trial is of much greater importance in determining the verdict of the jury than is the makeup of the jury itself. Macon (2000) also did not find scientific jury selection to be superior to selection by attorneys in the traditional method of selection. Indeed, one would hope that the finding reached by a jury is based on the evidence presented rather than on other factors such as age or income.

COURTROOM PROCESS AND PROCEEDINGS

The Fourth Amendment of the U.S. Constitution states that

the right of the people to be secure in their persons, houses, papers, and effects, against unreasonable searches and seizures, shall not be violated, and no Warrants shall issue, but upon probable cause, supported by Oath or affirmation, and particularly describing the place to be searched, and the persons or things to be seized.

It is this Amendment that prohibits anyone from being arrested without probable cause. **Probable cause** means that there is objective evidence to suggest that a crime was being committed or had been committed. Thus, a police officer stating that a person looked like a drug dealer would not constitute probable cause for arresting them. However, an officer performing a traffic stop on a speeding driver and then noting the odor of marijuana emanating from the vehicle, the presence of a white powdery substance under the driver's nose, and that the driver's speech was slurred would represent a very different case. In this case, there would be probable cause and the officer would be justified in further questioning and perhaps arresting the driver.

An **arrest** means that a law enforcement officer is legally detaining an individual and therefore their freedom of movement is being restricted. That person is then transported to jail, where the **booking** process takes place. Booking involves the gathering of demographic information from the accused, followed by the taking of mug shots and fingerprinting as well as recording the charges against that individual. On rare occasion, a psychologist might perform a mental health screening of the defendant, including questions to assess suicidality. More often, however, this mental health and suicide screening will be conducted by a nurse as part of a medical evaluation. After this process occurs, they will be seen by a judge or magistrate at the initial appearance, typically within 48 hours of having been arrested. At that point, the judge will review charges made by police and may choose to drop or dismiss charges if they determine that probable cause did not exist at the time of the arrest.

When the judge does find there to be sufficient probable cause, the judge will then determine under what circumstances (if any) the accused may be released from jail. For minor offenses or in cases where the accused has little or no criminal record and is not judged to be a flight risk or a danger to the community, the individual may be released under their own recognizance. This means that they are released without bail after having assured the court that they will appear at their next scheduled hearing.

For individuals with more serious offenses or who are judged to be of danger to the community or a risk of flight or who have a record of failing to attend past court hearings, the judge may decide to require that the accused post **bail**. Bail is money the defendant must lodge with the court to ensure their appearance at future court hearings. If and when the person complies with all such hearings, the money lodged with the court will be returned to them. There are occasions on which the judge may decide that bail will not be set for the individual and that they will not be released prior to further court hearings. Such refusal of bail might occur if the accused is found to be acutely mentally ill, have a high risk of flight, or be a threat of significant danger to a specific individual or to the community at large.

When the offense is serious or there is a potential risk if the accused is released into the community, the judge may ask a forensic psychologist for an evaluation of the accused. For example, if the defendant is accused of a serious assault on their spouse and the judge is concerned that if released, they may resume such abuse, the judge may request a psychological evaluation. The judge would then use the results of that evaluation to assist them in making a decision about whether to allow them an opportunity for bail. In Chapter 5, we discussed the challenges of psychologists in attempting to make predictions about future violent behavior; this is one example of where forensic psychologists face such challenges on a frequent basis.

The **initial appearance** is typically the accused's first appearance in court in front of a judge or magistrate. At that point, they will be informed of the charges against them, reminded of their rights, and allowed to make a plea of guilty, not guilty, or no contest (but this almost never happens, as it is too early in the process). The possible penalties for those charges are also explained. The defendant is informed of their right to a trial by jury and of their right to be represented by an attorney. The defendant is then allowed to make a plea and may be afforded the opportunity for bail or conditional release, as noted above. During the initial appearance, or at any other time the accused is interacting with a member of the court, if that defendant is displaying signs that might suggest mental health concerns, it is standard practice for the court to order a psychological evaluation to obtain more information about those concerns. Evaluations of competency to stand trial and evaluations for pleas of not guilty by reason of insanity will occur at a later point if necessary and will be discussed in detail in Chapter 10.

Courtroom Procedure: How Trials Are Conducted

The prosecution and the defense are each allowed to make an opening statement, with the prosecution often (but not always, depending on the jurisdiction) making their opening statement first. The prosecution tells jurors about the case they will be presenting and describes highlights of the facts and evidence that they will see and hear. The defense then has their opportunity to do exactly the same thing—except, of course, they are representing their own version of the events in question and will suggest that there is considerable doubt in regard to the prosecution's version of the events in question. Opening statements are not intended to be and are not allowed to be argumentative in nature; they are merely introducing the members of the jury to what they may expect to see and hear during the course of the trial.

Once the opening statements have been delivered, the prosecution begins by presenting the witnesses and evidence that it has prepared. Witnesses may provide **direct evidence**, which requires no interpretation or inferences. For example, direct evidence might include a security video of the accused entering the store that was robbed or the fingerprint of the accused on the murder weapon. Witnesses may also provide **circumstantial evidence**. Circumstantial evidence is evidence in which some type of inference must be made or conclusion reached. For example, perhaps there is testimony that the car at the scene of the offense was a blue Ford and the defendant happens to own a blue Ford, though it is not necessarily certain that the car observed was the same blue Ford. Circumstantial evidence might also involve the fact that the defendant was observed to be running from the police, suggesting that the defendant must have done something wrong and was attempting to elude the police.

The defense then has the opportunity to cross-examine the prosecution's witness. The purpose of the cross-examination is to *impeach* the witness, to demonstrate that their testimony could not be accurate or that they are not a credible witness. Cross-examination on the part of the defense is intended to provide the jury with reasonable doubt about the testimony provided by the prosecution's witness. Impeaching a witness may involve calling into question their ability to perceive the events in question ("You were not wearing your glasses at the time you witnessed the alleged offense?"). It may also involve questioning the witness's ability to recall these events objectively ("How many alcoholic beverages did you consume on the night in question?") or the reliability of the witness themselves ("Is it correct that you were promised a reduced sentence in exchange for your testimony today?"). During the cross-examination, **leading questions** are permitted. A leading question is a question phrased in such a manner that it prompts or encourages a certain answer. As you will see in the example below, leading questions can and do play an important role in influencing responses.

HOW FAST WAS THAT CAR GOING? THE INFLUENCE OF LEADING QUESTIONS

In 1974, psychologists Elizabeth Loftus and John Palmer conducted a seminal study on the flexibility of memory and how easily memory can be influenced by leading questions. A leading question is one that is phrased in such a manner that the wording of the question prompts or encourages a particular answer. Loftus and Palmer showed their subjects a film of a motor vehicle accident and then asked them to estimate the speed at which the vehicles were moving at the time of the accident. The wording of the question only varied by a single word in each condition. Subjects in one condition were asked, "About how fast were the cars going when they *smashed* into each other?" (emphasis added). In some conditions, the words *collided, bumped, hit,* or *contacted* were substituted for *smashed*. The subjects estimated the highest speed when asked how fast the vehicles were going when they *smashed*. They then provided progressively slower estimates of speed for the *collided* condition, the *bumped* condition, and the *hit* condition, with the slowest estimates for the *contacted* condition. This study (and subsequent ones) shows the profound impact even a single word can have on an individual's recall and their testimony in the courtroom. It also demonstrates the tremendous overlap between the science of psychology and the applications of that science to the courtroom. Lawyers are very much aware that the manner in which they phrase a question can have a significant impact on the answer they receive from the witness and may use leading questions in an effort to receive the answer they hope will strengthen their case.

The prosecution presents all its evidence and witnesses in the manner described above, with the defense being allowed to cross-examine each witness if it chooses to do so. Once the prosecution rests its case, it is the defense's turn to present their case and to refute the case presented by the prosecution. Remember that the burden of proof is on the prosecution; the defense does not have to prove that the defendant is innocent. Rather, the defense merely needs to convince the jury that the prosecution has not proved their case beyond a reasonable doubt. The Fifth Amendment of the Constitution protects the defendant from having to testify against themselves. The defendant cannot be required to testify, though they are certainly allowed to do so if they wish and if their attorney believes such testimony may be helpful. As the defense presents their witnesses, they engage in direct examination, and then the prosecution is allowed to engage in cross-examination of each of these witnesses. If the defendant chooses to testify, they are subject to cross-examination by the prosecution. The defendant cannot choose to testify in their own defense and then refuse cross-examination.

Once the defense rests its case, the prosecution has the opportunity for rebuttal. This means that the prosecution can present a witness or evidence that it has not already presented in order to attempt to refute evidence provided by the defense.

Each side will make a closing argument. Typically, the prosecution presents first, then the defense, with each side making the argument that the jury should decide in their favor. The prosecution has the last opportunity to make a rebuttal statement to refute the defense's case. Once both sides have made their closing arguments, the judge will then provide instructions to the jury. Such instructions include an explanation of the laws in question and remind the jurors that they are bound to make a determination based on those laws and the evidence that was presented to them during the trial.

The jury then moves to a separate room where they elect a foreperson who serves as an informal chairperson and spokesperson for the jury. The jury is *only* allowed to discuss the case in the jury room among the other jurors. They are not permitted to discuss the case with their family, friends, or anyone else or at any other time; to do so would be to risk a mistrial. The jury convenes in an effort to reach a verdict of guilty or not guilty. In criminal cases, that finding of guilt means that the jury has unanimously found the defendant to be guilty beyond a reasonable doubt, as discussed earlier in this chapter. If the jury does not believe the defendant is guilty beyond a reasonable doubt, they will deliver a verdict of not guilty. Often, it is the foreperson of the jury who reads that verdict in court. In the case of a finding of not guilty, the person is released and can no longer face criminal charges for that offense. In the case of a finding of guilt, the sentencing phase then begins, with the severity of the sentence determined by the judge, based on the seriousness of the offense and state guidelines.

THROUGH THE EYES OF THE VICTIM

It is difficult or impossible for us to understand the thoughts and emotions that survivors must face after they or their loved ones have been victimized in some manner. For some, it is hoped that being able to express the manner in which they have been harmed will help them to have some measure of emotional closure or at least begin the process of healing from the harm that has been done to them. The victim impact statement (VIS) is part of an attempt to allow victims to begin the healing process.

After a finding or a plea of guilty but before sentencing, victims may be permitted to make a VIS. In the courtroom, often with the offender present, they are allowed to describe to those present in the courtroom the manner in which the offender's actions harmed them. These statements are quite powerful and moving. Some victims are tearful, quietly expressing sadness at what they have lost; others anxiously describe how they are unable to function and no longer leave the house. Some angrily shout and yell profanities and threats at the offender, who is often seated across the room from them. In some cases, that anger boils over.

Larry Nassar was the physician for the U.S. Gymnastics Team and was later convicted of sexual assault on at least 265 young women who were part of that team (BBC News, 2018). More than 200 of those victims made VISs after he pleaded guilty, with those statements taking more than a week to complete (Rahal & Kozlowski, 2018). It is difficult to imagine the courage it would take for victims and their families to be able to compose themselves and to express to the court and to Nassar, mere feet away from them, the impact that his horrific crimes had on them. In at least one case, those feelings boiled over. Randall Margreaves, the father of three of Nassar's victims, asked to make such a statement. However, his feelings quickly boiled over, and he lunged at Nassar. Had he not been restrained by bailiffs, Margreaves would have done serious harm to Nassar. Although Margreaves was not charged with this attempted assault (Lacy, 2018), it certainly made clear how dire the consequences of having a loved one be victimized are and that being so close to the offender in the courtroom can retraumatize victims and their families.

CONCLUSION

Forensic psychologists are experts in regard to human thoughts, emotions, and behaviors. However, they may very well feel like a fish out of water when they first become involved in the courtroom or other legal settings. The legal system has its own terminology (much of it in Latin!), roles, and procedures and can be complex and overwhelming to the newcomer. It is important that the forensic psychologist become familiar with the manner in which the federal and state court systems work and the manner in which civil and criminal cases differ. As we learned in this chapter and will see in greater detail in Chapter 10, the fields of law and mental health overlap and intersect with great frequency, and negotiating such intersections can prove challenging indeed. It is hoped that this chapter will provide a foundation for Chapter 10, in which we will discuss in greater detail the manner in which these two fields coexist.

Exercises and Discussion Questions

1. The study by Loftus and Palmer (1974) discussed in this chapter demonstrated how easily witnesses may be influenced by even a single word in a leading question. That being the case, do you think that attorneys who are cross-examining witnesses should be allowed to use leading questions or not? Explain your rationale for allowing or prohibiting such questions.

2. In this chapter, we learned that potential jury members are selected based on driver's license data, voter registration lists, and other publicly available information. Nevertheless, there are times when there is little or no diversity in the jury that is selected. Do you think that the process can be fair without such diversity, or do you believe that juries should be required to include some diverse members to ensure a fair process and verdict? Explain your thoughts on this matter.

3. You are a practicing forensic psychologist, and a private defense attorney wants to hire you (for a considerable sum of money) as a trial consultant to aid in the defense of the client who is accused of a brutal homicide. As you become familiar with the case, it is your personal opinion that the client is guilty. Would you still accept the role of trial consultant, given that you don't know for sure that the client is guilty and that everyone accused is entitled to a defense? Explain your reasoning. Assuming for a moment that you did accept the trial consultant role, what suggestions might you make for the defendant in terms of dress, responding to questions, and courtroom demeanor?

KEY TERMS

Arrest
Bail
Booking
Challenges for cause
Circumstantial evidence
Defense attorney
Direct evidence
District attorney
District courts
Expert witness
Initial appearance
Judge
Lay witness

Leading question
Peremptory challenges
Plea bargain
Preliminary hearing
Preponderance of the evidence
Probable cause
Scientific jury selection
State courts
Trial consultant
U.S. circuit courts of appeal
U.S. Supreme Court
Voir dire

10 PSYCHOLOGY AND THE LAW

LEARNING OBJECTIVES

1. Identify the effects of deinstitutionalizing psychiatric facilities.

2. Describe three different types of specialized courts and the purpose of such courts.

3. Explain the conditions under which a forensic psychologist has a duty to warn others of a potentially dangerous client.

4. Describe the manner in which competence to stand trial may be assessed.

5. Compare and contrast *guilty but mentally ill* and *not guilty by reason of insanity*.

I looked at the man sitting in front of me and looked back again at his record on my desk. It didn't seem possible, but there it was, plain as could be. The inmate in front of me clearly had a very serious mental health diagnosis. Schizophrenia, to be specific, meaning that when he wasn't on medications, he heard voices whispering vile things to him. He saw shadows and moving shapes where none existed. He believed that the devil was trying to steal his soul, among other irrational beliefs. His hygiene at such times was atrocious and he was virtually incapable of performing daily living activities.

As he sat in front of me today, he was compliant with his psychotropic medications and doing relatively well, though his baseline functioning and hygiene were still fairly poor.

He had been in full-blown psychosis and homeless, living under a bridge in the winter in frigid southwest Pennsylvania when his offense occurred. He had wandered into the local supermarket, picked up a loaf of bread and a package of Oscar Mayer bologna, loitered for a few minutes to warm up, and walked out of the store without paying for the items he had picked up. The manager of the store called the police, who had subsequently placed him under arrest.

I looked down at his record in front of me. It couldn't be . . . and yet it was. For taking five dollars of bread and meat out of the grocery store, this poor man had been sentenced to one and a half to three years in state prison. I knew that the severely mentally ill are less likely to be paroled, meaning that in all probability, this man would be incarcerated for three full years, at a cost to the taxpayer of $33,000 per year to the tune of $99,000 in total for the offense of taking a little bit of food when he was starving and seriously mentally ill.

I knew this man did not need incarceration, and in fact, incarceration would do him far more harm than good. He should be getting treatment at a hospital or group home, not incarceration. And yet there he sat in front of me.

INTRODUCTION AND DEFINITIONS

As previously discussed in this text, the mental illnesses described in the *Diagnostic and Statistical Manual of Mental Disorders* (5th edition; DSM-5) are characterized by either a feeling of distress on the part of the effected individual or an impairment in some aspect of functioning, such as difficulty working or going to school, maintaining relationships, or performing daily living activities. In some cases, individuals with mental illness suffer both distress *and* an impairment in functioning. It seems self-evident that many such individuals who suffer from mental illness would benefit from support and an intervention of some type. Having a stable home, a source of income, and the ability to afford the basic necessities of daily life (with or without supervision) is certainly important. It is not difficult to imagine that the prison environment, while providing many of those basic necessities, is still an extremely difficult environment for *anyone* to exist in. For those who have mental health challenges, those difficulties are likely to be multiplied many times over. The prison environment is often stark, dangerous, and isolating. There are likely few, if any environments more poorly suited to those with mental health challenges than the prison setting.

In this chapter, we will discuss the challenges of balancing mental health treatment with criminal justice. As we will see, advancements in psychiatric treatment led to the release of many people with mental illnesses from inpatient psychiatric institutions. However, the communities into which these individuals were released were often unprepared to provide the support that was needed. Thus, many of those with mental health challenges eventually came into contact with the criminal justice system, which was even less well prepared to provide the necessary mental health services. Since that time, there have been efforts to divert the mentally ill from incarceration when this can be done without compromising the safety of the public.

Mental health experts and the justice system have collaborated (and at times, been at odds) in regard to the manner in which the mentally ill and society as a whole can be best served. In this chapter, we will discuss the manner in which mental health concerns must be taken into account before, during, and after the trial process. We will also examine how decisions are made concerning whether a person with mental illness is responsible for their offense and the best course of action for that person and for the community.

DEINSTITUTIONALIZATION OF PSYCHIATRIC HOSPITALS

The Declaration of Independence states that people have the inalienable right to "life, *liberty*, and the pursuit of happiness" (emphasis added). The Thirteenth Amendment of the U.S. Constitution states, "Neither slavery nor involuntary servitude, except as a punishment for crime whereof the party shall have been duly convicted, shall exist within the United States, or any place subject to their jurisdiction." Although psychiatric hospitalization certainly is not the equivalent of slavery or involuntary servitude, the Thirteenth Amendment does underscore the importance of not depriving any person of their freedom without due process and justifiable cause. Just as we would not confine a person to a medical hospital against their will, even if they had a physical ailment, it could be argued that we should not confine a person to a psychiatric institution simply because they are suffering from a mental illness.

Despite the inalienable rights outlined in the Declaration of Independence and the Thirteenth Amendment of the Constitution, up until the 1950s, the placement of severely mentally ill individuals (with or without their consent) was relatively commonplace; in 1955, there were 558,239 people in psychiatric hospitals, with a U.S. population of 164 million (Torrey, 1997). Psychiatric hospital beds were often readily available for those who needed them, and it was relatively easy for a mental health professional to commit an individual to such an institution (again, with or without their consent). On the one hand, this meant that those in need of psychiatric treatment were able to receive it. On the other hand, the quality of such treatment varied considerably, with some receiving adequate care but others simply being warehoused against their will in inadequate conditions for lengthy periods of time without any true due process.

With the development of Thorazine (a powerful and effective antipsychotic medication) and other psychotropic medications, it was conceivable that many of the individuals who were once treated in an inpatient psychiatric facility could be treated effectively on an outpatient basis. This afforded them the opportunity to live with their family or independently and could allow many to function effectively in the community with varying levels of support. Combined with the evolving idea that people should not be committed to psychiatric institutions against their will unless there was no other option, psychiatric hospitals began discharging many people to the community. So many were discharged, in fact, that many psychiatric institutions were permanently closed (or at the very least, substantially downsized).

In 1963, President Kennedy signed the **Mental Retardation Facilities and Community Mental Health Centers Construction Act**. This act was aimed at providing financial support from the federal government to community mental health treatment centers (DiGravio, 2013). The passing of this act was instrumental in the process of deinstitutionalization, as it provided support for local mental health treatment facilities by making large inpatient psychiatric facilities unnecessary.

By 1994, the more than 500,000 people psychiatrically hospitalized in 1955 had fallen significantly to only 71,619 with a U.S. population of 260 million. That means that 92% of the people who would have been in psychiatric hospitals in 1955 would not have been there in 1994 (Torrey, 1997).

Deinstitutionalization is the term used to describe the discharge of those in inpatient psychiatric facilities into the community, usually with the subsequent downsizing or closure of that facility. Such release and the subsequent freedom of movement allowed to the former patients on the surface seems to represent progress. On other hand, if such release into the community does not include the provision of supportive housing, mental health care, and other services, then perhaps what appears to be progress is only a recipe for further concerns for both those with mental illness and those in the community to which they are released. Without sufficient support and services, the chances of those who are severely mentally ill coming into contact with the criminal justice system at some point seem relatively high.

The closure of many psychiatric hospitals made both admission and/or readmission to such facilities much more difficult than it had previously been. The present author has traveled to many states as a speaker regarding mental health issues. One question I invariably asked my audience of mental health professionals was, "If you determined right now, today, that I needed long-term psychiatric hospitalization in your state, how long would I have to wait before you could get me admitted?" Although answers varied from state to state, the usual response involved people shaking their heads and saying things like, "Never," "Forget about it," or "Months." Yet when I asked those same people how long it would take me to be arrested and in the back of a police car if I chose to brandish a knife and threaten people in the hotel lobby, those same people responded, "Maybe ten minutes." It is sad but true: It is much easier for someone to be arrested and incarcerated than it is for that same person to receive psychiatric help. In fact, many inmates that I have known told me that they purposely committed offenses because they knew that soon after, they would be incarcerated and could therefore count on a bed, regular meals, and some form of medical and psychiatric care.

At present, the three facilities in the United States that hold the most individuals with mental illnesses are not psychiatric facilities but jails. The Los Angeles County Jail, the Cook County Jail in Chicago, and Rikers Island in New York City each hold more people with mental illnesses

Deinstitutionalization led to the release of many people from psychiatric units, with those units then closing or downsizing considerably.

istock/Derick Hudson

than any psychiatric facility in the United States (Penaloza, 2020). The Treatment Advocacy Center suggests that overall, the number of individuals with mental illness in jails and prisons in the United States is "ten times more than [the number] remaining in state psychiatric hospitals" (Torrey et al., 2014). It is not difficult to imagine that the stark and dangerous nature of incarceration would be extraordinarily unsettling for those already struggling with a mental illness.

Specialized Courts for the Mentally Ill

Jails and prisons are an ill-suited and expensive option for those who are mentally ill. The lack of privacy, threats to physical safety, and harsh environment are likely to only worsen an individual's mental health struggles. Incarcerating those who are mentally ill can cost two to three times more than incarcerating those who are not mentally ill (Riley, 2019). Furthermore, the prison environment is likely to exacerbate the symptoms for those who suffer from mental illnesses. For those with nonviolent or minor offenses, then, it makes sense to divert them from incarceration and instead assist them in finding treatment and supportive intervention. The goal of **mental health courts** is to divert some individuals with mental illness from incarceration.

Mental health courts represent a collaboration between mental health professionals and the criminal justice system. These courts were created by America's Law Enforcement and Mental Health Project in 2000 and later supported by the Mentally Ill Offender Treatment and Crime Reduction Act in 2004 (Bureau of Justice Administration, 2012). As of 2012, there were more than 150 mental health courts in the United States and that number continues to grow. Mental health courts employ judges, prosecutors, and defenders who have often received additional training in mental health issues. The atmosphere of the mental health court tends to be much less adversarial than that of criminal courts, with the courtroom work group working together in cooperation with the defendant to formulate a plan for supervising the defendant's behavior.

Mental health courts seek to place the defendant in the least restrictive environment that will still maintain their safety and the safety of those in the community. An individualized plan is developed for that client, with the plan likely to include conditions such as routine psychiatric appointments, monitored medication compliance (if prescribed), attendance of individual or group counseling sessions, and abstinence from alcohol and other drugs, among other possible conditions. The individual remains under judicial supervision and is assigned a case manager who will monitor their compliance with the stipulations of the court. Noncompliance may result in increased sanctions or (eventually) incarceration. Compliance may be met with gradually increased freedom from any restrictions. In addition, notable in mental health courts is the emphasis on support and positive reinforcement. In some such courts, those completing their requirements receive a certificate or a medal. Handshakes and hugs from the attorneys and even the judge are not unheard of when a defendant successfully graduates from mental health court.

A study by the RAND corporation of the mental health court in Allegheny County, Pennsylvania, demonstrated that mental health courts saved taxpayers a substantial amount of money while providing increased mental health services and decreasing the amount of time that participants spent incarcerated (Ridgely et al., 2007). Specifically, this study suggests that the Allegheny County mental health court saved taxpayers more than $3 million in a two-year period of time.

A 2017 study by Lowder, Rade, and Desmarais included a meta-analysis of 17 studies of the relationship between mental health courts and recidivism from 2004 to 2015. This meta-analysis suggested at least a small relationship between mental health courts and reduced recidivism and reduced jail terms for defendants. The authors also suggested that further study on this matter is likely to be beneficial.

In the board game Monopoly, there is a "Get Out of Jail Free" card that allows players to get out of the Jail square without having to pay a fine. Mental health courts should not be mistaken for a "Get Out of Jail Free" card. Violent offenders, mentally ill or not, will be seen in criminal court rather than mental health court. Those who are referred to mental health court are not absolved of their offenses but rather are ordered by the court to comply with a number of conditions aimed at stabilizing their mental health and promoting adaptive and law-abiding behavior. Thus, although some might see mental health courts as being soft on crime, it is important to consider both the detrimental impact on the mentally ill of incarcerating them when they have committed only minor offenses and the economic impact of paying for the lengthy and expensive incarceration of those who have done little or no harm to anyone other than themselves. Combined with the financial savings and decreased recidivism noted in the above research, it likely makes sense to think of mental health courts not as soft on crime but rather as smart on crime.

Veterans Treatment Courts (VTCs)

We owe the military veterans who have served our country a great debt. Veterans and their families have made many different types of sacrifices for our country; children have grown up with a military parent away from home for long periods of time, and military spouses are often tasked with taking care of all household responsibilities during that time. Some veterans have been

For those who have served our country and committed nonviolent offenses, veterans treatment courts can provide an alternative to incarceration.

istock/ iShootPhotosLLC

wounded, and others have made the ultimate sacrifice, giving their very lives for our country. Some of those who have served will, at one point or another, come into contact with the criminal justice system. The dilemma for society, then, is how to reconcile or balance their actions: the debt their country owes them balanced against a crime that they have committed. **Veterans treatment courts (VTCs)** are part of an attempt to achieve this balance for those who have committed minor or nonviolent offenses.

Similar to mental health courts, the goal of VTC is to divert those who have served our country from incarceration when possible. Those who have served in the military are as prone to mental health issues as anyone else, and those who have served in combat and other especially strenuous roles may be more prone to post-traumatic stress disorder (PTSD) and other mental illness than most other people are. According to the National Academy of Sciences (2018) 41% (1.7 million) of veterans who served in Operation Enduring Freedom, Operation Iraqi Freedom, and Operation New Dawn have a mental health need. A study by Elbogen et al. (2013) suggested that 43% of the veterans who served in Iraq and Afghanistan suffer from probable PTSD, major depressive disorder, and/or alcohol misuse.

VTCs may be helpful for those who have mental health and/or substance abuse issues. The structured court setting may be familiar and perhaps, in some cases, even comfortable to those who are accustomed to the structured life of the military, and VTCs clearly make use of this structure. It is not uncommon for the judge and the defendant to salute each other and to address each other as "sir" or "ma'am." As with drug and mental health courts, the VTC is not a "Get Out of Jail Free" card. A program is developed to meet the veteran's needs and to hold them accountable for following the conditions imposed upon them. In addition to the case manager, judge, and prosecuting and defense attorneys, it is not uncommon for the veteran to be assigned a peer support person who is a veteran themselves. Thus, the veteran has many officials to both support their efforts and hold them accountable for complying with the conditions set upon them.

The idea of VTC is to encourage people to participate in drug and alcohol rehab and to assist these veterans in finding stable housing and employment. Monitored compliance with medical and psychiatric appointments may also be established. Although evidence is still emerging, there is reason to believe that VTCs have been successful. Tsai et al. (2018) found that during a year of participation in a VTC, only 14% of those who participated were reincarcerated, which is substantially less than the 23%–46% recidivism rate of United States prisoners not participating in such a program (Durose et al., 2014). VTCs do appear to show considerable promise in helping those who have served and committed minor offenses in reestablishing a successful life in the community.

VETERANS TREATMENT COURTS: CARING FOR THOSE WHO SERVED THEIR COUNTRY

Tommy Rieman is the type of person who might be considered an all-American hero. He was serving in the Army in Iraq when his unit was ambushed. He and his crew were injured, and for his bravery in assisting his teammates and the injuries that he received while doing so, he earned both a Silver Star and a Purple Heart. In President Bush's 2007 State of the Union address, the president mentioned him by name, and Rieman received a well-deserved standing ovation. Little did others know that at the time, he was suffering from PTSD and alcoholism. By his own admission, he later attempted to kill himself by drinking and intentionally driving his vehicle into a tree. He was charged with driving under the influence (DUI). Given his service and the fact that his offense harmed no one other than himself, instead of being tried in criminal court, he was diverted to a VTC. He was assigned a case manager and a mentor who was also a veteran. He received treatment and was monitored for compliance with that treatment and for continued abstinence from alcohol and other drugs. He has now been the keynote speaker at a number of events, inspiring others with his story of overcoming adversity. His is a clear case of the benefits of the VTC providing treatment rather than punishment.

Drug Treatment Courts

As discussed earlier in this text, those struggling with mental illness at times self-medicate with alcohol and/or other drugs. To the user, it may seem that such use eases their emotional pain or at least temporarily numbs it. However, to the outside observer, it is often apparent that such use only exacerbates that person's mental health symptoms and further impairs their ability to function in a wide variety of ways. As the addicted individual develops a tolerance to the substance they are using, they use more and more to achieve the same effect, with an accompanying decrease in ability to function in the home, school, or work environment.

Those who suffer from alcohol and other drug addictions often come to the attention of law enforcement authorities, sometimes for offenses committed under the influence (such as a DUI) and other times for offenses committed as part of an effort to obtain money to support their addiction. When those offenses involve violence and harm to others, incarceration and treatment with the prison setting may be the only viable option. However, when their offenses are nonviolent, other treatments may be of greater benefit to the individual while being less costly to the community. As above with mental health courts and VTCs, it is hoped that drug treatment courts can divert some of those with addiction issues from incarceration.

The first **drug treatment court** was implemented in Miami in 1989 (Kirchner, 2014). At the present time, there are drug treatment courts in all 50 states, with more than 3,000 in total in the United States (Marlowe et al., 2016). Similar to mental health courts and VTCs, the purpose of drug treatment courts is to divert nonviolent offenders from incarceration when possible and when doing so appears to present little threat of harm to those in the community. Drug treatment courts require the screening and assessment of the offender as well as requiring that offender to attend treatment and remain abstinent from alcohol and other drugs. Drug courts, like the other specialized courts above, may be thought to utilize a "carrot and stick" approach: Positive reinforcement and increased privileges for those who comply with the court's requirements but increased sanctions and possible incarceration for those who fail to comply.

As discussed previously, incarceration by itself does not cure addiction or mental illness; it is only the person that can be locked up, not the addiction. If anything, the stress of incarceration might only serve to exacerbate either or both of these conditions. Furthermore, it is not impossible for those who are incarcerated to obtain alcohol or other drugs if they want to. In Chapter 11, we will learn about Bob, who after ten years of forced abstinence from alcohol while incarcerated, clearly expressed his intent to resume drinking the moment he was released. For now, it is sufficient to state that the forced abstinence people may endure while incarcerated is not a cure for alcoholism.

A ten-year-long study by National Institute of Justice researchers suggested that drug courts appear to lower rates of recidivism/rearrest and also save money (Finigan et al., 2007). Incarcerating drug offenders and providing them with treatment can cost between $20,000 and $50,000 per year. By way of contrast, a comprehensive drug court–mandated program typically costs a small fraction of this: $2,500 to $4,000 per year (Rich et al., 2005). Again, it would appear that with nonviolent offenders, drug courts (like other specialized courts) are not soft on crime but are smart on crime.

DUTY TO WARN

Therapist–client confidentiality is of great importance in the counseling setting. The client must be able to trust that the very difficult topics they are discussing with their therapist will not be revealed to others. This trust allows the therapeutic relationship to blossom and grow over time. However, there are situations in which the therapist can, and in some cases, *must* disclose to others what the client has told them during a session. Such limitations of confidentiality should be one of the very first things discussed by the therapist and client during their initial session. The therapist is required to inform the client that if the client makes any statement about harming themselves or others, the therapist is *permitted* in some cases to notify others of this threat (**permissive reporting**) and is *required* to do so in other cases (**mandated reporting**).

State laws vary as to whether a clinician is permitted or required to warn others when a client expresses violent or suicidal ideation, intent, or plan. For example, California, Pennsylvania, Montana, and Illinois are among the states that require mental health practitioners to report threats of violence or suicidality. Arizona, Texas, Connecticut, and Rhode Island are among the states that permit but do not require such reporting. Nevada, North Dakota, North Carolina, and Maine have no duty to warn in such cases (Hanson, 2022). It should be noted that the reporting requirements can change; in 2013, New York passed a law changing a permissive reporting statute to a mandated reporting statute. It is also important to note that the reporting requirements for one type of mental health clinician in a given state may be different from the requirements of a different type of clinician. It is vitally important that any mental health practitioner be quite clear on what the duty to warn requirements are for their state and their profession. The reason that permissive and mandated reporting guidelines exist in so many states, as we will see below, is a sad one indeed.

THE ORIGINS OF DUTY TO WARN

Prosenjit Poddar was a student at the University of California at Berkeley in 1968, when he met Tatiana Tarasoff. The two dated, but it seemed that Poddar was perhaps more taken by Tarasoff than she was by him. Poddar was noted to be emotionally upset when Tarasoff informed him that he was not the only one she was dating. His studies and grades declined after this revelation. In the summer of 1969, Tarasoff traveled to Brazil during summer break. Poddar began to see a psychologist for counseling to help him cope with his feelings about this potential breakup. At one point during their sessions, Poddar shared with the psychologist that he was having thoughts of killing Tarasoff. The psychologist then informed the campus police but did not inform the city police, Tarasoff, or her family of this threat. The campus police found no reason to hold or hospitalize Poddar, as he appeared calm and rational to them at the time. In October of 1969, after she returned to campus, Poddar did indeed carry through on his threat and stabbed Tarasoff to death. Her parents subsequently sued the school in the landmark case *Tarasoff v. Board of Regents* (1976). The court later ruled that mental health counselors have a duty to warn those who have been threatened, and that duty generally precludes the usual counselor–client confidentiality.

Not surprisingly, since the time of the Tarasoff case, counselors have been trained in the limitations of confidentiality and are required to inform their clients of these limitations. Furthermore, depending on the state in which they practice, counselors (including forensic psychologists and psychiatrists) may be required to inform not only the appropriate authorities but also any and all named potential victims when threats of harm are made during the counseling session. This duty to warn is especially important for those working in the forensic setting, as forensic clients have been known both to threaten others and, at times, to carry out those threats. Forensic clients, by the very nature of their involvement in the criminal justice system, must be monitored closely for threats toward themselves and others, with action taken when necessary.

To the uninitiated, it might seem simple to recognize exactly when a threat has been made and there is a duty to warn. For example, if a client were to say, "When I go to work tomorrow, I'm bringing my gun and I'm going to shoot my boss," that is a clear and simple threat that would trigger a duty to warn. However, in many situations, the statement made by the client is not clearly a threat. For example, a client might say, "I'm going to school tomorrow and I'm going to make a name for myself." Although such a statement would certainly be cause for concern, it is not a direct threat; the client could simply mean that they are hoping to go viral on social media for doing something silly on school property. It is the responsibility of the clinician in such cases to remind the client of the limitations of confidentiality and then to probe much further into such a statement in an effort to be as certain as possible as to whether the client is making a threat that permits or requires a duty to report. In the experience of the present clinician, one is never wrong to consult with colleagues or their state board of psychology (or other profession) about what steps to take when one is uncertain. Although the forensic psychologist may have some job duties that are quick and easy, decisions about duty to warn are not among such duties. Duty to warn situations must always be given careful consideration and consultation when needed.

COMPETENCY TO STAND TRIAL

In the last chapter, we discussed the manner in which those accused of criminal offenses may be taken into custody and how they are processed through the court system. At times, the judge, lawyers, or other criminal justice professionals may have reason to suspect that the accused has current mental health concerns. For example, the judge or lawyers may notice the defendant talking to themselves or expressing confusion at where they are or what is happening. Or perhaps the defendant appears to be intellectually limited. If the judge, district attorney, defense attorney, or anyone else involved in the case has reason to suspect that there are concerns about the defendant's mental health or intellectual functioning, they may request an evaluation of the defendant's competency to stand trial. **Competency to stand trial** refers to the state of mind of the accused at the time of the trial itself and the ability of that defendant to understand the charges against them and the court process itself. Competency to stand trial does not refer to the defendant's mind at the time of the offense; that issue we will consider shortly in regard to pleas of not guilty by reason of insanity.

In 1959, the 8th Circuit Court handed down what became known as the **Dusky standard**, which states that the accused must understand the trial process and that they must also be able to assist in their own defense (*Dusky v. United States*, 1959). The Dusky standard has two "prongs" or requirements. First, it is required that the defendant comprehends the charges against them and the potential penalties associated with those charges. Secondly, the defendant must have the ability to cooperate meaningfully and assist their attorney in their own defense. To say that the defendant must be able to assist in their own defense does not mean that they need to act as their own attorney, simply that they should be able to cooperate with their attorney and to answer their attorney's questions in a manner that allows their attorney to formulate a reasonable defense. Competency also means that the defendant is able to make reasonable choices as to what plea they want to enter. Regardless of how compelling the evidence against them may be, a defendant cannot be convicted of a crime if they are not mentally competent to stand trial.

According to *Pate v. Robinson* (1966), under 18 U.S.C. § 4241(a), the court must order a competency hearing if there is reason to believe that the accused has a mental health condition or intellectual limitation that might render them incapable of understanding the nature and consequences of the proceedings against them. Failure to do so would be to deny the accused a fair trial and would violate constitutional protections in place, including due process. Bringing to trial a person who is not competent is said to offend the dignity of the court, to undermine the credibility of the process itself, and to deprive a citizen of their rights.

In 1975, the court underscored the importance of the requirement of competency in the criminal process. In *Drope v. Missouri*, the court held that competency was "fundamental to an adversary system of justice." This decision also reaffirmed that it would be inappropriate to place on trial a defendant who lacked the capacity to understand the charges against them and the proceedings and possible consequences connected with being on trial. Given the protections noted above, it is perhaps no surprise that assessment of a defendant's competence to stand trial is the most common forensic evaluation performed in the United States. Defense attorneys have doubts about defendants' competency and request evaluations of competency to stand trial in 8%–15% of felony cases, and in 20%–30% of those cases, defendants are found not competent to stand trial (Noffsinger & Resnick, 2017).

Despite the importance of making certain that a defendant is competent to stand trial, there is no universally agreed-upon manner of doing so, with methods of performing such evaluations varying greatly between one mental health clinician and another. Some mental health professionals will make a determination as to competency based on a structured clinical evaluation. Others may make this determination using an unstructured evaluation, and still others may use a standardized instrument or a combination of different techniques. It is important to note that finding that the accused suffers from a mental disorder does not in and of itself mean that a person is incompetent to stand trial. For example, a person may be diagnosed with depression and anxiety and may be prescribed psychotropic medications for these conditions. However, if it is found that despite their mental health issues, the defendant meets the Dusky standard and is able to understand the charges against them and that they are able to assist counsel in their defense, then they will in all likelihood be deemed competent to stand trial.

The AAPL Practice Guideline for the Forensic Psychiatric Evaluation of Competence to Stand Trial (Mossman et al., 2007) provides guidelines for the assessment of competency to stand trial. It suggests that the examiner should conduct a thorough background review related to the defendant, including an examination of all available records, and should interview the defendant. The examiner is advised to inquire as to the defendant's basic knowledge of courtroom personnel and procedures and whether they are aware of the charges against them and the potential penalty if found guilty. This guideline also suggests that the examiner carefully assess the defendant's ability to behave safely and appropriately in the courtroom. This guideline does not recommend for or against the use of standardized competency assessment instruments but rather outlines the importance of a thorough and complete review of records and a detailed interview with the defendant.

If the defendant is found incompetent to stand trial, proceedings will be halted temporarily while action is taken to restore the defendant to competency. This may mean that the court mandates the defendant to receive inpatient or outpatient psychiatric treatment, counseling, and other steps to enable that individual to understand the court process and to be able to assist in their defense. If and when a mental health expert later deems the accused to be competent, trial proceedings will resume. Thus, similar to the discussion of specialized courts as not being a "Get Out of Jail Free" card, neither does being found not competent to stand trial mean that person will never be prosecuted. Instead, if and when that person is found to be competent to stand trial, the court process will resume.

Options for restoration of competency include state-run psychiatric hospitals, community or private psychiatric hospitals, or outpatient competency restoration (OCR) programs. OCR programs are less expensive and less restrictive and are generally used when the offense is a misdemeanor or a nonviolent felony (Hogg Foundation for Mental Health, 2013) Although not required by the Dusky standard, many statutes require that the examining psychiatrist express an opinion about whether restoration of competence is likely within some designated period of time. Furthermore, the psychiatrist may be asked for a recommendation as to whether the restoration of competency should take place in an inpatient or outpatient setting (Mossman et al., 2007).

There are cases in which attempts are made to restore the defendant to competency and it is determined that such restoration is never likely. For example, a defendant may be charged with a DUI in an accident that resulted in the death of two other people and serious head injury to the accused individual, rendering them incompetent to understand the trial proceedings; they may have little chance of ever being restored to competency. In other cases, it may be established that a defendant is so intellectually limited that they will never be able to understand the proceedings of the court in their case. In such cases, the court may order continued intermittent evaluations of competency and may decide to drop the charges or to pursue civil action to commit the person to a psychiatric facility for an undetermined period of time. In cases where the charges are less serious, it is also possible that the charges will be dropped entirely.

As noted above, competency can be assessed by a forensic psychologist, psychiatrist, or other mental health professional with an unstructured or structured interview or using a standardized instrument or some combination thereof. Several structured instruments are described below.

The Competence to Stand Trial Assessment Instrument (CAI)

The **Competence to Stand Trial Assessment Instrument (CAI)** was developed by a multidisciplinary team of lawyers and mental health experts in order to standardize both the process and the criteria for competency to stand trial. The CAI assesses thirteen different areas of the defendant's understanding and functioning. Among other areas, the CAI is designed to assess the defendant's ability to understand the legal defenses available to them, their ability to relate to their attorney, and their understanding of the charges against them and the potential penalties for those charges. Also assessed are the defendant's ability to testify appropriately on their own behalf and their understanding of the legal strategy of their own defense, including (but not limited to) understanding the implications of pleading guilty to lesser or reduced charges. Each of the thirteen areas assessed is rated by the clinician from 1 to 5, with lower ratings indicating more impairment than higher ratings. It is hoped that the CAI will provide the assessor with a valid means of evaluating competence to stand trial.

The MacArthur Competency Assessment Tool–Criminal Application (MacCAT–CA)

The **MacArthur Competency Assessment Tool–Criminal Application (MacCAT–CA)** consists of 22 items. Sixteen of these items are in the form of vignettes about a hypothetical crime and assess the defendant's understanding and reasoning about the prosecution of a defendant in those vignettes. The idea of using these vignettes is to distance the defendant from their own case and attempt to assess their understanding and reasoning about the criminal justice process itself. The remaining six items of the MacCAT–CA assess the defendant's attitudes and beliefs in regard to their own case and defense. The MacCAT–CA is designed to measure standards related to Dusky and typically takes 25 to 45 minutes to administer.

Similar to the discussion about specialized treatment courts not being the equivalent of a "Get Out of Jail Free" card, neither should the issue of incompetence be considered the equivalent of a person being able to get away with their offense. The ability of the accused to understand the proceedings of the courtroom is one of the most basic elements of due process. In most cases, a finding of not competent to stand trial merely postpones the proceedings until the accused can be rendered competent, at which time, the court will proceed as usual.

NOT GUILTY BY REASON OF INSANITY

In 1843, Daniel M'Naghten (sometimes referred to as *McNaughton*) was accused of killing Edward Drummond, whom M'Naghten incorrectly believed to be the prime minister of the United Kingdom. During his trial, it became obvious to everyone in the courtroom that M'Naghten was not of sound mind, as he ranted bizarre theories about the Tories intending to plot against him and kill him. M'Naghten's attorney claimed that he was too mentally ill to be found guilty and argued that it would be more appropriate to place him in a psychiatric institution than in prison. The court and jury agreed with this, and M'Naghten spent the remainder of his life in a psychiatric facility.

The M'Naghten case is considered the forerunner of the idea that those who do not fully understand that their actions are wrong should perhaps be held to a different standard of accountability for those actions. As discussed earlier in this text, a guilty mind (mens rea) is required in order to convict someone of most criminal offenses. If a person has severe mental health challenges or intellectual limitations, then they may not be fully capable of having a guilty mind. It is important to note that unlike *competency to stand trial*, which refers to the defendant's mental status at the time of the trial, *not guilty by reason of insanity* refers to the defendant's mental status at the time of the offense.

A TRIP TO THE CARNIVAL

During a summer between college semesters, the present author worked in a group home for individuals with severe intellectual limitations. One day, we took a group of those clients to the local carnival so that they could enjoy the rides, games, and food. Each staff member was assigned one of the clients to monitor. My client, whom I will refer to as Robert, functioned at the intellectual level of about a four- or five-year-old. As we walked around the grounds, Robert noticed a large pink stuffed bunny that was being offered as the grand prize at one of the games. He immediately grabbed the bunny, hugged it tight, and ran off with it. The carnival manager and I eventually caught up with him. I pleaded with Robert to let go of the bunny, but he refused, holding on as tight as he could. Knowing that Robert was not going to willingly return the bunny, I begged the manager to please not call the police, as Robert did not comprehend that his actions constituted stealing. Fortunately, the manager was more than sympathetic and happily allowed Robert to keep the bunny. Given his limitations, there was not—and could not be—a guilty mind.

When the defense claims that their client is not guilty by reason of insanity (NGRI), there are several consequences. First, it is acknowledged by the defense that the facts of the case are not in dispute; the defendant did indeed commit the act(s) in question. Therefore, there is no longer a burden on the prosecution to prove the facts of the case. Instead, the burden of proof shifts to the defense to prove that the defendant was legally insane at the time they committed those acts. According to the M'Naghten case, the defense must prove either (1) that at the time the offense was committed, the defendant did not know that what they were doing was wrong *or* (2) that they were acting in response to an irresistible impulse.

It is easy for the budding forensic psychologist (or anyone else for that matter!) to become confused in regard to NGRI claims, given that this is based on the defendant claiming to have been legally insane at the time of the offense. A close examination of the DSM-5 would yield absolutely no diagnosis of *insane*, as the word *insane* does not appear even a single time in that text. Thus, while there is a *legal* definition of insane, there is no *psychological* definition of the word. Insanity, then, is a legal term and defense, not a psychological one.

Perhaps because there have been some high-profile cases in which the insanity defense was successful (see the case of Andrea Yates, below) or perhaps because it is portrayed in popular television shows and movies, the public may believe that the insanity defense is commonplace, with the accused frequently getting away with offenses as the result of being found NGRI. The evidence strongly contradicts such a belief. The insanity defense is rarely used and is even less often successful. The NGRI defense is used in less than 1% of all cases, and in those cases where it is used, it is successful less than 25% of the time. This means that fewer than one in 400 defendants is found to be NGRI (Lewis, 2020).

A finding of NGRI in regard to a serious offense does not mean that the defendant is free to go with no consequences. Depending on the offense, they will likely be confined to a (perhaps locked) psychiatric unit. James McQuillan was charged with assault and intent to rape a minor in Michigan in 1970. He was found competent to stand trial and was subsequently found to be NGRI and was then committed to a psychiatric facility. After being held in that facility for several years, with little (if any) follow-up evaluations related to his mental state, the Michigan Supreme Court found that his constitutional rights were being violated, as he was being held in that facility for an indefinite period of time with no follow-up evaluations concerning his status (*People v. McQuillan*, 1974). Since that decision, it is required that individuals found to be NGRI must be regularly reevaluated as to their mental health status and fitness for release. Still, it is entirely possible that they will be confined in such a facility for at least as long, if not longer, than they would have been incarcerated had they pled or been found to be guilty. If and when those found to be NGRI are released, it will only be after they have been found to no longer be legally insane. Furthermore, they will not be released if there is reason to believe that they will be a threat to those in the community.

Not every state uses the M'Naghten rules to guide findings of NGRI, though the guidelines they do use tend to be similar in many ways. Some states use what is referred to as the **irresistible impulse test**; in other words, the defense claims that as the result of a mental illness or defect, their client was acting in response to an uncontrollable impulse and was incapable of resisting this urge. Other states utilize a **model penal code test**, meaning that due to a mental illness or defect, the defendant was incapable of understanding the criminal nature of their actions. Still other states make use of the **Durham rule**, which suggests that a mental illness led directly to the criminal behavior in question. Four states—Kansas, Montana, Idaho, and Utah—make no provision at all for the use of the insanity defense (Jacewicz, 2016).

NGRI: The Cases of Jeffrey Dahmer and Andrea Yates

Jeffrey Dahmer (1960–1994), also referred to as "The Milwaukee Cannibal," was an American serial killer who murdered 17 men and boys between the years of 1978 and 1991. The brutality and graphic nature of his offenses are almost beyond comprehension. His modus operandi was to drug his victims and physically abuse them. In some cases, he drilled holes in their heads and poured acid into their skulls while they were still alive in hopes of creating a "zombie love slave" (Mathias, 2022). Once the victims were dead, he attempted to destroy and dispose of some body parts while keeping other body parts as souvenirs and, in some cases, mummifying these body parts (Masters, 1993). He also committed sexual acts and acts of necrophilia with parts of victims' bodies. In short, to the layperson, it would be difficult to come to any other conclusion than that Dahmer was insane. After all, one might wonder, how could a sane person engage in such acts?

Despite the heinous nature of Dahmer's offenses, NGRI can still be very difficult to prove, given the conditions that must be met. As already mentioned, the defense must be able to prove either that the defendant did not know that what they were doing was wrong or that they were acting in response to an irresistible impulse. Dahmer was noted to have lied to the police on at least one occasion and was made multiple attempts to dispose of the bodies of his victims. He was also noted to have covered the air vents in his apartment, likely to try to prevent the smell from wafting over to neighboring apartments, which would have given him away. Such attempts to deceive the police, dispose of bodies, and hide the odor from others certainly suggest that Dahmer clearly knew that what he was doing was wrong and that he was trying to avoid capture. Thus, the defense was not able to prove to the jury that Dahmer did not know that what he was doing was wrong.

The other prong of the NGRI defense is that the defendant was acting in response to an irresistible impulse. Clearly, this was not the case for Dahmer, whose modus operandi was to meet a potential victim at a bar, get them drunk, and then lure them back to his apartment with offers of money, sex, and drugs. Dahmer patiently waited until the victim was impaired and securely in his apartment before he attacked them. Thus, the defense was not able to demonstrate that Dahmer was acting in response to an irresistible impulse. Despite the savage and almost incomprehensible nature of his offenses, the jury did not find that Dahmer was NGRI, and he was eventually sentenced to serve 16 life sentences. In 1994, after having served only two years of incarceration, Dahmer was assaulted and killed by another inmate at the Columbia Correctional Institution.

Andrea Yates (1964–present) was married and living in Houston, Texas, with her husband and five children. She had a history of severe mental illness, and her mental illness seemed to be becoming increasingly severe with the birth of each child, to such an extent that one of her psychiatrists warned her that she absolutely should not have any more children as this would be devastating to her mental health (Fox News Channel, 2015). However, she and her husband did go on to have a fifth child. Yates was psychiatrically hospitalized on a number of occasions as she was unable to care for herself and her children, and her willingness and ability to comply with her prescribed psychotropic medications varied considerably, only adding to her woes. On May 3, 2001, briefly left alone with her children, she filled the bathtub and drowned all five of them before calling the police and her husband.

At her first trial, a jury rejected her plea of NGRI and instead found her guilty of murder. She was sentenced to life in incarceration. However, this verdict was later overturned on appeal. In 2006, at the time of her retrial, she was found to be NGRI and was committed to Kerrville State Hospital in Texas, where she resides to this day.

Guilty But Mentally Ill

On March 30, 1981, President Ronald Reagan was being escorted from a hotel to his limousine when John Hinckley Jr. shot him and three other people who were with him, seriously wounding the president and critically wounding press secretary James Brady. Hinckley was subsequently found to be NGRI, and there was considerable public outcry about this, with many people feeling that justice had not been served and that if and when Hinckley was found to be sane, he would be released from the psychiatric facility that was holding him. At that time, of course, there was no way that the public could know that he would be confined for more than 30 years. Perhaps in response to this, a number of states developed statutes and guidelines for those who are both mentally ill *and* guilty of their offense.

Twenty states offer an alternative to the NGRI plea, called **guilty but mentally ill (GBMI)**. A GBMI plea means that the defendant is pleading guilty with the stipulation that they are also mentally ill. There has been considerable debate about the GBMI verdict. For example, Mental Health America (2020) has expressed the opinion that it may be confusing to jurors, making it difficult for them to decide if a defendant is NGRI or GBMI, and that it serves no clear purpose to society or to the victim of the offense. It is also noted that a finding of GBMI is not different in any meaningful way from a sentence of guilty. Neither the length of the sentence nor the conditions of confinement are necessarily different than that of an individual simply found to be guilty without condition of mental illness. The present author interacted with many offenders who had been found to be GBMI. During evaluations of those inmates, it was commonplace for them to claim that they had plead GBMI on the advice of their attorney in the hopes of receiving a shorter sentence. They also opined that they had not received a sentence that was any shorter than they would have received had they simply pled guilty.

Some of the GBMI offenders the present author was familiar with lived in a special needs unit, a unit dedicated to those with mental health challenges or intellectual limitations. However, others judged to be GBMI were able to live without problem in the general population. Some of them were receiving counseling or psychiatric services, while others reported that no such services were needed. In fact, some of these individuals demonstrated no mental health concerns at all. Toward the end of the author's career in the Pennsylvania Department of Corrections, it was decided that mental health professionals would closely monitor everyone who pled GBMI. More than a few of those inmates expressed frustration at this and even claimed that clinicians were harassing them by meeting with them regularly to monitor their mood, thoughts, and functioning. In short, in the experience of the present author, those inmates who pled GBMI often did not demonstrate more severe mental illness and did not demonstrate functional impairment compared to those who did not make such a plea.

Although being found GBMI does entitle the defendant to mental health services while incarcerated, it should be noted that all those who are incarcerated are entitled to such services, regardless of whether they plead GBMI. Reisner et al. (2013) points out that since everyone who is incarcerated is entitled to such services, the GBMI finding is of no special benefit to the individual convicted as GBMI and affords them no extra or better mental health services than any other incarcerated person.

Melville and Naimark (2002) express the concern that the option of a GBMI verdict may confuse juries who may already be struggling with the complexity of the NGRI option. Melville and Naimark also state that the purpose of the GBMI verdict was to reduce the probability of successful NGRI pleas. However, as mentioned earlier in this chapter, the frequency of such successful pleas is very low and according to Melville, there is no reason to believe that the option of the GBMI verdict actually does reduce the frequency of successful NGRI pleas.

INVOLUNTARY CIVIL COMMITMENT

Involuntary civil commitment means that a judge or other authorized individual acting in a similar capacity may issue an order that a person with a very serious mental health issue may be confined to an inpatient psychiatric facility (or, in some cases, that they may be mandated for treatment on an outpatient basis). Although each state has its own standards and procedures for this process, those procedures must comply with constitutional due process requirements. As a general rule, individuals may be involuntarily committed to a psychiatric facility only in very limited circumstances. An individual may be involuntarily committed if they pose a clear and immediate threat of harm to themselves or to a specific other individual in the community. Involuntary commitment is also possible in cases in which a person demonstrates an inability to care for themselves (sometimes referred to as a *grave disability*) to such an extent that some harm is likely to come to them. Even when an individual is involuntarily committed due to threats of harm or an inability to care for themselves, they may only be held for a limited period of time before being reviewed. The bar for involuntary commitment is set high—and rightfully so. It is important to carefully balance the rights of the individual and their due process rights with protecting that person and those in the community.

Involuntary commitment based on threats to oneself or others must be clear and unequivocal. Thus, a person who says, "One of these days, I'm going to do something that makes the whole world pay attention to me" could not be involuntarily committed simply based on that statement, as this statement does not represent a clear threat. After all, it is possible that this person means that their athletic ability, singing voice, or some other talent will eventually make them famous worldwide. In this example, the conscientious forensic psychologist would probe such a statement at length in an attempt to determine what exactly is meant. Only if it were determined (for example) that they intended to blow up the local municipal offices next week would an involuntary commitment be appropriate.

A threat in the absence of any identifiable mental illness would certainly be reason to call the police but would not automatically result in an involuntary civil commitment to a psychiatric facility. However, if there were obvious signs of mental illness at the time the threat was made or if those signs were identified by police at the time of their arrival, civil commitment to a psychiatric facility for further evaluation and possible treatment would be indicated.

As noted above, in addition to threats of self-harm and threats toward others, an individual may be involuntarily committed to a psychiatric facility if they are unable to care for themselves. Similar to threats of harm, the definition of an inability to care for oneself varies from state to state, but in general, such an inability is thought to consist of an inability to provide oneself with food, clothing, or shelter to such an extent that the individual is likely to come to harm. Inability to care for oneself is subject to interpretation. After all, a homeless person may be clothed, finding food in local dumpsters, and sleeping in an abandoned building. They have food, clothing, and shelter. Their circumstances are clearly less than ideal and might eventually lead them to harm, but there is no immediate concern in that regard. Would we really be helping them by committing them to a psychiatric facility or would we be depriving them of their freedom without sufficient reason? In regard to civil commitment, the safety of the individual and the community must be carefully balanced with the rights of that individual; this is not always an easy task.

The bar for involuntary civil commitment is high, and understandably so. We do not and cannot deprive someone of their liberty and their freedoms without very good justification. Furthermore, with deinstitutionalization and the closing of many psychiatric facilities, the number of psychiatric hospital beds is limited. For these reasons, such commitments can be very difficult to obtain. The World Health Organization (1996) recommends that mental health treatments should be as efficient as possible; hospitalization durations should be limited to the risk posed and used only if it is the only way for the patient to receive treatment. Typically, a person who is involuntarily committed to a psychiatric facility can be held for up to 72 hours against their will. After 72 hours, the person has the right to refuse treatment and to be released, unless the treating facility and professionals can demonstrate to a judge that continued treatment is required and necessary to avoid harm to the individual or to others.

THROUGH THE EYES OF THE VICTIM

Those of us fortunate enough to have slept in our own bed under a roof every night cannot possibly understand the plight of being homeless. Those who are homeless are forced to find shelter from the elements and the extremes of temperature. They may struggle to find enough to eat and may need to find a way to feed their children. Basic hygiene may be difficult or impossible. Threats to one's safety are ongoing. Members of the community may treat the homeless as social outcasts. In addition to these and other challenges, the homeless may be subject to physical and mental illnesses as well.

In New York City, more than 60,000 homeless people stayed in shelters in September 2022 alone, and there is no way to accurately estimate the number of homeless people who attempt to find shelter on the streets or subway stations of that city (Simone, 2022). Many of the homeless, both in shelters and on the street, struggle with mental illness. The present author, having spent some of his early life in New York City, was accustomed to seeing individuals who were homeless sleeping in the subway stations and on sidewalk gratings that vented hot air onto the sidewalk as part of an attempt to stay warm. Some of these individuals demonstrated signs of acute mental illness, talking to themselves, expressing bizarre beliefs, or appearing to respond to voices that only they could hear. Still others demonstrated no such signs but were clearly hungry, dirty, and tired, barely able to function.

It is impossible for us to comprehend what it would be like to be homeless and living with mental illness.

istock/ Gerry Justice

At the time this book was going to print, New York City Mayor Eric Adams (2022) was announcing new directives aimed at addressing the needs of those who were homeless and living with mental illness in the city. This directive provides for teams of clinicians from the New York City Department of Health and Mental Hygiene and the New York Police Department to evaluate those who appear to be acutely mentally ill and/or those who seem to be unable to care for themselves. Such evaluations may result in involuntary commitments to psychiatric facilities.

According to Mayor Adams, "It is not acceptable for us to see someone who clearly needs help and walk past them. For too long, there has been a gray area where policy, law, and accountability have been unclear, and this has allowed people in desperate need to slip through the cracks" (Adams, 2022). Mayor Adams's directive goes on to note that an inability to care for oneself can be sufficient grounds for involuntary commitment and the treatment that accompanies such commitment.

It is far too early to tell how Mayor Adams's directive will play out. The training and development of enough teams to evaluate the many thousands of homeless individuals would be a daunting task in and of itself. Furthermore, if even a fraction of the individuals being assessed were then involuntarily committed, there is no telling how many hundreds or thousands of additional psychiatric hospital bed placements would be required.

On the surface, Mayor Adams's directive appears to be well-intended; one can only be moved by the sight of a person who is homeless and suffering from mental illness sitting in the rain asking passersby for spare change so that they can buy something to eat. It is incumbent upon a forensic psychologist to give matters related to psychiatric commitment very careful consideration. After all, it is not the case that all who are homeless are mentally ill, and those who are mentally ill should have a role in decisions concerning their own care; autonomy is as important for those with mental illness as for those who do not suffer from it. Forensic psychologists must realize that what they perceive as the needs of an individual must be carefully weighed against the rights of that individual, and no one should be deprived of their freedom and autonomy except as a very last resort.

CONCLUSION

The release of hundreds of thousands of people with mental illness from inpatient psychiatric facilities into the surrounding communities in the 1950s and 1960s had a number of consequences. Some were expected: for example, the increased freedom and self-determination of those who were released. Other consequences were predictable: that the lack of mental health resources and supportive facilities in the community would eventually mean that many individuals with mental illness would end up running afoul of the criminal justice system.

Jails and prisons were unprepared for the influx of individuals with mental illness, and furthermore, the stark and violent nature of such institutions could only be expected to be detrimental to those already suffering from mental illnesses. In the years since, there has been an effort to divert those with mental illness and other extenuating circumstances from incarceration if they do not have a serious or violent offense. Furthermore, progress is being made at making sure that those individuals with mental illness who do enter into the criminal justice system are competent to do so and receive the services they require.

Exercises and Discussion Questions

1. In this chapter, we discussed specialized courts designed to divert veterans, those with mental illness, or those with drug and alcohol issues from the criminal courts and potential incarceration. In your opinion, do specialized courts allow those groups to get away with offenses that they should be punished for or do you believe that the diversion of these groups is warranted and beneficial to them without harming society? Explain your answer.

2. You are a forensic psychologist and you have been asked by the court to examine a defendant to determine whether they are competent to stand trial. What kind of questions would you ask them to determine if they understood the court process and if they would be able to assist their lawyer in formulating a defense? Why would you choose those questions?

3. As discussed in this chapter, some states allow a plea of NGRI. Some states make no allowance at all for such a plea. If you had the power to decide whether your state should allow such a plea, would you allow it or not? Explain your rationale.

4. In the United States, we hold freedom to be of the utmost importance. Civil commitment allows a judge, on the advice of a mental health professional, to have a person involuntarily committed to a psychiatric facility against their will, effectively taking that person's freedom away from them. Do you believe this is acceptable? Why or why not? Please explain.

KEY TERMS

Competency to stand trial

Competency to Stand Trial Assessment Instrument (CAI)

Drug treatment court

Durham rule

Dusky standard

Guilty but mentally ill (GBMI)

Involuntary civil commitment

Irresistible impulse test

MacArthur Competency Assessment Tool–Criminal Applications (MacCAT–CA)

Mandated reporting

Mental health courts

Mental Retardation Facilities and Community Mental Health Centers Construction Act

Model penal code test

Permissive reporting

Veterans treatment courts (VTCs)

11 THE CORRECTIONAL SYSTEM

LEARNING OBJECTIVES

1. Compare and contrast *punishment* and *rehabilitation*; list the perceived advantages and disadvantages of each of these approaches to correcting criminal behavior.

2. Define and explain the role of intermediate sanctions, including fines, community service, and probation.

3. Compare the United States to other countries when it comes to the rate of incarceration and the financial and social cost of such incarceration.

4. Define *evidence-based corrections* and explain why it is important to have empirical evidence that the programs employed in corrections are effective in reducing recidivism.

5. Discuss the disparities in the incarceration of people of color, women, and transgender individuals.

6. List and explain the arguments for and against the death penalty.

In Pennsylvania, as in many states, there are far more inmates than there are prison cells. The mathematical reality of that is quite simple; most cells, originally designed to house one inmate, now house two. Not surprisingly, inmates do not like this arrangement. After all, who would want to be locked in an 8-foot by 10-foot box with another person? Moving around in such a tiny space (most of which is taken up by the bunkbed and combination sink/toilet) is nearly impossible. And when one does need to use the toilet, with another person in the cell, they have no privacy whatsoever. It is no surprise that inmates greatly prefer to have a cell to themselves.

As a forensic psychologist, I had the ability to give the inmate a cell to themself. If I decided that the inmate is so mentally challenged or impaired that we can't possibly put another person in the cell with them, I could write a report to that effect and they will likely be granted the much-desired "Z-code." This means that for the remainder of their incarceration, they are no longer required to share a cell, permitting them (relative) peace and privacy. Inmates, of course, are aware of this rule and it is quite common for them to write me a letter stating that they want to be evaluated for that Z-code. My job at that point is to evaluate them and make a recommendation: Does this individual truly have a serious mental health diagnosis, or are they merely putting on an act to get a cell to themselves? It is important that the right recommendation is made. If they fake it and I believe them and give them a single cell, there will be a line of others outside my office door, all hoping that they can do the same. If I deny this individual a single cell and they truly have mental health issues and/or they hurt or kill their cellmate, I could be held responsible. There is little room for error.

It was an average day at the prison, and I had "Mr. Johnson" sent to my office so that I could per-
form a psychological evaluation to see if he was suitable to be paroled into the community. Did he have
mental health issues? If so, would he need mental health follow-up in the community? Was he likely
to pose a risk of harm to those in the community? Did he admit responsibility for his offense? Did he
appear remorseful? These and many other questions would all be part of my evaluation and my report
to the parole board. Mr. Johnson walked into my office, and before I could greet him or say a word to
him about the purpose of my calling for him, he screamed, "Doc, I'm crazy! Crazy as hell! I see little
green men running across the ceiling, Doc! I hear ducks quacking! Quack! Quack! You hear 'em, don't
you Doc?!" For the next few moments, he launched into the single worst impression of mental health
issues I'd ever seen, as he strutted around my office, bending his knees and flapping his bent arms back
and forth as he craned his neck and quacked like a duck.

After a few moments of this performance, I gathered myself. "Mr. Johnson, please wait a minute.
I think that you think that you are here for a single cell Z-code evaluation. In fact, the reason that I
called you here was to evaluate you to see if you are stable enough to be released to the community on
parole." He froze. I could see him thinking. "Oh," he said. "I'm cool. All good. Yeah, I'm ready to be
released!" In five seconds, he had stopped pretending to be mentally ill and had suddenly decided that
all was well and he was ready to go home.

INTRODUCTION

Written almost 4,000 years ago, the **Code of Hammurabi** is the first known attempt to make
the punishment fit the crime by dictating exactly what price should be paid for a wide variety of
offenses. This Code recognized that some crimes are, by their very nature, less serious than others and therefore warrant less severe penalties. In the present day, society continues the evolving
discussion of whether those who break laws should receive some sort of rehabilitation to help
them become a productive member of that society or whether they should be punished for their
wrongdoing as part of an effort to discourage them (and others) from engaging in that behavior
again. The economic, social, and ethical consequences of how our society treats those who break
laws are far-ranging and important.

In this chapter, we will discuss the use of intermediate sanctions for less-serious offenses and
the importance of diverting people from incarceration when possible. We will also examine growth
of the prison industry, which has been especially rapid in the United States (U. S.). We will examine
the manner in which jails and prisons serve very different purposes and discuss the special needs of
those who are incarcerated and who may also have substance abuse and/or mental health concerns.
The threats faced by those who are incarcerated will be discussed, as will the manner in which the
challenging environment of incarceration may exacerbate mental health issues. Of great debate is
the ultimate sanction—capital punishment, also known as the death penalty—and this chapter
will address some of the myths and realities of that sanction. Lastly, we will take a look at the issue
of those "hidden victims" of the prison system—the innocent children of those who are incarcerated, who (through no fault of their own) are deprived of one or both parents for a substantial
period of time, and the lasting consequences that such separation may have on them.

PUNISHMENT VERSUS REHABILITATION

Traditionally, there have been two competing approaches to how a society can respond when
a member of the community breaks a rule of law. One approach is to punish the wrongdoer
physically, emotionally, or perhaps financially, under the assumption that such punishment will

discourage future law breaking. The alternative approach seeks to rehabilitate the individual by providing education or training, with the assumption that such rehabilitation will help the wrongdoer become a productive member of that society.

Punishment is generally defined as the infliction of some type of penalty as retribution for a criminal offense. Depending on the time frame and society, punishment might involve incarceration, the infliction of physical pain (or even torture), or public humiliation. Some believe that punishment is the commonsense solution to all wrongdoing. If Johnny is told not to take a cookie out of the cookie jar but he is caught doing so anyway, some would believe that a spanking or removal of a privilege would lead Johnny to think twice before doing so again. As that train of thought goes, if Johnny *does* for some reason continue to take cookies without permission, the obvious solution is to punish him more severely. Sooner or later, it is believed that the punishment will be severe enough to prevent Johnny from continuing with this behavior.

But does this commonsense solution of punishment hold up to further examination? Perhaps rather than learning not to take cookies out of the cookie jar, Johnny will simply learn to wait until his parents are out of the house, when he is unlikely to be caught. In this manner, rather than teaching Johnny not to steal, perhaps punishing him when he is caught (and not punishing him when he manages to get away with it) is teaching him to be a more alert, cautious, and skillful thief.

Punishment may seem on the surface to make sense, and it may provide a sense of vengeance or satisfaction to the victim or to society. With punishment, the victim and society may feel that there has been some kind of retribution or that justice has been done in regard to the offender. However, it is important to keep in mind that punishment does not restore the victim from any financial, emotional, or physical losses they may have suffered. If Roberto is robbed of his wallet and physically assaulted and his offender is found and sentenced to a period of incarceration that is *not* the same as returning Roberto's wallet to him and may do little (or nothing) to restore Roberto's physical or mental well-being. It is also worth noting that if the offender is incarcerated and earning a few cents per hour for working a prison job, that offender is unlikely to ever be able to pay Roberto back for the cost of what was taken from him. Furthermore, the assumption that the offender will think twice before committing such an offense in the future is not necessarily a safe one; perhaps the offender will become even angrier and more violent while incarcerated.

Other members of society believe that the answer to wrongdoing is not punishment but **rehabilitation.** Rehabilitation involves teaching wrongdoers the error of their ways and showing them how to live as a productive, cooperative member of the community. After all, perhaps the person who grew up stealing came from a severely disadvantaged environment, where stealing was a necessary and acceptable means of survival. Or perhaps the person who broke the law did so because they have a substance use disorder, and during the course of their offense, they did not cause anyone any physical harm. A rehabilitation approach suggests that if the correctional system can help to provide such individuals with the education, coping skills, and job skills they need to earn a living, then they might well become productive members of society.

While the rehabilitation approach makes sense to some, others may question whether it does true justice to the victim. After all, if someone has been assaulted, and the correctional system rehabilitates the offender, teaching them anger management skills, job skills, and providing them with some education, then might the victim not feel that their offender has been given a number of advantages and opportunities rather than their just desserts?

Those who espouse a tough-on-crime attitude that supports the incarceration of offenders who have not committed violent acts may be missing a crucial piece of the correctional puzzle. It is not always the case that nonviolent offenders are sent to minimum-security (relatively safe) prisons. In a crowded correctional system, offenders are often placed in whatever facility has room for them. Thus, it is entirely possible for an individual with a nonviolent offense to be placed in a maximum-security prison that houses many violent offenders serving lengthy prison terms. The nonviolent offender placed in a maximum-security prison faces some extremely difficult decisions. If (or perhaps we should say *when*) they are confronted by a violent offender, the nonviolent individual can attempt to avoid a physical confrontation (in which case, they may be robbed of their meager possessions or physically or sexually assaulted or extorted) or they may attempt to defend themselves. In the latter case, the so-called correctional system may be just the opposite: instead of correcting that person's behavior, the environment is instead teaching them that violence may be required for survival. We can readily see how the offender (who was nonviolent when they were admitted to the facility) may learn to perpetrate violence against others. Thus, the nonviolent offender who went into the facility may be released as an individual who is now skilled, capable, and willing to perpetrate violent offenses. This is exactly the opposite of what we want the correctional system to do. Some have referred to state prisons as "gladiator schools," where inmates have the time to exercise, become stronger and healthier, and learn to become proficient in intimidation and physical violence.

Security Threat Groups (STGs)

Criminal street gangs are organized groups participating in a variety of often-illegal money-making activities. Such gangs are usually formed along racial or geographic lines and have a geographic area they consider to be theirs. Street gangs are prone to use violence to protect their profitable enterprises and their territory and act aggressively toward all those who oppose them or attempt to interfere with them. Although some gangs are more well-organized than others, to think of them as a chaotic mob with no one in charge and each member doing as they please would be inaccurate. Indeed, these groups typically have a paramilitary structure with a well-defined chain of command. Each member of the group has a rank and a well-defined role in that organization. Meetings are held and attendance is required. Rules and orders are issued and compliance is strictly enforced. The belief that a street gang is a loosely organized mob of individuals, each of whom does whatever they want, is misguided.

In the correctional system, such gangs are common and are typically referred to as **security threat groups (STGs)** by prison administration. Of the more than 1.5 million people incarcerated in 2016, it was estimated that more than 200,000 were gang-affiliated (Carson, 2018). According to the U.S. Department of Justice (2021), gangs in prison typically form along racial or ethnic lines and vary from disorganized to highly structured. STGs can be powerful and quite dangerous to the safe and secure running of the institution. Such groups are often well-organized and disciplined and are prepared for violence at all times. Street gang members who become incarcerated typically re-form with other members of their STG or an affiliated gang once they are incarcerated. The pressure on a new inmate to join a gang for protection can be strong, but those who do so then find themselves with a number of sworn enemies and are required by their own STG to participate in drug dealing, extortion, assaults, and other offenses. Refusal, or even expressed hesitancy, to participate in such activities for one's STG typically results in being assaulted by the members of one's own STG for being disloyal or disrespectful.

Unlike street gangs, who may be quite obvious in demonstrating their gang affiliation by means of wearing a particular color, graffiti on their turf, or obvious hand signs, prison STGs tend to be much more careful about identifying themselves so that they can conduct their illegal activities without being noticed by the prison authorities. Hand signs are kept small and discrete, meetings may be disguised as exercise or spiritual groups, and colors may consist of a single colored bead on a rosary necklace. All of this is done to make identification and tracking by prison authorities more complicated so that the STG's criminal enterprises are not discovered.

INTERMEDIATE SANCTIONS

The Code of Hammurabi is a Babylonian legal document that was quite literally "carved in stone" in a large piece of basalt rock in approximately 1754 BC. The Code is considered by many scholars to be the first known attempt at a legal code. It is comprised of nearly 300 if–then statements, noting a specific punishment for each of the named offenses. Thus, the Code of Hammurabi is commonly thought to be the first attempt to make the punishment fit the crime and to recognize that punishments should not be arbitrary or capricious and should be scaled to the severity of the offense. Though the code represented a first step toward *lex talionis* or "letting the punishment fit the crime," it was less than fair in this regard. Penalties for offenses committed by freemen were less harsh than the penalties applied to women and slaves who committed those same offenses. For example, a freeman striking another freeman would be fined "one gold mina," while a slave striking a freeman would "have his ear cut off" (King, 2008). The fact that these punishments are still wildly unequal is self-evident.

The Code of Hammurabi may have been the first attempt at intermediate sanctions—recognizing that not every offense merits harsh consequences. It makes no economic or moral sense to incarcerate everyone who jaywalks or litters. Regardless of whether we favor the punishment or rehabilitation of offenders (or some combination of the two), it stands to reason that minor offenses may be corrected through less severe measures than incarceration or capital punishment. Intermediate sanctions, then, are methods of attempting to correct wrongdoing through measures that are less harsh and restrictive than incarceration. Much like buying a suit or dress off the rack compared to having one tailored to fit, the notion of lex talionis suggests that it is important to tailor the consequence to fit the offense rather than a one-size-fits-all approach.

Fines

Fines have a long history of being used to punish minor offenses. We are all familiar with fines for violations such as speeding, failure to come to a complete stop at a stop sign, or other minor transgressions. The premise of such a fine is that this financial punishment will lead us to improve our driving habits so as to avoid any further costly sanctions. Unlike correctional measures such as probation and incarceration, fines add to the income of the state rather than subtracting from it. However, it could be argued that fines (as they are levied in the United States) are unfair in that they have little impact on the wealthy but pose an undue burden on those who are poor. The several-hundred-dollar fine for speeding means nothing to the wealthy celebrity in their exotic sports car but could be financially devastating to the single parent attempting to work three jobs to support their children.

Community Service

While fines may be used to punish relatively insignificant offenses, in cases of other minor infractions, the court may sentence an offender to a given number of hours of **community service**. Community service is typically assigned as a sentence for offenses that are minor in nature, such as trespassing or underage consumption of alcohol. Community service might involve picking up trash along a stretch of roadway, passing out meals at a homeless shelter, or painting a public picnic pavilion. Such service may be thought to comprise both punishment (the loss of one's free time) and rehabilitation (encouraging offenders to aid the community). Community service typically costs the taxpayers little or nothing, and taxpayers may be gratified to observe offenders picking up roadside trash or cleaning a public park. Those assigned to provide community service must typically provide documentation to the court that they have completed the requisite number of hours before the court will consider their sentence to be completed. Should they fail to do so, they may be assigned further (and likely more significant) consequences by the court.

Probation

Probation is a sentence imposed by the court instead of incarceration. In the case of probation, the court has decided that an offense is significant enough to warrant supervision and direction by the court but is not sufficiently severe enough to require incarceration and removal of the offender from the community. With probation, the court offers the offender an opportunity to remain in the community *if* that offender agrees to certain stipulations or conditions from the court.

Probation stipulations may be general (those that apply to everyone on probation) or specific (tailored to a particular offender). Common general stipulations of probation include regular meetings with a probation officer, drug and alcohol testing, and searches of the offender, their vehicle, and their living environment. Other general stipulations are likely to include that the probationer is not allowed to leave the area without permission and that they continue to attend school or maintain steady employment. Specific stipulations might be that an offender whose crimes occurred primarily at night have a curfew of 7:00 p.m., or that someone guilty of repeatedly driving under the influence have an ignition interlock installed in their car so that their car will only start if the probationer provides a negative breathalyzer result on that apparatus. If the offender complies with these rules and regulations, the probation officer may gradually relax those rules and permit increased autonomy. However, if they fail to comply, the court may decide to become more stringent in such stipulations or may eventually decide to revoke that individual's probation and instead sentence the offender to a period of incarceration.

Probation has a number of advantages compared to incarceration. First, it allows the offender to stay with their family rather than being removed (possibly a great distance) from it. It is important to consider the emotional as well as the economic impact of removing a provider/parent from the family; such removal by incarceration punishes not only the offender but their significant other and children. After all, incarceration removes the offender as a potential source of emotional and financial support to their loved ones. Furthermore, when it comes to making financial restitution to the victim, the offender is likely to be much more able to do so working even a minimum wage job in the community as opposed to a prison job, where they may make only pennies per hour. The offender sentenced to probation who continues to work a $12/hour job will eventually be able to make restitution to their victim for the $2,200 worth of belongings they burglarized. However, if that same offender is incarcerated and paying a portion of their $0.25/hour prison salary to the victim, the chances that full restitution will ever be made to the victim are slim indeed.

The costs of probation pale by comparison to those of incarceration, even when the costs of probation supervision, electronic monitoring, surveillance, and drug and alcohol testing are factored in. Specifically, at least one report indicates that the average cost of probation is $1,100 per offender per year, while the average cost of incarceration in a jail is almost $30,000 per offender per year, and the average cost of incarceration in a prison is slightly more than $45,000 per offender per year (Bradford, 2019). Furthermore, the probationer who is able to work even a low-wage job may be required to pay part (or all) of their own probation costs rather than placing this financial burden on the taxpaying public.

Parole

Parole is often confused with probation but is a very different sanction. Whereas probation is *instead of* incarceration, parole is served *after* incarceration. Although some may believe that everyone who is incarcerated should serve their maximum sentence, there are disadvantages to having them do so. When a person serves their maximum sentence, they are typically released to the community with no further form of supervision possible. The present author is aware of many cases in which an offender was maintained in a maximum-security (or in some cases, even super-maximum-security) housing unit until the final day of their sentence, at which time, there was no choice but to release them directly into the community with no further supervision possible—a frightening prospect indeed! Furthermore, the prospect of early release through parole, good conduct, or other incentives may help motivate some offenders to maintain safe and adaptive behavior while they are incarcerated.

Similar to probation, parole may carry with it both general and specific conditions. That is, the offender may be offered release back to the community subject to their agreement to follow certain conditions. In many cases, those conditions will be similar to those imposed on those who are on probation. For example, parolees will typically be required to report to a parole agent and to abstain from the use of alcohol and other intoxicants. They will also be required to maintain employment and will not be allowed to leave the immediate area without permission. Parolees typically cannot possess firearms and must submit to searches of their person, vehicle, and living quarters at the will of their parole agent.

In the case of some offenders, there will be stipulations that are specific to their offense. For example, a sex offender may be mandated to receive sex offender treatment or other counseling. Such offenders will not be allowed to own or possess pornography, and their phone, computer, or other electronics may be subject to search for that type of material. Sex offenders with child victims may be prohibited from being unsupervised in the presence of minors. Failure to follow these conditions, as with probation, may result in more severe restrictions being imposed or could result in a return to incarceration if the violation is serious enough.

THE STANFORD PRISON EXPERIMENT

In the summer of 1971, psychologist Philip Zimbardo recruited 24 college-age men to participate in a simulated prison environment in order to study the impact of incarceration on both the inmates and the guards. The participants would be paid to live (or, in the case of the guards, to work) for 14 days in a simulated prison environment in the basement of Jordan Hall at Stanford University in California. Mock prison cells were set up in the building, with mattresses and signs designating them the Stanford Prison. Guards were issued tan uniforms and mirrored sunglasses, and inmates were dressed in stocking caps and gowns with a number sewn on them. Inmates were to be addressed by these numbers and were instructed to refer to the guards as "Mr. Correctional Officer."

On only the second day of the experiment, the inmates had already rebelled to protest their conditions and treatment, and the guards had responded by spraying the prisoners with a fire extinguisher. By the fourth day, one prisoner appeared to be having a mental breakdown and was therefore released from further participation in the experiment. Conditions between the guards and inmates went from bad to worse, and by the fifth day, several of Zimbardo's colleagues had expressed grave concerns to him about whether this simulation even constituted an experiment. On the sixth day, Zimbardo ended the scenario, paying and debriefing the participants.

Zimbardo's study, cited countless times in introductory psychology, social psychology, and other texts, has been criticized on a number of fronts, with critics expressing the belief that it was of questionable scientific validity due to a number of flaws, including (but not limited to) biased and incomplete recording of data (Le Texier, 2019). Others have criticized this study for being unethical by not being completely forthcoming in terms of informed consent (McLeod, 2020). Certainly, the experiment could not be repeated today. A budding forensic psychologist might ask themselves, was Zimbardo's simulation worthwhile in terms of demonstrating how quickly the prison environment can lead the behavior of all involved to deteriorate, or was the emotional cost of the simulation too high a price to pay for whatever may have been learned from it?

THE INCARCERATION NATION

The U. S. may be considered to be the "Incarceration Nation," with far more people incarcerated per capita than any other nation on earth. The U. S. incarcerates 655 people per 100,000 compared to El Salvador (#2) with 618 per 100,000 and Rwanda (#3) with 464 per 100,000 (Walmsley, 2019). More than half of all countries in the world have rates below 150 per 100,000. The U. S. currently has a total of more than 2.1 million people incarcerated—more than are known to be incarcerated in any other nation on earth.

The number of individuals serving life sentences (with or without the possibility of parole) has continued to increase despite the fact that violent crime itself has steadily decreased for the past 20 or so years. One in nine inmates in prison are serving life sentences, with nearly one in three such lifers being sentenced to life without the possibility of parole. Such lengthy sentences have not been empirically proven to result in a public safety benefit. Of course, the social and economic impact of such lengthy sentences on the community, the inmate, and their family is difficult or impossible to accurately estimate (Nellis, 2021), though, as we will see below, McLaughlin et al. (2016) did make an effort to do just that.

The total economic cost of incarceration in the United States is staggering. The Bureau of Prisons (2018) estimates that in 2017, the average cost per federal inmate was $36,299.25 per year—a few cents less than $100 per day per federal inmate. The Vera Institute of Justice estimated state inmates costing an average of $33,274 per year in 2015.

Incredibly, the costs noted above may represent only a small fraction of the total costs of incarceration; researcher Carrie Pettus-Davis (in McLaughlin et al., 2016) suggested that for "every dollar in corrections costs, incarceration generates an additional $10 in social costs." McLaughlin et al. noted that few (if any) studies have attempted to calculate the social and economic costs associated with incarceration. For example, this study points out the income that will not be earned by those who are incarcerated, the visitation costs for the families who visit them, the divorces that may accompany incarceration, and factors such as the increased infant mortality associated with being the child of an incarcerated parent (Wakefield & Wildeman, 2014). When these and the other social costs associated with incarceration are added up, Pettus-Davis and her colleagues (McLaughlin et al., 2016) estimate a cost of a staggering one *trillion* dollars per year in the United States. The authors go on to note that one trillion dollars represents an incredible 6% of the U.S. Gross National Product for a year.

As we discussed with juvenile detention, incarceration typically costs far more than education does. This is true for adult offenders as well, even when we consider the cost of advanced education, including college tuition. As we can see in Table 11.1, the cost of in-state tuition and fees for a college student in Alabama in 2021 was less than half the cost of incarceration per year in 2015,

TABLE 11.1 ■ Cost of College versus Incarceration		
State	**In-State Tuition (2021)/ Year**	**Incarceration/ year (2015)**
Alabama	$7,051	$14,780
Delaware	$9,321	$39,080
Massachusetts	$8,827	$55,160

Note: Above data refers to College Tuition Compare (2021) and Vera Institute of Justice (2015).

despite the fact that college tuition costs likely increased considerably during the intervening years. Similarly, in-state tuition for college students in Delaware was a small fraction of the cost of incarceration; for Massachusetts, in-state tuition was an even smaller fraction of the cost compared to incarceration. In short, in many cases, it costs less to send a person to college than it does to incarcerate them. This is not to suggest that offenders should be sent to college rather than prison but is meant to illustrate the staggering cost of incarceration to taxpayers and society.

It seems that few people would object to the incarceration of violent offenders such as murderers, rapists, and child molesters. After all, the tax dollars spent on such imprisonment at the very least keeps those in the community safe from predation by those who are behind bars.

However, some might well question the necessity and cost of incarcerating those whose only offenses are drug related and/or nonviolent. Between 1980 and 2018, the number of people incarcerated for drug-related offenses skyrocketed from approximately 41,000 to more than 400,000 per year (Carson, 2020). While estimates are difficult and vary based on definition, according to the Associated Press (2014), the United States has spent more than $1 trillion on the so-called **War on Drugs**. Gil Kerlikowske, U.S. drug czar under President Obama, stated to the Associated Press, "In the grand scheme, [the War on Drugs] has not been successful. . . . Forty years later, the concern about drugs and drug problems is, if anything, magnified, intensified."

It is easy to wonder whether it is really worth putting someone in jail or prison for nonviolent and/or drug-related offenses. Is it worth the social or economic cost of incarcerating people who had a small amount of marijuana in their possession for their own personal consumption, especially when marijuana is available for recreational purchase and use in some states and for medicinal use in even more states? According to one study, 60% of Americans believe that marijuana should be legal for recreational and medical use, with an additional 30% of Americans believing it should be legal for medical use only. Thus, only 10% of Americans feel this substance should be completely illegal (Van Green, 2021). We could ask ourselves the same question about a person who stole copper pipe from the basement of an abandoned building to sell for scrap so that they could buy heroin. Is it necessary to remove that person from society and from their family and to spend tax dollars on incarcerating them when other options may well be available at a much lower cost? Some states are beginning to decide not to incarcerate nonviolent drug offenders. In November of 2020, Oregonians voted to decriminalize the personal use of *all* drugs. Measure 110 in Oregon states that possession of small amounts of drugs will be punishable by fine but not by incarceration. Measure 110 also goes on to expand access to addiction and other treatment services. Time will tell if other states follow Oregon's lead in this regard.

Types of Incarceration

Many years ago, jails were not intended to serve as punishment for committing a criminal offense. Rather, they were simply a means of holding the accused until a judge became available or until punishment could be administered. Early jails and prisons tended to be quite inhumane; those convicted were thought to suffer **civiler mortuus**, Latin for "civil death." This meant that the convicted had the same rights as a dead person (which is to say, none!). The courts left the running of prisons to the discretion of prison administrators and declined to hear or address the complaints of those who were incarcerated.

One early form of incarceration in the United States became known as the **Pennsylvania system**, for the state in which it originated. In Pennsylvania, Eastern State Penitentiary and Western State Penitentiary were built at approximately the same time, with Western State Penitentiary opening in 1882 and closing its doors for good in 2017. Interestingly, despite being named *penitentiaries*, both the Eastern and Western Penitentiary were designed for what was considered at the time to be *rehabilitation*. That is, the physical design was to maximize silence and isolation, theoretically so that prisoners could reflect on their misdeeds and study the Bible. It was believed that this would lead them to a better, more adaptive way of life. Ironically, as we will learn later in this chapter, it is that same isolation and silence that is now being considered more and more often by the courts as cruel and unusual punishment.

Eastern and Western State Penitentiaries are examples of what are commonly referred to as **first-generation prisons**. First-generation prisons were designed with long, straight rows of cells all facing in the same direction in order to discourage eye contact and communication between inmates. It is apparent from their construction that they were designed to discourage social interaction and any activities that today would be considered to constitute rehabilitation. Although the physical structure of first-generation prisons made it difficult for inmates to interact with one another, it also created supervision difficulties for the staff. Looking down a long, straight row of cells, staff could see little or nothing of what the inmates were doing inside their cells, unless that staff member stood directly in front of the cell looking in; even then, if the cell was dark inside, staff could see very little. There was absolutely no way to observe multiple cell occupants at the same time.

Developed in the years that followed, **second-generation prisons** and jails featured cells arranged in circular pods with a secure, raised enclosure or "bubble" that officers sat in so that they could observe many areas of the housing pod at once. In the bubble, staff sat behind reinforced glass, talked to the inmates through an intercom, and were able to open and close cell doors with the press of a button. This arrangement was relatively safe for staff but hindered communication and interaction with the inmates. Furthermore, being in such a locked enclosure meant a slower response time for being able to respond to emergency situations.

Newer prisons and jails often make use of a **third-generation prison** (sometimes referred to as *close supervision*) system in which specially trained officers are located in the unit with the inmates. Often, the officer's desk is in a common area and easily accessible to the inmates. This allows for easy and direct communication

Western Penitentiary was a first-generation prison, with cells in straight rows to limit inmates' ability to interact with one another. However, this made supervision of those inmates difficult for staff.

between the officer and the inmates and allows for close supervision of the inmates by the officer and rapid response time if there is an emergency in that unit. However, given that there are no structural barriers of any type between the officer and the inmates, the potential for staff being assaulted may be higher in a third-generation prison or jail.

Jails versus Prisons

Although many movies and television programs involving jails or prisons are available and often quite popular, it is important to keep in mind that few of these media portrayals are accurate and unbiased. After all, such portrayals depend on near-constant drama and excitement to obtain ratings, and accuracy can easily fall by the wayside. YouTube, television, movies, and other forms of media often portray jails and prisons as places where drugs are readily available and assaults and rapes are a near-daily occurrence. *Shawshank Redemption*, a critically acclaimed movie, clearly portrays the inmates as the heroes of the story while the prison warden and guards are uniformly corrupt and cruel. Similarly, *The Green Mile*, also critically acclaimed, portrays at least one of the guards as a sadistic villain. While all of the assaults portrayed in the media can and do occasionally happen in real-life jail and prison settings and while there are some staff members (as there are in any profession) who act inappropriately, it is important for the student of forensic psychology to keep in mind that media portrayals of the correctional system and process are not necessarily accurate.

However similar jails and prisons may be in physical appearance, they serve very different purposes. **Jails** are designed to hold those who are awaiting trial and those who have been deemed too dangerous to remain in the community while they await trial. Jails also house those who are charged with an offense and who are unable to post the bail that would allow them to remain free until they are seen by the court. Fully six out of ten people in jail are awaiting trial or plea bargain, and those who have not yet been found guilty of an offense account for 95% of the increase in jail population growth from 2000–2014 (Zeng, 2018). Jails are also used to hold those who have been sentenced to a relatively short term of incarceration (generally a sentence of less than two years). Because those in jail are being housed there for a relatively short period of time, jails often have limited opportunities for educational programs, vocational training, or recreation.

Prisons are different than jails in a number of ways. Everyone going to prison has pled guilty or been found guilty of an offense that is serious enough to warrant (generally) two or more years of incarceration. In some cases, they have been sentenced to spend many years or even the remainder of their natural lives in a correctional facility. Prisons generally have more educational opportunities, vocational opportunities, treatment groups, and recreational resources than jails do. Although those not familiar with prisons might wonder why that is the case, it is vitally important for the safety and security of the institution that those who are incarcerated for lengthy periods of time feel worthwhile and are productive. Jobs, education, recreation (in some places, video games or weights), a law library, trades, college classes, and vocational training all help to keep inmates active and motivated. Many prisons have intramural sports teams, including softball and basketball. While the public might object to the luxury of inmates being permitted to have televisions in their cells, staff seldom do: Television is an excellent means of keeping inmates occupied and out of trouble for lengthy periods of time.

Determinate versus Indeterminate Sentences

The manner in which individuals are sentenced to a term of incarceration varies according to the state that they are sentenced in. **Determinate sentencing** refers to sentencing an offender to a specific amount of time in a correctional institution. A determinate sentence of three years, for example, generally means that the offender would spend exactly three years incarcerated. After those three years had elapsed, the offender would not need to be seen by a parole board but would instead automatically be released. Determinate sentences are often seen as tougher on crime because they force an offender to serve the full amount of time that is specified in the sentence.

The idea of a determinate sentence is that every person sentenced for the same offense receives the same sentence and knows exactly how long they will be serving. This was thought to be fair so that people sentenced for the same offense did not receive widely different sentences. However, it is worth keeping in mind that "equal" crimes are not always equal after all. If I throw a stapler at you and it hits you, I could be charged with aggravated assault. The same charges could apply if I hit you with a baseball bat. However, it is likely that the baseball bat caused far more damage than the stapler. Thus, it could be argued that these "equal" offenses should actually receive different sentences according to the weapon used and the damage inflicted on the victim.

Indeterminate sentences do *not* mean that the offender is sentenced for an endless or undetermined period of time. Rather, an indeterminate sentence means that the individual is sentenced to a range of time. For example, an offender might receive an indeterminate sentence of 3–6 years, meaning that they will serve no less than three years and no more than six years. How long they serve depends on a decision made by the parole board. At regular intervals (often annually), the parole board conducts an interview and will examine the inmate's prison record, prior offenses, and the treatment that the offender has participated in. Also taken into consideration may be any expression of responsibility or remorse on the part of the offender, after which the board will then make a determination about releasing the inmate. One advantage of such a system is that it provides the inmate with some incentive to behave and act reasonably while incarcerated. An offender may not feel any inherent desire to participate in a drug and alcohol treatment group, an anger management group, or a sex offender group, but if they believe that doing so will lead them to be released earlier, they may decide to comply. It is certainly hoped that even if they inmate is only participating in such programs and cooperating with staff for the chance of early release, such groups will provide the offender with an opportunity for true and lasting change.

EVIDENCE-BASED CORRECTIONS

At times, the correctional system has employed punishments based on the belief that those punishments would serve to alter the offender's behavior. On other occasions, the correctional system has employed rehabilitative techniques, again with the hope that these techniques would lead the offender to live a more adaptive and law-abiding lifestyle. It is important for the forensic psychologist to realize that merely because a program of reward or punishment *seems* like it should be effective does not mean that it *actually* is. After all, it might seem that placing a person in prison for years would make them think twice about committing another offense after being released. However, given that 67.8% of all those released from incarceration return to incarceration with a new criminal offense within three years and more than 75% of all those released return with a new criminal offense within five years (Durose et al., 2014), the notion that incarceration in and of itself will change most people's behavior clearly is not empirically supported.

Evidence-based correction (EBC) is the fair and reasonable use of objective data and current research to guide decisions about the policies and practices implemented within the correctional system. The focus of EBC is to improve outcomes for inmates and to reduce the risk of their re-offending and therefore returning to incarceration. EBC involves the use of programs and policies that have been empirically demonstrated to be effective rather than programs that are thought or believed to be beneficial based on clinical judgment or anecdotal reports alone (Criminal Justice Institute, 2009).

It is important to distinguish between programs that offenders enjoy and those that are effective. Effective programs are ones that can empirically be shown to reduce the probability of a released offender returning to incarceration, either for a new offense or for a violation of the conditions of their release. Programs that do reduce recidivism may be economically and socially worthwhile even if they appear to be expensive to the taxpayer. For example, if it costs $5,000 per inmate to provide drug and alcohol treatment but evidence shows that such treatment significantly reduces the likelihood of recidivism and therefore saves $30,000 per year for every inmate who does not return to incarceration, there is tremendous economic benefit of having such programs. However, if such a program is not determined to reduce recidivism, it would be best to question whether it is worth the expense.

At times, prisons employ programs that appear to be beneficial and cost money but do not provide empirical evidence of their effectiveness. For example, inmates with a history of violent offenses or violent acts in the prison could be required to take a structured anger management program. The development and implementation of such a program will, of course, have an associated financial cost. If it is later determined that inmates who complete such a program are as likely to commit further acts of violence as inmates who have not participated in such programs, it would appear that the money spent on that program was wasted. It certainly seems logical to mandate anger management/violence reduction education for those who have committed violent offenses. However, it is just as important to be able to demonstrate that such a program actually works. It is the responsibility of the Departments of Corrections to make sure they are spending taxpayer dollars in a responsible manner.

Evidence-based correction hopes to ensure that the programs and education being offered to those who are incarcerated help to reduce the chances that they will return to incarceration once they are released.

Bob Daemmrich / Alamy Stock Photo

DISPARITY IN THE INCARCERATION OF MINORITIES

People of Color

It is vitally important for the forensic practitioner to understand that incarceration in the United States demonstrates evidence of great racial disparity, with Black Americans being incarcerated at nearly five times the rate of white Americans, and Latinx persons being incarcerated at 1.3 times the rate of non-Latinx white Americans (Nellis, 2021). It goes without saying that such disparity can have devastating long-lasting consequences, including (but not limited to) children growing up without the emotional or financial support of one (or in some cases, both) parents. The Sentencing Project found that in 12 states in the U. S., more than half of those incarcerated are Black (Nellis, 2021).

People of color, then, are overrepresented in the correctional system. For example, people who are Black make up 13% of the U.S. population but account for nearly 38% of all those people who are incarcerated. According to Carson (2020), Black men are six times as likely to be incarcerated as white men, and Hispanic men are 2.7 times as likely to be incarcerated as white men. For Black men in their thirties, a staggering one in 12 is in prison or jail on any given day in the United States.

Native Americans show a similar trend, making up only 1.3% of the population but representing 2.3% of all those who are incarcerated. White people, on the other hand, make up 76% of the U.S. population according to the U.S. Census (2022), but the Federal Bureau of Prisons (2023) indicates that white people make up 57% of all those incarcerated. Asians are underrepresented in correctional facilities, with Asians making up 6% of the U.S. population but only 1.5% of those who are incarcerated (Pariona, 2019). Pariona goes on to note that the impact on children of having a parent (or both parents) incarcerated can be "staggering," with people of color being far more likely than others to have a parent incarcerated. Of course, such disparity in incarceration for those of color can have a lasting and significant emotional, social, and economic impact.

Recent protests calling for a major reform of American policing tactics and policies has also brought racial injustice into focus in other areas of the criminal justice system, including the prison system (Sawyer, 2020). This is an area in which significant progress still needs to occur and much progress remains to be made.

Women

The number of women being incarcerated since 1980 is increasing at double the rate for men (Monazzam & Budd, 2023). In the United States, the number of incarcerated women has risen more than 750% since 1980 (Bilyeau, 2020). Furthermore, while the United States has only 4% of the world's female population, approximately 30%—nearly one in three—women who are incarcerated in the world are incarcerated in the United States (Kajstura, 2018). This is especially shocking when we consider that more than half of the women who are incarcerated here are incarcerated for drug-related offenses. Compared to incarcerated men, women disproportionately report a history of being diagnosed with mental health issues and challenges (Bronson & Berzofsky, 2017). Indeed, 67% of women reported a history of being diagnosed with a mental health disorder prior to or during incarceration compared to 40% of men.

The racial disparities noted above are not limited to men. Women of color are also disproportionately represented in prison, with Black women 1.6 times as likely to be incarcerated as white women, and Latinx women being 1.3 times as likely as white women to be locked up (The Sentencing Project, 2023). The continuing emotional and economic impact of such incarcerations is impossible to quantify or predict.

Further complicating the incarceration of women is the fact that some of these women are pregnant during incarceration. Between 5% and 10% of women who enter jails and prisons are pregnant when they do so, and approximately 2,000 babies per year are born to women who are incarcerated in the United States (Clark & Adashi, 2011). Such women naturally require considerable additional medical care. Furthermore, there is the vexing issue of what happens with their child if they happen to give birth before the expiration of their prison sentence. In some cases, the infant may live with the mother in a dedicated unit for mothers and children within the institution. In other cases, the infant may have to go into foster care or may be given to a relative of the inmate to care for until the inmate is released.

In addition to those women who are pregnant when they come into incarceration, there are many women who already have children and are then incarcerated, thereby removing them from those children. Indeed, the vast majority of women incarcerated are in jails rather than prisons, and 80% of those women incarcerated in jails have children (Sawyer & Bertram, 2018). This means that for at least brief periods of time (and sometimes not-so-brief periods of time), 2.3 million children in the United States will not have their mother present in the home environment.

Not surprisingly, it has been suggested that having a mother who is incarcerated has the potential to have a significant adverse impact on the child's mental health, social and emotional development, and behavior (La Vigne et al., 2008). More than 60% of women in state prisons have a child under the age of 18 (Glaze & Maruschak, 2009). The social and emotional impact on a child of any age whose mother is incarcerated is impossible to adequately quantify.

Transgender Individuals

Only recently has the Department of Correction begun to address the issue of housing inmates who are transgender. Transgender inmates are "almost never" housed according to their gender identity but instead are housed according to the sex they were assigned at birth (Sosin, 2020). This can create substantial safety issues for the transgender female housed in a correctional facility for cisgender males (individuals who are assigned male at birth and who do identify as male). According to NBC news (Sosin, 2020), of 4,890 transgender inmates in 45 states and Washington DC, only 15 are housed according to their lived gender. Transgender inmates' requests to be housed with those of their own gender are routinely denied, despite the fact that such inmates may be subject to frequent sexual harassment and physical assault as well as sexual assault.

The National Commission on Correctional Health Care (2020), in regard to the medical care provided to transgender and gender-diverse individuals, states that such individual should be provided with "the same fairness, dignity, and respect" and quality of medical care that any other person receives. The Commission goes on to state that if a transgender individual was receiving prescribed hormones prior to incarceration, they should continue to receive such hormones "without interruption." If they have not received such hormone treatment, they should be evaluated for their desire to do so and the medical appropriateness of such treatment. Similarly, in terms of gender-affirming surgical procedures, transgender and gender-diverse individuals should be evaluated on a case-by-case basis according to accepted medical standards in the community.

Substance Use and Abuse

It is important to note that incarceration by itself does nothing to treat or cure anyone of an addiction they have. People can be incarcerated; addictions cannot. Some clinicians would refer to those who are addicted to substances and incarcerated as being in "forced remission," meaning that they are only in remission because they do not have access to their drug of choice, not because they are choosing to abstain. In fact, individuals who are incarcerated and suffer from addictions may go to great lengths to obtain the substances they seek. Attempts to smuggle drugs and alcohol into the prison, to manufacture them in the prison itself, and to manipulate physicians and nurses into prescribing inappropriate, addictive medications are a constant game of cat-and-mouse in the prison setting. Drugs have been found to be brought in by visitors, dropped in at night by drones, launched over the wall inside a tennis ball, and smuggled in by corrupt staff members. Inmates have been found to brew homemade alcohol with rotten fruit and a few supplies stolen from the prison kitchen. Where there is a will, there is a way, and without treatment, simple incarceration would not appear to be the cure for substance abuse disorders.

ADDICTION CANNOT BE INCARCERATED

"Bob" was a model inmate. He was a hard worker who buffed the floors at the prison. He was consistently well-behaved and pleasant to both staff and other inmates. Bob didn't have a single disciplinary infraction during his incarceration. Bob frequently liked to regale the staff with stories about how much vodka he was able to consume prior to incarceration. He was serving 5–10 years, and upon seeing the parole board, the board informed Bob that he would be paroled with a few conditions, one of which was that he would have to abstain from alcohol and other drugs, attend Alcoholics Anonymous meetings, and be tested regularly by means of breathalyzer and blood tests for his compliance with this requirement.

In a very polite and matter-of-fact way, Bob informed the parole examiners that he intended to consume alcohol the moment he was released from prison. Naturally, the parole board then decided not to release him after all. At his six-, seven-, eight-, and nine-year parole review, the results were no different. The parole board offered him conditional release if he agreed not to consume alcohol. Each time, Bob politely assured them that he would drink the moment he stepped outside the prison door. Finally, as the last few days of his 10-year incarceration approached, he told me that his family would be picking him up and had promised to have a bottle of vodka in the car for him when they did so. He stated that he would finish the entire bottle in the minute it took them to get off the prison grounds. I implored him not to do so, as this might very well kill him. He laughed and said the prison doctor had recently given him a clean bill of health and that he couldn't wait to get back to drinking. Perhaps abstinence makes the heart grow fonder? Incarceration by itself certainly did nothing to cure Bob's alcoholism.

The Federal Bureau of Prisons provides a wide variety of substance abuse programming, depending on the inmate's assessed level of need. For those with less-serious histories of alcohol or other drug abuse, an educational program may be recommended for the inmate. Twelve-week nonresidential treatment involves a cognitive behavioral treatment approach with inmates who have substance abuse disorders that are more serious but who can still be treated while living in the general population of the institution. A residential drug abuse program (RDAP) is an intensive residential treatment program in which the inmates live in a "therapeutic community" within the prison, having limited or no contact with inmates in the institution who are not in the RDAP program. Such a program provides 24/7 therapeutic and recreational activities for those with the most intensive treatment needs. Many states are attempting similar models, providing varying levels of treatment to accommodate those with different levels of need.

Mental Health

THE INCARCERATION OF THOSE WITH MENTAL ILLNESS

I had a hard time believing what I was seeing in "Troy's" record. He had a history of homelessness, drug addiction, and mental illness. His criminal record was far from serious—a few trespassing charges, public intoxication, and a couple retail thefts. Most recently, he was living under a bridge during the winter months in Pittsburgh and was actively psychotic when he walked into a grocery store, took a pack of bologna and a loaf of bread, and walked out. The store manager called the police. Troy was subsequently arrested and, unbelievably, was sentenced to 1½–3 years in state prison at an average cost to the Pennsylvania taxpayer of $33,000 per year. Perhaps because he was mentally ill, certainly not due to any bad behavior while incarcerated (he turned out to be a model inmate), he served his entire three-year sentence. Given that he was on a number of costly psychotropic medications and required a single cell, his cost was likely substantially more than the $99,000 that would normally be estimated for three years of incarceration. While incarcerated, he lived in the special needs unit and staff made sure that he showered, that he saw a psychiatrist regularly, and that his medical needs were taken care of. Was this punishment for Troy, compared to living under a bridge? He now had a bed to call his own and three meals a day, but at what cost to his freedom and to the taxpayers? Could this money not have been more wisely and cost-effectively spent on sheltered housing, medications, and treatment in a supervised setting in which he was still able to maintain his freedom and autonomy?

Prisons have become de facto treatment centers of mental illness. Correctional staff used to express the belief that persons with mental illness "don't belong here." However, the reality is that many individuals with mental illness are incarcerated, and thus it is necessary to treat them and to make certain that they are treated to the same standards as any individual in the community. Persons with mental illness are overrepresented in the criminal justice system (Steadman et al., 2009). They continue to be incarcerated at an extremely high rate (James & Glaze, 2006) and they very often adjust poorly and are victimized in that setting (Abramsky & Fellner, 2003). Thus, it is vitally important that we provide them with treatment, both as a simple human right and also to help keep them and the community as safe as possible upon their release.

Jail and prison settings are quite harsh compared to living in the community. The loss of freedom, complete lack of privacy, drab gray walls, and lack of windows are only a few of the factors that can contribute to the often-dismal environment. Even for those who have never experienced mental illness, such a setting can easily be imagined to promote feelings of anxiety, depression, fear, and loneliness. For those already suffering with a mental disorder, the grim realities of incarceration may only exacerbate such difficulties.

Fortunately, there is hope for those who are struggling with mental illness and incarcerated. Stringer (2019) states that many prison systems are now using a variety of strategies to transform and improve mental health care in those settings. Individual recovery plans and regular reviews of treatment have been implemented in many prisons, as have multidisciplinary treatment reviews, similar to those conducted for individuals in the community. The Pennsylvania Department of Corrections (and others) are implementing some simple changes, such as paintings and artwork in specialized units and in some general population housing units. In Pennsylvania, nearly all such painting is performed by inmates chosen for their artistic ability. Bright and colorful paint, inspirational quotes, and pictures of sports stars, celebrities, and civil rights advocates are becoming more common. Once unheard of, outdoor scenes of the mountains, lakes, rivers, and sky are also brightening the atmosphere; such little changes can make a profound difference.

As one example of a program to assist inmates who have mental health challenges and who have run afoul of the law, Robert Morgan (Morgan et al., 2014) developed a program called Changing Lives and Changing Outcomes, a nine-module cognitive behavioral program that targets both mental health symptoms and the antisocial thinking patterns that often accompany criminal acts. Changing Lives and Changing Outcomes has shown promise in terms of decreasing reported symptoms of anxiety, depression, and other mental health symptoms and has also shown promise in terms of decreasing reactive criminal and antisocial thinking. It is important to remember that any interventions hoping to bring about change must target the whole person and must be tailored to that individual.

RESTRICTED HOUSING UNIT: THE JAIL WITHIN A JAIL

The **restricted housing unit (RHU)**. The segregated housing unit. Protective custody. Admax. The hole. The bucket. The side pocket. These are all synonyms for a housing unit that is essentially a prison within the prison. The RHU houses those inmates who, for one reason or another, cannot or will not be housed in the general prison population. Some are placed there for disciplinary infractions. Some are placed there because they are considered a threat to the institution as a whole or a specific individual in the institution. Others have asked to be placed there for their own safety. Some are there simply because they are too dangerous, violent, and impulsive to be housed in a regular prison setting. Some may only be there for a few days. Some are there indefinitely, at times for years. The RHU means that an inmate is placed in a single cell with minimal possessions. Books and magazines may be allowed in limited quantities. Radios and televisions are rare exceptions. Inmates have clothes, bedding, and a few toiletries. Often, inmates are allowed a maximum of one hour per day out of their cells, typically in a yard that is essentially a dog pen, to access some fresh air. Meals are delivered to the cell. Communication is only by means of yelling or attempting to "fish" (slide notes on pieces of paper) to another cell. Regular rounds are made by guards and other staff. RHU placement is difficult in the best of circumstances and is certainly not conducive to anyone's mental well-being. There is little to do but read and exercise. There are even those who serve the end of their sentence in the RHU, meaning that one day they are in a maximum-security setting and the next day they are walking free in the community. This is, of course, the worst possible transition back into society.

An RHU cell in the now-defunct Western Penitentiary. It is easy to see how such a stark environment could impact a person's mood and ability to function.

However unpleasant the RHU is, it is difficult to imagine running a prison without such a unit. It is indeed the case that some inmates rape or kill staff members or other inmates while they are incarcerated. The inmates that commit such acts must be treated with extreme caution in order to keep others in the institution safe. The present author can recall one inmate who was brought to his attention because he had repeatedly written letters to an A-list celebrity detailing exactly how he was going to kill, cook, and cannibalize that celebrity and his children. Upon interviewing him, it was apparent that he was entirely serious about this threat, and he became quite excited talking about this fantasy. There was no possibility of him being released from incarceration to carry out this threat, but it was certainly of concern that if released from the RHU to the general population of the prison, he might see fit to carry out his threats on someone less famous. In some cases, the RHU appears to be the only recourse to maintain the safety and security of those inside the prison.

The tide may be turning in regard to the once-frequent practice of placing inmates in the RHU setting. Haney (2018) notes that there is an "emerging consensus" among corrections professionals and mental health clinicians that solitary confinement has detrimental effects on those so housed and no demonstrable penological benefit. Both Basoglu et al. (2007) and Reyes (2007) compared the effects of isolation to those of physical torture. Such effects are especially profound for those with mental illness (Metzner & Fellner, 2010). It is difficult to imagine the impact of such isolation on someone who is already depressed, anxious, or psychotic. Although the United States Supreme Court has not yet issued a ruling on whether solitary confinement violates the cruel and unusual punishment clause of the Eighth Amendment, there are many who argue that it does indeed do so. Cherian (2019) notes that while solitary confinement may appear to be less barbaric than execution or whipping, it is simply a more subtle form of punishment that is indeed cruel and unusual.

The United Nations General Assembly (2016), in its Minimum Rules for the Treatment of Prisoners, called any period of isolation longer than 15 days "prolonged" and recommended that solitary confinement should only be used "in exceptional cases as a last resort for as short a time as possible." The Assembly went on to suggest that solitary should be "prohibited in the case of prisoners with mental or physical disabilities, when their conditions would be exacerbated by such measures." In keeping with this recommendation, the state of New York recently passed the Humane Alternatives to Long-Term (HALT) Solitary Confinement Act (The New York State Senate, 2021). This act limits RHU placement to 15 days or fewer and proposes several alternatives to such placement; it appears that the age of extended RHU placements may be coming to an end.

DEATH PENALTY

Arguments for and against capital punishment abound and are often a subject of vigorous debate. Those in favor of the death penalty may state that execution is the just dessert of those who have committed murder. Some proponents express the belief that executing the murderer will bring some type of solace and emotional closure to the family of the victim. Others argue that it is expensive and morally reprehensible to allow a murderer to live out their natural life in prison while their victim is deceased. Still others who support the death penalty feel it is the only way of being certain that the murderer will never commit another offense. Advocates of the death penalty may also express the belief that this ultimate penalty will deter people from committing murders, as the potential offender will be too afraid of the consequences of their actions and will therefore not harm anyone.

Those opposed to the death penalty often argue that the penalty itself is hypocritical. That is, if murder is wrong, then it is hypocritical to penalize murder by executing the offender. Opponents of the death penalty note that it is possible that innocent people will be executed, an incredibly serious miscarriage of justice. If an incarcerated person is found to be innocent, they can be released but obviously, if a person is executed and later found to be innocent, no reversal of their sentence is possible. Opposition to the death penalty includes the argument that it is not necessarily less costly than incarceration and that it is inherently racially biased. In this section, we will examine some of the above positions in regard to the death penalty. Although everyone (including forensic psychologists) is entitled to have a personal opinion regarding the death penalty, it is important for those involved in the criminal justice process to have a thorough understanding of both sides of the issue.

The United States is one of 55 countries in the world that have and impose capital punishment, also known as *the death penalty* (Ali, 2020). The remaining 142 countries in the world never had the death penalty or have abolished it. Belarus is the only European country to have the death penalty. Few Western countries other than the U.S. impose capital punishment. Other countries that do so include China, North Korea, Pakistan, and Iran. It is worth noting that worldwide, execution statistics are difficult or impossible to calculate, as countries such as China and North Korea are suspected of carrying out many executions but little or no reliable data is available.

As of 2023, 24 states and the federal government have the ability to impose the death penalty. Twenty-three states have abolished it and three (California, Oregon, and Pennsylvania) currently have a moratorium on imposing this penalty (World Population Review, 2023), meaning that the penalty will not be carried out on anyone (pending further review). Texas has by far the most completed executions with 574 since 1976.

The Death Penalty Is a Deterrent—Or Is It?

We might imagine that the death penalty would deter people from committing the crime of homicide. After all, the reasoning goes, if an individual knows that murdering someone might well lead to their own execution, then it would seem to stand to reason that they would decide not to follow through with it. However, the evidence does not suggest that this is the case. The Death Penalty Information Center (2020), using the Federal Bureau of Investigation's data, points out that states that have the death penalty do *not* in fact have a lower rate of homicide than states without the death penalty. In fact, states with the death penalty have a slightly higher homicide rate than states without this penalty. A survey conducted by the *New York Times* reinforced the notion that states without a death penalty have a lower homicide rate than do states with the death penalty. Specifically, the *New York Times* noted that 10 of the 12 states that do not have a death penalty have lower rates of homicide than the national average rate (Table 11.2; Fessenden, 2000). International data suggest the same: Countries that had the death penalty and abolished it tended to see *decreased* murder rates after abolishing this penalty (Abdorrahman Boroumand Center for Human Rights in Iran, 2018.) This suggests the death penalty is not a deterrent.

TABLE 11.2 ■ Homicide Rate in Death Penalty States versus Non–Death Penalty States			
States Without the Death Penalty	**Murder Rate**	**States with the Death Penalty**	**Murder Rate**
Connecticut	2.92	Alabama	7.3
Michigan	5.57	Georgia	6.16
New Jersey	2.95	Kansas	3.6
West Virginia	4.35	Missouri	9.78

Adapted from Death Penalty Information Center (2020).

As a forensic psychologist, imagine a person who is enraged enough to commit a homicide or who is panicked over a crime gone wrong. In such cases, does it seem likely that the individual would be rational enough to stop, consider the potential consequences of their actions, and then decide not to engage in homicide because the death penalty might be imposed at some future time? Or does it seem more likely that their extreme emotional state might override any rational thought and that the death penalty would not serve as a deterrent? It would appear that the evidence suggests that the latter is correct.

Racial Bias

Many aspects of the death penalty are subject to vigorous (and healthy) debate. However, when it comes to the subject of racial bias and the death penalty, the evidence seems unequivocal: "Racial disparities are present at every stage of a capital case and get magnified as a case moves through the legal process," said Robert Dunham, Death Penalty Information Center's executive director and the report's editor (Death Penalty Information Center, 2020). This study includes a 2015 meta-analysis of 30 studies showing that the killers of white people were more likely than the killers of Black people to face capital prosecutions. The Death Penalty Information Center goes on to state that eliminating the death penalty would be one way of assuring that people of color are not unfairly charged, sentenced, and executed.

According to the Vera Institute of Justice (2015), there is no question that the death penalty in the United States has been carried out in a fashion that is racially biased. According to the Institute, individuals convicted of killing white people are 17 times as likely to be sentenced to death than those who killed Black people. Furthermore, this same article notes that while only 13% of the U.S. population is Black, Black people make up more than 40% of people on death row on both a state and federal level (Rahman & Schmidt, 2021).

A *New York Times* article (Liptak, 2020) cites a 1990 study by the General Accounting Office in which 23 of the 28 studies reviewed indicated that the race of the victim played a significant role in the likelihood of an individual being sentenced to execution. The study went on to note that this finding was "remarkably consistent across data sets, states, data collection methods and analytic techniques." It is vitally important for the forensic practitioner to realize that such disparities exist and to educate others and take steps to intervene whenever possible.

Cost

On the surface, it might appear that the cost of execution would save a considerable sum of money when compared to the cost of lengthy incarceration of the guilty party. After all, how much can a lethal injection cost compared to the cost of feeding and housing the offender for many years? However, is as the case with many aspects of the death penalty, there is more to the final cost of this sanction than meets the eye.

It is important to realize that from a legal standpoint, death penalty cases are handled much differently than any other criminal case. Because of their seriousness and complexity, a death penalty case costs far more than other types of trials (Amadeo, 2019). Amadeo notes that in Kansas, the median cost for death penalty trials is more than $500,000 per trial compared to $33,000 for non–death penalty cases. The cost of the full case in which the death penalty is sought is, on average, $1.2 million compared to $740,000 for non–death penalty cases (Kansas State Library, 2023, p. ii). These costs include additional security and a more extensive due process. Because the penalty is by definition a permanent one, the defendant often has greater grounds for appeal and more appeals are permitted. Jury selection is more complex, and matters taken into account may include the defendant's mental health impairments and/or intellectual deficiency. Also, capital case trials *automatically* receive an appeal at the state appellate court (Amadeo, 2021). Thus, death penalty cases cost more than non–death penalty trials at every step and it is not necessarily clear that the death penalty costs less than life in prison.

A DAY IN THE LIFE OF A FORENSIC PSYCHOLOGIST IN CORRECTIONS

Perhaps the most common question asked of a forensic psychologist working in the prison system is, "What is an average day like?" The best answer to that question is likely, "There is no such thing as an average day." For those hoping for a stable and relatively unchanging daily routine, this is hardly an ideal occupation. However, for the clinician who might become bored with such a routine or who wishes to see up-close and personal examples of some of the extremes in human thoughts, actions, and emotions, correctional psychology might be a career worth considering.

The duties of a mental health professional in a correctional setting are numerous and varied. On any given day, one might be conducting group treatment, assessing incoming individuals for mental health needs, providing crisis intervention, making a determination as to whether it is advisable to place an inmate on suicide precautions, or providing individual counseling. Duties might also include determining whether an inmate belongs in a particular specialized unit or whether they would benefit from a higher level of mental health care. Psychological evaluations of those being considered for release into the community are a common task. Consultations with psychiatry, nursing, security staff, and administration are also commonplace. In the event of routine training or emergency situation, the correctional psychologist could also be tasked with searching the facility, helping to prepare and deliver meals, or negotiating for the release of a hostage. It is also worth noting that whatever is scheduled for the day is subject to change at any given moment if the forensic clinician gets a call stating that their services are immediately required for a crisis intervention.

For those who are easily bored, correctional psychology may be an excellent career choice. Remember that some of those who are incarcerated are in the greatest need of mental health treatment and may have histories of severe trauma. There are daily challenges, and there is rarely a lack of work to be done. Such work can be extremely rewarding, as in helping someone learn to cope adaptively with their anger or when successfully intervening in a case where an inmate was threatening or attempting suicide. Furthermore, the knowledge that the forensic report written about a truly dangerous individual may help to keep the community safe by assuring that person remains incarcerated can also be rewarding.

As might be expected, while the duties of a correctional psychologist will rarely be boring, the excitement of the job may come at a price. Being verbally threatened and insulted is a commonplace occurrence. At times, the people that the psychologist is attempting to help will refuse that help. Although assaults are infrequent, they can and do occur at times. Thus, the excitement and reward of the job are often accompanied by a considerable amount of stress. It is important for the correctional psychologist to self-monitor and to maintain self-care. The wise clinician begins to establish healthy self-care habits early in life, ideally before their career even begins. The importance of regular exercise, proper sleep habits, strong relationships, and relaxing hobbies, to name a few aspects of self-care, cannot be overstated.

THERE ARE NO SECRETS IN PRISON

In the Pennsylvania Department of Corrections (and many others), staff are not allowed to have any keys in their pockets, where they can be picked or fall out. All keys—personal *and* prison keys—must be secured to your belt by a metal clip. Most employees are careful to have a personal key ring that has the bare minimum of personal keys that they need: usually a car key and a house key. Each staff member has a numbered metal tag or "chit" that they give to the officer in the control booth, who then issues the staff their prison keys for the day. Staff put their prison keys on top of their personal keys on the metal clip attached to their belt. In my particular case, I was always careful to park in a part of the parking lot where inmates could not see (otherwise they know every staff member and what car they drive). I told no one when I traded in my Jeep for a Subaru. A few days after doing so, one of the inmates approached me in the hall and said, "Doc, you got a new car!" I was stunned, confused, and walked off muttering to myself. I had told no one. I parked around a corner. How could he possibly know this? A week later, I saw the inmate again in the hall. He looked directly at the metal clip and keys on my belt. He was letting me know that under all my prison keys, he had noticed that my Jeep key had been replaced by a Subaru one. That is the level of scrutiny that staff are under from inmates; it is worth remembering.

THROUGH THE EYES OF THE VICTIM

In this text is a discussion of victim impact at the end of each chapter. Many times, it is easy to identify the victim of a crime: a man has been shot, a woman has been robbed, or a child has been sexually assaulted. It is self-evident that they have been victimized, and it is just as evident that those who love them have been victimized as well. We would be remiss in not addressing some often-unrecognized victims: the innocent children of offenders, who (through no fault of their own) are now deprived of a relationship with one (or in some cases, both) of their parents. Children of incarcerated parents face significant obstacles in their lives in addition to the usual challenges of growing up.

Since the "War on Drugs" began in the 1980s, the rate of children whose mothers are incarcerated has risen 100% and the rate of children whose fathers are incarcerated has risen 75% (Raeder, 2012). Thus, it is important to consider not only the impact on the offender and the cost of incarcerating those with nonviolent drug- and alcohol-related offenses but also the subsequent impact on the families and children of such individuals. The total number of children who have had a parent incarcerated at some point during their lives is estimated to be 1.7 million to 2.7 million. At present, there are approximately 2.3 million people incarcerated in jails and prisons in the United States. More than 5 million children have a parent who was at some point incarcerated (Murphey & Cooper, 2015). Approximately 50%–75% of incarcerated individuals report having a minor child (Roxburgh & Fitch, 2014), and those children are more likely to experience adverse events than other children (Murphey & Cooper, 2015). When considering whether it is worth incarcerating someone for a nonviolent offense, it is important to think about the potential impact of removing that person from their family and loved ones and the social, financial, and emotional cost of doing so to all involved.

Not surprisingly, growing up with an incarcerated parent has been found to have an impact on the mental health of children (La Vigne et al., 2008). The social stigma of having a parent who is incarcerated should not be underestimated. The challenge of a child explaining to their friend why their parent is not attending their football game or dance recital is difficult to comprehend and making up a story about that parent being in the military or working can be incredibly burdensome for that young person.

In cases where there may be no choice but to incarcerate an individual who is a parent, it certainly seems to be worth considering what can be done to mitigate the impact of that incarceration on the children. Perhaps the offender could be incarcerated in an institution relatively close to their home so that visits are less expensive and burdensome for that person's family. Perhaps technology could be utilized to allow face-to-face video visits so that the parent and child may interact without the child having to go through the unpleasant process of being searched when coming to the institution's visiting room. The question of whether offenders should be rehabilitated or punished is open to considerable debate; however, no one would argue that the innocent children of those who have committed offenses should be punished for their parents' transgressions.

CONCLUSION

As we learned in this chapter, the United States incarcerates many more people per capita than any other nation on earth. Such incarceration comes with an extremely high price tag not only financially but also in terms of the social and societal impact of incarcerating those who may not have committed a violent offense. Such individuals' only motivation for doing so may have been addiction to a substance, and those with mental health challenges may have those challenges exacerbated by their placement in a jail or prison. In such cases, it is important to achieve some balance between protecting society and deciding how best to address the offending individuals; do they need education and training so that they can be released back into society as law-abiding, productive citizens? Alternatively, does providing them with such opportunities do a disservice to the victims and their families, who (in some cases) were significantly impacted by the offender? The answers to such questions are not simple. Especially in thinking about sentencing an individual to execution, we must take a hard look at our criminal justice system and be certain that we are doing more good than harm . . . and that is no easy task. In addition, we must never forget that the sentence we impose on an offender, whether it be punishment or rehabilitation, impacts the family of that offender as well.

Exercises and Discussion Questions

1. Imagine that you are the warden of your own very unique and innovative correctional system, with unlimited funds and the ability to structure that program however you think is best. What would this system look like? Would it be punishment-based, rehabilitation-based, some combination of the two, or something completely unique? Describe your plan in detail.

2. Prior to reading this chapter, would you have said that you were in favor of the death penalty or opposed to it? Has that opinion changed or remained the same after having read the chapter? If you have changed your opinion, what was it that you learned that changed how you look at this sanction?

3. We have discussed the potential emotional, social, and financial impact on children when a parent is incarcerated. What, if anything, do you believe can be done to minimize the negative impact on the child? What could be done as part of an attempt to maintain the bond between a child and their incarcerated parent? Please be specific.

4. We have discussed the enormous financial cost of incarcerating so many people in the United States. Do you think this money could be better spent in other programs (such

as schools, after-school programs, mentor programs, etc.), with the end result being that fewer people would be incarcerated? Be specific as to how such money could be spent.

5. Prisons sometimes house extremely violent individuals. Some may be so dangerous that they pose a risk to inmates and staff if housed in the general population. Yet we have seen that long-term solitary confinement is being viewed more and more often by the courts as cruel and unusual. What might you suggest we do in order to allow institutions to run in a safe and humane manner without placing people in solitary confinement for lengthy periods of time?

KEY TERMS

Civiler mortuus

Code of Hammurabi

Community service

Determinate sentencing

Fines

First-generation prisons

Indeterminate sentencing

Jail

Parole

Pennsylvania system

Prison

Probation

Punishment

Rehabilitation

Restricted housing unit (RHU)

Second-generation prisons

Security threat group (STG)

Third-generation prisons

War on Drugs

GLOSSARY

Abduction: An action taken, often by a noncustodial parent, to obtain possession of a child.

Abnormal: Deviating from the average.

Acquaintance rape: Rape and/or sexual assault when committed by a perpetrator known to the victim.

Actus reus: Latin for "guilty act."

Adam Walsh Act: The Adam Walsh Child Protection and Safety Act supplements Megan's Law sex offender registration requirements and implements a three-tier system for classifying sex offenders.

Adjudicative hearing: A hearing at which the master hears prosecution and defense and renders a verdict.

Aggravated assault: An act, often involving a weapon, that attempts to or does inflict serious bodily injury to another person.

Aggravated indecent assault: Penetration, no matter how slight, of the vagina, mouth, or anus of a non-consenting person by any body part or foreign object used by the offender.

Aggression: A behavior intended to inflict some type of harm on another person.

American Psychological Association (APA): A scientific and professional organization representing psychologists.

Antisocial personality disorder: A pattern of stable traits characterized by a lack of conscience or remorse; this lack often leads the individual to harm others around them in some manner.

Arraignment hearing: A hearing at which the juvenile is advised of the charges against them.

Arrest: The process of a person being legally detained by a law enforcement officer.

Atavistic: Cesare Lombroso's idea that criminals are "primitive" or "savages."

Bail: Money or collateral levied by the court upon an individual's release from jail in order to assure that they will appear in court at a later time.

Behavioral Analysis Unit (BAU): The current name of the Federal Bureau of Investigation's five units devoted to crimes against children, terrorism, counterterrorism, violent crime, and criminal profiling, including teaching, research, and strategy.

Behavioral evidence analysis (BEA): A fusion of profiling techniques in which deductive reasoning is used to create a profile.

Behavioral Sciences Unit (BSU): The original designation of what is now known as Federal Bureau of Investigation Behavioral Analysis Unit #5.

Belief perseverance: A tendency to maintain one's belief even in the presence of evidence that directly contradicts that belief.

Booking: The process of taking fingerprints and photographs when a person is brought to jail.

Borderline personality disorder: A personality disorder distinguished by unstable and intense personal relationships.

Bullying: Unwanted aggressive behavior toward another where there is a power imbalance.

Challenges for cause: The ability of the prosecution or defense to dismiss a potential juror with reason.

Child abuse: Actions which lead to the physical, emotional, or sexual harm of a child.

Child pornography: Any sexually provocative depiction of a minor (a person less than 18 years of age).

Child sexual abuse: The use of force or coercion in order to engage in sexual activity with a victim younger than 13 years old when the perpetrator was at least five years older, or with a victim 13–16 years of age when the offender is at least 10 years older than the victim.

Circumstantial evidence: Evidence that involves making an inference or reaching a conclusion.

Civiler mortuus: Latin for "civil death"; the notion that a prisoner has the same rights as a dead person.

Code of Hammurabi: Ancient Babylonian legal code and the first attempt to scale punishment to fit specific crimes.

Cognitive behavioral therapy: Psychotherapy predicated upon the notion that by helping people change how they think, those same people can change how they feel and therefore change how they act.

Cognitive load: The amount of information a person can retain or process at one time.

Cognitive load approach: An approach to detecting deception by increasing cognitive load on the subject.

Cognitive processing therapy: A form of talk therapy that involves teaching an individual to recognize the thoughts that are causing them emotional distress and how to challenge and change such thoughts.

Community service: A sentence from the court to perform a given number of hours of work for the community in reparation for one's offense.

Competency to stand trial: Refers to whether the defendant at the time of the trial has the ability to understand the proceedings and to assist their lawyer in adequately defending them.

Competency to Stand Trial Assessment Instrument (CAI): A formalized method of rating 13 areas of a defendant's ability to understand the court process and to assist in their defense.

Compliant false confession: A false confession provided by a subject in order to comply with the demands of the interrogator.

Conduct disorder (CD): A condition in which a juvenile repeatedly violates norms and the rights of others.

Consent: An informed, voluntary, and willing decision to engage in sexual activity.

Control question test/comparison question test (CQT): A polygraph technique in which responses to nonthreatening questions, likely lies, and relevant questions are compared.

Courtroom work group: The professionals working in the courtroom setting.

Crime action profiling (CAP): A profiling technique used to describe both the criminal actions that have occurred and the prediction of offender characteristics based on those actions.

Criminal investigative analysis (CIA): A technique used in the early days of the Federal Bureau of Investigation's Behavioral Sciences Unit to systematically study violent crimes, sometimes involving interviews of violent criminals as part of an attempt to gain insight into their offenses and motivations.

Critical Incident Response Group (CIRG): The Federal Bureau of Investigation group that integrates tactical responses, negotiations, behavioral analysis, and other crisis management services into one cohesive structure.

Critical incident stress debriefing (CISD): A formalized method of interacting with those who have responded to crisis events, intended to decrease the probability that they will develop post-traumatic stress disorder (PTSD).

CSI effect: The idea that television programs have led many people to believe that numerous complex and involved scientific, investigative, and DNA tests can be quickly and easily performed and are required for a finding of guilt.

Cyberbullying: Using electronic or social media to threaten, demean, or embarrass others.

Date rape: Rape and/or sexual assault in the context of a date or dating relationship.

Defense attorney: An attorney tasked with providing a vigorous legal defense for the accused.

Deinstitutionalization: The process of discharging individuals with mental illness from psychiatric facilities into the community and then closing or downsizing those facilities.

Determinate sentencing: A sentence for a specified period of time.

Deviant arousal pattern: An abnormal pattern of sexual arousal; for example, a sexual arousal by an adult in regard to prepubescent children and/or nonconsenting adults.

Diagnostic and Statistical Manual (DSM): Published by the American Psychiatric Association, the DSM-5 (5th edition) is the diagnostic manual used to assist in the diagnosis of mental health disorders.

Differential risk: An area in which one group is at distinctly greater risk than another group.

Diffusion of responsibility: As the number of bystanders increases, the probability of any one person providing assistance to someone in distress decreases.

Direct evidence: Factual evidence that requires no inferences or conclusions to be reached.

District attorney: The chief law enforcement officer representing the state; their job is to prosecute the defendant.

District courts: The 94 trial courts of the federal court system.

Diversion: Treatment, counseling, or community service in lieu of juvenile detention.

Diversity, equity, and inclusion: Principles of fairness and equality and treating all individuals with respect and dignity.

Drug treatment court: Similar to the other specialized courts, this is intended to divert nonviolent offenders with alcohol- or drug-related issues from incarceration and instead requires compliance with a treatment program.

Duping delight: Lying simply for the excitement of doing so.

Durham rule: Suggests that a mental illness led directly to the criminal behavior in question.

Dusky standard: In order to be found competent to stand trial, an individual must be able to understand the charges against them and the court process and must also be able to assist their lawyer in their defense.

Dynamic risk factors: Risk factors that are amenable to change.

Emotional aggression: Aggression, often impulsive, to express anger or other strong negative emotion.

Ethics: The moral principles guiding one's behavior.

Evidence-based corrections: The use of research to determine which correctional programs reduce recidivism.

Expert witness: A person who is qualified as an expert on a given topic and allowed to provide testimony and opinion to the court on that topic.

Exposure therapy: A form of therapy that involves teaching the client to relax in the presence of thoughts or actual stimuli that were once traumatic for them.

Eye movement desensitization reprocessing (EMDR): A form of therapy that involves using bilateral eye movements while discussing or imagining traumatic events, with the goal of decreasing one's response to those events.

False confession: A statement of guilt made by an individual who knows that they are not guilty.

Fetal alcohol syndrome (FAS): A medical condition seen in some infants born to mothers who drank alcohol excessively while pregnant.

Fines: A sentence from the court to pay a given amount of money for one's offense.

First-degree homicide: A homicide in which that act was premeditated and there was specific intent to kill another person.

First-generation prisons: A jail or prison with cells arranged in straight lines to discourage inmates from interacting with one another.

First responders: Volunteer or professional workers including police, firefighters, emergency medical services, military, corrections, and other related personnel who respond to crisis situations.

Fitness for duty evaluation (FFDE): An evaluation conducted by a mental health professional with the goal of determining whether or not a first responder is fit to continue performing their duties with or without assistance/intervention.

Forcible rape: Defined by the Federal Bureau of Investigation as sexual penetration, no matter how slight, without the consent of the victim.

Forensic digital analyst: An individual who analyzes computer data and other data to assist in solving criminal offenses.

Forensic entomologists: Individuals who use their knowledge of insect populations and insect development to assist in solving crimes.

Forensic evidence: Evidence obtained scientifically for use in court.

Forensic meteorologist: An individual who uses their knowledge of weather patterns to assist in solving accidents and criminal offenses.

Forensic psychology: Application of psychological research and knowledge to the legal and court systems.

Forensics: The use of scientific techniques to detect and solve crimes.

Gangs: Groups with a defined hierarchy, rules, and territory who often engage in illegal activities.

Grooming: Actions taken by a sex offender to maximize their chances of being able to commit a sex offense against a child; this often involves special favors, treatment, or gifts.

Guilty but mentally ill (GBMI): A plea allowed in some states, equivalent to a plea of guilty but suggests that mental illness was present at the time of the offense.

Guilty knowledge test (GKT): A polygraph technique in which people respond to multiple-choice questions about an offense.

Hare Psychopathy Checklist–Revised: A test developed by Robert Hare as a psychological assessment tool for the presence or absence of psychopathy.

Hate crimes/bias crimes: Defined by the Federal Bureau of Investigation as offenses committed toward a person or their property based on hostility toward that person due to their race, gender, sexual orientation, religion, disability, or other factors related to that person.

Indecent assault: Touching a private region of a non-consenting individual's body, either over or under their clothing.

Indeterminate sentencing: A sentence that includes a minimum and a maximum amount of time that will be served as determined by a parole board or other agency.

Initial appearance: A hearing at which the charges are formally read to the defendant and the defendant is allowed to enter a plea.

Instrumental aggression: Aggression (often premeditated) to achieve a specific goal.

International Association of Forensic Criminologists (IAFC): An organization with an established code of ethics and written practice standards that provides credentialing and verification of expertise in criminal profiling.

Interrogation: The process of attempting to obtain a confession for a crime.

Intimate partner violence (IPV): Violence between any two current or former domestic partners, regardless of age or gender.

Inveiglement: Use of trickery or deception to take, abuse, harm, abduct, or kidnap a victim.

Investigation: A meeting to gather information about a given topic of offense.

Investigative psychology (IP): The methodological review and study of closed police cases as part of an attempt to identify ideographic themes.

Involuntary civil commitment: The authorized placement of an individual with severe mental illness in an inpatient psychiatric facility against their will.

Irresistible impulse test: Similar to the not guilty by reason of insanity plea; used in some states by defendants who claim that they were acting in response to an irresistible impulse.

Jail: Confinement for those awaiting trial who cannot post bail or confinement for offenses with sentences of less than two years.

Judge: An elected or appointed official who has the responsibility of making certain that the prosecution and defense conduct the trial in accordance with the principles of law.

Juvenile delinquency: The participation of a person less than 18 years old in criminal activity.

Juvenile petition: A legal document used to initiate legal action against a juvenile.

Juveniles: People under the age of 18 years old.

Kidnapping: An action taken to obtain possession of a child in order to achieve some other goal, such as a monetary ransom for that child.

Lay witness: An individual who is allowed to testify to facts relevant to the case in question.

Leading question: A question phrased in such a manner that it prompts or encourages a certain answer.

Long-term stress: Stress of greater or lesser intensity for a relatively lengthy period of time.

MacArthur Competency Assessment Tool–Criminal Applications (MacCAT–CA): A formalized measure designed to assess the defendant's understanding and reasoning in regard to the court and criminal justice process.

Major depressive disorder (MDD): Defined by the *Diagnostic and Statistical Manual* (5th edition) by the occurrence of symptoms such as sadness, change in sleep and appetite, loss of energy, and thoughts of death much of the day, every day, for at least two weeks.

Mandated reporting: In some states, the requirement that a mental health professional warn police that a client has expressed violent and/or suicidal ideation and intent.

Mass murderer: An individual who kills three or more people in one place at one time.

Megan's Law: A federal law requiring that sex offenders register their address with local law enforcement agencies and that the community be provided with information about that offender.

Mens rea: Latin for "guilty mind."

Mental health courts: A specialized court intended to divert those with mental illness from incarceration and instead requires treatment and supportive intervention.

Mental Retardation Facilities and Community Mental Health Centers Construction Act: An act intended to provide federal funding to community mental health centers.

Minnesota Multiphasic Personality Inventory (MMPI): A 567-item psychological instrument that may be used in the hiring process for many first responders.

Model penal code test: Similar to the not guilty by reason of insanity plea; used in some states by defendants who claim that due to a mental illness at the time of the offense, they did not understand that their actions were criminal in nature.

Modus operandi (M.O.): Latin for "method of operation;" the manner in which an offender commits and attempts to get away with committing a crime.

Narcissistic personality disorder: A personality disorder distinguished by a grandiose sense of self-importance.

National Center for Analysis of Violent Crime (NCAVC): The mission of the

NCAVC was to assist with investigations into violent offenses and to provide training and support as needed to federal, state, and local law enforcement agencies.

Neglect: Failure to provide for the basic medical, nutritional, educational, or other needs of a child.

Normal: Average or typical.

Not guilty by reason of insanity (NGRI): A finding by a jury that a person was legally insane at the time that they committed their offense.

Obedience to authority: The tendency of people to comply with orders from authority figures.

Occupational stress: Stress due to the specific demands of one's employment.

Oppositional defiant disorder (ODD): A condition in which a child is unusually angry and irritable.

Organizational stress: Stress due to organizational demands such as long work hours, restrictive policies, or budgetary concerns within the organization.

Own-race bias (ORB): The tendency of people to be more accurate in identifying members of their own race.

Paraphilia: An intense and persistent sexual interest other than sexual activity with a consenting adult partner.

Paraphilic disorder: A paraphilia becomes a paraphilic disorder when the individual is intensely bothered by their own paraphilia or when they act on their desire in such a manner as to cause harm or potential harm to themselves or others.

Parole: Early conditional release from incarceration.

PEACE model: A five-stage interrogation model that is less confrontative than some other models.

Pennsylvania system: An early system of incarceration that emphasized silence and isolation as forms of rehabilitation.

Peremptory challenges: The ability of the prosecution or defense to dismiss a potential juror without having to provide a reason for doing so.

Permissive reporting: In some states, mental health professionals are permitted (but not required) to forgo confidentiality and inform police or others if a client has expressed suicidal or violent ideation, intent, or plan.

Personality: A pattern of stable traits that differentiates us from others.

Personality disorder: Stable and enduring traits that are significantly distressing to the individual having those traits or that are harmful to them or others in some way.

Personal stress: Stress not due to one's employment but instead due to factors such as finances, relationship concerns, or legal difficulties.

Phrenology: Franz Gall's idea that the shape of an individual's skull could provide us with meaningful and important information about their personality; this was later discredited.

Plea bargain: The accused agrees to plead guilty to some or all of the charges against them. In return, the prosecution will typically drop some of the charges or impose charges of a lesser severity.

Polygraph: A machine that records and measures a number of physiological functions that may be used as part of an attempt to detect deception.

Positivist criminology: Cesare Lombroso's idea that criminals are born, not made.

Post-traumatic stress disorder (PTSD): As defined in the *Diagnostic and Statistical Manual* (5th edition), a response to having experienced or witnessed a life-threatening event, often characterized by reexperiencing that event while awake or asleep, dysphoric mood, and attempts to avoid reminders of the trauma.

Prefrontal cortex: The portion of the brain involved in decision making, judgment, and suppression of urges.

Preliminary hearing: A hearing at which the district attorney/prosecution must demonstrate that they have sufficient evidence or probable cause that a crime occurred and that the crime was the responsibility of the defendant.

Preponderance of the evidence: The burden of proof in civil cases.

Pre-sentence investigation: A report written by the probation officer to help the court reach an appropriate sentencing decision.

Prison: Confinement of those convicted of crimes and serving at least two years of incarceration.

Probable cause: Objective evidence to suggest that a crime was being committed or had been committed.

Probation: A conditional sentence by the court instead of incarceration in which the offender must follow a given set of stipulations.

Protective factors: Factors that may serve to decrease an individual's risk of offending.

Psychological first aid (PFA): A formal technique for providing emotional support to those who have responded to a crisis event.

Psychopathy: A personality disorder distinguished by a complete and utter lack of remorse and by sadistic pleasure in the suffering of others.

Psychosis/psychotic: A thought disorder characterized by the experience of hallucinations, delusions, and impaired thought and behavior.

Punishment: The idea that imposition of a penalty will deter further illegal behavior.

Rape: Sexual intercourse by physical force or forcible compulsion.

Rehabilitation: The idea that treatment and education can serve to restore a person to adaptive and legal behavior.

Reid technique: A nine-step confrontative technique for eliciting a confession.

Relevant–irrelevant: A polygraph technique that involves comparing responses to questions that are relevant to the offense to those that are not.

Restricted housing unit (RHU): A specialized unit within a prison for inmates who are thought to be dangerous and therefore are separated from the general population.

Risk factors: Factors that may serve to increase an individual's risk of offending.

Ritualistic behavior: A behavior repeatedly engaged in by an offender that is not necessary for the commission of the offense or as part of getting away with the offense.

Robbery: Usually defined as the unlawful taking of another person's property through force or threat of force.

Salem Witch Trials: The false accusations and subsequent conviction and execution of those accused of being witches in and around Salem, Massachusetts, in the late 1600s.

Scientific jury selection: An attempt by the defense or prosecution to use scientific techniques to pick a jury that will provide a verdict favorable to that side.

Second-degree homicide: A homicide in which that act was not premeditated but there was specific intent to kill another person.

Second-generation prisons: A jail or prison in which housing units are circular pods and officers are able to observe from a raised enclosure in the middle of that pod.

Security threat group (STG): A gang within the prison that may be a threat to the security of the institution through violence or drug smuggling.

Self-fulfilling prophecy: Acting in such a manner as to increase the probability that a prediction about oneself does in fact come to be.**Serial killer:** An individual who kills three or more people in different places at different times with a cooling-off period between kills.

Sexually violent predator (SVP): An individual having a mental abnormality of personality disorder that increases the probability of that individual committing sex offenses in the future.

Short-term stress: Stress of greater or lesser intensity for a relatively brief period of time.

Simple assault: An act that puts an individual in reasonable fear of being injured; typically no weapon is involved.

Social learning theory: Bandura's theory that children learn by imitating adults.

Spree killer: An individual who kills three or more people in different places at different times but without a cooling-off period between kills.

State courts: Trial courts for matters pertaining to state laws.

Static-2002R: The most widely used means of predicting sex offender recidivism.

Static risk factors: Risk factors that are not amenable to rapid change.

Status offense: An action that is illegal for a certain group of people (often people under 18 years of age).

Statutory rape: Rape or sexual assault perpetrated by a person above the age of consent upon a person who is not of the legal age of sexual consent.

Stress: Mental or emotional strain on an individual that leads to the activation of their sympathetic nervous system.

Substance use disorder (SUD): Defined by the *Diagnostic and Statistical Manual* (5th edition) as using more of a given substance than was intended, unsuccessful attempts to reduce usage, a need for more of the substance to achieve intoxication, and withdrawal symptoms if/when the substance is not used.

Suicide: The voluntary and willful act of ending one's own life.

Testosterone: The primary male sex hormone, often associated with aggressive behavior.

Third-degree homicide: An act, typically reckless in nature, resulting in the death of another person; the act was not premeditated and there was no clear intent to kill another person.

Third-generation prisons: A jail or prison in which the officers are in the housing unit with the inmates, often with no physical barrier between the staff member and inmates.

Trial consultant: An individual with experience in the behavioral sciences who may be consulted regarding a wide variety of courtroom practices.

U.S. circuit courts of appeal: The 13 courts that oversee appeals from U.S. district courts.

U.S. Supreme Court: The highest court in the U. S., overseen by nine justices.

Veterans treatment courts (VTCs): A specialized court similar to a mental health court but focused on diverting military veterans from incarceration and instead requires treatment and supportive intervention.

Victim impact statement (VIS): A statement made to the court by the victim or their family detailing the physical, emotional, financial, or other losses they may have suffered as a result of the offense.

Victim–offender mediation: A process in which a victim (or the family member of a victim) is allowed to meet with the offender in a supervised setting in the hopes of achieving some emotional closure or resolution of their suffering.

Violent Crime Apprehension Program (ViCap): A computer-based program designed to assist law enforcement agencies in the apprehension of serial violent offenders.

Voir dire: Latin for "to tell the truth"; a process of questioning jurors and witnesses about the testimony they may give or hear.

Waiver: Action taken to allow a juvenile to be tried in adult court.

War on Drugs: An effort on the part of U.S. law enforcement and military to decrease the importation, manufacture, distribution, and used of drugs by U.S. citizens.

REFERENCES

CHAPTER 1

American Psychological Association. (2017). *Ethical principles of psychologists and code of conduct*. Effective date June 1, 2003, with amendments effective June 1, 2010, and January 1, 2017.

Bandura, A., Ross, D., & Ross, S. A. (1961). Transmission of aggression through imitation of aggressive models. *Journal of Personality and Social Psychology, 63*, 575–82.

Burl, J., Shah, S., Filone, S., Foster, E., & DeMatteo, D. (2012). A survey of graduate training programs and coursework in forensic psychology. *Teaching of Psychology, 39*(1), 48–53.

Chawkins, S. (2015, April 15). Martin Reiser dies at 87; LAPD's first staff psychologist. *LA Times*. https://www.latimes.com/local/obituaries/la-me-martin-reiser-20150417-story.html

Earley, P. (2007). *Crazy: A father's search through America's mental health madness*. Berkley Books.

Joshi, A. S., & Kline, C. T. (2015, September 1). *Lack of diversity: A national problem with individual consequences*. American Bar Association.

Nellis, A. (2021, October 13). *The color of justice: Racial and ethnic disparity in state prisons*. The Sentencing Project.

Packer, I., & Borum R. (2003). Forensic training and practice. In A. M. Goldstein & I. B. Weiner (Eds.), *Handbook of psychology* (pp. 21–32). Wiley.

Torres, A. N., Boccaccini, M. T., & Miller, H. A. (2006). Perceptions of the validity and utility of criminal profiling among forensic psychologists and psychiatrists. *Professional Psychology Research and Practice, 37*, 51–58.

Ward, J. T. (2013, September). What is forensic psychology? *Psychology Student Network*. American Psychological Association.

CHAPTER 2

American Foundation for Suicide Prevention (AFSP). (2017, May). *Suicide statistics*. https://afsp.org/suicide-statistics/

American Psychiatric Association. (2013). *Diagnostic and statistical manual* (5th ed.). American Psychiatric Publishing.

American Psychological Association. (2017, July 31). *Eye movement desensitization and reprocessing (EMDR) therapy*.

American Psychological Association. (2022). Developing resilience in response to stress and trauma. Tsai, J., Batastini, A. B., & Kearney, L. K. (Eds.). *Psychological Services, 19*(1).

Anderson, M. K. (2020, September 30). *The most effective ways to combat stress: Comparing stress levels and coping mechanisms from alcohol to exercise and peer support in first responders*. EMS1.

Barber, E., Newland, C., Young, A., & Rose, M. (2015). Survey reveals alarming rates of EMS provider stress and thoughts of suicide. *Journal of Emergency Medical Services 40*(10), 30–34.

Barrett, A. E., Kesling, B., & Gurman, S. (2020, May). Justice department says that George Floyd's death a priority. *Wall Street Journal*.

Ben-Porath, Y. S., & Tellegen, A. (2020). *Minnesota Multiphasic Personality Inventory-3 (MMPI-3): Manual for administration, scoring, and interpretation*. University of Minnesota Press.

Bentley, M. A., Crawford, J. M., Wilkins, J. R., Fernandez, A. R., & Studnek, J. R. (2013). An assessment of depression, anxiety, and stress among nationally certified EMS professionals. *Prehospital Emergency Care 17*(3), 330–338. https://doi.org/10.3109/10903127.2012.761307

Bishop, S. A., Piquero, N. L., Worrall, J. L., & Piquero, A. R. (2018, March). Negative affective responses to stress among urban police officers: A general strain theory approach. *Deviant Behavior, 40*(6), 635–654. https://doi.org/10.1080/01639625.2018.1436568

Bowler, R. M., Kornblith, E. S., Li, J., Adams, S. W., Gochera, V. A., Schwarzer, R., & Cone, J. E. (2016). Police officers who responded to 9/11: Comorbidity of PTSD, depression, and anxiety 10–11 years later. *American Journal of Industrial Medicine, 59*(6), 425–436.

Brooks, S. K., Dunn, R., Amlot, R., Greenberg, N., & Rubin, G. J. (2016). Social and occupational factors associated with psychological distress and disorder among disaster responders: A systematic review. *BMC Psychology, 4*, 18. https://doi.org/10.1186/s40359-016-0120-9

Cambell, J. M. (2019, November 1). *US firefighter injuries in 2018*. National Fire Prevention Association.

Conts, C. R. (2018, November 13). *Research analysis: More than 1-in-20 EMT deaths are due to suicide*. EMS1. https://www.ems1.com/paramedic-chief/articles/research-analysis-more-than-1-in-20-emt-deaths-are-due-to-suicide-7nGmXiNq3q0ezZlc/#:~:text=Death%2Dby%2Dsuicide%20occurred%20in,the%20MOR%20dropped%20to%201.39.

Corey, D. M., & Ben-Porath, Y. S. (2020). *MMPI-3 user's guide for the police candidate interpretive report*. Regents of the University of Minnesota.

Davis, H. (2019). *Police officer suicide rate more than doubles line of duty deaths in 2019 study shows*. Fox News. https://www.foxnews.com/us/texas-police-officer-suicide-rate

Denhof, M. D., & Spinaris, C. G. (June 2013). *Depression, PTSD, and comorbidity in United States corrections professionals: Prevalence and impact on health and functioning*. Desert Waters Outreach.

DePietro, A. (2020, April 23). Here's how much money police officers earn in every state. *Forbes*. https://www.forbes.com/sites/andrewdepietro/2020/04/23/police-officer-salary-state/?sh=46a68b372010

Everly, G. S. (2018, October 9). *Psychological first aid*. Psychology Today. https://www.psychologytoday.com/us/blog/when-disaster-strikes-inside-disaster-psychology/201810/psychological-first-aid

Fleischmann, M. H., Strode, P., Broussard, B., & Compton, M. T. (2016). *Law enforcement officers' perceptions of and responses to traumatic events: A survey of officers completing crisis intervention team training*. Policing and Society.

Forehand, J. A., Peltzman, T., Westgate, C. L., Riblet, N. B., Watts, B. V., & Shiner, B. (2019). *American Journal of Preventive Medicine, 57*(2), 145–152.

George, L. (2020, December 8). Police shot in the line of duty hits record high, statistics show. *American Military News*.

Governor's Task Force on Police Suicide. (2009). *New Jersey police suicide task force report*. https://www.nj.gov/oag/library/NJPoliceSuicideTaskForceReport-January-30-2009-Final(r2.3.09).pdf

Haddock, C. K., Poston, W. S. C., Jahnke, S. A., & Jitnarin, N. (2017). Alcohol use and problem drinking among women firefighters. *Women's Health Issues, 27*(6), 632–638. https://doi.org/10.1016/j.whi.2017.07.003

Harris, M. B., Baloglu, M., & Stacks, J. R. (2002). Mental health of trauma-exposed firefighters and critical incident stress debriefing. *Journal of Loss and Trauma, 7*(3), 223–238. https://doi.org/10.1080/10811440290057639

Harvard Medical School. (2017). *National comorbidity survey*. https://www.hcp.med.harvard.edu/ncs/

Harvard Medical School. (2020). *Understanding the stress response: Chronic activation of this survival mechanism impairs health*. https://www.health.harvard.edu/staying-healthy/understanding-the-stress-response

Hayes, C. (2018, April 11). *Silence can be deadly: 46 officers were fatally shot last year: more than triple that—140—committed suicide*. USA Today.

Heavey, S. C., Homish, G. G., Andrew, M. E., McCanlies, E., Mnatsakanova, A., Violanti, J. M., & Burchfield, C. M. (2015). Law enforcement officers' involvement level in Hurricane Katrina and alcohol use. *International Journal of Emergency Mental Health and Human Resilience, 17*(1), 267–273.

Heyman, M., Dill, J., & Douglas, R. (2018, April). *The Ruderman white paper on mental health and suicide of first responders*. https://dir.nv.gov/uploadedFiles/dirnvgov/content/WCS/TrainingDocs/First%20Responder%20White%20Paper_Final%20(2).pdf

International Association of Chiefs of Police. (2009). *Psychological fitness-for-duty psychological evaluation guidelines*. IACP.

International Association of Firefighters. (2019, October 2). *Legislation supports fire fighters' mental health*. https://www.iaffrecoverycenter.com/blog/legislation-supports-fire-fighters-mental-health/

Jahnke, S. A., Poston, W. S., Haddock, C. K., Jitnarin, N., Hyder, M. L., & Horvath, C. (2012). The health of women in the U.S. fire service. *BMC Women's Health, 12*(39). https://doi.org/10.1186/1472-6874-12-39

Kerr, M. (2018, August 20). *Depression and military families*. Healthline. https://www.healthline.com/health/depression/military-service

Konda, S., Tiesman, H., Reichard, A., & Hartley, D. (2013). US Corrections officers killed or injured on the job. *Corrections Today, 75*(5), 122–123.

Kraska, P. B., & Kapeller, V. E. (1988). Police on-duty drug use: A theoretical and descriptive examination. *American Journal of Police, 7*(1), 1–28.

Lee, J. H., Kim, I., Won, J. U., & Roh, J. (2016). PTSD and occupational characteristics of police officers in the republic of Korea: A cross-sectional study. *BMJ Open, 6*(3).

McCanlies, E. C., Mnatsakanova, A., Andrew, M. E., Burchfiel, C. M., &

Violanti, J. M. (2014). Positive psychological factors are associated with lower PTSD symptoms among police officers: Post Hurricane Katrina. *Stress & Health, 30*(5), 405–415. https://doi.org/10.1002/smi.2615

Merlo, L. J., Singhakant, S., Cummings, S. M., & Cottler, L. B. (2013). Reasons for misuse of prescription medication among physicians undergoing monitoring by a physician health program. *Journal of Addiction Medicine, 7*, 349–353.

Military-Ranks.org. (2023). [Website]. https://www.military-ranks.org/

Mitchell, J., & Everly, G. (1996). *Critical incident stress debriefing: An operations manual for the prevention of traumatic stress among emergency services and disaster workers* (2nd ed.). Chevron.

National Institute of Mental Health. (2022). *Mental health and mass violence: Evidence-based early psychological intervention for victims/survivors of mass violence—A workshop to reach consensus on best practices*. U.S. Government Printing Office.

Office of the Press Secretary, The White House. (2003, December 17). *Homeland Security Presidential Directive HSPD-8*. https://irp.fas.org/offdocs/nspd/hspd-8.html

Pietrangelo, A. (2020, May 29). *The effects of stress on your body*. Healthline.

Robertson, I. T., Cooper, C. L., Sarkar, M., & Curran, T. (2015). Resilience training in the workplace from 2003–2014: A systematic review. *Journal of Occupational and Organizational Psychology, 88*(3), 533–562.

Skeffington, P. (2016, August 2). *One in five police officers are at risk of PTSD—here's how we need to respond*. The Conversation.

Spitzer, A. (2020, July 28). First responders and PTSD: A literature review. *Journal of Emergency Medical Services*.

Stanley, I. H., Hom, M. A., & Joiner, T. E. (2016). A systematic review of suicidal thoughts and behaviors among police officers, firefighters, EMTs, and paramedics. Clinical Psychology Review, 44,

25–44. https://doi.org/10.1016/j. cpr.2 015.12.002

U.S. Bureau of Labor Statistics. (2019a). *Occupational employment & wages*, May 2019. *29-2040 Emergency medical technicians and paramedics.* https://www.bls.gov/oes/2019/may/oes292040.htm

U.S. Bureau of Labor Statistics. (2019b). *Occupational employment & wages*, May 2019. *33-3012 Correctional officers and jailers.* https://www.bls.gov/oes/2019/may/oes333012.htm

Van Emmerick, A. A., Kamphuis, J. H., Hulsbosch, A. M., & Emmelkamp, P. M. (2002). Single-session debriefing after psychological trauma: A meta-analysis. *The Lancet, 360*(9335), 766–771.

Werner, E. E. (1992). The children of Kauai: Resiliency and recovery in adolescence and adulthood. *Journal of Adolescent Health, 13*(4), 262–268.

World Health Organization. (2003). *Mental health in emergencies: Mental and social aspects of health of populations exposed to extreme stressors.* https://aps.who.int/iris/handle/10665/67866

CHAPTER 3

American Polygraph Association. (2011). Meta-analytic study of criterion accuracy of validated polygraph techniques. *Polygraph, 40*(4).

American Polygraph Association. (2019). *APA Bylaws and standards.* https://www.polygraph.org/apa-bylaws-and-standards

American Psychological Association. (2004a). The polygraph in doubt. *Monitor on Psychology, 35*(7). https://www.apa.org/monitor/julaug04/polygraph

American Psychological Association. (2004b). *The truth about lie detectors (aka polygraph tests).* https://www.apa.org/topics/cognitive-neuroscience/polygraph

Aracena, V. L. (2017, April 16). Own-race bias: Why some people might look the same to you. *CogBlog—A Cognitive Psychology Blog.* https://web.colby.edu/cogblog/2017/04/16/own-race-bias-why-some-people-might-look-the-same-to-you/

Arndorfer, A., & Malloy, L. C. (2013, July). Interrogations, confessions, and the vulnerability of youth. *American Psychology-Law Society.* https://www.apadivisions.org/division-41/publications/newsletters/news/2013/07/interrogations

Badenhausen, K. (2019, February 12). The NBA's highest paid players in 2019: LeBron James leads with $89 million. *Forbes.*

Bond, C. F., & DePaulo, B. M. (2006). Accuracy of deception judgments. *Personality and Psychology Review, 10*(3), 214–234.

Borger, J. (2006, August 9). DNA rules out man who said he killed JonBenet Ramsey. *The Guardian.*

Brauer, A. (1999). Biofeedback and anxiety. *Psychiatric Times, 16*(2). https://www.psychiatrictimes.com/view/biofeedback-and-anxiety

Chappell, B. (2020, June 3). *Chauvin and 3 former officers face new charges over George Floyd's death.* NPR. https://www.npr.org/2020/06/03/868910542/chauvin-and-3-former-officers-face-new-charges-over-george-floyds-death

Chew, S. L. (2018, August 20). *Myth: Eyewitness test is the best kind of evidence.* Association for Psychological Science.

Darley, J., & Latane, B. (1968). Bystander intervention in emergencies: Diffusion of responsibility. *Journal of Personality and Social Psychology, 8*(4), 377–383.

Death Penalty Information Center. (n. d.). *Innocence: Executed but possibly innocent.* https://deathpenaltyinfo.org/policy-issues/innocence/executed-but-possibly-innocent

DePaulo, B. M., Kashy, D. A., Kirkendol, S. E., Wyer, M. M., & Epstein, J. A. (1996). Lying in everyday life. *Journal of Personality and Social Psychology, 70*(5), 979–995.

Drizin, S. A., & Leo, R. (2004). The problem of false confessions in the post-DNA world. *North Carolina Law Review, 82*, 891–1008.

Ekman, P. (2009). *Duping delight: Getting away with lies.* Paul Ekman Group.

Gansberg, M. (1964, March 27). 37 who saw murder didn't call the police: Apathy at the stabbing of Queens woman shocks inspector. *The New York Times.*

Honts, C. R., Thurber, S., & Handler, M. (2020, December 18). A comprehensive meta-analysis of the comparison question polygraph test [Special issue]. *Applied Cognitive Psychology, 35*(2), 411–427.

Innocence Project. (2020). *How eyewitness misidentification can send innocent people to prison.*

Jellison, J. J. (1977). *I'm sorry, I didn't mean to, and other lies we love to tell.* Chatham Square Press.

Kassin S., & Wrightsman L. (1985). Confession evidence. In S. Kassin & L. Wrightsman (Eds.), *The psychology of evidence and trial procedure* (pp. 67–94). SAGE.

Kozinski, W. (2018). The Reid interrogation technique and false confessions: A time for change *Seattle Journal for Social Justice, 16*(2), Article 10.

Lipchik, G. L. (1998). Ohio University headache treatment and research project. *Headache, 9*(2).

Loftus, E. (1996). *Eyewitness testimony.* Harvard University Press.

Mandelbaum, J., & Crossman, A. (2014). *No illusions: Developmental considerations in adolescent false confessions.* American Psychological Association.

McFadden, R. D. (2016, April 4). Winston Moseley, who killed Kitty Genovese, dies in prison at 81. *The New York Times.*

Meissner, C. A., & Brigham, J. C. (2001). Thirty years of investigating the own-race bias in memory for faces: A meta-analytic review. *Psychology, Public Policy, and Law, 7*(1), 3–35.

Milgram, S. (1963). Behavioral study of obedience. *Journal of Abnormal and Social Psychology, 67*(4), 371–378.

National Research Council. (2003). *The polygraph and lie detection.* The National Academies Press. https://doi.org/10.17226/10420.

The News-Gazette. (2013, July 5). *Man sues over wrongful conviction.* https://www.news-gazette.com/news/man-sues-over-wrongful-conviction/article_75ba2a4c-ec63-5bc6-b4bb-f0715ad14d4a.html

Ofshe, R., & Leo, R. (1997). The social psychology of police interrogation: The theory and classification of true and false confessions. *Studies in Law, Politics, and Society, 16,* 189–251.

Possley, M. (2021, August 18). Andre Davis. *The National Registry of Exonerations.*

Possley, M., & Warden, R. (n. d.). *Andre Davis: Nearly 32 years behind bars—and innocent.* Bluhm Legal Clinic Center on Wrongful Convictions.

Redlich, A. D., Silverman, M., Chen, J., & Steiner, H. (2004). The police interrogation of children and adolescents. In G. Lassiter (Ed.), *Interrogations, confessions, and entrapment* (pp. 107–125). Kluwer Academic/Plenum Publishers.

Rogal, L. (2017). Protecting persons with mental disabilities from making false confessions: The Americans with Disabilities Act as a safeguard. *New Mexico Law Review, 47*(1).

Saad, G. (2011, November 30). *How often people lie in their daily lives. The Pinocchio effect: Lying in daily life.* Psychology Today.

Schafer, J. (2014, March 11). *How to detect a liar.* Psychology Today.

Schafer, J. (2020, September 28). *Three simple techniques to detect deception.* Psychology Today.

Schatz, S. J. (2018). Interrogated with intellectual deficiency: The risks of false confessions. *Stanford Intellectual and Developmental Disability Law and Policy Project, 70.*

Scheck, B., Neufeld, P., & Dwyer, J. (2000). *Actual innocence: Five days to execution, and other dispatches from the wrongly convicted.* Random House.

Stern, B. A., & Krapohl, D. J. (2004). The efficacy of detecting deception in psychopaths using a polygraph. *Polygraph, 33*(4).

U.S. Census Bureau. (2022). *Real median personal income in the United States.* FRED, Federal Reserve Bank of St. Louis.

Verschuere, B., Crombez, G., Koster, E. H. W., & DeClercq, A. (2007). Antisociality, underarousal and the validity of the concealed information polygraph test. *Biological Psychology, 74*(3), 309–331.

Vrij, A., Mann, S. A., Fisher, R. P., Leal, S., Milne, R., & Bull, R. (2008). Increasing cognitive load to facilitate lie detection: The benefit of recalling an event in reverse order. *Law and Human Behavior, 32*(3), 253–265.

Wells, G. (2002). Eyewitness testimony. In W.G. Jennings (Ed.), *The encyclopedia of crime and punishment.* John Wiley & Sons.

Wong, H. K., Stephen, I. D., & Keeble, D. R. T. (2020). The own-race bias for face recognition in a multiracial society. *Frontiers in Psychology, 11.* https://doi.org/10.3389/fpsyg.2020.00208

CHAPTER 4

Abel, E. L., & Sokol, R. J. (1987). Incidence of fetal alcohol syndrome and economic impact of FAS-related anomalies: Drug alcohol syndrome and economic impact of FAS-related anomalies. *Drug and Alcohol Dependency, 19*(1), 51–70.

Anderson, M. (2018). *A majority of teens have experienced some form of cyberbullying.* Pew Research Center.

Arain, M., Haque, M., Johal, L., Mathur, P., Nel, W., Rais, A., Sandhu, R., & Sharma, S. (2013). Maturation of the adolescent brain. *Neuropsychiatric Disease and Treatment, 9,* 449–461.

Baglivio, M. T., & Wolf, K. T. (2017). *Prospective prediction of juvenile homicide: Attempted homicide among early-onset juvenile offenders.* PubMed Central.

Barbaree, H., & Marshall, W. (2006). *The juvenile sex offender* (2nd ed.). The Guilford Press.

Barbaree, H., Marshall, W., & Hudson, S. (1993). *The juvenile sex offender.* The Guilford Press.

Bartol, C. R., & Bartol, A. M. (2008). *Current perspectives in forensic psychology and criminal behavior.* SAGE.

Batrinos, M. L. (2012). Testosterone and aggressive behavior in men. *International Journal of Endocrinological Metabolism, 10*(3), 563–568.

Butts, J. A., Bazemore, G., & Meroe, S. A. (2010). *Positive youth justice—framing justice interventions using the concepts of positive youth development.* Coalition for Juvenile Justice.

Carol, L. (2016). *How the war on drugs affected incarceration rates.* Politifact—The Poynter Institute.

Centers for Disease Control and Prevention. (2021). *School-associated violent death study.* https://www.cdc.gov/violenceprevention/youthviolence/schoolviolence/SAVD.html

Currie, J., & Tekin, E. (2007). *Does child abuse cause crime?* National Bureau of Economic Research Working Paper 12171.

Death Penalty Information Center. (2023). *Executions of juveniles in the U.S. 1976–2005.*

Dopp, A., Borduin, C., & Brown, C. (2015). Evidence-based treatments for juvenile sexual offenders: Review and recommendations. *Journal of Aggression, Conflict and Peace Research, 7,* 223–236.

Ethen, M. K., Ramadhani, T. A., & Scheuerle, A. E. (2008). Alcohol consumption by women before and during pregnancy. *Maternal and Child Health Journal, 13*(2), 274–285.

Fernald, C. D., & Gettys, L. (1980). Diagnostic labels and perceptions of children's behavior. *Journal of Clinical Child Psychology, Academic Search Premier, 9*(3).

Finckenauer, J. O., & Gavin, P. W. (1999). *Scared straight: The panacea phenomenon revisited.* Waveland Press, Inc.

Finkelhor, D., & Turner, H. (2016). *National Survey of Children's Exposure to Violence II, 1993–2012 [United States].* Inter-university Consortium for Political and Social Research [distributor]. https://doi.org/10.3886/ICPSR36177.v1

Galaif, E. R., Stein, J. A., Newcomb, M. D., & Bernstein, D. P. (2001). Gender differences in the prediction of problem alcohol use in adulthood: Exploring the influence of family factors and childhood maltreatment. *Journal of Studies on Alcohol*, *62*, 486–493. https://doi.org/10.15288/jsa.2001.62.486

Gest, T. (2020). *Juvenile homicides rose amid overall crime decline*. The Crime Report. https://thecrimereport.org/2020/06/22/juvenile-homicides-rose-amid-overall-crime-decline/

Gladden, M. R., Vivolo-Kantor, A. M., Hamburger, M. E., & Lumpkin, C. D. (2014). *Bullying surveillance among youths: Uniform definitions for public health and recommended data elements, version 1.0*. National Center for Injury Prevention and Control, Centers for Disease Control and Prevention, and U.S. Department of Education.

Haapasalo, J., & Tremblay, R. E. (1994). Physically aggressive boys from ages 6 to 12: Family background, parenting behavior, and prediction of delinquency. *Journal of Consulting and Clinical Psychology*, *62*(5), 1044–1052.

Harp, C. (2020, June). *Juvenile arrests, 2018*. Juvenile Justice Statistics National Report Series Bulletin.

Heide, K. M. (2020). Juvenile homicide offenders look back 35 years later: Reasons they were involved in murder. *International Journal of Environmental Research and Public Health*, *17*(11), 3932.

Herrenkohl, T. I., Hawkins, J. D., Chung, I., Hill, K. G., & Battins-Pearson, S. (2001). School and community risk factors and interventions. In R. Loeber & D. Farrington (Eds.), *Child delinquents: Development, intervention, and service needs* (pp. 211–246). SAGE.

Hockenberry, S., & Puzzanchera, C. (2020). *Juvenile court statistics*. National Center for Juvenile Justice.

Howell, J. C. (1997). *Youth gangs. OJJDP Fact Sheet, #72*. Office of Juvenile Justice and Delinquency Prevention.

Howell, J. C. (1998). *Youth gangs: An overview. Juvenile Justice Bulletin*. Office of Juvenile Justice and Delinquency Prevention.

Howell, J. C. (2000). *Youth gang programs and strategies: Summary*. Office of Juvenile Justice and Delinquency Prevention.

Jessor, R., Turbin, M. S., & Costa, F. M. (1998). Risk and protection in successful outcomes among disadvantaged adolescents. *Applied Developmental Science*, *2*(4), 194–208.

Johnson, J. G., Cohen, P., Smailes, E., Kasen, S., Oldham, J., Skodol, A., & Brook, J. (2000). Adolescent personality disorders associated with violence and criminal behavior during adolescence and early adulthood. *American Journal of Psychiatry*, *157*(9), 1406–1412.

Justice Policy Institute. (2020). *Sticker shock: The cost of youth incarceration*. https://justicepolicy.org/research/policy-brief-2020-sticker-shock-the-cost-of-youth-incarceration/

Juvenile Law Center. (2020). *Sex offender registration of children (SORNA)*. https://jlc.org/issues/juvenile-sex-offender-registry-sorna

Kagan, E., & Supreme Court of the United States. (2011). *U.S. Reports: Miller v. Alabama, 567 U.S. 460*. https://www.loc.gov/item/usrep567460/

Katsiyannis, A., Zhang, D., Barrett, D. E., & Flaska, T. (2004). Background and psychosocial variables associated with recidivism among adolescent males: A 3-year investigation. *Journal of Emotional and Behavioral Disorders*, *12*(1), 23–29.

Kendziora, K., & Osher, D. (2004). Deconstructing the pipeline: Using efficacy, effectiveness, and cost-benefit data to reduce minority youth incarceration. *New Directions for Youth Development*, *99*, 91–120.

Kennedy, A. M., & Supreme Court of the United States. (2004). *U.S. reports: Roper v. Simmons, 543 U.S. 551*. https://www.loc.gov/item/usrep543551/

Kvalevaag, A. L., Ramchandani, P. G., Hove, O., Eberhard-Gran, M., Assmus, J., Havik, O. E., Sivertsen, B., & Biringer, E. (2014). Does paternal mental health in pregnancy predict physically aggressive behavior in children? *European Child & Adolescent Psychiatry*,

23(10), 993–1002. https://doi.org/10.1007/s00787-014-0587-y

Lansford, J. E., Dodge, K. A., Pettit, G. S., Criss, M. M., Shaw, D. S., & Bates, J. E. (2009). Trajectories of physical discipline: Early childhood adolescents and developmental outcomes. *Child Development 80*(5), 1385–1402.

Leiter, V. (1993). *Special analysis of data from the OJJDP conditions of confinement study*. Abt Associates.

Lilienfeld, S. O., Lynn, S. J., Ruscio, J., & Beyerstein, B. L. (2010). *50 great myths of popular psychology: Shattering widespread misconceptions about human behavior*. Wiley-Blackwell.

Liptak, A., & Bronner, E. (2012, June 25). Justices bar mandatory life terms for juveniles. *The New York Times*.

Lynch, J. P., & Sabol, W. J. (1997, August 1). *Did getting tough on crime pay? Crime policy report #1*. The Urban Institute.

McCann, K., & Lussier, P. (2008). Antisociality, sexual deviance, and sexual reoffending in juvenile sex offenders: A meta-analytical investigation. *Youth Violence and Juvenile Justice*, *6*, 363–385.

McClelland, G. M., Teplin, L. A., & Abram K. M. (2004). Detection and prevalence of substance use among juvenile detainees. *Juvenile Justice Bulletin*. U.S. Department of Justice.

McCord, J. (1979). Some child-rearing antecedents of criminal behavior in adult men. *Journal of Personality and Social Psychology*, *37*(9), 1477–1486.

McCord, J. (1997, April). *Some unanticipated consequences of summer camps* [Paper presentation]. The biennial meetings of the Society for Research in Child Development, Washington DC, United States.

McCord, J., Widom, C. S., & Crowell, N. A. (Eds.). (2001). *Juvenile crime, juvenile justice*. Panel on Juvenile Crime: Prevention, Treatment, and Control. National Academy Press.

Miller, E. K., & Wallis, J. D. (2009). Executive functioning and higher-order cognition: Definitions and neural substrates. In L. R. Squire (Ed.),

Encyclopedia of neuroscience (Vol. 4, pp. 99–104). Academic Press.

Miller, W. (1982, March–April). Youth gangs: A look at the numbers. *Children Today, 11*(2), 10–11.

Mims, C. (2007, July 5). *Strange but true: Testosterone alone does not cause violence*. Scientific American.

Moffitt, T. E. (1993). Adolescence-limited and life-course-persistent antisocial behavior: A developmental taxonomy. *Psychological Review, 100*(4), 674–701.

Moffitt, T. E. (2018). Male antisocial behavior in adolescence and beyond. *Natural Human Behavior, 2*, 177–186.

Office of Juvenile Justice and Delinquency Prevention. (2020). *Decline in arrests of juveniles continued through 2019*. https://www.ojjdp.gov/ojstatbb/snapshots/DataSnapshot_UCR2019.pdf

Ogloff, J., Cutajar, M., Mann, E., & Mullen, P. (2012). Child sexual abuse and subsequent offending and victimization: A 45-year follow-up study. *Trends and Issues in Crime and Criminal Justice, 440*, 421–440. https://www.aic.gov.au/publications/tandi/tandi440

Ortega-Barón, J., Buelga, S., Ayllón, E., Martínez-Ferrer, B., & Cava, M-J. (2019). Effects of intervention program Prev@cib on traditional bullying and cyberbullying. *International Journal of Environmental Research and Public Health, 16*(4), 527–540. https://www.ncbi.nlm.nih.gov/pmc/articles/PMC6406646/

Osher, D. M., Quinn, M. M., Poirier, J. M., & Rutherford, R. B. (2003). Deconstructing the pipeline: Using efficacy, effectiveness, and cost-benefit data to reduce youth minority incarceration. *New Directions in Youth Development, 99*, 91–120.

Palumbo, S., Mariotti, V., Iofrida, C., & Pellegrini, S. (2018). Genes and aggressive behavior: Epigenetic mechanisms and underlying individual susceptibility to aversive environments. *Frontiers in Behavioral Neuroscience, 12*(117).

Pardini, D. A., & Fite, P. J. (2010). Symptoms of conduct disorder, oppositional defiant disorder, attention-deficit/hyperactivity disorder, and callous-unemotional traits as unique predictors of psychosocial maladjustment in boys: Advancing an evidence base for DSM-5. *Journal of American Academic Adolescent Psychiatry, 49*(11), 1134–1144.

Petrosino, A., Turpin-Petrosino, C., & Buehler, J. (2002). "Scared straight" and other juvenile awareness programs for preventing juvenile delinquency. *The Cochrane Database of Systematic Reviews, 4*, CD002796. https://doi.org/10.1002/14651858.CD002796.pub2

Phillppi, S., Thomas, C. L., & Lentini, K. (2020). Translation of national juvenile drug treatment court guidelines into statewide standards and practices: A case study. *American Journal of Criminal Justice, 4*, 483–495.

Prison Policy Initiative. (2020). *2019–2020 annual report*. https://static.prisonpolicy.org/reports/PPI_Annual_2019-2020.pdf

Puzzachera, C. (2018). *Juvenile arrests 2018*. Juvenile Justice Statistics National Report Series Bulletin.

Reilly, J. (2012). *Risk and protective factors of delinquency: Perspectives from professionals working with youth*. St. Catherine University. https://sophia.stkate.edu/cgi/viewcontent.cgi?article=1076&context=msw_papers

Sawyer, W. (2019). *Youth confinement: The whole pie*. Prison Policy Initiative.

Schaffer, L. M. (2018, November 2). *Can a juvenile get life in prison?* FindLaw.

Shader, M. (2003, January). *Risk factors for juvenile delinquency: An overview*. U.S. Department of Justice Programs.

Sickmund, M., Sladky, T. J., Kang, W., & Puzzanchera, C. (2019). *Easy access to the census of juveniles in residential placement (EZACJRP)*. National Institute of Corrections. https://www.ojjdp.gov/ojstatbb/ezacjrp/

Siegel, L. J. (2002). Juvenile delinquency. Wordsworth Group.

Sissons, C. (2018). *Typical testosterone levels in males and females*. Medical News Today.

Statista Research Department. (2018, September 28). *U.S.—Number of serious violent crimes by youth 1980–2018*. https://www.statista.com/statistics/477466/number-of-serious-violent-crimes-by-youth-in-the-us/

Sturm, R. A., & Larsson, M. (2009). Genetics of human iris colour and patterns. *Pigment Cell Melanoma Research, 22*(5), 544–562. https://doi.org/10.1111/j.1755-148X.2009.00606.x

Tremblay, R. E., & LeMarquand, D. (2001). Individual risk and protective factors. In R. Loeber & D. Farrington (Eds.), *Child delinquency: Delinquency, intervention, and service needs* (pp. 137–164). SAGE.

U.S. Department of Health and Human Services. (2015). *Child maltreatment 2013*.

Wasserman, G. A., Keenan, K., Tremblay, R. E., Cole, J. D., Herrenkohl, T. I., Loeber, R., & Petechuk, D. (2003, April). Risk and protective factors of child delinquency. *Child Delinquency Bulletin Series*. Office of Juvenile Justice and Delinquency Prevention.

Werner, E. (2000). Protective factors and individual resilience. In J. P. Shonkoff & S. J. Meisels (Eds.), *Handbook of early childhood intervention* (2nd ed., pp. 115–132). Cambridge University Press.

Widom, C. S., Czaja, S. J., Bentley, T., & Johnson, M. S. (2012). A prospective investigation of physical health outcomes in abused and neglected children: New findings from a 30-year follow up. *American Journal of Public Health, 102*, 1135–1144. https://doi.org/10.2105/AJPH.2011.300636

Williams, L. M., Debattista, C., Duchemin, A. M., Schatzberg, A. F., & Nemeroff, C. B. (2016). Childhood trauma predicts antidepressant response in adults with major depression: Data from the randomized international study to predict optimized treatment for depression. *Translational Psychiatry, 6*(5), e799. https://doi.org/10.1038/tp.2016.61

CHAPTER 5

ABC News. (2009, January 7). *Benoit's brain showed severe damage from multiple concussions, doctors and dad say.* https://abcnews.go.com/GMA/story?id=3560015#:~:text=They%20found%20that%20Benoit's%20brain,of%20head%20trauma%2C%20said%20Bailes.

Ægisdóttir, S., White, M. J., Spengler, P. M., Maugherman, A. S., Anderson, L. A., Cook, R. S., Nichols, C. N., Lampropoulos, G. K., Walker, B. S., Cohen, G., & Rush, J. D. (2006). The meta-analysis of clinical judgment project: Fifty-six years of accumulated research on clinical versus. statistical prediction. *The Counseling Psychologist, 34*(3), 341–382.

Arain, M., Haque, M., Johal, L., Mathur, P., Nel, W., Rais, A., Sandhu, R., & Sharma, S. (2013). Maturation of the adolescent brain. *Neuropsychiatric Disease and Treatment, 9,* 449–461.

Ball, J. C., Rosen, L., Flueck, J. A., & Nurco, D. N. (1982). Lifetime criminality of heroin addicts in the United States. *Journal of Drug Issues, 12*(3), 225–239.

Batrinos, M. L. (2012). Testosterone and aggressive behavior in man. *International Journal of Endocrinology and Metabolism, 19*(3), 563–568.

Berkowitz, L. L. (1967). Weapons as aggression-eliciting stimuli. *Journal of Personality and Social Psychology, 7,* 202–207.

Black, M. C., Basile, K. C., Breiding, M. J., Smith, S. G., Walters., M. L., Merrick, M. T., Chen, J., & Stevens, M. R. (2011). *The National Intimate Partner and Sexual Violence Survey (NISVS): 2010 summary report.* National Center for Injury Prevention and Control, Centers for Disease Control and Prevention.

Brockell, G. (2019, April 20). Bullies and black trench coats: The Columbine shooting's most dangerous myths. *The Washington Post.*

Bureau of Justice Statistics. (2005). *Family violence statistics.* NCJ 207846.

Bushman, B. J., & Huessman, L. R. (2006). Short-term and long-term effects of violent media on aggression in children and adults. *Archives of Pediatric Adolescent Medicine, 160*(4), 348–352.

Centers for Disease Control and Prevention. (n. d.). *Risk and protective factors.* https://www.cdc.gov/violenceprevention/youthviolence/riskprotectivefactors.html

Cooley, B. (2018). *Will my red car get me more tickets?* CNET.

Copping, L. (2017). *Gender differences in violence and aggression.* Wiley Online Library. https://doi.org/10.1002/9781119057574.whbva005

Donaldson-Evans, C. (2015, May 18). *Wrestler Chris Benoit double murder-suicide: Was it 'roid rage'?* Fox News.

Duke, A. A., Smith, K. M., Oberleitner, L. M., Westphal, A., & McKee, S. A. (2018). Alcohol, drugs, and violence: A meta-meta-analysis. *Psychology of Violence, 8*(2), 238–249.

Fagan, J. (1990). Intoxication and aggression. *Crime and Justice, 13,* 241.

Fazel, S., & Danesh, J. (2002). Serious mental disorder in 23,000 prisoners: A systematic review of 62 studies. *The Lancet, 359*(9306), 545–550.

Fazel, S., Långström, N., Hjern, A., Grann, M., & Lichtenstein, P. (2009). Schizophrenia, substance abuse, and violent crime. *Journal of the American Medical Association, 301*(19), 2016–2023.

Ferguson, C. J., & Wang, J. C. (2019). Aggressive video games are not a risk factor for future aggression in youth: A longitudinal study. *Journal of Youth and Adolescence, 48*(8), 1439–1451.

Floden, D., Alexander, M. P., Kubu, C. S., Katz, D., & Stuss, D. T. (2008). Impulsivity and risk-taking behaviour in focal frontal lobe lesions. *Neuropsychologia, 46*(1), 2013–223.

Goldstein, D. (2015). *Too old to commit crime? Why people age out of crime, and what it could mean for how long we put them away.* The Marshall Project.

Goldstein, P. J., Brownstein, H. H., Ryan, P. J., & Bellucci, P. A. (1989). Crack and homicide in New York City, 1988: A conceptually based event analysis. *Contemporary Drug Problems, 16*(4), 651–687.

Grove, W. M., Zald, D. H., Lebow, S., Snitz, B. E., & Nelson, C. (2000). Clinical vs. mechanical prediction: A meta-analysis. *Psychological Assessment, 12,* 19–30.

Harlow, C. W. (1999). *Prior abuse reported by inmates and probationers.* U.S. Department of Justice, Bureau of Justice Statistics.

Krug, E. G., Dahlberg, L. L., Mercy, J. A., Zwi, A. B., & Lozano, R. (Eds). (2002). *World report on violence and health.* World Health Organization. https://apps.who.int/iris/bitstream/handle/10665/42495/9241545615_eng.pdf

McAvennie, M. (2023, May 16). What are normal testosterone levels by age? *The Edge.*

Monahan, J., Steadman, H. J., Robbins, P. C., Appelbaum, P., Banks, S., Grisso, T., Heilbrun, K., Mulvey, E. P., Roth, L., & Silver, E. (2005). An actuarial model of violence risk assessment for persons with mental disorders. *Psychiatry Services 56,* 810–815.

National Center For Missing and Exploited Children. (2022). *NCMEC data.* https://www.missingkids.org/ourwork/ncmecdata

National Children's Alliance. (2018). *National statistics on child abuse.* https://www.nationalchildrensalliance.org/media-room/national-statistics-on-child-abuse/

National Crime Information Center. (2018). *2017 NIC mission person and unidentified person statistics.* FBI. https://www.fbi.gov/file-repository/2018-ncic-missing-person-and-unidentified-person-statistics.pdf/view

National Crime Information Center. (2021). *2021 NCIC missing person and unidentified person statistics.* FBI. https://www.fbi.gov/file-repository/2021-ncic-missing-person-and-unidentified-person-statistics.pdf/view

Niolan, P. H., Kearns, M., Dills, J., Rambo, K., Irving, S., Armstead, T. L., & Gilbert, L. (2017). *Preventing interpersonal violence across the lifespan: A technical package of programs, policies, and practices.* National Center for Injury Prevention and Control Centers for Disease Control and Prevention.

Nyce, C. M. (2016). Dress codes after Columbine. *The Atlantic*.

Office of the Inspector General. (2009). The Federal Bureau of Investigations efforts to combat crimes against children. *Audit Report 09-08*. U.S. Department of Justice.

Peralta, R., & Novisky, M. (2015). When women tell: Intimate partner violence and the factors related to police notification. *Violence Against Women, 21*(1), 65–86.

Rafael, D. (2017). *Floyd Mayweather–Connor McGregor pulled in 4.3 million domestic PPV buys, $600M*. ESPN. https://www.espn.com/boxing/story/_/id/21770652/floyd-mayweather-conor-mcgregor-43-million-domestic-ppv-buys-600-million

Rao, V., Rosenburg, P., Bertrand, M., Salehinia, S., Spiro, J., Vaishnavi, S., Rastogi, P., Noll, K., Schretlen, D. J., Brandt, J., Cornwell, E., Makley, M., & Miles, Q. S. (2009). Aggression after brain injury: Prevalence and correlates. *Journal of Neuropsychiatry and Clinical Neuroscience, 21*(4), 420–429.

Shao, R., & Wang, Y. (2019). The relationship of violent video games to adolescent aggression. *Frontiers of Psychology, 10*, 384. https://doi.org/10.3389/fpsyg.2019.00384

Sherman, L. W., & Berk, R. A. (1984). *The Minneapolis domestic violence experiment*. Police Foundation.

Sifferlin, A. (2015, August 17). Violent videogames are linked to aggression, study says. *TIME*.

Silverman, A. B., Reinherz, H. Z., & Giaconia, R. M. (1996). The long-term sequalae of childhood and adolescent abuse: A longitudinal study. *Child Abuse and Neglect, 20*(8), 709–723.

Smith, S. G., Zhang, X., Basile, K. C., Merrick, M. T., Wang, J., Kresnow, M., & Chen, J. (2018). *The national intimate partner and sexual violence survey (NISVS): 2015 data brief—updated release*. National Center for Injury Prevention and Control, Centers for Disease Control and Prevention.

Statista Research Department. (2020). *Violent crime in the United States*. https://www.statista.com/study/13105/viole nt-crime-in-the-united-states-statista-dossier/

Statista Research Department. (2022). *Number of child abuse cases in the United States in 2020, by age of victim*. https://stagingfr.statista.com/statistiques/203838/number-of-child-abuse-cases-in-the-us-by-age/

Swanson, A. (2015, December 15). Why violence is so contagious. *The Washington Post*.

Szczerba, R. J. (2014, April 3). Mixed martial arts and the evolution of John McCain. *Forbes*. https://www.forbes.com/sites/robertszczerba/2014/04/03/mixed-martial-arts-and-the-evolution-of-john-mccain/?sh=328424ae2d59

Tefft, B. C. (2017). *Rates of motor vehicle crashes, injuries, and deaths in relation to driver age, United States, 2014–2015*. AAA Foundation for Traffic Safety.

Truman, J. L., & Morgan, R. E. (2014). *Nonfatal domestic violence, 2003–2012*. NCJ 244697.

U.S. Department of Health & Human Services, Administration for Children and Families Children's Bureau (2018). *Child maltreatment 2018*. https://www.acf.hhs.gov/sites/default/files/documents/cb/cm2018.pdf

USA Today. (2019, August 14). *50 of the most dangerous cities in the world*. https://www.usatoday.com/picture-gallery/travel/news/2019/07/24/most-dangerous-cities-world-tijuana-caracas-cape-town/1813211001/

Wasserman, E., & Ellis, C. A. (2010). Chapter 6: Impact of crime on victims. *National Victim Assistance Academy Track 1: Foundation-Level Learning*. Office for Victims of Crime Training & Technical Assistance Center.

CHAPTER 6

Arizona Coalition to End Sexual and Domestic Violence. (2022). *Sexual violence myths and misconceptions*. https://www.acesdv.org/about-sexual-domestic-violence/sexual-violence-myths-misconceptions/

Association for the Treatment of Sexual Abusers. (2010). *Registration and community notification of adult sex offenders*. ATSA.com

Beesley, K. (2017, November 14). *Sexual assault is about power: How the #MeToo campaign is restoring power to victims*. Psychology Today. https://www.psychologytoday.com/us/blog/psychoanalysis-unplugged/201711/sexual-assault-is-about-power

Black, M. C., Basile, K. C., Breiding, M. J., Smith, S. G., Walters, M. I., Merrick, M. T., Chen, J., & Stevens, M. R. (2011). *National intimate partner and sexual violence survey—2010 summary report*. Centers for Disease Control and Prevention, National Center for Injury Prevention and Control.

Bureau of Justice Statistics. (1997). *An analysis of data on rape and sexual assault: Sex offenses and offenders*. NCJ 163392.

Bureau of Justice Statistics. (2013). *Sexual victimization in prisons and jails reported by inmates 2011–2012*. NCJ 241399.

California Legislating Information. (1998). *California welfare and institution code*. https://leginfo.legislature.ca.gov/faces/codes_displayText.xhtml?lawCode=WIC&division=6.&title=&part=2.&chapter=2.&article=4.

Centers for Disease Control and Prevention. (2014). Prevalence and characteristics of sexual violence, stalking, and intimate partner violence. *Morbidity and Mortality Weekly Report, 63*(8).

Centers for Disease Control and Prevention. (2021, July). *National intimate partner and sexual violence survey*.

Chancellor, A. S. (2012). *Investigating sexual assault cases*. Jones and Bartlett Learning.

Chivers-Wilson, K. A. (2006). Sexual assault and posttraumatic stress disorder: A review of the biological, psychological and sociological factors and treatments. *McGill Journal of Medicine, 9*(2), 111–118.

Clark, S. K., Jeglic, E. L., Calkins, C., & Tatar, J. R. (2016). More than a nuisance: The prevalence and consequences of frotteurism and exhibitionism. *Sexual Abuse, 28*(1), 3–19. https://doi.org/10.1177/1079063214525

Cortoni, F., Hanson, R. K., & Coache, M. E. (2010). The recidivism rates of female sex offenders are low: A meta-analysis. *Sexual Abuse: A Journal of Research and Treatment, 22,* 387–401.

Cullen, F., Fisher, B., & Turner, M. (2000). *The sexual victimization of college women*. NCJ 182369.

Epperson, D. L., Kaul, J. D., Huot, S. J., Hesselton, D., Goldman, R., & Alexander, W. (1998). *Minnesota sex offender screening tool-revised (MnSOST-R)*. Minnesota Department of Corrections.

Finkelhor, D. (1984). *Child sexual abuse: New theory and research*. Free Press.

Glasser, M., Kolvin, I., Campbell, D., Glasser, A., Leitch, I., & Farrelly, S. (2001). Cycle of child sexual abuse: Links between being a victim and becoming a perpetrator. *British Journal of Psychiatry, 179,* 482–494. https://doi.org/10.1192/bjp.179.6.482

Gold, C., & Jeglic, E. (2017). *Non-contact sex offenders and public perception: The importance of victim type and crime location* [Student thesis]. John Jay College of Criminal Justice.

Groth, N. (1979). *Men who rape: The psychology of the offender*. Plenum Press.

Guideline Law. (2022). *Romeo and Juliet laws by state in the U.S. in 2022*. https://www.guidelinelaw.com/romeo-and-juliet-law/

Hammond, E. M., Berry, M. A., & Rodriquez, D. N. (2011). The influence of rape myth acceptance, sexual attitudes, and belief in a just world on attributions of responsibility in a date rape scenario. *Legal and Criminal Psychology, 16*(2), 242–252.

Hanson, R. K., Bourgon, G., Helmus, L., & Hodgson, S. (2009). The principles of effective correctional treatment also apply to sexual offenders: A meta-analysis. *Criminal Justice and Behavior, 36*(9), 865–891.

Hanson, R. K., & Morton-Bourgon, K. E. (2005). The characteristics of persistent sexual offenders: A meta-analysis of recidivism studies. *Journal of Consulting and Clinical Psychology, 73*(6),

1154–1163. https://doi.org/10.1037/0022-006X.73.6.1154

Hanson, R. K., & Thornton, D. (1999). *Static-99: Improving actuarial risk assessments for sex offenders (User Report 99-02)*. Department of the Solicitor General of Canada.

Hanson, R. K., & Thornton, D. (2003). *Notes on the development of Static-2002.* (Corrections Research User Report No. 2003-01). Department of the Solicitor General of Canada.

Harris, A. J. R., & Hanson, R. K. (2004). *Sex offender recidivism: An updated meta-analysis*. Public Safety and Emergency Preparedness Canada.

Harris, G. T., Rice, M. E., & Quinsey, V. L. (1993). Violent recidivism of mentally disordered offenders: The development of a statistical prediction instrument. *Criminal Justice and Behavior, 20,* 315–335.

Jenkins, A., & Petherick, W. (2014). *Profiling and serial crime* (3rd ed.). Elsevier.

Kansas v. Hendricks. 521 U.S. 346, 356-358 117 S.Ct. 2072, 138 L. Ed. 2d. 501. (1997).

Koenen, K. (2015). *Helping victims of sexual violence overcome PTSD*. Harvard School of Public Health.

Koss, M. P., & Burkhart, B. R. (1989). A conceptual analysis of rape victimization. *Psychology of Women Quarterly, 13*(1), 27–40. https://doi.org/10.1111/j.1471-6402.1989.tb00983.x

Lanyon, R. I. (1986). Theory and treatment in child molestation. *Journal of Consulting and Clinical Psychology, 54*(2), 176–182.

Lerner, M. J., & Montado, L. (1998). An overview: Advances in belief in a just world theory and methods. In L. Montado & M. J. Lerner (Eds.), *Responses to victimizations and belief in a just world: Critical issues in social justice*. Plenum.

MacPherson, G. (2003). Predicting escalation in sexually violent recidivism: Use of the sVR-20 and PLC: SV to predict outcome with non-contact recidivist and contact recidivists. *The Journal of Forensic Psychiatry and Psychology, 14*(3), 615–627.

McGrath, R., Cumming, G., Burchard, B., Zeoli, S., & Ellerby, L. (2010). *Current practices and emerging trends in sexual abuser management: The safer society 2009 North American survey*. Safer Society Press.

Milaniak, I., & Widom, C. S. (2015). Does child abuse and neglect increase risk for perpetration of violence inside and outside the home? *Psychological Violence, 5*(3), 246–255. https://doi.org/10.1037/a0037956

Monson, C. M., & Shnaider, P. (2014). *Treating PTSD with cognitive-behavioral therapies: Interventions that work*. American Psychological Association.

Morgan, R. E., & Kena, G. (2016). *Criminal victimization, 2016: Revised*. U.S. Department of Justice, Bureau of Justice Statistics.

Myers, D. G. (2015). *Exploring social psychology* (7th ed.). McGraw Hill Education.

National Sexual Violence Resource Center. (2011). *Child sexual abuse prevention: Overview*. https://www.nsvrc.org/publications/child-sexual-abuse-prevention-overview

Office of Justice Programs. (2012). *Chapter 8: Sex offender management strategies*. Office of Justice Programs, Sex Offender Management and Planning Initiative.

Plummer, M., & Cossins, A. (2018). The cycle of abuse: When victims become offenders. *Trauma Violence Abuse, 19*(3), 286–304. https://doi.org/10.1177/1524838016659487

Quinsey, V. L., Harris, G. T., Rice, M. E., & Cormier, C. A. (2006). *Violent offenders: Appraising and managing risk* (2nd ed.). American Psychological Association.

Resnick, H. S., Kilpatrick, D. G., Dansky, B. S., Saunders, B. E., & Best, C. L. (1993). Prevalence of civilian trauma and post-traumatic stress disorder in a representative national sample of women. *Journal of Consulting and Clinical Psychology, 61,* 984–991.

Seltzer, L. F. (2015, July 8). *Trauma and the freeze response: Good, bad, or both?* Psychology Today.

Smith, M. D. (2004). *The encyclopedia of rape*. Greenwood.

Smith, S. G., Chen, J., Basile, K. C., Gilbert, L. K., Merrick, M. T., Patel, N., & Jain, A. (2017). *The National Intimate Partner and Sexual Violence Survey (NISVS): 2010-2012 state report*. Centers for Disease Control and Prevention, National Center for Injury Prevention and Control.

U.S. Department of Justice (2015). *Child pornography*. https://ojjdp.ojp.gov/taxonomy/term/child-pornography?page=16

U.S. Department of Justice, National Institute of Justice. (1993). *Acquaintance rape: When the rapist is someone you know*. https://www.ojp.gov/ncjrs/virtual-library/abstracts/when-rapist-someone-you-know

U.S. Department of Veterans Affairs. (2023). *PTSD: National center for PTSD*. https://www.ptsd.va.gov/

Walsh, C. (2020, February 27). What the nose knows. *The Harvard Gazette*.

Ward, T., & Stewart, C. A. (2003). The treatment of sex offenders: Risk management and good lives. *Professional Psychology: Research and Practice, 34*(4), 353–360. https://doi.org/10.1037/0735-7028.34.4.353

Whatley, M. A., Rhodes, A., Smith, R. H., & Webster, J. M. (1999). The effect of a favor on public and private compliance. How internalized is the norm of reciprocity? *Basic and Applied Social Psychology, 21*(3), 251–259.

Yates, C. (2013). Evidence-based practice: The components, history, and process. *Counseling Outcome Research and Evaluation, 4*(1), 41–54.

CHAPTER 7

Associated Press. (1986, May 9). *Night Stalker's love of killing quoted in court documents*. https://apnews.com/article/e316fa8a9ce6ef6c1dffb5c87343c1a3

BBC News. (1999, April 27). *Columbine killers planned to kill 500*. http://news.bbc.co.uk/1/hi/world/americas/329303.stm

Bourgoin, S. (2020, March 5). Kemper kept souvenirs. *Edmund Kemper stories: Documenting the co-ed killer case*. https://edmundkemperstories.com/blog/2020/03/05/kemper-kept-souvenirs/

Brooks, D. (April 24, 2004). The Columbine killers. *The New York Times*.

Brown, B., & Merritt, R. (2002). *No easy answers: The truth behind death at Columbine*. Lantern books.

Brown, J. (1999, April 23). Doom, Quake, and mass murder. *Salon*.

Calhoun, B. (2016, August 30). *Yesterday's crimes: Big Ed Kemper the butcher*. SF Weekly.

Campbell, J. H., & Denevi, D. (Eds.). (2004). *Profilers: Leading investigators take you inside the criminal mind*. Prometheus.

Cauchon, D. (1999, April 13). *Zero-tolerance policies lack flexibility*. USA Today.

Centers for Disease Control and Prevention. (2019). *School-associated violent death study*. https://www.cdc.gov/violenceprevention/youthviolence/school-violence/SAVD.html

Chase, A. (2004). A mind for murder: *The education of the Unabomber and the origins of modern terrorism*. W. W. Norton & Company.

Chester, D. S. (2020, April 26). *How do people develop into 'successful' psychopaths?* Psychology Today.

Cleckley, H. (1955). *The mask of sanity: An attempt to clarify some issues about the so-called psychopathic personality* (3rd ed.). CV Mosby Co.

CNN. (1999, August 18). *Columbine tragedy was 'wakeup call' for the nation's SWAT teams*. http://www.cnn.com/US/9908/18/columbine.SWAT.01/

CNN. (2008, January 19). *Letter from Timothy McVeigh to the Union-Sun & Journal*. https://web.archive.org/web/20080119111020/http://www.cnn.com/US/OKC/faces/Suspects/McVeigh/1st-letter6-15/index.html

Cullen, D. (1999, September 23). Inside the Columbine High investigation. *Salon*.

Cullen, D. (2010). *Columbine*. Twelve (Hatchet Publishing Group).

Cullen, R. (1994). *The killer department: Detective Viktor Burakov's eight-year hunt for the most savage serial killer of our times*. Orion Media.

Doyle, A. C. (1891, June 25). A scandal in bohemia. *The Strand*.

Everytown Research and Policy. (2020). *The impact of active shooter drills in schools: Time to re-think reactive school safety strategies*. https://everytownresearch.org/report/the-impact-of-active-shooter-drills-in-schools/

Federal Bureau of Investigation. (n. d.). *What we investigate: Terrorism*. https://www.fbi.gov/investigate/terrorism

Girard, J. E. (2013). *Criminalistics: Forensic science, crime, and terrorism*. Jones & Bartlett Publishers.

Hare, R. (1993). *Without conscience: The disturbing world of the psychopaths among us*. Guilford Press.

Hare, R. D., Harper, T. J., & Hakistan, A. R. (1989). Two-factor conceptualization of psychopathy: Construct validity and assessment implications. *Psychological Assessment, 1*(1), 6–17.

Huchzermeier, C., Geiger, F., Bruss, E., Godt, N., Kohler, D., Hinrichs, G., & Aldenhoff, J. B. (2007). The relationship between DSM-IV Cluster B personality disorders and psychopathy according to Hare's criteria: Clarification and resolution of previous contradictions. *Behavioral Sciences and the Law, 25*(6), 901–911.

Jefferson County Sheriff's Office. (2018, October 7). Columbine High School—OOL deceased. *Columbine High School 99-7625 Evidence*. http://www.acolumbinesite.com/reports/cr/p11867-11870.pdf

Jefferson County Sheriff's Report. (1999). *Columbine High School shootings investigation records, April 20, 1999*. https://archives.jeffco.us/repositories/2/resources/24

Kiehl, K. A. (2014). *The psychopath whisperer: The science of those without a conscience*. Crown Publishers/Random House.

Kirklin, L. (2019). *Ripples of Columbine: Lance Kirklin* [YouTube video]. https://www.youtube.com/watch?v=abb3vN6kkbE

Lane, B. (1993). *Chronicle of 20th century murder*. Virgin Books.

Liebelson, D. (2013, April 8). *Where did the money donated to Columbine, Aurora, and Virginia Tech Shooting Victims Go?* Mother Jones.

Masters, B. (1993). *The shrine of Jeffrey Dahmer*. Hodder & Stoughton.

McVeigh, T. (2001, May 6). The McVeigh letters: Why I bombed Oklahoma. *The Guardian*.

Michel, H., & Herbeck, L. (2001). *American terrorist: Timothy McVeigh and the Oklahoma city bombing*. HarperCollins.

Mitchell, H., & Aamodt, M. G. (2005). The incidence of child abuse in serial killers. *Journal of Police and Criminal Psychology, 20*(1).

Moghadam, A. (2008). *The globalization of martyrdom: Al Qaeda, Salafi Jihad, and the diffusion of suicide attacks*. Johns Hopkins University Press.

Morton, R. J., & Hilts, M. A. (Eds.). (2005, September 2). *Serial murder: Multi-disciplinary perspectives for investigators*. U.S. Department of Justice, Office of Justice Programs.

Mullins-Sweat, S. N., Peters, N., Derefinko, K., & Miller, J. D. (2010). The search for the successful psychopath. *Journal of Research in Personality, 44*(4), 554–558.

Norris, J. (1992). *Jeffrey Dahmer*. Pinnacle Press.

Pankratz, H., & Simpson, K. (1999, November 13). Judge gives man 6 years. *The Denver Post*.

Pettigrew, M. (2019). The preference for strangulation in a sexually motivated serial killer. *International Journal of Offender Therapy and Comparative Criminology, 63*(5), 781–796. https://doi.org/10.1177/0306624X18803829

Russakoff, D., & Kovaleski, S. F. (1995, July 2). An ordinary boy's extraordinary rage. *The Washington Post*, p. A01.

Sandy Hook Advisory Commission. (2015, February). *Final Report to of the Sandy Hook Advisory Commission*, presented to Governor Dannel P. Malloy, State of Connecticut. http://www.governor.ct.gov/malloy/lib/malloy/SHAC_Doc_2015.02.13_draft_version_of_final_report.pdf

Seattle Post-Intelligencer. (2003, November 4). *Green River Killer confesses*. https://www.seattlepi.com/local/article/Green-River-Killer-confesses-1128925.php

Verona, E., Patrick, C. J., & Joiner, T. E. (2001). Psychopathy, antisocial personality, and suicide risk. *Journal of Abnormal Psychology, 110*(3), 462–470.

Walsh, E. (1992, February 4). Psychiatrist says Dahmer has a "terrible sickness." *Washington Post*. https://www.washingtonpost.com/archive/politics/1992/02/04/psychiatrist-says-dahmer-has-a-terrible-sickness/e939e3f7-1be1-4b99-91c4-f1572f33ba01/

Wright, G., & Millar, S. (1999, April 22). A clique within a clique, obsessed with guns, death, and Hitler. *The Guardian*.

CHAPTER 8

Bonn, S. A. (2020, September 27). *Skeptical of FBI profilings' validity?* Psychology Today.

Boysun, M. (2011, January 23). Portrait of "Mad Bomber," considered by police to be most dangerous man in town unexpected. *New York Daily News*.

Burney, I., & Pemberton, N. (2012). Making space for criminalistics: Hans Gross and fin-de-siecle CSI. *Studies in History and Philosophy of Biological and Biomedical Scenes, 44*(1), 16–25.

Canter, D., & Youngs, D. (2009). *Investigative psychology: Offender profiling and the analysis of criminal actions*. Wiley and Sons.

Carra, G. (2004). Images in psychiatry: Cesare Lombroso M.D., 1835–1909. *The American Journal of Psychiatry, 161*(4), 624.

Craker, W. D. (1997). Spectral evidence, non-spectral acts of witchcraft, and confession at Salem in 1692. *The Historical Journal, 40*(2), 332.

Elder, R. K. (2008, May 18). A brother lost, a brother found. *Chicago Tribune*.

Federal Bureau of Investigation. (2011). *Behavioral interview program: Attempting to understand violent offenders*. https://www.fbi.gov/news/stories/behavioral-interview-program

Federal Bureau of Investigation. (2014). *Overview of the behavioral analysis units* [audio]. https://www.fbi.gov/audio-repository/news-podcasts-thisweek-overview-of-the-behavioral-analysis-units.mp3/view

Grassberger, R. (1957). Pioneers in criminology XIII—Hans Gross. *Journal of Criminal Law & Criminology, 47*(4), 397–405.

Hannam, J. (2011). *The genesis of science*. Regnery Publishing Inc.

Hedgepeth, M. (2012, May 26). *The thirteenth juror: The "CSI effect."* Campbell Law Observer.

The International Association of Forensic Criminologists. (n. d.). [Website]. https://www.iafc-abp.org/

Kocsis, R. N. (Ed.). (2007). *Criminal profiling: International theory, research, and practice*. Humana Press.

Kocsis, R. N., Hayes, A. F., & Irwin, H. J. (2002). Investigative experience and accuracy in psychological profiling of a violent crime. *Journal of Interpersonal Science, 17*(8), 811–823.

Kocsis, R. N., & Palmero, G. B. (2016). Criminal profiling as expert witness evidence: The implications of the profiler validity research. *The International Journal of Law and Psychiatry, 49*, Part A, 55–65.

Kushner, H. (2013). Deficit or creativity: Cesare Lombroso, Robert Hertz, and the meanings of left-handedness. *Laterality, 18*(4), 416–436.

Leidy, L. (2020, August 28). *Top Gun was made to re-brand the military after Vietnam*.

Leonard, D. P. (2001). Character and motive in evidence law. *Loyola of LA Law Review, 34*, 439–536.

Louw, D. (2015). Forensic psychology. In J. Wright (Ed.), *International* encyclopedia of the social and behavioral sciences (2nd ed.). Pergamon.

MacGillis, A., Del Quentin, W., & Barker, J. (2002, October 4). Random shootings target victims in Montgomery during a 16-hour period. *The Baltimore Sun.*

Office for Victims of Crime. (2000). *Directory of victim–offender mediation programs in the United States.* https://ovc.ojp.gov/library/publications/directory-victim-offender-mediation-programs-united-states

Pedrini, C. J. (2007). A byte out of history: The beltway snipers: Part 1. *Federal Bureau of Investigation.* https://archives.fbi.gov/archives/news/stories/2007/october/snipers_102207

Popper, K. R. (1959). *The logic of scientific discovery.* Basic Books

Ramsland, K. (2015, February 10). *Henry Lee Lucas: Prolific serial killer or prolific liar?* Crime Library.

Reis, E. (1997). *Damned women: Sinners and witches in Puritan New England.* Cornell University Press.

Ribeiro, R. A. B., & Soeiro, C. B. B. (2021). Analysing criminal profiling validity: Underlying problems and future directions. *International Journal of Law and Psychiatry, 74.*

Roach, M. K. (2002). *The Salem witch trials: A day-to-day chronicle of a community under siege.* Cooper Square Press.

Scherer, J. A., & Jarvis, J. P. (2014). Criminal investigative analysis: Practitioner perspectives. *Federal Bureau of Investigation Law Enforcement Bulletin.* https://leb.fbi.gov/articles/featured-articles/criminal-investigative-analysis-practitioner-perspectives-part-one-of-four

Sirota, D. (2011, March 16). *How your taxpayer dollars subsidize pro-war movies and block anti-war movies.* HuffPost. https://www.huffpost.com/entry/how-your-taxpayer-dollars_b_836574

Staum, M. S. (2003). *Labeling people: French scholars on society, race and empire, 1815–1848.* McGill-Queen's University Press.

Stevens Point Daily Journal. (1957, November 21). *Gein pleads innocent by reason of insanity,* p. 1, cols. 7–8. https://www.newspapers.com/article/24095567/gein_pleads_innocent_by_reason_of/

Tefft, B. C. (2017). *Rates of motor vehicle crashes, injuries, and deaths in relation to driver age, United States, 2014–2015.* AAA Foundation for Traffic Safety.

Thompson, S. (2022, August 23). Jerry Bruckheimer reflects on billion-dollar box office unicorn Top Gun: Maverick. *Forbes.*

Torres, A. N., Boccaccini, M. T., & Miller, H. A. (2006). Perceptions of the validity and utility of criminal profiling among forensic psychologists and psychiatrists. *Professional Psychology: Research and Practice, 37*(1), 51–58.

Turvey, B. E. (2012). *Criminal profiling: An introduction to behavioral evidence analysis* (4th ed.). Elsevier.

Umbreit, M. S. (2001). *The handbook of victim mediation: An essential guide for practice and research.* Jossey-Bass.

CHAPTER 9

BBC News. (2018, January 31). *Larry Nassar case: USA gymnastics doctor "abused 265 girls."* https://www.bbc.com/news/world-us-canada-42894833

Bieber, C. (2023, January). How much do lawyers cost? 2023 guide. *Forbes.*

Bui, J. (2022, December 23). *The differences between a criminal case and a civil case.* FindLaw.

Clio. (2022). *2022 legal trends report.* https://www.clio.com/resources/legal-trends/2022-report/

Devers, L. (2011, January 24). *Plea and charge bargaining: Research summary.* U.S. Department of Justice, Bureau of Justice Administration.

Eisenstein, J., & Jacob, H. (1977). *Felony justice: An organizational analysis of criminal courts.* Little & Brown.

Fitzgibbons v. Integrated Healthcare Holdings Incorporated. California

Fourth Appellate District, Division 3 (Super. Ct. No. 30-2008-001088081). (2015.

Hernandez v. Texas, 347 U.S. 475 (1954.

Kressel, N. J., & Kressel, D. F. (2004). *Stack and sway: The new science of jury consulting.* Westview Press.

Lacy, E. (2018, February 13). Father who tried to attack Larry Nassar won't face charges. *Lansing State Journal.*

Lesh, E. (2015). State courts 101: Structure and selection. *Justice out of balance.* Lambda Legal.

Loftus, E. F., & Palmer, J. C. (1974). Reconstruction of auto-mobile destruction: An example of the interaction between language and memory. *Journal of Verbal Learning and Verbal Behavior, 13,* 585–589.

Macon, R. (2000). Inside the black box: What empirical research tells us about decisionmaking by civil juries. In R. E. Litan (Ed.), *Verdict: Assessing the civil jury system* (p. 151). The Brookings Institution.

Moreno v. Texas. 586 S.W. 3d 472, 478-86 (Tex App—Dallas 2019). (2018.

National Center for State Courts. (2018). *Court statistics project.* State Court Caseload Digest.

Offices of the United States Attorneys. (n. d.). *Introduction to the federal court system.* U.S. Department of Justice.

Ogborn-Mihm, LLP. (2015, August 21). *Diversity of jury pool critical to fair outcomes.* https://www.omtrial.com/diversity-of-jury-pool-critical-to-fair-outcomes/

Rahal, S., & Kozlowski, K. (2018, February 14). 204 Victim impact statements, 9 days, 2 counties, and a life sentence for Larry Nassar. *The Detroit News.*

Sweeney, A., & Dizikes, C. (2013, March 27). The balancing act of jury selection. *Chicago Tribune.*

United States Courts. (2019, May 9). *Courts seek to increase jury diversity.* https://www.uscourts.gov/news/2019/05/09/courts-seek-increase-jury-diversity

CHAPTER 10

Adams, E. (2022). *Mayor Adams announces plan to provide care for individuals suffering from untreated mental illness across New York City*. The official website of the city of New York. https://www.nyc.gov/office-of-the-mayor/news/870-22/mayor-adams-plan-provide-care-individuals-suffering-untreated-severe-mental#/0

Bureau of Justice Administration. (2012, February 19). *Mental health courts program*. https://bja.ojp.gov/program/mental-health-courts-program/overview

DiGravio, V. (2013). *The last bill JFK signed—and the mental health work still undone*. WBUR.

Drope v. Missouri, 420 U.S. 162. (1975.

Durose, M. R., Cooper, A. D., & Snyder, H. N. (2014). *Recidivism of prisoners released in 30 states in 2005: Patterns from 2005 to 2010*. NCJ 244205. http://www.bjs.gov/content/pub/pdf/rprts05p0510.pdf.

Dusky v. United States, 271 F.2d 385, 395, 8th Cir. Mo. (1959). https://casetext.com/pdf-email?slug=dusky-v-united-states-2

Elbogen, E. B., Wagner, H. R., Johnson, S. C., Kinneer, P., Kang, H., Vasterling, J. J., Timko, C., & Beckham, J. C. (2013). Are Iraq and Afghanistan veterans using mental health services? New data from a national random-sample survey. *Psychiatric Services, 64*(2), 134–141.

Finigan, M. W., Carey, S. M., & Cox, B. A. (2007). *Impact of a mature drug court over 10 years of operation: Recidivism and costs—Final report*. Office of Justice Programs. https://www.ojp.gov/pdffiles1/nij/grants/219225.pdf

Fox News Channel. (2015, January 13). *Doctor: I warned Andrea Yates not to have any more children*. https://www.foxnews.com/story/doctor-i-warned-andrea-yates-not-to-have-any-more-children

Hanson, K. (2022, March 16). *Mental health professionals' duty to warn*. National Conference of State Legislatures.

Hogg Foundation for Mental Health. (2013). *Restoration of competency to stand trial*. https://hogg.utexas.edu/project/competency-restoration-policy-brief

Jacewicz, N. (2016). *With no insanity defense, seriously ill people end up in prison*. NPR.

Kirchner, L. (2014). Remembering the drug court revolution. In C. D. Clark (Ed.), *In the recovery revolution*. Columbia University Press.

Lewis, S. J. (2020, February 6). *Not guilty by reason of insanity: What it means to be insane according to the law*. Psychology Today.

Lowder, E. M., Rade, C. B., & Desmarais, S. L. (2017, August 15). Effectiveness of mental health courts in reducing recidivism: A meta-analysis. *Psychiatric Services, 69*(1), 15–22. https://doi.org/10.1176/appi.ps.201700107

Marlowe, D. B., Hardin, C. D., & Fox, C. L. (2016, June). *Painting the current picture: A national report on drug courts and other problem-solving courts in the United States*. National Drug Court Institute.

Masters, B. (1993). *The shrine of Jeffrey Dahmer*. Hodder & Stoughton.

Mathias, G. (2022, September 29). Cannibal killer Jeffrey Dahmer wanted to turn his victims into 'zombie love slaves.' *The Daily Star*.

Melville, J. D., & Naimark, D. (2002). Punishing the insane: The verdict of guilty but mentally ill. *The Journal of the American Academy of Psychiatry and the Law, 30*(4), 553–555.

Mental Health America. (2020). *Position statement 57: In support of the insanity defense*. https://mhanational.org/issues/position-statement-57-support-insanity-defense#:~:text=(1)%20A%20person%20is%20not,the%20requirements%20of%20the%20law.

Mossman, D., Noffsinger, S. G., Ash, P., Frierson, R. L., Gerbasi, J., Hackett, M., Lewis, C. F., Pinals, D. A., Scott, C. L., Sieg, K. G., Wall, B. W., & Zonana, H. V. (2007). AAPL practice guideline for the forensic psychiatric evaluation of competency to stand trial. *Journal of the American Academy of Psychiatry and the Law Online, 35*(4), S3–S72.

National Academies of Sciences, Engineering, and Medicine, Health and Medicine Division, Board on Health Care Services, & Committee to Evaluate the Department of Veterans Affairs Mental Health Services. (2018). *Evaluation of the Department of Veterans Affairs mental health services*. National Academies Press.

Noffsinger, S. G., & Resnick, P. J. (2017). Criminal competencies. In R. Rosner & C. L. Scott (Eds.), *Principles and practice of forensic psychiatry* (3rd ed.). Taylor & Francis.

Pate v. Robinson, 383 U.S. 375, 378 (1966.

Penaloza, M. (2020). *America's mental health crisis behind bars*. NPR.

People v. McQuillan, Sup. Ct. of Michigan 392 Mich 511 221N.W. 2d 569. (1974.

Reisner, A. D., Peil, J., & Makey, M. (2013). Competency to stand trial and defendants who lack insight into their mental illness. *American Academy Psychiatry Law Journal, 41*, 85–86.

Rich, J. D., McKenzie, M., Shield, D. C., Wolf, F. A., Key, R. G., Poshkus, M., & Clarke, J. (2005). Linkage with methadone treatment upon release from incarceration: A promising opportunity. *Journal of Addictive Diseases, 24*(3), 49–59. https://doi.org/10.1300/J069v24n03_04

Ridgely, M. S., Engberg, J., Greenberg, M. D., Turner, S., DeMartini, C., & Demboskey, J. W. (2007). *Justice, treatment, and cost—an evaluation of the fiscal impact of Allegheny County mental health court*. RAND Technical Report. http://www.rand.org/pubs/technical_reports/TR439.

Riley, R. (2019, May 19). The cost of caring for mentally ill inmates. *The Gazette*.

Simone, J. (2022). *State of the homeless in 2022: New York at a crossroads*. Coalition for the Homeless.

Tarasoff v. Regents of University of California, 17 Cal.3d 425, Supreme Court of California. (1976.

Torrey, E. F. (1997). *Out of the shadows: Confronting America's mental health crisis.* John Wiley & Sons.

Torrey, E. F., Zdanowicz, M. T., Kennard, A. D., Lamb, H. R., Eslinger, D. F., Biasotti, M. C., & Fuller, D. A. (2014). *The treatment of persons with mental illness in prisons and jails: A state survey.* Treatment Advocacy Center.

Tsai, J., Finlay, A., Flatley, B., Kasprow, W. J., & Clark, S. (2018). A national study of veterans treatment court participants: Who benefits and who recidivates. *Administration and Policy in Mental Health and Mental Health Services Research, 45,* 236–244. https://doi.org/10.1007/s10488-017-0816-z

World Health Organization. (1996). *Mental health care law: Ten basic principles.* https://apps.who.int/iris/handle/10665/63624

CHAPTER 11

Abdorrahman Boroumand Center for Human Rights in Iran. (2018, December 13). *What happens to murder rates when the death penalty is scrapped? A look at eleven countries might surprise you.* https://www.iranrights.org/library/document/3501

Abramsky, S., & Fellner, J. (2003). *Ill-equipped: U.S. prisons and offenders with mental illness.* Human Rights Watch.

Ali, M. (2022). Infographic: Which countries still have the death penalty? *Alijazeera.*

Amadeo, K. (2019, November 29). What criminal sentence costs more: Death or life in prison? *The Balance.*

Associated Press. (2014). *AP impact: After 40 years, $1 trillion, US war on drugs has failed to meet any of its goals.* Fox News Channel.

Basoglu, M., Livanou M., & Crnobaric C. (2007). Torture vs. other cruel, inhuman and degrading treatment: Is the distinction real or apparent? *Arch Gen Psychiatry, 64,* 277–285.

Bilyeau, N. (2020). *The trauma of women in prison.* The Crime Report.

Bradford, M. (2019, February 15). *Criminal justice series: Probation and parole.* Primer House Appropriations Committee (D).

Bronson, J., & Berzofsky, M. (2017). *Indicators of mental health problems reported by prisoners and jail inmates, 2011–12.* NCJ 250612.

Bureau of Prisons. (2018). *Annual determination of average cost of incarceration.* Document 2018-09062. https://www.govinfo.gov/content/pkg/FR-2018-04-30/pdf/2018-09062.pdf

Carson, E. A. (2018). *Prisoners in 2016.* Bureau of Justice Statistics.

Carson, E. A. (2020). *Prisoners in 2018.* Bureau of Justice Statistics.

Cherian, M. (2019). Cruel, unusual, and unconstitutional: An originalist argument for ending solitary confinement. *Georgetown Law, 56*(4).

Clarke, J. G., & Adashi, E. Y. (2011). Perinatal care for incarcerated patients: A 25-year-old woman pregnant in jail. *Journal of the American Medical Association, 305*(9), 923–929.

College Tuition Compare. (2021). *Tuition, fees, and college costs by state.* https://www.collegetuitioncompare.com/compare/tables/

Criminal Justice Institute. (2009). *Implementing evidence-based policy and practice in community corrections* (2nd ed.). U.S. Department of Justice, National Institute of Corrections.

Death Penalty Information Center. (2020). *Ending injustice: The persistence of racial discrimination in the U.S. death penalty.* https://deathpenaltyinfo.org/facts-and-research/dpic-reports/in-depth/enduring-injustice-the-persistence-of-racial-discrimination-in-the-u-s-death-penalty

Durose, M. R., Cooper, A. D., & Snyder, H. N. (2014). *Recidivism rate of prisoners released in 30 states in 2005: Patterns from 2005–2010—Update.* NCJ 244205.

Federal Bureau of Prisons. (2023). *Inmate race.* https://www.bop.gov/about/statistics/statistics_inmate_race.jsp

Fessenden, F. (2000, September 22). Deadly statistics: A survey of crime and punishment. *New York Times,* Section A, p. 23.

Glaze, L. E., & Maruschak, L. M. (2009). *Parents in prison and their minor children.* Bureau of Justice Statistics.

Haney, C. (2018). Restricting the use of solitary confinement. *Annual Review of Criminology, 1,* 285–310.

James, D. J., & Glaze, L. E. (2006). *Mental health problems of prison and jail inmates.* NCJ 213600.

Kajstura, A. (2018). *Women's incarceration: The whole pie 2018.* Prison Policy Initiative.

Kansas State Library. (2003). *Costs incurred for death penalty cases: A K-GOAL audit of the Department of Corrections.* https://cdm16884.contentdm.oclc.org/digital/collection/p16884coll58/id/266

King, L. W. (Trans.). (2008). *The code of Hammurabi.* Yale School of Law—Lillian Goldman Library.

La Vigne, N. G., Davies, E., & Brazzell, D. (2008). *Broken bonds: Understanding and addressing the needs of children with incarcerated parents.* The Urban Institute Justice Policy Center.

Le Texier, T. (2019). Debunking the Stanford prison experiment. *American Psychologist, 74*(7), 823–839. https://doi.org/10.1037/amp0000401

Liptak, A. (2020, August 3). A vast racial gap in death penalty cases, new study finds. *New York Times.*

McLaughlin, M., Pettus-Davis, C., Brown, D., Veeh, C., & Renn, T. (2016). *The economic burden of incarceration in the U.S.* Institute for Justice Research and Development: Florida State University.

McLeod, S. (2020). *The Stanford prison experiment.* Simply Psychology.

Metzner, J. L., & Fellner, J. (2010). Solitary confinement and mental illness in U.S. prisons: A challenge for medical ethics. Journal of the American Academy of Psychiatry and the Law Online, *38*(1), 104–108.

Monazzam, N., & Budd, K. M. (2023). *Incarcerated women and girls.* The Sentencing Project. https://www.sentenci

ngproject.org/fact-sheet/incarcerated-women-and-girls/

Morgan, R. D., Kroner, D. G., Mills, J. F., Bauer, R. L., & Serna, C. (2014). Treating justice-involved persons with mental illness: Preliminary evaluation of a comprehensive treatment program. *Criminal Justice and Behavior, 41*(7), 902–915.

Murphey, D., & Cooper, M. (2015). *Parents behind bars: What happens to their children*? Child Trends.

National Commission on Correctional Health Care. (2020). *Transgender and gender diverse health care in correctional settings.* https://www.ncchc.org/position-statements/transgender-and-gender-diverse-health-care-in-correctional-settings-2020/

Nellis, A. (2021). *The color of justice: Racial and ethnic disparity in state prisons.* The Sentencing Project.

The New York State Senate. (2021, March 18). *Senate passes the "HALT" solitary confinement act.* https://www.nysenate.gov/newsroom/press-releases/senate-passes-halt-solitary-confinement-act

Pariona, A. (2019). *US prison population by race.* WorldAtlas.

Raeder, M. (2012). Making a better world for children of incarcerated parents. *Family Court Review, 50*(1), 23–35.

Rahman, I., & Schmidt, L. (2021). *Ending the death penalty is a step toward racial justice.* Vera Institute of Justice.

Reyes, H. (2007). The worst scars are in the mind: Psychological torture. *International Review of the Red Cross, 89*(867), 591–617.

Roxburgh, S., & Fitch, C. (2014). Parental status, child contact, and well-being among incarcerated men and women. *Journal of Family Issues, 35*(10), 1394–1412.

Sawyer, W. (2020). *Visualizing the racial disparities in mass incarceration.* Prison Policy Initiative.

Sawyer, W., & Bertram, W. (2018). *Jail will separate 2.3 million mothers from their children this year.* Prison Policy Initiative.

The Sentencing Project. (2023). *Incarcerated women and girls.* https://www.sentencingproject.org/fact-sheet/incarcerated-women-and-girls/

Sosin, K. (2020, February 26). *Trans, imprisoned—and trapped.* NBC News.

Steadman, H. J., Osher, F. C., Clark-Robbins, P. C., Case, B., & Samuels, S. (2009). Prevalence of serious mental illness among jail inmates. *Psychiatric Services, 60*, 761–765.

Stringer, H. (2019). Improving mental health for inmates. *American Psychological Association Monitor of Psychology, 50*(3), 46.

U.S. Census. (2022). *Quick facts.* https://www.census.gov/quickfacts/fact/table/US/PST045222

United Nations General Assembly. (2016, January 8). *United Nations standard minimum rules for the treatment of prisoners (the "Nelson Mandela rules").* 70th Session, Agenda Item 106.

United States Department of Justice. (2021). *Prison gangs.* https://www.justice.gov/criminal-ocgs/gallery/prison-gangs

Van Green, T. (2021). *Americans overwhelmingly say that marijuana should be legal for recreational or medical use.* Pew Research Center.

Vera Institute of Justice. (2015). *Prison spending in 2015.* https://www.vera.org/publications/price-of-prisons-2015-state-spending-trends/price-of-prisons-2015-state-spending-trends/price-of-prisons-2015-state-spending-trends-prison-spending

Wakefield, S., & Wildeman, C. (2014). *Children of the prison boom.* Oxford University Press.

Walmsley, R. (2019). *World prison brief.* Institute for Crime & Justice Policy Research. http://www. prisonstudies.org/world-prison-brief

World Population Review. (2023). *Death penalty status.* https://worldpopulationreview.com/state-rankings/death-penalty-states

Zeng, Z. (2018). *Jail inmates in 2016.* NCJ 251210.

INDEX

ABOUT THE AUTHOR

Growing up, Kenneth B. Cairns never imagined that one day, he would be on death row.

During the time that he was working on his bachelor's degree at Adelphi University, and later when he was completing his master's degree and doctoral degree in clinical psychology at Case Western Reserve University, Dr. Cairns fully intended to spend his career counseling in a private practice setting. Soon after earning his degree, his interests turned to forensics and the darkest depths of the human mind, and Dr. Cairns applied for a job as a psychological services specialist at the State Correctional Institution in Pittsburgh. During the course of what was to become a 20-year career in corrections, Dr. Cairns worked in medium-security, maximum-security, and super-maximum-security units, including death row. During his career, he interviewed and counseled thousands of offenders and served as a member of the Department of Corrections Hostage Negotiation Team. Prior to retiring, Dr. Cairns oversaw the delivery of mental health care services to 16,000 inmates in nine State Correctional Institutions in Pennsylvania, giving him a unique and personal perspective on the challenges of those who are incarcerated and mentally ill. Dr. Cairns's work was recognized in 2018 when he won the Department of Corrections Outstanding Employee Performance Award.

Since retiring from corrections in 2019, Dr. Cairns has enjoyed teaching both criminal justice and psychology at Waynesburg University in the southwestern part of Pennsylvania. In 2022, he was honored to receive the Lucas-Hathaway Award for Excellence in Teaching and was later promoted to department chair of criminal justice and social sciences. Dr. Cairns is incredibly grateful to Waynesburg for the support he has received from the University in writing the present book.

It is Dr. Cairns's desire and intention to help educate the next generation of law enforcement personnel and forensic psychologists. He enjoys spending his spare time with family and friends and volunteering at a local animal rescue center. In his spare time, Dr. Cairns enjoys going for walks, while making sure to greet and pet every dog he meets along the way.